VIEWS FROM THE BENCH

CHATHAM HOUSE SERIES ON CHANGE IN AMERICAN POLITICS
edited by Aaron Wildavsky
University of California, Berkeley

VIEWS FROM THE BENCH
The Judiciary
and Constitutional Politics

Foreword by

WARREN E. BURGER
Chief Justice of the United States

Collected and Edited by

Mark W. Cannon
and
David M. O'Brien

With Introductions by David M. O'Brien

Chatham House Publishers, Inc.
Chatham, New Jersey

VIEWS FROM THE BENCH
The Judiciary and Constitutional Politics

Chatham House Publishers, Inc.
Box One, Chatham, New Jersey 07928

Publisher: Edward Artinian
Interior design: Quentin Fiore
Jacket and cover design: Lawrence Ratzkin
Composition: Chatham Composer
Printing and binding: Hamilton Printing Company

Library of Congress Cataloging in Publication Data
Main entry under title:

Views from the bench.

(Chatham House series on change in American politics)
Bibliography: p.
Includes index.
1. Judicial process—United States—Addresses, essays,
lectures. 2. Courts—United States—Addresses, essays,
lectures. 3. Political questions and judicial power—
United States—Addresses, essays, lectures. I. Cannon,
Mark W. II. O'Brien, David M. III. Series.
KF8775.A75V53 1985   347.73′5   85-9990
ISBN 0-934540-34-9   347.3075
ISBN 0-934540-33-0 (pbk.)

Manufactured in the United States of America
10   9   8   7   6   5   4   3   2   1

FOR
RUTH AND CLAUDINE
AND COURT WATCHERS EVERYWHERE

Contents

PART III
The Judiciary and the Constitution

Foreword

This collection seeks to introduce students and the general public to the judicial process and the role of the judiciary in our increasingly complex and litigious society. An understanding of the history, dynamics, and role of the judiciary is particularly important as we approach the celebration of the bicentennial of the United States Constitution.

Most people know, or think they know, what the President and Congress are expected to do under our Constitution. Far fewer have a clear idea of what goes on in the courts generally and in the Supreme Court of the United States in particular. Even though hundreds of thousands of visitors a year have gone through the Supreme Court building and its museum exhibits, and perhaps have observed oral arguments briefly, for most it has remained a remote, austere "marble temple" housing nine seldom-seen jurists who periodically issue pronouncements on the law of the land.

This is not because the justices prefer remoteness, but chiefly because they are engrossed in the confining task of reviewing cases and writing opinions. It is surely not because they do not want people to understand the judicial function in our system; unfortunately there are relatively few people qualified to interpret and explain the Court's role in terms widely understood, and even fewer who undertake to address the public on the subject. Happily this is changing, and this book will make a contribution to that change.

Courts, like the other branches of government, belong to the American people; they serve the individual and the public interest through legal processes slowly and carefully evolved over centuries. An independent judiciary need not be a mysterious area of government or appear to be an occult priesthood. Indeed, of all branches of the government, it can be seen as the most open; all its hearings are public, and all its decisions are promptly made public. No one may address arguments to the Court except in public sessions of the Court and by printed briefs available to public examination. Justices who disagree with the majority have their dissenting views printed with the Court opinion.

It has been said that, except for its decision conferences, the Supreme Court literally operates "in a goldfish bowl." Like all institutions, it consists of flesh-and-blood mortals with individual personalities, the normal human traits; their lives and activities are available to any person diligent enough to inquire.

This collection is noteworthy in providing "a view from the bench," a unique opportunity for students and citizens alike to read what a diverse and representative group of leading state and federal judges think and to understand how judges themselves approach their function and the role of the judiciary in our constitutional system of free government.

Warren E. Burger

Chief Justice of the United States

Preface

To a reporter's question, "Does the average American understand the judicial process?" former congressman and now federal Court of Appeals Judge Abner J. Mikva responded: "No. In a sense [people] know less about the courts than they do about the Congress. They may have a lot of mistaken views about Congress, but the problem with the courts is that they are so mysterious. I worry about that a great deal. Some of my colleagues on the bench think that is why the judicial branch is given a great deal of respect, that it isn't as well known as the other two branches. I hate to think that we're only beloved in ignorance."[1] Courts and the judicial process are generally open and accessible, though particular aspects are closed or open only to professional observers. Whatever mystery surrounds the judiciary undoubtedly stems from what Judge Jerome Frank calls "the cult of the robe"[2] and Justice Felix Frankfurter felicitously describes as "judicial lockjaw."[3]

The "tradition" of judicial lockjaw, honored more often in rhetoric than in practice, evolved because of a number of institutional, political, and historical considerations. Article III of the Constitution, which vests the judicial power in one Supreme Court and in such lower federal courts as Congress may establish, provides that the judiciary shall decide only actual cases or controversies. From the earliest days, federal courts have therefore refused to render advisory opinions or advice on abstract and hypothetical issues.[4] Intimately related to the view that advisory opinions would violate the principle of separation of powers and compromise judicial independence, justices and judges contend that they should not offer off-the-bench commentaries on their decisions and opinions. As Justice William Brennan once recounted:

> A great Chief Justice of my home State [New Jersey] was asked by a reporter to tell him what was meant by a passage in an opinion which has excited much lay comment. Replied the Chief Justice, "Sir, we write opinions, we don't explain them." This wasn't arrogance—it was his picturesque, if blunt, way of reminding the reporter that the reasons behind the social policy fostering an independent juciciary also require that the opinions by which judges support decisions must stand on their own merits without embellishment or comment from the judges who write or join them.[5]

Explanations of judicial opinions have also been thought to be ill advised for more prudential reasons: Justice Hugo Black, among others, felt that off-the-bench remarks might prejudge issues that could come before the courts;[6] and Justice Harlan Stone counseled that such public discussions might actually invite litigation.[7]

Judicial opinions, whether those of trial or appellate judges, of course do not purport to describe the decision-making process. They are intended to justify the decision in a particular case. Judicial opinions, moreover, reveal merely the surface of the judicial process. As Justice Frankfurter once noted: "The compromises that an opinion may embody, the collaborative effort that it may represent, the inarticulate considerations that may have influenced the grounds on which the case went off, the shifts in position that may precede final adjudication—these and like factors cannot, contemporaneously at all events, be brought to the surface."[8]

The constraints of judges' "self-denying ordinance,"[9] which Justice Benjamin Cardozo abided throughout his tenure on the high bench, further inhibit disclosures about the deliberative and decision-making processes. Justices' revelations inexorably must prove modest given the institutional and political realities of judicial decision making. Unlike legislative decisions, judicial decisions, particularly in the Supreme Court and multijudge appellate courts, are collegial, incremental, and reached in an atmosphere that Justice Lewis Powell has described as one of "the last citadels of jealously preserved individualism."[10] Off-the-bench remarks about the deliberative process are therefore controlled by self-imposed standards of propriety that appear necessary to preserving the confidentiality—institutionally and personally—required of life-tenured judges who must sit together and collegially decide cases. For as Chief Justice Earl Warren, after his retirement, recollected, "when you are going to serve on a court of that kind for the rest of your productive days, you accustom yourself to the institution like you do to the institution of marriage, and you realize that you can't be in a brawl every day and still get any satisfaction out of life."[11]

The lessons of history also incline members of the judiciary to refrain from voicing their views on matters not only pertaining to the judicial process and law but also on politics more generally. During the founding period, judges in fact engaged in intensely partisan debates over differing views of constitutional principles. Chief Justice John Jay ran for the governorship of New York but did not campaign, as did Justice William Cushing for that office in Massachusetts; and Justice Samuel Chase campaigned for the election of John Adams as President.[12] By the late 1840s and 1850s, however, there emerged considerable opposition to judges', and specifically Justice John McLean's, active participation in partisan politics.[13] Still, throughout the late nineteenth and twentieth centuries, justices and judges have continued to undertake some extrajudicial roles and activities, such as arbitrating boundary disputes and heading special commissions. Charles Evans Hughes resigned from the bench to run for the Presidency in 1916 against Woodrow Wilson, and Chief Justice William Howard Taft advised the Republican party on a range of matters; Justices Frankfurter and Louis Brandeis had a long, close relationship with President Franklin Roosevelt. Members of the Court have also in extraordinary circumstances accepted extrajudicial assignments; notably, Justice Owen Roberts headed a presidential commission to investigate Pearl Harbor, and Justice Robert Jackson served as chief prosecutor of Nazi leaders at the Nuremburg trials. Chief Justice Earl Warren reluctantly headed an investigation of the assassination of President John Kennedy.

During the early part of the nineteenth century, the principal forum for judges' pronouncements on judicial and political issues was provided by Congress's requirement that justices of the Supreme Court travel to the various circuits and sit on cases as well as deliver charges to grand juries there. Although most members of the Court confined their grand jury charges to discussions of their views of consititional principles or newly enacted legislation, others used the occasion to issue political broadsides and thus enter into the heated debates raging between Federalists and Jeffersonian Republicans. This practice culminated in 1805 with the impeachment and trial of Justice Samuel Chase for "disregarding the duties and dignity of his judicial character." Specifically, the eighth article of impeachment charged the justice with "pervert[ing] his official right and duty to address the grand jury . . . on matters coming within the province of the said jury, for the purpose of delivering to the said grand jury an intemperate and inflammatory political harangue, . . . a conduct highly censurable in any, but peculiarly indecent and unbecoming in a judge of the supreme court of the United States."[14]

A more typical, less objectionable, and still prevalent form of off-the-bench commentary may be found in various justices' and judges' works on the Constitution and public law. Among his numerous treatises, Justice Joseph Story's *Commentaries on the Constitution of the United States*[15] became a classic; it was required reading for generations of lawyers, judges, and court watchers.[16] Justices James Wilson[17] and Henry Baldwin[18] also wrote major works in the early nineteenth century, as did Justices Samuel Miller[19] and Benjamin Curtis[20] in the latter part of the century. In the twentieth century, comparable works tend to place the Court in a more political context, and to emphasize individual justices' avowed judicial and political philosophies. Justice Robert Jackson's two books[21] are illustrative of contemporary judges' recognition of the expressly political role of courts in our system of free government;[22] works by Justices Hugo Black,[23] William O. Douglas,[24] and Wiley Rutledge[25] are representative of the style of recent judicial scholarship and the personal expression of judges' avowed "political jurisprudence."[26]

Despite institutional, political, and historical considerations, and despite the relentlessness of Court business and acquired judicial habits, off-the-bench commentaries are the prominent tradition and norm. There have been, to be sure, some especially reclusive judges: Chief Justices Roger Taney, Morrison Waite, Edward White, and Harlan Fiske Stone, as well as Justices Benjamin Cardozo and Thurgood Marshall, with rare exception ventured forth after they assumed their seats on the bench. Still, even those judges—notably Justice Frankfurter—professing "judicial lockjaw" often publicly addressed a wide range of judicial and extrajudicial matters.[27]

While justices and judges, like other political actors, reserve their most personal observations for private correspondence, they communicate their views and insights in numerous and diverse forums: from university and law school commencements to celebrations, annual meetings of law-related organizations, and bar association conventions; with newspaper, magazine, and broadcast interviews; and with polished scholarly articles and books. Occasionally, judges have also written to congressmen and testified before Congress on pressing issues confronting the courts and the country.[28]

The topics addressed by justices and judges are no less numerous and diverse; they run from rather rare comments about specific decisions to more frequent observations about the operation of the judiciary and the administration of justice. Despite the self-imposed credo that members of the bench "should not talk about contemporaneous decisions,"[29] judges have occasionally sought to clarify, explain, or defend their rulings. Chief Justice John Marshall, writing to a newspaper under the pseudonym "A Friend to the Union," defended his landmark decision in *McCulloch v. Maryland;*[30] and in 1979 five justices sought to explain their ruling in a controversial case involving public access to judicial proceedings.[31] More typically, judges who publicly address matters of public law—such as the constitutional protection afforded private property,[32] the meaning of the First Amendment,[33] or the evolution of administrative law and regulatory politics[34]—do so from a historical and doctrinal perspective or by means of judicial biography or autobiography.[35] There are, however, some matters, such as judicial administration and legislation affecting the courts, on which, as Judge Irving Kaufman has said, "judges must speak out."[36] Indeed, in recent years not only the chief justice, who has responsibility for overseeing the federal judiciary, but an increasing number of state and federal judges have voiced their views on rising caseloads, the operation of the judicial process, and innovations in the administration of justice, as well as on the litigiousness of our society.

The value of off-the-bench commentaries naturally depends on what they reveal about the way judges think, and what they think is important in understanding the judicial process. Their value in part turns on the relationship between judges' rhetoric and the reality of the judicial process and behavior. Judges, like other political actors, of course are neither always in the best position to describe their role nor able to detach themselves and critically assess their presuppositions and the way in which their policy orientations affect their decisions and the judicial process. The tradition of judicial lockjaw and the operation of the judicial system, moreover, provide judges with fewer opportunities than those of other political actors to explain their decision-making process and role. Judges' explanations of the deliberative process, for example, thus tend to be more inhibited, rather formal in emphasizing the rule-bound nature of the process. Their explanations are therefore only partial and must be supplemented with what we learn from social science, history, and philosophy.[37] What judges say remains nonetheless crucial for understanding the judicial process and the role of courts in American politics. This is so precisely because the Constitution structures the political process, and judges occupy a unique position and vantage point within our system of governance. Off-the-bench commentaries, no less than judicial opinions, may thus prove instructive about the governmental process, public policy, and enduring political principles.

This collection presents the views of leading justices and judges on the judicial process, the function of judging, and the role of courts—particularly the Supreme Court—in our increasingly litigious society. It provides a unique view of the judicial process, the dilemmas of deliberation and decision making, and other matters about which court watchers and the general public may otherwise only speculate. No less important than the insights they offer about the operation of and the problems confronting courts, the selections make accessible contemporary justices' and judges' thinking about judicial activism and self-restraint, and the role of courts in the political process.

We hope this collection makes the judiciary and the judicial process more understandable and encourages readers to think about the qualities of judges— their temperament, character, judicial philosophies, and political views—as well as the role of the courts and judicial review in our constitutional system of free government.

NOTES

1. A.J. Mikva, Q. and A.: "On Leaving Capitol Hill for the Bench," *New York Times* B8, col. 1 (12 May 1983).

2. J. Frank, "The Cult of the Robe," 28 *Saturday Review* 12 (13 October 1945).

3. F. Frankfurter, "Personal Ambitions of Judges: Should a Judge 'Think Beyond the Judicial'?" 34 *American Bar Association Journal* 656 (1948).

4. In 1793, the Supreme Court's refusal to answer a set of questions submitted to Secretary of State Thomas Jefferson, on behalf of President George Washington, concerning the interpretation of treaties with Britain and France. See C. Warren, *The Supreme Court in United States History,* Vol. I, 110-111 (Boston: Little, Brown, 1922). See also *Muskrat v. United States,* 219 U.S. 346 (1911).

5. W. Brennan, Jr., Address, Student Legal Forum, University of Virginia, Charlottesville, Va. (17 February 1959).

6. See H. Black, Address, 13 *Missouri Bar Journal* 173 (1943).

7. See H.F. Stone, "Fifty Years Work of the Supreme Court of the United States," 14 *American Bar Association Journal* 428 (1928).

8. F. Frankfurter, " 'The Administrative Side' of Chief Justice Hughes," 63 *Harvard Law Review* 1, 1 (1949).

9. Quoted by G.S. Hellman in *Benjamin N. Cardozo: American Judge* 271 (New York: McGraw-Hill, 1940).

10. L.F. Powell, "What the Justices Are Saying . . . ," 62 *American Bar Association Journal* 1454, 1454 (1976).

11. E. Warren, "A Conversation with Earl Warren," WGBH-TV Educational Foundation (1972).

12. See Warren, supra note 4, Vol. 1, at 269-276.

13. See A. Westin, ed., *An Autobiography of the Supreme Court* 6-10 (New York: Macmillan, 1963). See also A. Westin, "Out of Court Commentary by United States Supreme Court Justices, 1790-1962: Of Free Speech and Judicial Lockjaw," 62 *Columbia Law Review* 633 (1962); and R. Wheeler, "Extrajudicial Activities of the Early Supreme Court," *1973 Supreme Court Review* 123.

14. Quoted in Westin, *Autobiography,* supra note 13, at 18-19.

15. J. Story, *Commentaries on the Constitution of the United States,* 3 vols. (Boston: Little, Brown, 1833).

16. No less important in the late nineteenth century was Judge Thomas Cooley's *A Treatise on the Constitutional Limitations* (Boston: Little, Brown, 1868).

17. J. Wilson, Lectures, "Of the Judicial Department," in *The Works of James Wilson,* Vol. 2 (Chicago: Callaghan, 1896).

18. H. Baldwin, *A General View of the Origin and Nature of the Constitution and Government of the United States* (Philadelphia: J.C. Clark, 1837).

19. S. Miller, *Lectures on the Constitution* (Washington: Morrison, 1880).

20. B. Curtis, *Jurisdiction, Practice, and Peculiar Jurisdiction of the Courts of the United States* (Boston: Little, Brown, 1880).

21. R. Jackson, *The Struggle for Judicial Supremacy* (New York: Knopf, 1941); and *Supreme Court in the American System of Government* (Cambridge: Harvard University Press, 1955).

22. See also, from a different perspective, Judge Richard Neely, *How Courts Govern America* (New Haven: Yale University Press, 1981).

23. H. Black, *A Constitutional Faith* (New York: Knopf, 1969).

24. W.O. Douglas, *We the Judges* (Garden City, N.Y.: Doubleday, 1956).

25. W. Rutledge, *A Declaration of Legal Faith* (Lawrence: University of Kansas Press, 1947).

26. For further discussion, see symposium "Whither Political Jurisprudence," Harry Stumpf, Martin Shapiro, David Daneleski, Austin Sarat, and David O'Brien, 36 *Western Political Quarterly* 533 (December 1983).

27. See Selected Bibliography (303-316). See also R. Wheeler, "Of Standards for Extra-Judicial Behavior," 81 *Michigan Law Review* (1983) (Book Review).

28. See, e.g. the testimony of Justice Willis Van Devanter on the passage of the Judges' Bill of 1925 in U.S. Congress, 68th Cong., 2d Sess., H.R. Committee on the Judiciary, *Hearings on the Jurisdiction of Circuit Courts of Appeals and of the Supreme Court of the United States* (Washington, D.C.: Government Printing Office, 1925); Letter of Chief Justice Charles Evans Hughes to Senator Burton Wheeler on proposed reorganization of the federal judiciary, reprinted in U.S. Congress, 75th Cong. 1st Sess., Senate, Committee on the Judiciary, *Hearings on the Reorganization of the Federal Judiciary,* S. Rept. No. 711, at 38 (Washington, D.C.: Government Printing Office, 1937).

29. F. Frankfurter, *Proceedings in Honor of Mr. Justice Frankfurter and Distinguished Alumni* 11, Occasional Pamphlet No. 3 (Cambridge: Harvard University Press, 1960).

30. See *Philadelphia Union* (28 April, 1 May 1810) (New York Historical Library Collection), and discussed by Westin, supra note 13, at 19.

31. "Brennan Assails Media Criticisms of Court Decisions," *Washington Post* A12, col. 1 (18 October 1979); "Justice Marshall Hits Colleagues on Rights," *Seattle Post-Intelligencer* B2 (3 June 1979); John Paul Stevens, "Some Thoughts on a General Rule," 21

Arizona Law Review 599 (1979); and *New York Times* A14, col. 1 (9 September 1979) (quoting Justice Stevens's view that "members of the general public, including the press, could not assert rights guaranteed to the accused by the Sixth Amendment"); *New York Times* A17, col. 1 (9 August 1979) (quoting Chief Justice Burger "that the opinion referred to pretrial proceedings only"); *New York Times* A13, col. 1 (14 August 1979) (reporting Justice Powell's address to a panel at the annual meeting of the American Bar Association and explanation that *Gannett* was based only on the Sixth Amendment); and *New York Times* A15, col. 1 (4 September 1979) (reporting Justice Blackmun's view that after *Gannett v. DePasquale* [1979] closure of trials is permissible).

32. See, e.g., D. Brewer, "Protection of Private Property from Public Attack," 10 *Railway and Corporation Law Journal* 281 (1891).

33. See, e.g., W. Brennan, Address, 32 *Rutgers Law Review* 173 (1979); P. Stewart, "Or of the Press," 26 *Hastings Law Journal* 631 (1975); J.P. Stevens, "Some Thoughts about a General Rule," 21 *Arizona Law Review* 599 (1979).

34. See, e.g., H. Leventhal, "Principled Fairness and Regulatory Urgency," 25 *Case Western Reserve Law Review* 66 (1974); and "Environmental Decisionmaking and the Role of the Courts," 122 *University of Pennsylvania Law Review* 509 (1974); J. Wright, "Rulemaking and Judicial Review, 30 *Administrative Law Review* 461 (1978); and D. Bazelon, "The Impact of Courts on Public Administration," 52 *Indiana Law Journal* 101 (1976).

35. See, e.g., citations to Justice Frankfurter's writings in the Selected Bibliography.

36. I. Kaufman, "Judges Must Speak Out," *New York Times* A23 (30 January 1982).

37. See, for example, C. Warren, *The Supreme Court in United States History,* 3 vols. (Boston: Little, Brown, 1922); W. Murphy, *Elements of Judicial Strategy* (Chicago: University of Chicago Press, 1964); W. Murphy and J. Tanenhaus, *The Study of Public Law* (New York: Random House, 1972); H.J. Abraham, *The Judicial Process,* 5th ed. (New York: Oxford University Press, 1985); S. Wasby, *The Supreme Court in the Federal Judicial System* (New York: Holt, Rinehart and Winston, 1978); W. Murphy and C.H. Pritchett, eds., *Courts, Judges, and Politics,* 4th ed. (New York: Random House, 1985); S. Goldman and A. Sarat, eds., *American Court Systems: A Reader* (San Francisco: Freeman, 1978); J. Grossman and R. Wells, eds., *Constitutional Law and Judicial Policy Making,* 2d ed. (New York: Wiley, 1980); C. Sheldon, *The American Judicial Process* (New York: Dodd, Mead, 1974); G. Schubert, ed., *Judicial Behavior* (Chicago: Rand McNally, 1964); J. Schmidhauser, *Justices and Judges* (Boston: Little, Brown, 1979); J.W. Howard, Jr., *Courts of Appeals in the Federal Judicial System* (Princeton: Princeton University Press, 1981); R. Carp and C.K. Rowland, *Policymaking and Politics in the Federal District Courts* (Knoxville: University of Tennessee Press, 1983); and A.T. Mason, *The Supreme Court From Taft to Burger,* 3d ed. (Baton Rouge: Louisiana State University Press, 1979).

Acknowledgments

We are grateful to the following justices, judges, and publishers for their support and permission to print excerpts from the off-the-bench commentaries included herein:

Chief Justice Warren E. Burger for an abridged version of his Presidential Address, delivered to the Bentham Club, University College, London (1 February 1972).

Harvard University Press for excerpts from *The Supreme Court in the American System of Government* by Robert H. Jackson, Cambridge, Mass.: Harvard University Press, Copyright © 1955 by William Eldred Jackson and G. Bowdoin Craighill, Jr., Executors, © 1983 by William Eldred Jackson.

Judge Marvin E. Frankel for excerpts from the Third Annual Tom Sealy Law and Free Society Lecture at the University of Texas School of Law (20 November 1975), which appears in 54 *Texas Law Review* 465 (1976).

Judge Frank M. Coffin and Houghton Mifflin Company for excerpts from *The Ways of a Judge* by Frank M. Coffin, Copyright © 1980 by Frank M. Coffin.

Judge Alvin B. Rubin for his presentation at the Seminar on the Administration of Justice, sponsored by the Brookings Institution (1980) and appearing in 55 *Notre Dame Lawyer* 648 (1980).

Justice Lewis F. Powell, Jr., for his remarks delivered at the Southwestern Legal Foundation (1 May 1980).

Justice William H. Rehnquist for the Ninth Annual Will E. Orgain Lecture, at the University of Texas School of Law (12 May 1976), which also appears in 54 *Texas Law Review* 693 (1976).

Justice John Paul Stevens for an excerpt from the James Madison Lecture, New York University School of Law (27 October 1982), which was published in 58 *New York University Law Review* 1 (1983).

Cornell University Law Review for permission to reprint portions of "The Role of Oral Argument," by Justice John M. Harlan, Jr., from 41 *Cornell Law Review* 6 (1955), Copyright Cornell University.

Retired Chief Justice Walter V. Schaefer for excerpts from the Ernst Freund Lecture, University of Chicago Law School (21 April 1955), and appearing in 34 *University of Chicago Law Review* 3 (1966).

Judge Edward A. Tamm and retired Justice Paul C. Reardon for excerpts from their article in 3 *Brigham Young University Law Review* 448 (1981).

Chief Judge William Wayne Justice for excerpts from his article in 52 *University of Colorado Law Review* 19 (1980).

Justice Dallin H. Oaks for his speech at Utah State University (29 April 1982).

Judge J. Clifford Wallace for his lecture delivered at the National Law Center, George Washington University (25 September 1981), appearing in 50 *George Washington Law Review* 1 (1981).

Judge Robert H. Bork for the Francis Boyer Lectures on Public Policy given at the American Enterprise Institute. Copyright © 1984 by the American Enterprise Institute for Public Policy Research, Washington, D.C., and London.

The Association of the Bar of the City of New York City for permission to reprint portions of Justice Felix Frankfurter's essay from 2 *Record of the Association of the Bar of the City of New York* 213 (1947), Copyright Association of the Bar of the City of New York.

Judge Carl McGowan for his Sixth Sulzbacher Memorial Lecture at Columbia Law School, appearing in 77 *Columbia Law Review* 1119 (1977).

Judge Antonin Scalia for an abridged version of his article, adapted from the Frank J. Donahue Lecture delivered at Suffolk University Law School on 28 March 1983, appearing in 4 *Suffolk University Law Review* 881 (1984).

The *New York University Law Review* for permission to reprint excerpts from Justice Hugo L. Black's article "The Bill of Rights," from 35 *New York University Law Review* 865 (1960).

Justice William J. Brennan, Jr., for his address before the New Jersey State Bar Association, appearing in 15 *The Judges' Journal* 82 (1976).

Justice Hans A. Linde for excerpts from his lecture at the University of Baltimore School of Law (16 May 1979), which appears in 9 *University of Baltimore Law Review* 379 (1980).

Justice Sandra Day O'Connor for sections from her article in 22 *William and Mary Law Review* 801 (1981).

Judge Ruggero J. Aldisert for his address, as part of the Bicentennial Observation of the American Bar Association (9 August 1976), which appears also in 38 *University of Pittsburgh Law Review* 437 (1977).

Judge Henry J. Friendly for excerpts from his article in 33 *University of Miami Law Review* 21 (1978).

Judge Frank M. Johnson, Jr., for his address at the University of Georgia School of Law in 1977, which also appears in 16 *The Judges' Journal* 7 (1977).

Chief Judge Howard T. Markey for his remarks to the Federal Bar Association (19 June 1981).

Judge Ralph K. Winter and the American Enterprise Institute for permission to print portions of a paper written and presented at the AEI while the author was William K. Townsend Professor of Law at Yale Law School, in December 1978.

C. Herman Pritchett, Henry J. Abraham, Jack Peltason, Alpheus T. Mason, Russell Wheeler, and Jeffrey Morris read portions of the Introductions, and we appreciate their kind service and words of encouragement. We are also grateful for the assistance of Connie Fore and Lisa Lett, as well as for the commendable typing of Bunny Stinnett and Kathy Fast of the University of Virginia.

PART I

Judicial Review and American Politics: Historical and Political Perspectives

JUDICIAL REVIEW was not fully comprehended during the founding period and remains controversial in American politics. The U.S. Constitution, in Article III, vests the judicial power in one Supreme Court and in any lower courts that Congress may establish. Yet, neither the nature nor the scope of that power is defined. Instead, Chief Justice John Marshall in *Marbury v. Madison* established the power of judicial review—the power to strike down laws enacted by Congress or the states and to declare official government action unconstitutional. The historical background, the political drama, and the enduring significance of that decision is eloquently described in chapter 1 by Chief Justice Warren E. Burger. After *Marbury* the Court did not invalidate another act of Congress, and thereby invite national political controversy, until 1857 in *Dred Scott v. Sandford*—a decision Chief Justice Charles Evans Hughes characterized as a "self-inflicted wound." The Court nonetheless struck down some 40 state and local laws prior to the Civil War, thus legitimating the role of the national government and the power of judicial review.

Subject to the constitutional restriction that the Court decide only actual cases or controversies, the justices are not self-starters—they must await an appeal in an actual case or controversy in a properly framed lawsuit. But whereas the President and the Congress are restrained by the ballot box and the processes of democratic government, as well as by judicial review, Chief Justice Harlan Fiske Stone pointed out, "the only check on [the justices'] exercise of power is [their] own sense of self-restraint."[1] Chief Justice Stone was only partially correct, for the Court depends upon the cooperation of other branches of government and compliance by the people; as an irate President Andrew Jackson declared: "John Marshall has made his decision, now let him enforce it."[2] Accordingly, the Court evolved other, self-imposed rules governing its power. Justice Tom Clark summarizes these self-imposed constraints:

> The case or controversy presented must be a genuine dispute [with real and adverse litigants], raising a substantial question. The Court does not deal in advisory opin-

ions [or abstract or hypothetical questions], moot questions [already resolved by changing circumstances], or political issues [more appropriately resolved by the President or Congress, or which the Court is incapable of resolving]. Traditionally it shies away from deciding constitutional questions; not rendering such a decision unless it is absolutely necessary to the disposition of the case. Even though a substantial constitutional issue is presented it will not be passed upon if the case can be disposed of on a non-constitutional ground. An appeal from the highest state court is dismissed if that court's judgment can be sustained on an independent state ground [i.e., if the decision is based on the state's constitution, the Court will defer to the state supreme court in recognition of the principle of comity]. A statute is not construed unless the complaining party shows that he is substantially injured by its enforcement. An attack on an act of Congress on constitutional grounds is by-passed in the event a construction of the statute is fairly possible by which the constitutional question may be avoided.[3]

The power and prestige of the Court fundamentally lie with the justices' recognition of the responsibility imposed by judicial independence under the Constitution and in a system of free government. The Constitution provides for judicial independence with the selection and appointment of members of the federal judiciary by the President with the advice and consent of the Senate. Presidential appointment and senatorial confirmation are the principal means by which democratic values are infused into the judiciary. In addition to seeking meritorious individuals with outstanding professional qualifications, Presidents have also sought to ensure some measure of geographic, ethnic, and religious representation on the federal bench.

The selection and appointment of state court judges varies from state to state, according to each state's constitutional provisions. The methods of appointment include popular—partisan or nonpartisan—election in 25 states; selection by governors in eight and by legislatures in four states; and in 13 states some combination of both methods, or a so-called merit system—under which a commission provides a list of nominees from which the governor makes an appointment and then, after one year of service, the judges's name is placed on a ballot with voters deciding whether the judge should be retained or not, for either a specified or unspecified term.[4]

All federal judges hold their offices during good behavior subject to impeachment for high crimes and misdemeanors (only nine judges have been impeached and only four of those convicted.). Federal judges enjoy essentially life tenure. The fourth chief justice, John Marshall, served for 34 years, surpassed by Justice William Douglas's record of 36 years and 7 months; several other justices have served 20 years or more on the bench.

Judicial independence, though constitutionally provided for, was actually secured by Chief Justice Marshall. For as Chief Justice Earl Warren observed:

Insistence upon the independence of the judiciary in the early days of our nation was perhaps John Marshall's greatest contribution to constitutional law. He aptly stated the controlling principle when, in speaking of the Court during his tenure, he said that he had "never sought to enlarge the judicial power beyond its proper bounds, nor feared to carry it to the fullest extent that duty required." That is precisely the obligation of the judiciary today.[5]

The essence of judicial independence, Judge Irving Kaufman similarly notes, "is the preservation of a separate institution of government that can adjudicate cases or controversies with impartiality."[6] The history of the judiciary is replete with examples of judges' assertions of independence; the first decision that federal District Court Judge Murray Gurfein had to make upon ascending the bench, for example, was to deny the administration that had just appointed him its request for an injunction to suppress the publication of the Pentagon Papers. And Chief Justice Burger, also appointed by President Richard Nixon, wrote for a unanimous court in *United States v. Nixon*, denying the President's generalized claim to executive privilege as a shield against turning over the so-called Watergate tapes.

Despite the fact that courts are not self-starters, the self-imposed limitations on judicial review, and given the tradition of judicial independence, the judiciary has proven to be neither the least dangerous branch, as Alexander Hamilton envisioned,[7] nor quiescent "under the chains of the Constitution,"[8] as Thomas Jefferson hoped. Prior to the 1983 ruling in *Immigration and Nationalization Service v. Chadha*—striking down a one-house veto provision for federal regulations, but therewith throwing into question the validity of over 200 other statutes with similar provisions—the Supreme Court had invalidated over 110 congressional statutes and 1050 state laws or municipal ordinances. The Court also reversed its own prior decisions some 175 times. By comparison, Congress and the states passed constitutional amendments overturning Supreme Court decisions only four times in almost 200 years.[9]

The Supreme Court and the judiciary loom large in American politics in part because, as Alexis de Tocqueville observed: "Scarcely any political question arises in the United States that is not resolved, sooner or later, into a judicial question."[10] Justice Felix Frankfurter likewise commented, "almost every question in the history of the United States is ultimately shaped for adjudication by the Supreme Court."[11] Justice Jackson proclaimed more boldly: "*This is government by lawsuit.* These constitutional lawsuits are the stuff of power politics in America."[12]

The overwhelming work of state and federal courts actually involves rather mundane civil, criminal, and regulatory matters—disputes over contracts, personal injuries, government benefits, labor relations and the regulation of businesses, public utilities, and health and safety services. The judiciary is nevertheless drawn into political conflicts precisely because the Constitution's separation of powers among the three branches of government amounts to a prescription for political struggle and conflict. The doctrine of separation of powers, Justice Louis Brandeis pointed out, "was not to promote efficiency but to preclude the exercise of arbitrary power. The purpose was, not to avoid friction, but, by means of the inevitable friction incident to the distribution of the governmental powers among three departments, to save the people from autocracy."[13] In the twentieth century (as further discussed in part 5), the judiciary also assumed a role as guardian of civil rights and liberties, and thus often invited political contests by countering the coercive powers of the national government and the states.

The Supreme Court provides a forum for resolving political conflicts, but a forum of last resort. Recourse to the Court, James Madison explained, "must necessarily be deemed last in relation to the authorities of the other departments of government, not in relation to the rights of the parties to the constitutional compact, from which the judicial, as well as the other departments hold their delegated trusts."[14] The Court provides an "auxiliary precaution," not the primary check on political passions and conflicts. Denied the power of both the sword and the purse, the Court depends on the cooperation of the coequal branches of government and ultimately public acceptance. In a system of free government, Chief Justice William Howard Taft, the only member of the Court to serve previously as President, observed: "The fact is that the judiciary, quite as much as Congress and the Executive, is dependent on the cooperation of the other two, that government may go on."[15]

As a political institution and unit of government sharing power, Justice Jackson explains in chapter 2, the Court confronts vexatious disputes between the President and Congress, for example, and over the exercise of federal and state powers and from the competition among the states, as well as arising from persistent and perennial demands to balance majoritarian democracy with the rights of individuals and minorities.

As a guardian of the Constitution and the symbols and instruments of free government, the Supreme Court was destined for controversy. The exercise of judicial review inevitably proves problematic for, as Justice Jackson said, the judiciary "is an institution of distinctive characteristics which were intended to give it independence and detachment, but which also tend to make it antidemocratic." There is no "evading the basic inconsistency between popular government and judicial supremacy."[16] Nor is the Court "saved from being oligarchic because it professes to act in the service of humane ends." Justice Frankfurter reminds us: "The powers exercised by this Court are inherently oligarchic."[17] The power and prestige of the Court rests on a paradox. The power of judicial review is at once antidemocratic and countermajoritarian, yet that power, in Chief Justice Edward White's words, "rest[s] solely upon the approval of a free people."[18]

Judicial review cannot be reconciled with democratic governance. Nevertheless, the Constitution does not prescribe a democracy pure and simple, but a republic—a mixed form of government—in which political power is diffused among institutions that remain dependent on and accountable to the people in a variety of ways.[19] In a system of free government, majorities are constantly in flux and constrained by constitutional checks and balances. So, as Madison argued, "[a] dependence on the people is . . . the primary control on the government."[20] The judiciary fulfills an important albeit limited role as an auxiliary precaution against both the abuse of governmental power by a tyrannical minority and the excesses of majoritarian democracy. Far from being antithetical, judicial review is essential to the promise and performance of free government.

NOTES

1. *United States v. Butler*, 297 U.S. 1, 79 (1936) (Stone, J., dis. op.).

2. Quoted by E. Corwin, *The Doctrine of Judicial Review* 22 (New Haven: Yale University Press, 1914).

3. T.C. Clark, "Random Thoughts on the Court's Interpretation of Individual Rights," 1 *Houston Law Review* 75, 78 (1963).

4. For a further discussion, see W. Murphy and C.H. Pritchett, *Courts, Judges, and Politics* 122-161 (New York: Random House, 3d ed., 1979); and H.J. Abraham, *Justices and Presidents* (New York: Oxford University Press, 2d ed., 1985).

5. E. Warren, Address, American Law Institute, 20 (20 May 1959).

6. I. Kaufman, "The Essence of Judicial Independence," 80 *Columbia Law Review* 671, 688 (1980).

7. A. Hamilton, *The Federalist*, No. 78, at 465, ed. by C. Rossiter (New York: New American Library, 1961).

8. T. Jefferson, "Resolutions Relative to the Alien and Sedition Laws," in *The Writings of Thomas Jefferson*, Vol. 17, 389, ed. by A. Lipscomb and R. Bergh (Washington, D.C.: N.p., 1904-1905).

9. The Eleventh Amendment (the only amendment removing part of the jurisdiction of federal courts) was passed in response to the Court's decision in *Chisholm v. Georgia* (2 Dallas 419, 1793); the passage of the Thirteenth and Fourteenth amendments overturned *Dred Scott v. Sandford* (19 Howard 393, 1857); the Court's decision striking down a federal income tax, in *Pollock v. Farmers' Loan and Trust Co.* (158 U.S. 601, 1895), was overturned by the Sixteenth Amendment; and the Twenty-sixth Amendment, extending the franchise to eighteen-year-olds, overturned the Court's five-four decision in *Oregon v. Mitchell* (400 U.S. 112, 1970).

10. A. de Tocqueville, *Democracy in America* 151, ed. by P. Bradley (New York: Doubleday, 1945).

11. F. Frankfurter, *Proceedings in Honor of Mr. Justice Frankfurter and Distinguished Alumni* 8, Occasional Pamphlet No. 3 (Cambridge: Harvard Law School, 1960).

12. R. Jackson, *The Struggle for Judicial Supremacy* 287 (New York: Knopf, 1941).

13. *Meyers v. United States*, 272 U.S. 52, 293 (1926) (Brandeis, J., dis. op.).

14. Quoted by E. Corwin, *The Doctrine of Judicial Review* 22 (New Haven: Yale University Press, 1914).

15. *Ex parte Grossman*, 267 U.S. 87, 119-120 (1925).

16. Jackson, supra note 12, at vii and 311.

17. *AFL v. American Sash & Door Co.*, 335 U.S. 538, 555-556 (1949) (footnotes omitted).

18. E. White, "The Supreme Court of the United States," 7 *American Bar Association Journal* 341 (1921).

19. For a further discussion, see D.M. O'Brien, "Judicial Review and Constitutional Politics: Theory and Practice," 48 *University of Chicago Law Review* 1052 (1981).

20. J. Madison, *The Federalist,* No. 51, supra note 2, at 322.

1

The Doctrine of Judicial Review:
Mr. Marshall, Mr. Jefferson, and Mr. Marbury

Warren E. Burger
Chief Justice, Supreme Court of the United States

Lord Bryce once observed:

> No feature of the government of the United States has awakened so much curiosity in the European mind, caused so much discussion, received so much admiration, and been more frequently misunderstood, than the duties assigned to the Supreme Court and the functions which it discharges in guarding the Ark of the Constitution.[1]

I should add that in some quarters, the Supreme Court's guardianship of that Ark probably has received more guarded praise than in distant places where its impact is purely theoretical.

Lord Bryce, of course, had reference to the doctrine of judicial review, sometimes described as the doctrine of judicial supremacy, in the interpretation of constitutional terms and principles. . . .

It is helpful to an understanding of this subject to examine it in the setting in which *Marbury v. Madison* was decided in 1803 with all its momentous consequences for our country and to suggest to you that this great case had its antecedents in our colonial experience, and its taproots in the declarations of fundamental rights of Englishmen back to Magna Carta.

Marbury v. Madison: Act 1, The Setting

Very early in the history of our country the colonial experience of living under a parliamentary system with no check on the legislative or executive branch, except that of popular will in a limited way, led our Founding Fathers to feel strongly the need for limitations on all branches of government. The intellectual spadework for the system ultimately adopted for our federal government had been done, of course, by such seventeenth- and eighteenth-century polit-

This chapter is excerpted from the Presidential Address delivered by Chief Justice Burger to the Bentham Club, University College, London, England, on 1 February 1972.

ical theorists as Hobbes and Locke.[2] As we know, the great rationalist Montes-quieu contributed the notion of a separation of powers within the government itself, in order that each branch might act as a sort of brake upon the others.[3] As the system works today, one of the checks exercised by the Supreme Court involves measuring executive or legislative action against the Constitution when-ever a challenge to such action is first properly brought within the framework of a "case" or "controversy,"[4] and then properly brought within the "appellate jurisdiction"[5] of the Supreme Court.

It has been suggested from time to time that the subject of judicial review of Congressional Acts was not in the minds of the delegates to the Constitu-tional Convention in 1787. However, such an obviously important question could not have entirely eluded their attention. Some of the delegates, without doubt, looked to an independent judiciary with fixed tenure as a means of pro-tecting the states against the powers of the new national government, whose scope was as yet unseen and unknown and therefore feared. Others, particular-ly the propertied classes, probably regarded a Supreme Court and an indepen-dent Federal Judiciary as a source of protection against the egalitarian popular government advocated by Jefferson. They could not fail to be aware that the exercise of such powers by the judiciary must in some way involve limitations on legislative and executive action.

Some residual controversy remains as to the exercise of judicial review to-day, but it is largely as to scope, not basic power. It is now accepted that the original assertion of the power was not judicial usurpation as Jefferson con-sidered it.[6] Needless to say, the major challenges to the power have occurred during those periods when, for whatever reason, the Supreme Court has been under attack for its role in contemporary affairs.

As an example, many polemics as well as some of the most thoughtful and scholarly challenges were written during the 1930s when, to many of its critics, the Supreme Court represented the dead hand of the past impeding legitimate experimentation and innovation in trying to cope with a crisis. At present, it is fair to say that, absent some unforeseeable convulsion of great magnitude, the doctrine of judicial review, as announced by Chief Justice John Marshall in 1803 in *Marbury v. Madison,*[7] is likely to remain part of the Amer-ican system.

It is often assumed that the doctrine was the invention of Chief Justice Marshall in that most famous of all his opinions. It is true, of course, that Chief Justice Marshall first announced this keystone doctrine of our constitu-tional law in the *Marbury* case; and it is also true that our written Constitu-tion makes no reference to the theory in defining judicial power.[8] But Marshall was not and never claimed to be the originator of the doctrine since he was well aware of a growing acceptance of the idea that constitutional adjudica-tion was inherent in the very nature of a written constitution. This is not to disparage Marshall, for he was the one who recognized the need to enunciate the doctrine as part of Federal jurisprudence and seized—some might say forced

—the first opportunity to assert the power of the Court to measure an act of Congress by the yardstick of the Constitution.

But this takes me ahead of my story, and I must turn back to 1776, the very year of the Declaration of Independence. In that year the people of the town of Concord, Massachusetts, held a Town Meeting and adopted a resolution that "a Constitution alterable by the Supreme Legislative is no security at all to the subject, against encroachment of the Governing Part on any or on all their rights and privileges." Earlier, when the Colony of Massachusetts Bay was under British Colonial rule, the sturdy farm people of Berkshire County refused to let the Colonial courts sit from 1775 to 1780 until the people of Massachusetts adopted a Constitution with a Bill of Rights enforceable by judges.

Notice the premise in these events, 25 years before *Marbury*, that a written constitution would govern the acts of a legislature and protect fundamental liberties. And notice also the tacit assumption that the judicial branch was the appropriate vehicle for providing that protection.

In 1793, ten years before Marshall's decision in *Marbury v. Madison*, Spencer Roane, a great judge of the Virginia Court and an intimate of Thomas Jefferson, said, in the case of *Kamper v. Hawkins,*

> If the legislature may infringe this Constitution [of Virginia], it is no longer fixed; . . . and the liberties of the people are wholly at the mercy of the legislature.[9]

To be sure, Judge Roane was speaking to the power of the state courts to strike down legislative acts contrary to the Virginia Constitution, but conceptually the doctrine is indistinguishable from *Marbury*. In 1793 the Commonwealth of Virginia, of course, regarded itself as a sovereign at least equal to the new National Government. Some lawyers, including very good ones of that day, would later hesitate and ponder before taking the final step to make the doctrine equally applicable to a Federal Constitution and a Federal Legislature, but very quickly their strong sense of the rights of the states, that were widely viewed as sovereign in the eighteenth and early nineteenth centuries, would impel them to accept such a restraint on the federal legislative body. Their hesitation was no more than that of thoughtful men chary of granting open-ended power to anyone.

Although I attributed a certain uniqueness to the American doctrine of judicial review as formally articulated in *Marbury v. Madison*, it is quite clear that this, like almost all else in our law, has its roots in English legal thought.

Magna Carta, of course, was primarily intended by the Barons as a limitation on King John; but it has come to stand for a limitation on princes and parliaments alike. In one of the very early opinions of the Supreme Court of the United States,[10] one of many containing references to Magna Carta, it was said:

> . . . after volumes spoken and written [about the guarantees of Magna Carta], the good sense of mankind has at length settled down to this: *that they were in-*

tended to secure the individual from the arbitrary exercise of the powers of government. . . . (Emphasis supplied.)

Another thread of influence originates with the struggle between Lord Coke and the Stuart kings. Coke's writings and Reports were well known to the American colonists, and even though the dictum in *Dr. Bonham's Case* has never been very closely followed in England, it has been seminal in our law. In that case Coke asserted that

> . . . in many cases, the common law will controul Acts of Parliament, and sometimes adjudge them to be utterly void: for when an Act of Parliament is against common right and reason, or repugnant, or impossible to be performed, the common law will controul it, and adjudge such Act to be void.[11]

And even that super authoritarian, Cromwell, said, 150 years before *Marbury v. Madison:*

> In every government, there must be something fundamental, somewhat like a Magna Carta which would be unalterable. . . .[12]

I doubt that the stern Mr. Cromwell intended to propound the idea that a judicial body like our Supreme Court, independent of both the executive and legislative branches, should be empowered to act as a sort of umpire, but obviously he was concerned about unbridled legislative power.

A very important point of departure from England's jurisprudence was the American insistence on written guarantees that would be definite and would narrow the area for interpretation. Each of the thirteen original states of the Union had a written constitution, giving tangible expression to what the farmers of Concord and Berkshire, Massachusetts, demanded as early as 1775. Having said that the idea of written guarantees in a constitution departed in a sense from England's precedents, I am bound to note that even this idea traces directly back to Magna Carta and to the written charters of the colonies.

An important function of a constitution is its organic allocation of powers of government, and in this area alone the authority must reside somewhere for a binding pronouncement that, for example, treaty-making power is shared by the Executive and the Senate, that the veto power is exclusively for the Executive, the overriding power exclusively in the Congress. More than a decade before *Marbury,* Justices of the Supreme Court sitting on circuit held that state laws contrary to the Federal Constitution were invalid, and this was confirmed in *Van Horne Lessee v. Dorrance.*[13] In his opinion in that case Justice Paterson, sitting on circuit, asserted flatly:

> I take it to be a clear position; that if a legislative act oppugns a constitutional principle, the former must give way, and . . . it will be the duty of the Court to adhere to the Constitution, and to declare the act null and void.[14]

We see, therefore, that long before *Marbury* American political leaders, including many of the most distinguished lawyers and judges in the Colonies and in the original thirteen states, accepted it as fundamental that a written Constitution was a restraint on every part of the federal government. It does not disparage John Marshall's greatness as a judge or a statesman to say that when he wrote the opinion in *Marbury* he was doing little more than declaring what was widely accepted by so many of the best legal minds of his day—at least when they could divorce politics from reason! If it had not come in *Marbury,* it would have come later, but John Marshall was not a man to wait for perfect opportunities if a plausible one offered itself. It had to be said, and *Marbury* was the fortuitous circumstance that made it possible to establish this great principle early in our history.

The setting in which this great case developed is important. The incumbent President Adams was defeated by Thomas Jefferson in the election of November 1800. But between the time of the election and the following March when Jefferson actually took office, Adams remained in control of the government and in control of what we call a "lame duck" Congress.[15] One of the first things he did after his defeat was to encourage the ailing Chief Justice Ellsworth to resign. The Federalist Adams was, of course, deeply concerned about the future of the country, and undoubtedly about the future of the Supreme Court in the hands of Jefferson and his Republicans. . . .

An interesting footnote to history, often overlooked in the appropriate recognition of John Marshall and the wisdom of John Adams in appointing him, emerges from the circumstance that Marshall was not Adams' first choice for Chief Justice after Ellsworth resigned. John Jay, who had served as the first Chief Justice of the United States by appointment of George Washington, resigned as Chief Justice in 1795 to become Governor of New York State. Adams wrote to Jay urging him to return to his old position as Chief Justice but he declined. Interestingly, Jay refused because, as he put it, "I left the [Supreme] Bench perfectly convinced that under a system so defective, it would not obtain the energy, weight and dignity which are essential to its affording due support to the National Government, nor acquire the public confidence and respect which, as the last resort of the justice of the nation, it should possess."[16] His decision not to return to the court in that frame of mind, thus opening the way for Marshall, was one of the most fortuitous events in the two centuries of our history.

Whatever Jay may have thought of the office, you may be sure that Jefferson was anything but overjoyed at the eleventh hour appointment of John Marshall, who was his distant kinsman but not a friend.

Jefferson's deep and bitter hostility toward John Marshall is one of the unplumbed mysteries of this complex man. Some historians explain it in terms of his opposition to Marshall's judicial philosophy, but other explanations are also suggested.[17]

Jefferson's choice for Chief Justice, had Marshall not been appointed, was Spencer Roane, an able Virginia judge. Yet Judge Roane, described by Professor Charles Warren[18] as "an ardent strict constructionist of the Constitution," showed his basic agreement with Marshall in an opinion for the Virginia court in 1793, stating:

> It is the province of the judiciary to expound the laws. . . . It may say too, that an act of assembly has not changed the Constitution [of Virginia], though its words are expressly to that effect. . . . [I]t is conceived, for the reasons above mentioned, that the legislature have not power to change the fundamental laws. . . . [W]ould you have them [judges] to shut their eyes against that law which is of the highest authority of any . . . ?[19]

From the day Jefferson took office as President on 4 March 1801, those who were even slightly aware of his hostility toward the Supreme Court, the Federal Judicial Branch as a whole, and John Marshall in particular, could sense that these events foreshadowed a collision of two strong men who had quite different views as to how the United States could best fulfill its destiny.

Underlying the impending conflict was a very fundamental difference between the Federalist belief that a strong national government was the key to the future of the new nation and the opposing belief of the Jeffersonian radical Republicans who feared all centralized power and wanted to keep the states the strong and indeed the dominant political power. When he took office Jefferson still looked with considerable favor on the French Revolution, notwithstanding its later excesses and horrors. Jefferson had been largely aloof from the hardships of our war of rebellion; he lacked the firsthand experience that Washington, Hamilton, and even Marshall, as a junior officer, shared in a war in which thirteen quarrelsome and disunited colony-states, functioning through an impotent confederation and a parochial Congress, fumbled and almost failed in raising, equipping, and maintaining armies. Jefferson's lifelong passion for minimal government had never been subjected to the acid test of trying to conduct a war with a truly "minimal" government.

Jefferson's remarkable political instincts enabled him to see, far ahead of his contemporaries, that the latent power of the National Judiciary, and especially the Supreme Court, could be a major obstacle to his dream of a simple, loose-jointed, national confederation, linking but not binding the several states.[20] But Jefferson was at heart a majoritarian. What the People wanted, the People would have.

Whatever his earlier beliefs, by 1800 Jefferson's distrust of and opposition to the federal judiciary had hardened. From 1800 onward, Jefferson did not waver in this attitude, and in 1820 we find him declaring that

> to consider the judges as the ultimate arbiters of all constitutional questions. . . would place us under the despotism of an oligarchy.[21]

Similarly, in a letter to a friend dated 18 August 1821, Jefferson wrote — some would say, prophetically —

> It has long . . . been my opinion, and I have never shrunk from its expression . . . that the germ of dissolution of our federal government is in the Constitution

of the federal judiciary; an irresponsible body (for impeachment is scarcely a scarecrow), working like gravity by night and by day, gaining a little today and a little tomorrow, and advancing its noiseless step like a thief, over the field of jurisdiction, until all shall be usurped from the States, and the government of all be consolidated into one. To this I am opposed; because when all government, domestic and foreign, in little as in great things, shall be drawn to Washington as the centre of all power, it will render powerless the checks provided of one government on another, and will become as venal and oppressive as the government from which we separated.[22]

From the time he was President to the end of his life, Jefferson did not alter his hostility either to strong central government or to the federal judiciary, and the Supreme Court, in particular, was the target of repeated bitter comments. Of course, in the United States we judges have had to learn to accept philosophically all manner of "slings and arrows," and by modern standards Jefferson's characterization of Federal judges as "thieves" is a fairly moderate comment. If he ever recognized that the unsound pronouncements of the Supreme Court could be "reversed" through the constitutional amending process by the People he trusted so much, I have not discovered evidence of it. However, Jefferson would also well understand difficulties of the amending process.

Marbury v. Madison: The Second Act

So much for the setting. We now come to the final act.

As sometimes is true of great events in history, *Marbury v. Madison* was an accident. But it was an accident which the solid, steady, and resourceful Marshall exploited to the fullest. The accident of fortuitous combination was the coincidence of a need, an opportunity, and a man—a man with the foresight, the wit, and the courage to make the most of his chance.

Adams, as I have noted, was a "lame duck" President after November 1800, with a "lame duck" Congress on hand for five months after the election. Naturally he made as many appointments as possible. Persuading Ellsworth to resign to make way for Marshall as Chief Justice was one step. The appointment of a goodly number of Federal judges was another. But the far lesser post of Justice of the Peace was the grist of Marbury's case.

The story is too well known to be chronicled in detail. Marbury was one of those whose commission as a Justice of the Peace was signed by President Adams and sealed by Marshall (who was still acting as President Adams' Secretary of State even after being appointed Chief Justice and confirmed by the Senate). But Marbury's commission was not delivered. Legend, supported by letters, tells us this was because of Marshall's careless error as he hastened to complete his duties as Secretary of State and don his robe as Chief Justice before 4 March 1801.

The minor office of Justice of the Peace was hardly worth a lawsuit, but Marbury was a spunky fellow and he sought a direct mandamus in the Supreme Court against Madison, Jefferson's Secretary of State, to compel what Marbury rightly claimed was the purely ministerial act of delivering the commissions that Madison's predecessor Marshall, as Secretary of State, had forgotten to mail out. In the Supreme Court it can be assumed that the first reaction was, "of course," since the Judiciary Act provided that precise remedy—mandamus by an original action in the Supreme Court.

Marshall saw it otherwise. If mandamus issued and Jefferson's Administration ignored it—as was likely—the first confrontation between court and Executive would be lost—and all of it over a Justice of the Peace commission! The court could stand hard blows, but not ridicule, and the ale houses would rock with hilarious laughter. If the court simply refused to issue mandamus in the face of the very explicit authority of the Federalist-drafted Judiciary Act of 1789, this, too, would be an ignominious retreat by the court—a court fearing to act because it would not be obeyed.

But if, as no one had even remotely suspected up to that time, Congress could not vest original jurisdiction in the Supreme Court in any cases except those specifically recited in Article III, then the court could say, "Yes, Marbury was duly confirmed"; and "Yes, the Commission was duly signed and sealed"; and "Yes, this court may examine into the manner in which the Executive conducts its own affairs"; and "Yes, delivery is a purely ministerial act," and "Yes, it is shameful that the new administration will not perform the simple, ministerial act of delivery"; but the court could also say, "However, this court has no power under the Constitution to entertain any original action except those specified in Article III, and hence section 13 of the Judiciary Act of 1789[23] purporting to give the Supreme Court such authority is invalid and, sadly, this action to compel the Executive to do its duty cannot be entertained here as an original action."

And this is precisely what Marshall persuaded the court to do in a straight-faced, long-winded opinion that exhaustively, and exhaustingly, explored every possible alternative. After doing so, he sadly concluded that the Federalist Congress of 1789 had passed, and the Federalist President, George Washington, had signed, an Act—drafted by no less than Ellsworth, Marshall's distinguished predecessor—that everyone had thought excellent for 13 years, but section 13 of which was void because it conflicted with Article III of the Constitution.

Jefferson's Secretary of State, Madison, had won the battle; Marbury, the Federalist, had lost, and the real war, the great war over the supremacy of the Supreme Court in constitutional adjudication, had been won by Marshall—and by the United States.

Because it was a small case—almost a joke—few people cared. But Jefferson the lawyer and politician saw that he had been outmaneuvered by the holding of the court near the time of an election—1803—when it would be very difficult to make an issue of a case decided in his favor and against Marbury, his political opponent. Not even a Pyrrhic Victory! Small wonder he likened the federal judiciary to thieves in the night!

For salt and vinegar in Jefferson's wounds, in the same Term the Supreme Court announced in solemn tones with respect to another section of the same Judiciary Act of 1789 (as to which its section 13 had now been declared void) that

> practice and acquiescence under it [the Act of 1789] for a period of several years [13 years!], commencing with the organization of the judicial system . . . has . . . fixed the construction . . . [and] is too strong . . . to be shaken . . . is at rest, and ought not now to be disturbed.

Marshall is spared the charge of judicial hypocrisy for, having sat as the trial judge on circuit, he took no part in the case in which this was said, *Stuart v. Laird.*[24]

Not for 54 years after *Marbury* did the court hold another Act of Congress unconstitutional.[25] In another irony of history, the court decided in 1857 that Congress had no power to ban slavery in the Louisiana Territory under an 1820 Act known as the Missouri Compromise. This case was the infamous *Dred Scott* decision[26] that added fuel to the fires leading to our Civil War.

Another interesting footnote to Mr. Marbury's case is that after 10,000 words, more or less, Marshall held that the court had no jurisdiction on the case since the statute purporting to create jurisdiction was void. So we have, perhaps, the most important single opinion of the court in nearly 200 years pronounced in the context of a holding that the court had no jurisdiction at all! From this, of course, we authoritatively conclude that the court always has jurisdiction to decide its own jurisdiction!

As with so many great conceptions, the idea of judicial review of legislation now seems simple and inevitable in the perspective of history. People, not governments, delegated certain powers to the national government and placed limits on those powers by specific and general reservations. The people having flatly stated certain guarantees relating to religious freedom, to speech, to searches, seizures, and arrests, would it be reasonable to think that legislative action could alter those rights? The very explicit procedures for constitutional amendments, standing alone, negate the idea that a written constitution could be altered by legislative or executive action.

The language of Article III vesting judicial power "in one Supreme Court" for "all Cases, in Law and Equity, arising under this Constitution, the Laws of the United States, and Treaties . . ." would be sterile indeed if the Supreme Court would not exercise that judicial power by deciding conflicts between the Constitution, federal laws and treaties on the one hand, and Acts of Congress, the Executive or States on the other.

Epilogue

To speak of the doctrine of judicial review and of *Marbury,* and fail to add at least a few more words on Marshall, would be to serve a great claret without letting it breathe and in a thick porcelain mug.

When one speaks of the "Great Chief Justice" . . . every literate person knows the reference is to John Marshall. It does not disparage his unique qualities but rather emphasizes his unparalleled gifts to note that he had no formal education and read law at William and Mary College for a mere few weeks before he was admitted to practice. This becomes more important when we remember that his contemporaries included Alexander Hamilton, Thomas Jefferson, James Madison, and Aaron Burr who were all highly educated in the classics, all deeply read and trained in law.

There are several other factors, all relating to the political climate of the day, that may help to understand Marshall and his place in history. Going back to the appointment of the first court in 1790, we must recall that there were no political parties and it was then devoutly hoped that none would evolve. But men who risk all to conduct a revolution must be passionate believers, and our Founding Fathers were just that.

It is not at all surprising, therefore, that when the newly created Supreme Judicial Court of the United States[27] met for the first time on 1 February 1790, it was composed of men who tended to reflect the views of George Washington and his administration. In short, they were all federalists—the word was not uniformly capitalized then—and they were firm believers in the need for a strong federal or national government as a condition of survival. The Federalists remained in power until Jefferson defeated them in 1800—over 12 years. Quite naturally, then, when Marshall came to the Supreme Court every one of its members shared his political and judicial philosophy.

Since the court had delivered opinions in only a handful of cases when John Marshall was appointed, there could hardly be a more propitious moment for a judge of great intellectual capacity and remarkable qualities of statesmanship to ascend the highest court in the country. He had every advantage in his favor: he was very literally writing on a clean slate, with the support of five colleagues who shared his basic philosophy, and he had the wit and courage to make the most of his opportunity. As a soldier in the Continental Army, he had learned the need for a unified and strong national government to ensure the cohesiveness essential to survival of a new nation composed of three million highly individualistic and scattered people. As a political leader of Virginia, a member of its legislature, a member of the national Congress and a Secretary of State, he understood government. Moreover, as one of the leaders in the Virginia struggle to secure adoption of the new Constitution over the vigorous opposition of men of such stature as Thomas Jefferson and Patrick Henry, he knew how fragile were the ties that held the former colonies together.

Thus the everlasting benefit of a country begotten in revolution and weaned in confusion and conflict, the United States of America was to be tutored in constitutional law for 34 formative years by a man who knew precisely what was needed to make a strong nation.

Small wonder, then, that John Adams in 1823, looking back, saw his appointment of John Marshall to the Supreme Court of the United States as one of his greatest contributions to his country. How indeed could there have been a greater one?

NOTES

1. James Bryce, *The American Commonwealth,* Vol. I, 242 (New York: Macmillan, 1931).

2. Thomas Jefferson, in writing the Declaration of Independence, relied heavily upon Locke's *Second Treatise on Government,* almost to the point of plagiarism.

3. Montesquieu's *L'Esprit des Lois* contains the clearest expression of the principle.

4. "The judicial Power shall extend to . . . Cases . . . [and] Controversies. . . ." U.S. Const. Art. III. § 2, cl. 1.

5. "[T]he supreme Court shall have appellate Jurisdiction both as to Law and Fact, with such Exceptions, and under such Regulations as the Congress shall make." U.S. Const. Art. III. § 2, cl. 2.

6. Although most scholars agree that Article III (granting the judicial power and extending it to "Cases . . . arising under this Constitution, [and] the Laws of the United States . . .") coupled with the Supremacy Clause in Article VI, cl. 2, necessarily includes the power to disregard state or federal statutes found to be unconstitutional, several major efforts to lay a scholarly basis for the contrary conclusion have been made. See, e.g., L. Boudin, *Government by Judiciary* (New York: Godwin, 1932); and W. Crosskey, *Politics and the Constitution in the History of the United States* (Chicago: University of Chicago Press, 1953). However, the understanding of the Constitutional Convention seems to have been quite clearly in favor of such a power, see, e.g., M. Farrand, *The Framing of the Constitution* (New Haven: Yale University Press, 1913); and C. Warren, *The Making of the Constitution* (Chicago: University of Chicago Press, 1937 ed.). See generally H.M. Hart and H. Wechsler, *The Federal Courts and the Federal System* 7-37 (Mineola, N.Y.: Foundation Press, 1973).

7. 1 Cranch 137 (1803).

8. The reasons for not writing it into the Constitution are speculative at best. Perhaps it would have been too controversial for some; it could have delayed the final draft; others may have thought it part of the warp and woof of a system of delegated and divided power. In any event, since our Constitution is a document to divide and assign powers and governing functions, the choice of the "one supreme Court" to construe and enforce "the supreme Law of the Land" seems simple, and the grant of power a necessary corollary of that choice. Thus the omission of any reference to the theory may have been due to an unwillingness to elucidate the obvious.

9. *Kamper v. Hawkins,* 1 Virginia Cases 20, 38 (1793). This is by no means the only state case in which state legislative acts were declared unconstitutional by state courts or in which the principle of judicial review was announced. In addition to Virginia, a number of states had each either announced the principle or strongly hinted at it. Among them were Maryland (*Whittington v. Polk,* 1 Harris & Johnson 236, 241 [1802]), South Carolina (*Lindsay v. Comm'rs.,* 2 Bay 38, 61-62 [1796]); also *Bowman v. Middleton,* 1 Bay 252, 254 (1792), a conspicuous case in which the court declared an act void because it was against "common right" and "magna charta"), North Carolina (*State v. _____,* 1 Haywood 28, 29, 40 [1794]), Kentucky (*Stidger v. Rogers,* 2 Kentucky

52 [1801]), New Jersey (*State v. Parkhurst*, 4 Halstead 427 [1802]), and Pennsylvania (*Austin v. Univ. of Pennsylvania*, 1 Yeates 260 [1793]). For further detail and a more complete list of early state cases, see R. McLaughlin, *A Constitutional History of the United States* 312, n. 34 (New York: Appleton, 1935).

10. *Bank of Columbia v. Okley*, 4 Wheat. 235, 244 (1819).

11. (1610) 8 Co. 113b, 118a, 77 E.R. 646, 652. For a more complete discussion, see C. Haines, *The American Doctrine of Judicial Supremacy* 29-43 (New York: Russell & Russell, 1959).

12. Oliver Cromwell, *Letters and Speeches*, ed. by T. Carlyle (New York: AMS Press, 1974), Part 7, Speech 3 (12 September 1654).

13. 2 Dallas 304 (1795). S. 25 of the Judiciary Act of 1789 in terms granted federal appellate jurisdiction to review judgments of state courts concerning the validity of a treaty or statute of the United States under the Federal Constitution. S. 1, Statutes at Large 85.

14. Ibid., at 309.

15. In Marshall's time, the old Congress met in December after the November elections, and the newly elected Members did not take their seats until the following March. Since some of the old Members had been voted out of office, the December to March sitting came to be called a "lame duck Congress." The problem has been solved by the 20th Amendment which shortens the delay between the time a Member is elected and the time he takes his seat.

16. C. Warren, supra note 6, at 173.

17. S.E. Morison, *The Oxford History of the American People* (New York: Oxford University Press, 1965), at 362 states: "Toward Marshall his kinsman Jefferson entertained an implacable hatred because he [Marshall] had shown him up and broken the sentimental . . . bubble in the XYZ affair."

18. C. Warren, *Congress, The Constitution and the Supreme Court* 58-59 (Boston: Little Brown, 1935 ed.).

19. *Kamper v. Hawkins*, 1 *Virginia Cases* 20, 38 (1793).

20. Somewhere along the line in the development of his political philosophy, Jefferson had lost trust in the belief, expressed in a letter to a friend in 1798, that "the laws of the land, administered by upright judges, would protect you from any exercise of power unauthorized by the Constitution of the United States." Jefferson to Rowan, 26 September 1798: Ford ed., *Writings*, Vol. VIII, 448 (New York: Putnam's, 1892-98).

21. Jefferson to Jarvis, 28 September 1820: Ford ed., *Writings*, Vol. XII, 162.

22. H.A. Washington, ed., *The Writings of Thomas Jefferson*, Vol. VII, 216 (New York: H.W. Derby, 1861).

23. S. 13 of the First Judiciary Act provided: "The Supreme Court . . . shall have power to issue writs of . . . mandamus . . . to any courts appointed, or persons holding office . . . of the United States." 1 Stat. 81.

24. 1 Cranch 299, 309 (1803).

25. However, in *Martin v. Hunter's Lessee*, 1 Wheaton 304 (1816), Justice Story for the Court firmly asserted the power of the Supreme Court to invalidate a state statute contrary to the Federal Constitution.

26. *Dred Scott v. Sandford*, 19 Howard 393 (1857).

27. The Journal of the Court used this title for the Court until the February 1791 session.

2

The Supreme Court in
the American System of Government

ROBERT H. JACKSON

Justice, Supreme Court of the United States

No sound assessment of our Supreme Court can treat it as an isolated, self-sustaining, or self-sufficient institution. It is a unit of a complex, interdependent scheme of government from which it cannot be severed. Nor can it be regarded merely as another law court. The Court's place in the combination was determined by principles drawn from a philosophy broader than mere law.

Our foundations were quarried not only from the legal ideas but also from the political, social, philosophical, scientific, and theological learnings of the eighteenth century, "the silver age of the Renaissance." All these were dominated by a belief in "the laws of nature and of nature's God." Faith in a "higher law," which had achieved a venerable place in the history of ideas through the speculations of jurists, monks, and scholars, burst forth toward the end of the eighteenth century into a fanatical creed that took over French and American liberal thinking and led in each case to a violent revolution.

Our judicial, executive, and legislative branches all were grounded in a belief that they were bound by the authority of a clear and universally acceptable natural law, revealed by man's reason and always and everywhere the same. Its fundamentals were proclaimed self-evident truths, as indisputable as the axioms of geometry, which needed only to be declared to be acknowledged as right and just by the opinion of mankind. These truths of natural law to that age stood as the ultimate sanction of liberty and justice, equality and toleration. The whole constitutional philosophy of the time was based on a system of values in which the highest was the freedom of the individual from interference by officialdom—the rights of man. To supplement this natural order, little man-made government was thought to be needed, and the less the better.

To make certain that these natural rights should have some man-made sanctions, the forefathers added ten Amendments to the original instrument, translating their version of the rights of man into legal limitations on the new government. They did not stop, as the French did, at reciting these in a preamble to the Constitution, where they served as an admonition only to a parliament that was all-powerful because there could be no judicial review of its legislation. On the contrary, the forefathers established a Bill of Rights which conferred as a matter of law, enforceable in court, certain immunities and rights upon citizens which correspondingly limited the power of the majority duly expressed through governmental action. . . .

Against this background a study of the Supreme Court can hardly fail to be instructive. . . .

The Supreme Court as a Unit of Government

We ought first to inquire what kind of institution the Supreme Court really is, the degree of its independence, the nature of its power, and the limitations on its capacity and effectiveness.

The Supreme Court of the United States was created in a different manner from most high courts. In Europe, most judiciaries evolved as subordinates to the King, who delegated to them some of his functions. . . .

The status of the Court as a unit of the Government, not as an institution subordinate to it, no doubt has given it prestige, for the people do not regard the Justices as employees of the Government of the day or as civil servants, as in continental Europe. Also, federal judges enjoy two bulwarks of independence—life tenure (except for impeachable misbehavior) and irreducible salaries (except by taxation and inflation).

Nonetheless, the Constitution-makers left the Court in vital respects a dependent body. The political branches nominate and confirm the Justices, a control of the Court's composition which results in a somewhat lagging political influence over its trend of decision, and any party that prevails in the Federal Government through several presidential terms will gradually tend to impress its political philosophy on the Court. The political branches also from time to time may alter the number of Justices, and that power was used to influence the course of decision several times before it was again proposed by President Roosevelt.

The Court also is dependent on the political branches for its powers in other vital respects. Its only irrevocable jurisdiction is original, and that reaches only cases affecting Ambassadors, public Ministers, or Consuls, or cases in which a state is a party. In all other cases it has appellate jurisdiction, but "with such exceptions and under such regulations as Congress shall make."

The Court also is dependent upon the political branches for the execution of its mandates, for it has no physical force at its command. The story is traditional that President Jackson once withheld enforcement, saying, "John Marshall has made his decision:—*now let him enforce it!*" Also, the Court, of course, depends upon Congress for the appropriation of funds with which to operate. These all add up to a fairly formidable political power over the Supreme Court, if there were a disposition to exert it.

But perhaps the most significant and least comprehended limitation upon the judicial power is that this power extends only to cases and controversies.

We know that this restriction was deliberate, for it was proposed in the Convention that the Supreme Court be made part of a Council of Revision with a kind of veto power, and this was rejected.

The result of the limitation is that the Court's only power is to decide lawsuits between adversary litigants with real interests at stake, and its only method of proceeding is by the conventional judicial, as distinguished from legislative or administrative, process. This precludes the rendering of advisory opinions even at the request of the nation's President and every form of pronouncement on abstract, contingent, or hypothetical issues. It prevents acceptance for judicial settlement of issues in which the interests and questions involved are political in character.

It also precludes imposition on federal constitutional courts of nonjudicial duties. Recent trends to empower judges to grant or deny wiretapping rights to a prosecutor or to approve a waiver of prosecution in order to force a witness to give self-incriminating testimony raise interesting and dubious questions. A federal court can perform but one function—that of deciding litigations—and can proceed in no manner except by the judicial process. . . .

The judicial power of the Supreme Court, however, does extend to all cases arising under the Constitution, to controversies to which the United States is a party, and to those between two or more states. Thus, the Court must face political questions in legal form, for surely a controversy between two separately organized political societies does present a political question, even if waged with the formalities of a lawsuit. And any decision which confirms, allocates, or shifts power as between different branches of the Federal Government or between it and a constituent state is equally political, no matter whether the decision be reached by a legislative or a judicial process.

Our Constitution was the product and expression of a virile political philosophy held by those who wrote it. Controversies over its meaning often spring from political motives, for the object of politics always is to obtain power. Such controversies have to be solved either by consideration of the experiences and statements of the framers [themselves] which indicate the original will, or by reference to some relevant subsequent events and currents of opinion deemed controlling. And all constitutional interpretations have political consequences.

We must not forget that, at bottom, the Civil War was fought over constitutional doctrine. It oversimplifies that tragedy to say that it was a war over slavery, an institution which many southern leaders had come to deplore and one which Mr. Lincoln did not propose to abolish in the states where it existed.

The controversy was over the power of the Federal Government to control the spread of slavery into new territory, and over the voluntary or compulsory character of the federal compact. These, like most other questions which have deeply agitated our people, found their way to the Supreme Court in the guise of private controversies between litigating parties. . . .

Executive v. Legislative

It is hard to conceive a task more fundamentally political than to maintain amidst changing conditions the balance between the executive and legislative branches of our federal system. The Supreme Court often is required to arbitrate between the two because litigation in one form or another raises questions as to the legitimacy of the acts of one branch or the other under the doctrine of separation of powers. In such cases the Court has found no precedent from any other country or in the judicial interpretation of any similar written instrument, and it has had to devise its own doctrine from time to time.

The Court, both before and after the Roosevelt influence was felt in its appointments, has tended strongly to support the power of the President in matters involving foreign affairs. On the other hand, where only internal affairs are involved, the Court has been more inclined to restrict executive power. It halted a presidential effort indirectly to control the policies of the administrative agencies by removal of a Federal Trade Commissioner. In the cases striking down the NIRA, the Court refused to sanction the congressional practice of delegating power to the President to make codes for industry that would be the equivalent of new laws.

The Court has kept the Executive from usurping the adjudicative function through military trials of offenders by holding such trials illegal in *Ex parte Milligan,* after, however, they had been running riot for a number of years.

In the more recent Steel Seizure case the Court refused to sanction a presidential seizure of private property without congressional authorization, holding that the President has no such inherent power under the Constitution. But I felt constrained in that case to point out the inadequacies of judicial power to appraise or control the realistic balance of power between Congress and the President. This is because of the gap that exists between the President's paper powers and his actual powers. The real potency of the Executive office does not show on the face of the Constitution. The relative influence of the President and of the Congress has fluctuated widely, depending on the personal and political strength of the particular President as compared with that of the congressional leadership. A Congress stampeded by a powerful leader like Thaddeus Stevens may cripple a President who is politically vulnerable, and a senatorial coalition may break the foreign policy of even an able and strong President like Wilson. On the other hand, a White House tenant who is a skillful manipulator of his extralegal influences may force an unwelcome program through Congress.

What are these sources of presidential strength? First, the Executive power is concentrated in a single head in whose choice the whole nation has a part, making him the focus of public hopes and expectations. No collection of local representatives can rival him in prestige. None can gain such ready and effective access to the modern means of communication with the masses or exert such influence on public opinion; this is one of his most effective leverages upon those in Congress who are supposed to balance his power. As the nation's activities have spread, the President wields the power of appointment and promotion over a vast multitude of our people. He is not merely the Chief Magistrate of the Republic; he is the titular and usually the actual head of the prevailing political party, whose loyalties and interest enable him to win as political leader what he could not command under the Constitution. Woodrow Wilson summed it all up in the observation that "if he rightly interpret the national thought and boldly insist upon it, he is irresistible. . . . His office is anything he has the sagacity and force to make it."

Yet it depends not upon the President alone but upon his sagacity and force measured against that of the Congress as manifested in its leadership. If Congress forfeits the respect of the country, it will not be able to balance the power of the Executive. No matter what the Supreme Court opines, only Congress itself can keep its power from slipping through its fingers.

Federal Power v. State Power

It is the maintenance of the constitutional equilibrium between the states and the Federal Government that has brought the most vexatious questions to the Supreme Court. That it was the duty of the Court, within its own constitutional functions, to preserve this balance has been asserted by the Court many times; that the Constitution is vague and ambiguous on this subject is shown by the history preceding our Civil War. It is undeniable that ever since that war ended we have been in a cycle of rapid centralization, and Court opinions have sanctioned a considerable concentration of power in the Federal Government with a corresponding diminution in the authority and prestige of state governments.

Here again the principal causes of this concentration have not been within judicial control. Improved methods of transportation and communication; the increasing importance of foreign affairs and of interstate commerce; the absorption of revenue sources by the nation with the consequent appeal by distressed localities directly to Washington for relief and work projects, bypassing the state entirely; the direct election of Senators; and various other factors —all have contributed to move the center of gravity from the state capital to that of the nation.

I think it is a mistake to lump all states' rights together as is done so frequently in political discussions. . . . It was early perceived that to allow the Federal Government to spend money for internal improvements would aggrandize its powers as against those of the states. It was not until the famous decision holding the Social Security Act constitutional that this controversy over the federal power to tax and spend for the general welfare was settled, and settled in favor of the existence of that power in the Federal Government. I believe that this controversy was rightly settled, but there is no denying that the power is vast and, uncontrolled, leads to the invasion of sources of revenue and builds up the Federal Government by creating organizations to make the expenditures. But here we are dealing with powers granted to the Federal Government, if not entirely without ambiguity, at least in language which fairly admits of the construction given it and which fairly warned those who adopted the Constitution that such results might follow.

Considerations of a different nature arise from interferences with states' rights under the vague and ambiguous mandate of the Fourteenth Amendment. The legislative history of that Amendment is not enlightening, and the history of its ratification is not edifying. I shall not go into the controversy as to whether the Fourteenth Amendment, by a process of incorporation or impregnation, directs against the states prohibitions found in the earlier Amendments. Whether it does or not, I think the Fourteenth Amendment has been considerably abused.

For more than half a century the Supreme Court found in the Fourteenth Amendment authority for striking down various social experiments by the states. The history of judicial nullification of state social and economic legislation is too well known to justify repetition here. It came to its culmination when the Court wound up the October 1935 Term by declaring that there was no power in either state or nation to enact a minimum wage law, a position repudiated within a few months by the conventions of both political parties and retracted by the Court itself with some haste. That retraction probably brought an end to the use of the Fourteenth Amendment to prevent experiments by the states with economic and social and labor legislation. . . .

Today, however, we have a different application of the Fourteenth Amendment. Today it is being used not to restrain state legislatures but to set aside the acts of state courts, particularly in criminal matters.

It is a difficult question and always will remain a debatable question where, in particular instances, federal due process should step into state court proceedings and set them aside. When the state courts render harsh or unconsidered judgments, they invite this power to be used. But I think in the long run the transgressions of liberty by the Federal Government, with its all-powerful organization, are much more to be feared than those of the several states, which have a greater capacity for self-correction.

State v. State

Another clearly political type of litigation is that of state against state. It was logical that in a federation the different units should have some arbiter to settle their differences. Congress was made a supervisor of their separate compacts or agreements. The Supreme Court was made the arbiter of their controversies.

To what source may the Court look for law to govern such controversies? The actual practice perhaps is well illustrated in Mr. Justice Cardozo's opinion in *New Jersey v. Delaware*. His search carried him through many ancient documents, which he interpreted according to the common law of property, and he compared the claims of the two states in the light of that body of learning. But this was inadequate for the solution of the case and resort was had to international law. He traced international law through the Court's own decisions and through all of the conventional authorities, American and foreign. He found international law inconclusive and no positive law applicable. He declared that "international law, or the law that governs between states, has at times, like the common law within states, a twilight existence during which it is hardly distinguishable from morality or justice, till at length the *imprimatur* of a court attests its jural quality." He concluded that in these circumstances it was within the power of the judicial process to develop and apply a formula consonant with justice and with the political and social needs of the interstate or international legal system. Reduced to its simplest terms, what the Court seemed to be saying in that case was that it found no controlling law and was obliged to declare some, in the light of the experience and learning of the law in similar situations. The Court has no escape in many cases of this character from the undesirable alternatives of refusing to obey its duty to decide the case or of devising some rule of decision which has no precedent or positive law authority.

I know that it is now regarded as more or less provincial and reactionary to cite the Tenth Amendment, which reserves to the states and the people the powers not delegated to the Federal Government. That Amendment is rarely mentioned in judicial opinions, rarely cited in argument. But our forefathers made it a part of the Bill of Rights in order to retain in the localities certain powers and not to allow them to drift into centralized hands.

Majority v. Individual

Perhaps the most delicate, difficult and shifting of all balances which the Court is expected to maintain is that between liberty and authority. It is not so easy as some people believe to determine what serves liberty best by way of restriction of authority. For example, the removal of the Japanese from the West Coast during the War, which seemed to me plainly unconstitutional as applied to citizens, was rationalized as a service to ultimate liberty. And I suppose no one would be more likely than Abraham Lincoln to win recognition by common vote as the greatest servant of freedom; yet President Lincoln, at the outset of his administration, suspended the writ of habeas corpus and resorted to wholesale arrest without warrant, detention without trial, and imprisonment without judicial conviction. Private mail was opened, and Cabinet officers simply sent telegrams ordering persons to be arrested and held without communication or counsel. The power was given to generals of various of the northern states to suppress newspapers and suspend the writ. President Lincoln, in his famous letter to Erastus Corning and others, defended his conduct, saying all that ever could be said and what always will be said in favor of such policies in time of emergency. Those policies were sharply but unavailingly condemned in May of 1861 by the aged Chief Justice Taney, and he has said all that can be said on the other side. Had Mr. Lincoln scrupulously observed the Taney policy, I do not know whether we would have had any liberty, and had the Chief Justice adopted Mr. Lincoln's philosophy as the philosophy of the law, I again do not know whether we would have had any liberty.

Lord Acton has said that liberty is a term of 200 definitions. About all I am sure of is that it is something never established for the future, but something which each age must provide for itself. I think we are given the rough outlines of a free society by our Bill of Rights. Liberty is not the mere absence of restraint, it is not a spontaneous product of majority rule, it is not achieved merely by lifting underprivileged classes to power, not is it the inevitable by-product of technological expansion. It is achieved only by a rule of law. . . .

The Supreme Court, in the exercise of its power, has repeatedly come into collision with the strong executives of the nation. Jefferson, Jackson, Lincoln, and Franklin Roosevelt have been in open conflict with it. The clash has occurred where the Court was believed to be entering political realms through the passageway of private litigation. It would serve no purpose to review the merits of the conflict here, but in almost every instance it has occurred in such form as really to raise the question of minority and individual rights against majority rule; in each instance the President has been the representative of a powerful, popular majority. This is one of the great dilemmas of judicial power and one most avoided in discussion of the subject. So far as I can see, nothing has been accomplished in any of the controversies to settle or put at rest the questions which cause them. Judicial power to nullify a law duly passed by the representative process is a restriction upon the power of the majority to govern the country. Unrestricted majority rule leaves the individual in the minority unprotected. This is the dilemma and you have to take your choice. The Constitution makers made their choice in favor of a limited majority rule.

PART II

The Dynamics of the Judicial Process

"WE ARE very quiet here, but it is the quiet of a storm center, as we all know."[1] Courts—and particularly the Supreme Court, as Justice Oliver Wendell Holmes observed—are indeed a storm center—facing the panoply of human problems, crowded dockets, and unrelenting work schedules. Moreover, in Justice Benjamin Cardozo's memorable words, "the great tides and currents which engulf the rest of men, do not turn aside in their course, and pass judges by."[2] Not surprisingly, then, as Judge Irving Kaufman has said:

> Much tension accompanies the job of deciding the questions that all the rest of the social matrix has found too hard to answer. . . . For the job of adjudication is to decide those questions according to particular rules and free of the influences that often affect decisions made outside the courtroom. We represent a third value that is not, and is trusted not to be, the prisoner of either wealth or popular prejudice. . . . Thus all the pleasing mummery in the courtroom, all our political insulation, indeed all our power, is designed to support a message: "Whichever side you're on, we are not on your side or your opponent's side; you must persuade us not that you've got money or that you've got votes, but that your cause is lawful and just."[3]

The political nature of courts and judges inexorably poses tensions and influences the process of judgment. Judges are political actors, and not surprisingly, their political presuppositions and policy orientations affect their decisions and the process of decision making. Still, what remains essential in judging, Justice Felix Frankfurter argued, is "first and foremost, humility and an understanding of the range of the problems and [one's] own inadequacy in dealing with them: distinterestedness . . . and allegiance to nothing except the effort to find [that] path through precedent, through policy, through history, through [one's] own gifts of insights to the best judgment that a poor fallible creature can arrive at in that most difficult of all tasks, the adjudication between man and man, between man and state, through reason called law."[4]

The experience of appointment to the bench and the challenge of serving varies from judge to judge. Chief Justice Charles Evans Hughes related that when he was appointed, a friend wrote: "You are entering upon a life of slavery." He replied: "Yes; I know that. I have experienced freedom but even freedom has its illusions. I rejoice both in the responsibilities and the privileges."[5] Appointment to the Court, Justice Lewis Powell recalls, was more "like being struck by lightning."[6] Chief Justice Earl Warren reminisced that "perhaps the most lonesome day I ever had in my life was the day I arrived at the Supreme Court":

> [O]n Monday morning, I walked in about ten o'clock in the morning, and the Court didn't convene then until noon, and so I walked into the office of the Chief Justice and there was Mrs. McCue who had been the secretary for Chief Justice Vinson . . . and there were three law clerks, . . . [and] two old messengers. . . . And that was my staff, that's all there was, and here I came on four days notice, with no preparation and no knowledge of [the cases] in the Court at that time . . . to make the adjustment to the Supreme Court from [the Governorship of California], was really an adjustment.[7]

The adjustment to the bench usually takes some time. There is a kind of "freshman affect" on new appointees. Justice Tom Clark suggested as much when recounting a conversation with Justice Robert Jackson, whom he had asked: " 'How long did it take you to get acclimated here, Bob?' And he said, 'You know I asked Chief Justice Hughes that.' And I said, 'What did the Chief Justice say?' 'He said it would take about three years.' So I said, 'What do you think?' He said, 'Oh I'd say it's nearer to five.' "[8]

The experiences of judges and the dynamics of the judicial process are significantly different in trial and appellate courts. Former Court of Appeals Judge Thurman Arnold explained that he resigned because he found the work of a judge much duller than that of an advocate; though he "might have liked the trial court but on the appellate court we sat in groups of three and all we did was to listen to argument and write opinions."[9] At the trial level, the central function of the judge, sitting alone, is to oversee the adversarial process and umpire the factual determination of legal culpability. At the appellate level, judges, sitting three or more, review the records of lower courts' decisions for procedural errors or misapplication of the law. The trial judge, in other words, is primarily "a trier of facts"; whereas appellate judges clarify and "declare the law" in written opinions. This functional distinction imposes different responsibilities and represents a basic allocation of judicial power with important public policy consequences.

TRIAL JUDGES AND THE ADVERSARIAL PROCESS

The role and responsibilities of trial judges are often underestimated or neglected, perhaps because trial courts are but the first tier in the judicial system or because of an "upper court bias." We read and hear more about appellate courts, especially the Supreme Court. Still, as Judge Charles Wyzanski points out:

The task of writing opinions is as nothing compared with the duty of so conducting a trial, particularly a jury trial, that the jurors, the parties, the witnesses, the counsel, and the spectators not only follow the red threads of fact and of law but leave the courtroom persuaded of the fairness of the procedure and the high responsibility of courts of justice in advancing the values we cherish most deeply.[10]

Trial judges in both the federal and state systems, in fact, handle the bulk of judicial business. In 1982, for example, there were 189,479 civil cases and 31,889 criminal cases terminated in the 94 federal district courts; federal courts of appeals, now numbering 13, faced a total of 27,946 filings.[11] A substantial number of federal criminal defendants do not even go to trial or plead guilty, often as a result of plea bargaining, and a small percentage (14 percent) of those criminal cases that do go to trial are subsequently appealed. As one federal judge observed: "Justice stops in the district. They either get it here or they can't get it at all."[12] In most instances, trial courts, especially state trial courts, are courts of first and last resort. The discretion exercised by trial judges therefore is a crucial feature of our judicial system. As Judge Henry J. Friendly emphasizes: "In some instances the trial court is accorded broad, virtually unreviewable discretion, as is the case with criminal sentencing in the federal system. In others, the trial judge's discretion is accorded no deference beyond its persuasive power."[13]

Because lower court judges preside over trials among other things—including management of case processing, approval of plea bargains, supervision of the settlement process, and monitoring remedial decrees[14]—they, to a greater degree than appellate judges, experience the drama of the adversary process. Judge Marvin Frankel, in chapter 3, describes the work of a trial judge. He underscores the tensions between the role of a judge as an impartial arbitrator and the realities of a judge embattled, frustrated by the adversary process—a process some judges describe as legalized gambling based on a sporting theory of justice. The adversary system has long been criticized for its excesses, abusive treatment of witnesses, procedural delays, and high financial costs. Judge Jerome Frank eloquently argues that the system is based not on a "theory of truth" but on a " 'fight' theory, a theory which derives from the origin of trials as substitutes for private out-of-court battles":

> Many lawyers maintain that the "fight" theory and the "truth" theory coincide. They think that the best way for a court to discover the facts in a suit is to have each side strive as hard as it can, in a keenly partisan spirit, to bring to the court's attention the evidence favorable to that side. Macaulay said that we obtain the fairest decision "when two men argue, as unfairly as possible, on opposite sides," for then "it is certain that no important consideration will altogether escape notice."[15]

This spectacle of partisan justice uniquely replayed in each trial, as Judge Frankel shows, inevitably influences judicial decision making and behavior. A judge is not a mechanical scale or computer, Judge Frank reminds us: "Trial judges, being human, vary in their respective qualities of intelligence, perceptiveness, attentiveness—and other mental and emotional characteristics operative while they are listening to, and observing witnesses."[16] After presiding over a trial and reflecting on the evidence and law, the judge "experiences a gestalt"[17] on which he renders a final decision and then may rationalize in a written opinion.

APPELLATE JUDGES AND THE "CASELOAD CRISIS"

"No judge writes on a wholly clean slate,"[18] especially appellate court judges who review the decisions of lower courts and administrative agencies. The process of deciding appeals and the work cycle of an appellate judge is described in considerable detail by Judge Frank M. Coffin in chapter 4.

The collegial nature of appellate decision making needs to be emphasized and contrasted to the individualized decision making of trial judges. Federal appellate judges, for instance, sit in rotating panels of three. Occasionally, on especially important or divisive cases, the entire court sits as a panel or *en banc*. The dynamics of decision making therefore varies with the rotation of judges and the number of judges sitting *en banc*.

In response to the rising number of appeals during the last few decades, Congress increased the number of appellate judges, and in 1981 the Fifth Circuit was reorganized and split into a new Fifth Circuit and a new Eleventh Circuit (see appendix C, Jurisdictional Map of the U.S. Courts of Appeals and U.S. District Courts). Given the collegial nature of appellate decision making, the number, rotation, and location of judges in a circuit directly affects decision making. Chief Judge John Godbold, who serves on the Eleventh Circuit, explains some of the dimensions and problems of appellate decision making:

> I came on the former Fifth [Circuit] when there were twelve judges. We went to thirteen, then to fifteen, and finally to twenty-six. On the former Fifth, we had either thirty-five or thirty-six, counting the senior judges, at one time. That number gave more than seven thousand different possible combinations of judges sitting in panels of three. . . . [Moreover] as the [court] grew in size to twenty-six, it tended to fragment into several groups. I don't mean just in opinion writing, but also in differing views of the law. . . . A smaller *en banc* court performs the process of adjudication in the traditional manner. Usually, there is one view in one direction and an opposing view, with debate back and forth, and maybe people change their minds, but ultimately the court concludes with probably two views and maybe three once in a while. . . . In contrast the twenty-six-person *en banc* performed somewhat like a legislative body. It divided up into groups, with judges seeking accommodation on some ground that, while maybe not ideal for everybody, was at least agreeable to a majority. Its function became almost legislative and, therefore, antithetical to the way that appellate courts normally operate.[19]

The growing numbers of appeals and appellate judges strain working relationships and threaten the stability and continuity of law: more cases, more judges, and more opinions. In 1982 the Ninth Circuit alone issued nearly 4000 opinions. In the Fifth, Eighth, and Eleventh Circuits, for instance, a judge trying to keep abreast of caselaw developments faced reading between 1500 and 2000 new opinions each year. One appellate judge, Donald Lay, tells of his frustration: "A few months ago I was reading an opinion from our court; after reading several pages on a certain point, I wondered who wrote it. I was amazed to find that I had authored the opinion some 10 years before. The point is we read so much that we can no longer even recognize — let alone remember — our own opinions."[20]

In order to handle expanding caseloads, the number of law clerks assigned to a judge rose from one to two to three (and, at the Supreme Court, to four). There are also more staff attorneys and other office personnel. The chapter by Judge Coffin provides one view of collaborating with law clerks during the decision-making and opinion-writing process. Another federal judge tersely commented: "My law clerks write 90 percent of the opinion, and I write 100 percent." The increased number of law clerks and staff requires judges to spend more time managing their offices and perhaps less time deliberating and reflecting on their cases and decisions. Some appellate judges thus fear, as Judge Alvin Rubin explains in chapter 5, the bureaucratization of the federal courts.

Whether the increased number of law clerks and support staff will indeed prove to be the "carcinoma of the federal judiciary"[21] and turn courts into "opinion writing bureaus"[22] depends on the personalities and qualities of judges as well as the extent to which they actually relinquish their responsibilities to clerks or become preoccupied with supervising their staffs. "I don't think people are shocked any longer to learn that an appellate judge receives a draft of a proposed opinion from a law clerk." So remarked Justice William Rehnquist, adding: "I think they would be shocked, and properly shocked, to learn that an appellate judge simply 'signed off' on such a draft without fully understanding its import and in all probability making some changes in it. The line between having law clerks help one with one's work, and supervising subordinates in the performance of *their* work, may be a hazy one, but it is at the heart . . . [of] the fundamental concept of 'judging.' "[23] Some judges dismiss the threat of "bureaucratic justice,"[24] while others warn of its dangers — too many, too long, too footnoted, law review-type, patchwork opinions.[25] There is no gainsaying that the role and importance of law clerks in the judicial process has changed dramatically.

THE SUPREME COURT AND THE JUDICIAL PROCESS

The Supreme Court is often depicted as the most secretive, inaccessible institution in government. Yet, as Justices Lewis Powell and William Rehnquist explain in chapters 6 and 7, except for the justices' conferences and deliberations prior to handing down a ruling, "the Marble Temple" is open to public view.

Briefs for cases are available from the offices of the clerk and public information officer, and members of the public and media may listen to oral arguments and the "handing down" of decisions as well as obtain copies of final published opinions.

Life at the Supreme Court—once described as being of "unremitting toil"— is in fact much less glamorous than popularly imagined and largely centers in the cloistered chambers of the justices. Justice John Harlan, Jr., characterized the justices' chambers as "nine little law firms"—an apt description if one notes that law firms rarely work together; rather, they move in different if not opposite directions. "As much as 90 percent of our total time," Justice Powell similarly observed, "we function as nine small, independent law firms":

> I emphasize the words *small* and *independent*. There is the equivalent of one partner in each chamber, three or four law clerks [seven of the justices each use four clerks; the Chief Justice employs an additional assistant as well; while Justices William Rehnquist and John Paul Stevens rely on three and two, respectively], two secretaries, and a messenger. The informal interchange between chambers is minimal, with most exchanges of views being by correspondence or memoranda. Indeed, a justice may go through an entire term without being once in the chambers of all of the other eight members of the Court.[26]

Justice Powell entered the caveat that in other respects a modern law firm and the Supreme Court are light years apart. For one thing, he noted, he averages 60 hours per week: "This is considerably more than my chargeable hours ever were at the peak of a large and demanding law practice."[27] Similarly, Justice Harlan cautioned that "decisions of the Court are not the product of an institutional approach, as with a professional decision of a law firm or policy determination of a business enterprise. They are the result merely of a tally of individual votes cast after the illuminating influences of collective debate. The rule of ultimate individual responsibility is the respected and jealously guarded tradition of the Court."[28] The traditions and processes of decision making at the Supreme Court are indeed unlike those in law firms; but, like the heads of law firms, the justices are shrewd, strong-willed individuals—in Justice Harry Blackmun's words, "all prima donnas."[29]

The business of the Supreme Court, like that of other federal courts, continues to grow: from a bare 565 cases on the docket in 1920 to over 1300 in 1950, over 2300 in 1960, 4212 in 1970, and 5311 by the end of the 1970s. Unlike other courts, the modern Supreme Court's docket is largely discretionary. Therefore, to a considerable degree, the justices may determine their own agenda. The cornerstone of the Court's operations, Justice Harlan remarked, "is the control it possesses over the amount and character of its business."[30]

The Court must give full, plenary consideration to cases that come either under its original jurisdiction, as specified by the Constitution,[31] or as mandatory rights of appeal, as statutorally provided by Congress. Until 1925 the Court was required to hear and decide the merits of every case, except for a small number in which it exercised discretionary jurisdiction after the creation of Circuit Courts of Appeals in 1891.[32] Because of the expanding number of cases arising from the Industrial Revolution and government regulation at the turn of the century, the Court eventually could not keep abreast of its docket. Congress, passing the Judges' Act in 1925,[33] temporarily alleviated the Court's problem by largely replacing mandatory rights of appeal with petitions for *writs of certiorari*—petitions requesting the Court to exercise its discretion to hear the merits of cases, thus giving the Court power to refuse plenary consideration and enabling it to control its agenda.

Prior to 1925, 80 percent of the Court's docket was on appeal and 20 percent on certiorari. By contrast, today approximately 95 percent of all filings are on certiorari. During the 1981 term, the Court disposed of 4433 cases from its docket of 5311 cases, carrying over to the next term 878 cases. The cases disposed of included six on original jurisdiction, 242 on appeal, and 4089 petitions for writ of certiorari, as well as 96 others petitioning for extraordinary remedies. The Court granted review and disposed of 468 cases, either by full opinion or summarily (without oral argument or with a written opinion), and another 28 cases were withdrawn by consent of the parties. The Court thus gave plenary consideration to less than 9 percent of its docket; hearing oral argument in 184 and (after consolidation) disposing of 170 with 141 full opinions and ten by *per curiam* (unsigned) opinions, and scheduling four cases for reargument. The bulk of the cases—over 3900—were either denied as appeals or dismissed as a matter of discretion; the remaining cases were carried over to the next term.

Deciding what to decide, therefore, is one of the most important steps in the Court's decision-making process. The review of "cert." petitions, Justice Harlan Stone once claimed, is very laborious.[34] But as Justice Harlan underscores:

> The certiorari system affords the Court opportunities for more mature deliberation in the decision of cases than would otherwise be possible. For a large volume of unfinished business is bound to have an unfortunate impact on the decisional process, in that a court working under the compulsion of keeping its docket reasonably current inevitably has to deny itself the opportunity for unhurried reflection which is so indispensable to sound decision in all but the perfunctory type of case.[35]

Still, as Justice Byron White indicates, if the Court no longer can review more than 10 to 20 percent of the docket and give plenary consideration "to only 4½ percent of all cases,"[36] for the overwhelming number of cases is it not a matter of petition denied, justice denied? Justice Hugo Black provides a partial response to that question:

> I don't think it can fairly be said that we give no consideration to all who apply. I think we do. You can't decide the case, you can't write long opinions, but when we meet, we take up the cases that are on our docket that have been brought up since we adjourned. Frequently I'll mark up at the top [of a petition] "Denied— not of sufficient importance," "No dispute among the circuits," or something else.

And I'll go in and vote to deny it. Well, I've considered it to that extent. And every judge does that same thing in [our] conference.[37]

As Justice Black suggests, every case is given some consideration by each justice, and of course no case is entitled to "unlimited" review. In obviously doubtful, difficult, and important appeals or cert. petitions, two justices may be assigned to independently write full memoranda on the issues presented, prior to the justices' voting on whether to grant review. No less crucial but often overlooked is the fact that the vast majority of the cases on the Court's docket do not appear to merit review or are frivolous. Testifying before Congress in 1937, Chief Justice Charles Evans Hughes observed:

> I think that it is safe to say that almost 60 percent of the applications for certiorari are wholly without merit and ought never to have been made. There are probably about 20 percent or so in addition which have a fair degree of plausibility, but which fail to survive critical examination. The remainder, falling short, I believe, of 20 percent, show substantial grounds and are granted.[38]

Even prior to the introduction of the certiorari system, which encouraged the filing of questionable cases, Justice John Clarke in 1922 expressed his "surprise at the great number of cases finding their way into [the] court which are of entirely negligible importance, whether considered from the point of view of the principles of law or of the property involved in them. That impression has been intensified as time has passed, for their number constantly increases."[39] Similarly, Justice Harlan estimated that "more than one-half [of all appeals are] so untenable that they never should have been filed."[40]

The number of frivolous cases, in particular frivolous cert. petitions, largely stems from the Court's *in forma pauperis* (in the form of a pauper) practice — a congressionally established practice that gives every citizen the right to file without payment of fees upon an oath of indigency.[41] *In forma pauperis* petitions (IFPs) have steadily increased from 22 to 1930 to over 1000 in 1960 to almost half of the Court's present docket — 2354 in the 1981 term. Justice Harlan, among others, concluded that "more than nine-tenths of the [IFP] petitions [are] so insubstantial that they never should have been filed."[42] Individuals, without the cost of attorneys or payment of filing fees, thus may petition the Court with absolutely gratuitous claims. Clarence Brummett, for one, repeatedly asked the Court to assist him in a war of extermination he vowed against Turkey.[43] Justice William Brennan illustrates some of the frivolous petitions currently arriving:

> "Are Negroes in fact Indians and therefore entitled to Indians' exemptions from federal income taxes?" "Are the federal income tax laws unconstitutional insofar as they do not provide a deduction for depletion of the human body?" "Is the 16th Amendment unconstitutional as violative of the 14th Amendment?" and . . . "Does a ban on drivers turning right on a red light constitute an unreasonable burden on interstate commerce?"[44]

The largest and growing category of IFPs come from "jailhouse lawyers," indigent prisoners claiming some constitutional violation or deprivation. "The claims made are often fantastic, surpassing credulity," commented Justice William O. Douglas.[45] Although "98% or 99% of them are frivolous," he added, "We read them all because they produce classic situations like *Gideon* and *Miranda* and so on."[46] Even after a case has been granted review and after further deliberations, the justices may still dismiss a case as improvidently granted.

Deciding what to decide occurs during the Court's conferences. Conferences are held during the last week of September to consider the more than 1000 petitions that come in over the summer and, thereafter, when the Court is in session, on Wednesdays and Fridays to consider both petitions and cases on which oral argument was presented earlier in the week. Summoned by a buzzer five minutes before the hour, only the justices are present in the conference room, an oak-paneled chamber lined with books from floor to ceiling, located directly behind the courtroom. Over the mantle of an exquisite marble fireplace at one end hangs a portrait of Chief Justice John Marshall. Next to the fireplace stands a large rectangular table where the justices sit, surrounded by carts full of petitions, briefs, and other books. The chief justice sits at the east end and the senior associate justice at the west end. Along the right-hand side of the chief justice, next to the fireplace, sit Justices Thurgood Marshall, Harry Blackmun, and Byron White; on the left-hand side, Justices Powell, Rehnquist, Stevens, and Sandra Day O'Connor, the most junior justice. Sitting closest to the outside door, the junior justice by tradition receives and sends messages that come and go via knocks on the door—a tradition about which Justice Tom Clark wryly commented: "For five years I was the highest-paid doorkeeper in the world."[47]

The conferences for obvious reasons are conducted in absolute secrecy. (Prior to 1910, when a leak was suspected, two page boys were also present to run errands for the justices.) Like Justice Rehnquist (in chapter 7), Justice Brennan emphasizes: "But the secrecy is as to our deliberations. There is no secrecy as to how we operate at the conference."[48] Each conference begins with the justices' customary shaking of hands—a custom begun by Chief Justice Melville Fuller, which reminded Justice James Byrnes of "the usual instruction of the referee in the prize ring."[49] A typical conference, Chief Justice Burger tells, "opens with a discussion of the applications for review in this court; and then we move to a consideration of which opinions are ready for announcement; and from that we go to a discussion of the argued cases."[50]

The role of the chief justice in opening discussions of cases is not insignificant, for it provides the opportunity of fixing the relative import of a case within the context of the Court's entire deliberations, and perhaps to suggest (if not determine) the amount of time to be spent on each case during the more than 40 conferences each term. Chief Justice Hughes, a respected task leader, reportedly strove to limit discussion of cert. petitions to three and a half minutes and was largely successful for, as Justice Owen Roberts recalls, "[s]o complete were his summaries that in many cases nothing needed to be added by any of his associates."[51] With an average of 70 to 100 petitions to consider at each Friday conference, Chief Justice Earl Warren observed: "It may be fairly said that a majority of the time of our conferences is devoted to this purpose."[52]

Because the chief justice presides over the conference and is the executive officer for the Court, he also has an equally important role as a social leader—a role that in fact dovetails with that of task leader. Accomplishing the work of the Court requires cooperation among the justices, but that may prove at times difficult among strong-willed individuals with their own habits, prejudices, and philosophies. Justice James McReynolds, an avowed anti-Semite, for example, refused to even talk to newly appointed Justice Brandeis for three years. Chief Justice White was apparently unsuccessful in easing the situation, whereas the amiable Chief Justice Taft had somewhat greater success. The chief justice's role as social leader may hence prove vexing, for he cannot command collegiality or good feelings among the justices.

Chief Justice Hughes stands out as one of the most popular task leaders and social leaders. In Justice Frankfurter's words, "he made others feel his moral superiority, they merely felt a fact . . . all who served with him recognized [his] extraordinary qualities. . . . To see him preside was like [seeing] Toscanini leading an orchestra."[53]

During the conferences, the chief justice's skills as a task and social leader are especially crucial and instrumental to avoiding open conflict and promoting teamwork and cohesion. The responsibilities are particularly vexatious given crowded dockets and the limited time available for discussion of each case on the Court's agenda. Some chief justices are more successful than others in fulfilling their roles as task and social leaders. Whereas Chief Justice Hughes was largely successful in both roles, Stone's elevation from associate to chief justice led to severe tension and serious conflict, in part because he was unable to control the conference process and cut off debate, or to mediate conflicts when they arose. When a chief justice is unable to fulfill one or the other of these two important functions, it usually falls to one of the associate justices to take the initiative, or, alternatively, there emerges a competition among the justices for influence.[54]

As a decisional rule for granting cert. petitions review, the justices vote on the basis of an informal Rule of Four. That is, at least four justices must agree that a case is certworthy and hence merits oral argument and full consideration. The rule, like other practices and traditions at the Court, emerged incrementally in response to changing caseload demands. As the rule became established, it was occasionally breached if three or even two justices felt particularly strongly about hearing a case.

During his tenure as chief justice, Hughes explained the liberal application of the rule and that "certiorari is always granted if four justices think it should be, and, not infrequently, when three, or even two, justices strongly urge the grant."[55] Justice John Paul Stevens in chapter 8 further discusses the history and operation of the Rule of Four. Notably, he also suggests that, in view of the Court's crowded docket and the need for review of fewer cases and more deliberation, the rule should be revised to grant cert. on the basis of a majority vote.

The Rule of Four ostensibly has no bearing on the merits of a case or the lower court decision. Though Justice Robert Jackson contended that denial of cert. carries tacit approval of the lower court ruling, most justices maintain that "a denial nowise implies agreement" on the merits. Rather, for at least six members "the issue was either not ripe enough or too moribund for adjudication; that the question had better wait for the perspective of time or that time would bury the question or, for one reason or another, it was desirable to wait and see; or that the constitutional issue was entangled with nonconstitutional issues that raised doubt whether the constitutional issue could be effectively isolated; or for various other reasons not related to the merits."[56]

The chapter by Justice Stevens also draws attention to some of the changes that have occurred, due to increasing caseloads, in the process of preparing for conference and deciding what to decide. Given the steady increase in IFPs since Chief Justice Hughes's time, Justice Stevens points out, the chief justice assumed the task of circulating a so-called dead list identifying the cases he deemed unworthy of conference discussion. It was also the practice for some chief justices to prepare an outline of the issues presented by each cert. petition and to distribute it to the other justices prior to their Friday conference.

Current practice is for the chief justice to circulate a *discuss list*—a list of appeals and the cert. petitions he deems worthy of discussion, to which the other justices may add cases they think worth discussing. Moreover, six of the justices—the chief justice and Justices White, Powell, Blackmun, Rehnquist, and O'Connor—rely on *cert. pool memos,* which are two- or three-page memos each prepared by one of their clerks and circulated among the justices, explaining the facts and issues and stating a recommendation to grant or deny a petition. Those justices who chose not to participate in the cert. pool system must screen 100 or more petitions each week. Justice Brennan describes his screening process and use of law clerks:

> I try not to delegate any of the screening function to my law clerks and to do the complete task myself. I make exceptions during the summer recess when their initial screening of petitions is invaluable training for next Term's new law clerks. And I also must make some few exceptions during the Term on occasions when opinion work must take precedence. When law clerks do screening, they prepare a memorandum of not more than a page or two in each case, noting whether the case is properly before the Court, what federal issues are presented, how they were decided by the Courts below, and summarizing the positions of the parties pro and con the grant of the case.[57]

Justice Stevens has also found "it necessary to delegate a great deal of responsibility in the review of certiorari petitions to my law clerks. They examine them all and select a small minority that they believe I should read myself.

As a result, I do not even look at the papers in over 80 percent of the cases that are filed."[58]

Given crowded dockets, the justices necessarily rely on their law clerks (and on five research librarians, as well as, since 1975, two legal officers at the Court for assistance with cases on original jurisdiction or involving extraordinary remedies or requiring expedition—as with motions to stay the execution of a death penalty pending an appeal—and the like). Speculations about the Court's screening process are perhaps inevitable. Chief Justice Hughes, among others, dispelled the myth that petitions are distributed to the justices according to their circuit assignments.[59] When deciding what to decide, the justices do not operate via committees or panels. Another suspicion, Justice Jackson over 30 years ago reported, is that clerks "constitute a kind of junior court which decides the fate of certiorari petitions."[60] But every justice ultimately must decide and vote to grant or deny based on the justices' understanding of the issues, familiarity with other pending cases, and their own experience. Reminiscent of Judge Frank's description of a trial judge's decision, Justice Harlan observed: "Frequently the question whether a case is 'certworthy' is more a matter of 'feel' than of precisely ascertainable rules."[61]

Immediately after conference, the present practice is for the junior justice to report to the clerk of the Court which cases have been granted and which denied. (The chief justice also tallies the votes, and every justice has a large, docket book in which he or she may note votes and discussions for personal records.) The clerk, then, notifies both sides in a case granted review, as well as other individuals or organizations permitted to file *amicus curiae* (friends of the court) briefs, that they have 30 days to file supporting briefs. Once all briefs (40 copies of each) have been submitted, the clerk schedules the case for oral argument.

The Court's current argument calendar permits it to hear approximately 180 cases each term—far more than some justices feel advisable given the complexity of the cases on the Court's agenda and the necessity for reflection and collegial deliberation. "As a rule of thumb," Justice White, for one, has said, "the Court should not be expected to produce more than 150 opinions per term in argued cases, including per curiam opinions in such cases."[62] More than 30 years ago, when the Court was reviewing fewer cases and handing down fewer opinions, Justice Frankfurter complained that the Court's "schedule crowds the mind and thereby tends to force us toward premature judgments. There is such a thing as an intellectual traffic jam." Like Justice Frankfurter before him, Justice Stevens has complained that often "we [are] too busy to decide whether there was anything we could do about the problem of being too busy."[63]

The opportunity to argue a case before the Supreme Court, Justice Harlan reputedly said, is an opportunity to lose, not win, a case. Justice Harlan in chapter 9 further discusses the value of oral argument, but it is worth noting Justice Wiley Rutledge's observation that the function of oral presentation is controlled by two factors: "One is its brevity. The other is the preparation with which the judge comes to it."[64]

The importance of providing a concise bird's-eye view of the central facts and controlling issues in a case is underscored by the Court's strictly enforced time limits. Until about 1846 there was unlimited argument of each case before the Court. As the docket became more crowded, the length of time permitted became more limited, thus requiring more brevity from counsel. In Chief Justice Edward White's tenure the summary docket was invented; if an appeal could not be dismissed or a writ denied and the Court did not deem the case meriting unlimited argument time, each side was allowed 30 minutes. After the Judges' Act enlarged the Court's discretion as to which cases it would hear, Chief Justice Taft established another practice that further relieved the Court of the burden of hearing full argument in questionable cases. If the petitioner made an opening argument failing to sustain his contention, the Court would then announce that it would not hear the respondent. Noted for his rigorous enforcement of the rules governing oral argument, Chief Justice Hughes reportedly called time on an attorney in the middle of uttering the word "if." During Chief Justice Warren's tenure the time allotted per side was reduced from two hours to one hour, and the Court heard arguments only three days a week. Since 1972, the Court allows only one-half hour per side (though exceptions may be made). Although undoubtedly adding to the pressure on the advocates, the reduced time for oral argument not only permits the Court to hear more arguments but to spend more time preparing for and deliberating cases. Furthermore, prior to the Court's limiting argument time, Justice Frankfurter disclosed that Justice Jackson and he once agreed that the best arguments are those by counsel who have only a half an hour, adding that "a number of lawyers think it is a constitutional duty to use an hour when they have got it."[65]

Naturally, justices differ in the premium they place on oral argument. Justice Douglas insisted that "oral arguments win or lose the case,"[66] whereas Chief Justice Warren found oral arguments "not highly persuasive."[67] Accordingly, preparation for oral arguments varies among the justices. Most justices currently come prepared with "bench memos" identifying central facts, issues, and possible questions. Justice Holmes, however, rarely found oral argument influential, often taking catnaps while on the bench. Instead, he relied primarily on lower court records and to some extent the briefs. Justice Frankfurter, who claimed to never read the briefs, would consume large segments of an attorney's time—sometimes exasperating both counsel and other justices. In one instance, Justice Frankfurter interrupted counsel 93 times during a 120-minute oral argument.[68] On another occasion of F.F.'s interrogations, Justice Douglas intervened to help counsel with a useful answer, whereupon Justice Frankfurter asked the attorney, "I thought *you* were arguing the case?" The attorney responded, "I am, but I can use all the help I can get."[69] Oral argument provides the justices with an opportunity to probe the factual basis and limits of the logic of counsel's arguments, and to exchange views with each other.

During the Wednesday and Friday conferences (as Justices Powell and Rehnquist note in their chapters), the chief justice by tradition begins the discussion of cases on which the Court heard oral argument earlier in the week. Chief Justice Burger explains the procedure:

> The Chief Justice gives a brief summary of what the case is about, as he sees it, what the issues are, and perhaps in some of them indicating his view of the matter; that is not always the case because as the discussion goes around the table then, from the Chief Justice to the senior [Associate] Justice and in seniority, it is not uncommon for a Justice to say he would like to hear the full discussion before he comes to a conclusion. This might mean that he waits until the junior Justice has expressed his views, and then a general discussion may take place.[70]

There is a good deal of give and take in the process, and Justice White adds, "by the time that everyone has had his say, the vote is usually quite clear; but, if not, it will be formally taken."[71]

The traditional manner of voting has been said to be that the justices vote in ascending order of their seniority, with the chief justice voting last. Justice Tom Clark, for one, explained the rationale for this manner of voting: "Ever since Chief Justice John Marshall's day the formal vote begins with the junior Justice and moves up through the ranks of seniority, the Chief Justice voting last. Hence the juniors are not influenced by the vote of their elders."[72] But there are good reasons for doubting that the procedure is always followed, in view of the fact that the justices sit together year in and year out; their views become known over time if not during the course of a particular conference. Moreover, Justice Blackmun claims, "we vote by seniority, as you know, despite [the fact] that some texts say we vote by juniority."[73] He thus echoes Justice Black's admonition that it is "a fiction that everybody always waits for the youngest man to express himself, or vote, as they say. Well that's fiction."[74] Furthermore, as Justice Harlan stressed, by "common consent all conference votes are tentative."[75] "The books on voting are never closed until the decision actually comes down. Until then any member of the Court is perfectly free to change his vote, and it is not an unheard-of occurrence for a persuasive minority opinion to eventuate as the prevailing opinion."[76]

The tentative nature of initial conference votes underscores the important role of the chief justice in assigning the Court's opinion when he is the majority. If the chief justice is not in the majority, then the senior justice who is in the majority, by tradition, may either draft the opinion or assign it to another. Occasionally, at the initial conference a clear majority inclined toward disposing of a case in a particular way does not emerge, and thus the case may be carried over to another conference. Chief Justice Warren reported that *Brown v. Board of Education* was carried over week after week. Indeed, the arguments in that case were held in the middle of November, but the Court did not vote until the middle of February and after two prior conferences devoted to simply discussing the issues in that watershed decision.[77] In such situations, Chief Justice Burger tells:

The practice has grown up of assigning . . . one Justice to simply prepare a memorandum about the case, and at that time all other Justices are invited if they want to submit a memorandum; and then out of that memorandum usually a consensus is formed and someone is identified who can write an opinion that will command a majority of the Court.[78]

The responsibility for opinion assignments presents the chief justice with several options and considerations that may enhance or frustrate the working relationships among the justices. The assignment of opinions is made after each two-week session of oral arguments and conferences, unlike the prior practice of assigning cases the day after each conference. Hence, the chief justice has some flexibility in distributing the workload relatively evenly among the justices, while weighing in the selection, for example, how a particular justice views precedents and policy bearing on a particular case. The chief justice may assign an opinion to a justice in the majority whose views are closer to those of the minority in order to perhaps accommodate the other justices' views and thereby achieve a larger consensus if not a unanimous opinion. Of course, in unanimous decisions and those so-called landmark or watershed cases in which the chief justice is in the majority, he may choose to write the Court's opinion—as did Chief Justices Warren in *Brown* and Burger in *United States v. Nixon* (an opinion on which he worked 42 days straight and over 80 hours per week).

The drafting of opinions occurs in each of the justices' chambers with the justices and their law clerks collaborating long hours. It is usually weeks before an acceptable, initial draft is circulated to other justices. In the average case an opinion requires three weeks of work in preparation before it is circulated to each of the justices: "Then the fur begins to fly."[79] The circulation of draft opinions is pivotal in the justices' deliberative and decision-making process, providing opportunities for shifting votes and either further coalition building or fragmentation within the Court. As Justice Brennan explains:

I have converted more than one proposed majority opinion into a dissent before the final decision was announced. I have also, however, had the more satisfying experience of rewriting a dissent as a majority opinion for the Court. Before everyone has finally made up his mind a constant interchange among us by memoranda, by telephone, at the lunch table, continues while we hammer out the final form of the opinion. I had one case . . . in which I circulated 10 printed drafts before one was approved as the Court opinion.[80]

The circulation of numerous drafts is the norm and the switching of votes, even the conversion of a majority into a dissenting opinion, or vice versa, not uncommon. Once, for example, when the justices divided eight to one, Justice Stone, the lone dissenter, managed to persuade Chief Justice Taft, who assigned himself the opinion, to reconsider the majority's position. The result was that some weeks later when the draft opinion was circulated, the following note was appended: "Dear Brethren: I think we made a mistake in this case and have written the opinion the other way. Hope you will agree. W.H.T."[81] The new revised opinion became the decision for a unanimous court.

Although all votes are tentative until a decision is finally handed down, the psychological pressures on a justice assigned an opinion are complex and an important dimension of the Court's decision-making process. The justice assigned the task of formulating the position registered by a majority must carefully craft an opinion persuasive to a majority, and, if possible, not occasion separate, concurring, or, worse yet, dissenting opinions. Each justice copes differently with the psychological pressures of this responsibility—and assumes a particular style and approach; each may as well employ various strategies for marshaling the other justices. In Justice Holmes's view, drafting an opinion requires that a "judge can dance the sword dance; that is, he can justify an obvious result without stepping on either blade of opposing fallacies."[82] Crafting an opinion requires delicate balancing of opposing views, persuasive argumentation, and often subtle or not so subtle negotiation and bargaining. In one instance, Justice Stone candidly told Justice Frankfurter: "If you wish to write [the opinion] placing the case on the ground which I think tenable and desirable, I shall cheerfully join you. If not, I will add a few observations for myself."[83] On another occasion, Justice McReynolds gently appealed to Justice Stone: "All of us get into a fog now and then, as I know so well from my own experience. Won't you 'Stop, Look, and Listen'?"[84] For Justice Holmes, the task of writing the Court's opinion proved to be especially vexing; he complained: "The boys generally cut one of the genitals out of mine, in the form of some expression that they think too free."[85]

The author of a concurring or dissenting opinion, by comparison, does not carry the burden of speaking for the Court. Comparatively speaking, the dissenter, in Justice Cardozo's words, "is irresponsible. The spokesman of the Court is cautious, timid, fearful of the vivid word, the heightened phrase. . . . Not so the dissenter. . . . For the moment he is the gladiator making a last stand against the lions."[86] Dissenting opinions, in the view of Hughes, one who rarely wrote dissents, appeal "to the brooding spirit of the law, to the intelligence of a future day, when a later decision may possibly correct the error into which the dissenting judge believes the court to have been betrayed."[87] A dissenting opinion is a way of potentially undercutting the majority's opinion, but also a potentially useful tactic in negotiating with other justices; for the threat of dissent may persuade the majority to narrow its holding or tone down the language of its opinion. Some cases, of course, are "small fish," and a justice may not write a dissent in the hope of persuading the case-author to side with him in some future case. Justice Pierce Butler, for instance, once wrote to his colleague: "I voted to reverse. While this sustains your conclusion to affirm, I still think reversal would be better. But I shall in silence acquiesce. Dissents seldom aid in the right development of the law. They often do harm. For myself I say: 'I lead us not into temptation.' "[88]

The drafting and circulation of opinions is therefore central, if not the hallmark of the Supreme Court's deliberative process. The circulation of drafts permits the refinement of ideas and promotes negotiation and reflection prior to the handing down of a case on Opinion Day (which until the mid-1960s was only on Mondays, but now is on any day the Court is in session) when the justices either read verbatim or, more often, summarize their ruling and opinions. The dynamics of this part of the Court's decision-making process and the value of judicial opinions—majority, dissenting, concurring, and separate opinons—is eloquently examined in greater detail by Chief Justice Walter Schaefer in chapter 10.

Throughout the Supreme Court's decision-making process the chief justice occupies a special role: structuring the conference agenda; leading discussions of appeals, cert. petitions, and argued cases; and assigning memoranda and opinions. As first among equals, the chief justice inspires special attention. For, as Chief Justice Hughes explained: "Popular interest naturally centers on the Chief Justice as the titular head of the Court. He is its executive officer; he presides at its sessions and its conference, and announces its orders. By virtue of the distinctive function of the Court he is the most important judicial officer in the world; he is the Chief Justice of the United States."[89] The Office of the Chief Justice, moreover, has an increasingly important but nonetheless often overlooked administrative side. Judge Edward Tamm and Justice Paul Reardon in chapter 11 survey the administrative responsibilities—enumerated in over 50 statutes—of the Office of the Chief Justice and assess the accomplishments of Chief Justice Warren E. Burger in overseeing the federal judicial system and in promoting innovations in the administration of justice.

NOTES

1. O.W. Holmes, "Law and the Court," in *Collected Legal Papers* 292 (New York: Harcourt, Brace, 1921).

2. B.N. Cardozo, *The Nature of the Judicial Process* 168 (New Haven: Yale University Press, 1921).

3. I. Kaufman, Address, reprinted in *Time* 70 (5 May 1980).

4. F. Frankfurter, quoted by Justice Tom C. Clark in his address, "Some Thoughts on Supreme Court Practice," at the University of Minnesota Law School Alumni Association, 11-12 (13 April 1959).

5. C.E. Hughes, Address, American Law Institute (1930).

6. L.F. Powell, Jr., "Supreme Court Film," transcript at 1 (Film shown to visitors of the Supreme Court of the United States, Washington, D.C.).

7. E. Warren, "A Conversation with Earl Warren," *Brandeis Television Recollections,* WGBH-TV, Boston, transcript at 1-2 (Boston: WGBH Educational Foundation, 1972).

8. T.C. Clark, "Supreme Court Film," supra note 6, at 8.

9. T. Arnold, *Selections from the Letters and Legal Papers of Thurman Arnold* 3 (Washington, D.C.: Merkle Press, 1961).

10. C. Wyzanski, *Whereas—A Judge's Premises* 4 (Boston: Little, Brown, 1964).

11. See *Annual Report of the Director 1982* (Washington, D.C.: Administrative Office of the United States Courts, 1983). The number of filings in courts of appeals do not include those for the Court of Appeals for the Federal Circuit, which began operation in October 1982.

12. Quoted by R. Carp and R. Wheeler, "Sink or Swim: The Socialization of a Federal District Judge," 21 *Journal of Politics* 359, 361 (1972).

13. H. Friendly, "Indiscretion About Discretion," 31 *Emory Law Journal* 747 (1982).

14. See, generally, A. Levin and R. Wheeler, *The Pound Conference* (St. Paul: West, 1979); R. Peckham, "The Federal Judge as a Case Manager: The New Role in Guiding a Case from Filing to Disposition," 69 *California Law Review* 770 (1981); W. Hoffman, "Plea Bargaining and the Role of Judges," 53 *Federal Rules Decisions* 499 (1971); and H. Will, R. Merhige, Jr., and A. Rubin, *The Role of the Judge in the Settlement Process* (Washington, D.C.: Federal Judicial Center, 1977).

15. J. Frank, *Courts on Trial* 80 (Princeton: Princeton University Press, 1949).

16. Ibid., at 153.

17. Ibid., at 171.

18. F. Frankfurter, *The Commerce Clause Under Marshall, Taney, and Waite* 12 (Raleigh: University of North Carolina, 1937).

19. J. Godbold, "Interview," 15 *The Third Branch* 1, 2 (July 1983).

20. D. Lay, "Will the Proposed National Court of Appeals Create More Problems Than It Solves?" 66 *Judicature* 437, 437 (1983).

21. See P. Higginbotham, "Bureaucracy—The Carcinoma of the Federal Judiciary," 31 *Alabama Law Review* 261 (1980); and W. McCree, Jr., "Bureaucratic Justice: An Early Warning," 129 *University of Pennsylvania Law Review* 777 (1981).

22. W. Rehnquist, "Are the Old Times Dead?" MacSwinford Lecture, University of Kentucky (23 September 1983).

23. W. Rehnquist, Remarks, Ninth Circuit Conference, Coronado, California, at 24 (27 July 1982).

24. See McCree, supra note 21.

25. See H.T. Edwards, "A Judge's View on Justice, Bureaucracy, and Legal Method," 80 *Michigan Law Review* 259 (1981).

26. L.F. Powell, "What the Justices Are Saying . . . ," 62 *American Bar Association Journal* 1454, 1454 (1976).

27. L.F. Powell, Address, Eleventh Circuit Conference, at 4 (8 May 1983).

28. J.M. Harlan, Jr., "A Glimpse of the Supreme Court at Work," 11 *University of Chicago Law School Record* 1 (1963).

29. H. Blackmun, "A Justice Speaks Out: A Conversation with Harry A. Blackmun," *Cable News Network, Inc.,* Transcript at 4 (4 December 1982).

30. Harlan, supra note 28, at 4.

31. U.S. Constitution, Article III, sec. 2, cl. 1 and 2.

32. Circuit Court of Appeals Act of 1891 (3 March 1891).

33. Judiciary Act of 1925 (13 February 1925).

34. H.F. Stone, "Fifty Years' Work of the United States Supreme Court," 14 *American Bar Association Journal* 428, 436 (1928).

35. J.M. Harlan, Jr., "Some Aspects of the Judicial Process in the Supreme Court of the United States," 33 *Australian Law Journal* 108 (1959).

36. B. White, "The Case for the National Court of Appeals," 23 *Federal Bar News* 134, 140 (1976).

37. H. Black, "Justice Black and the Bill of Rights," *CBS News Special,* Transcript at 5 (New York: CBS News, 3 December 1968).

38. Letter to Senator Burton Wheeler, reprinted in U.S. Congress, Senate, Committee on the Judiciary, *Hearings on the Reorganization of the Federal Judiciary,* S. Rept. No. 711, 75th Cong., 1st Sess., at 40 (Washington, D.C.: Government Printing Office, 1937).

39. J. Clarke, "Observations and Reflections on Practice in the Supreme Court," 8 *American Bar Association Journal* 263, 263 (1922).

40. J.M. Harlan, Jr., "Manning the Dikes," 13 *Record of the New York City Bar Association* 541, 546 (1958).

41. See, 27 Stat. 252 (1892), 28 U.S.C. § 1915 (1948).

42. Harlan, supra note 40, at 547.

43. See *Ex parte Brummett,* 295 U.S. 719 (1935); 299 U.S. 514 (1936); 302 U.S. 644 (1937); 303 U.S. 570 (1938); 306 U.S. 615 (1939); 309 U.S. 625 (1940); *Ex parte Brummitt,* 304 U.S. 545 (1938); 311 U.S. 614 (1940); 313 U.S. 548 (1941); and 314 U.S. 585 (1941).

44. W.J. Brennan, Jr., "The National Court of Appeals: Another Dissent," 40 *University of Chicago Law Review* 473 (1973).

45. W.O. Douglas, "The Supreme Court and Its Case Load," 45 *Cornell Law Quarterly* 401, 407 (1960).

46. W.O. Douglas, "Mr. Justice Douglas," *CBS Reports,* Transcript at 12 (New York: CBS News, 6 September 1972).

47. Quoted in "The Supreme Court: How It Operates in Private Chambers Outside Courtroom," *Smithsonian* (Washington, D.C.: Smithsonian Institution, 1976).

48. W. Brennan, Jr., "State Court Decisions and the Supreme Court," 31 *Pennsylvania Bar Association Quarterly* 393, 403 (1960).

49. J.F. Byrnes, *All in One Lifetime* 154 (New York: Harper & Bros., 1958).

50. W.E. Burger, "Supreme Court Film," supra note 6, at 11.

51. O. Roberts, Address, Meeting of the Association of the Bar of the City of New York and the New York County Lawyers' Association (12 December 1946).

52. E. Warren, Remarks, American Law Institute, at 7 (Washington, D.C.: American Law Institute, 1956).

53. F. Frankfurter, *Of Law and Men* 133, 148 (New York: Harcourt, Brace, 1956).

54. For a further discussion, see David Danelski, "The Influence of the Chief Justice in the Decisional Process." Paper presented in New York City at the 1960 annual meeting of the American Political Science Association, and abridged and reprinted in W. Murphy and C.H. Pritchett, *Courts, Judges and Politics* 695 (New York: Random House, 3d ed., 1979).

55. C.E. Hughes, "Reason as Opposed to the Tyranny of Force," Speech delivered to the American Law Institute (6 May 1937), and reprinted in *Vital Speeches of the Day* 458, 459 (1937).

56. Brennan, supra note 48, at 402-403.

57. Brennan, supra note 44.

58. J.P. Stevens, "Some Thoughts on Judicial Restraint," 66 *Judicature* 177, 179 (1982).

59. See Brennan, supra note 44.

60. Quoted by T. Clark, "Internal Operation of the United States Supreme Court," 43 *Journal of the American Judicature Society* 45, 48 (1959).

61. Quoted in ibid.

62. B. White, "The Work of the Supreme Court: A Nuts and Bolts Description," 54 *New York State Bar Journal* 346, 383 (1982).

63. Stevens, supra note 58, at 177. For at least the last ten years of his tenure on the bench, Justice Frankfurter at the close of every term circulated memoranda to the other justices complaining of the Court's heavy workload and urging various changes in conference procedures. See unpublished Internal Memorandum, 1951-1961.

64. W. Rutledge, "The Appellate Brief," 28 *American Bar Association Journal* 251, 251 (1942). See also J.C. Godbold, "Twenty Pages and Twenty Minutes-Effective Advocacy on Appeal," 30 *Southwestern Law Journal* 801 (1976); and I. Kaufman, "Advocacy as Craft—There Is More to Law Schools than a 'Paper Chase,' " 28 *Southwestern Law Journal* 495 (1974).

65. F. Frankfurter, *Proceedings in Honor of Mr. Justice Frankfurter and Distinguished Alumni* 18 (Cambridge: Harvard University Law School, Occasional Paper No. 3, 1960).

66. Quoted in *Philadelphia Inquirer* (9 April 1963), and by H. Abraham, *The Judicial Process* 203 (New York: Oxford University Press, 1980).

67. E. Warren, "Seminar with Mr. Chief Justice Warren," University of Virginia Legal Forum, at 9 (25 April 1973).

68. See J. Frank, *The Marble Palace* 104-105 (New York: Knopf, 1958).

69. As reported by A. Lewis in "The Justices' Supreme Job," *New York Times Magazine* (11 June 1961), and quoted by Abraham, supra note 66, at 203 (emphasis added).

70. Burger, "Supreme Court Film," supra note 6, at 12.

71. White, supra note 62, at 383.

72. Clark, supra note 60, at 50.

73. Blackmun, supra note 29, at 21.

74. Black, supra note 37, at 5.

75. Harlan, supra note 35, at 21.

76. Harlan, supra note 28, at 7.

77. Warren, supra note 7, at 12.

78. Burger, "Supreme Court Film," supra note 6, at 12.

79. Clark, supra note 60, at 51.

80. Brennan, supra note 48, at 405.

81. Quoted by A.T. Mason, *Harlan Fiske Stone: Pillar of the Law* 222 (New York: Viking Press, 1956).

82. Quoted by A.T. Mason, Book Review of *The Holmes-Einstein Letters,* in *New York Review of Books* 60 (22 November 1964).

83. Quoted by Mason, supra note 81, at 501.

84. Quoted by A.T. Mason, *The Supreme Court from Taft to Burger* 65 (Baton Rouge: Louisiana University Press, 3d ed., 1979).

85. Quoted by D.M. O'Brien, *The Public's Right to Know: The Supreme Court and the First Amendment* 75 (New York: Praeger, 1981).

86. Quoted by T. Clark, "Some Thoughts on Supreme Court Practice," Address, University of Minnesota Law School (13 April 1959).

87. C.E. Hughes, *The Supreme Court of the United States* 68 (New York: Columbia University Press, 1928).

88. Quoted by Danelski, supra note 54, at 21; and Abraham, supra note 66, at 227.

89. Quoted by Abraham, supra note 66, at 208.

3

The Adversary Judge:
The Experience of the Trial Judge

MARVIN E. FRANKEL

*District Judge, U.S. District Court
for the Southern District of New York*

The Role as Written

There is an unhappily wide consensus that excellent trial judges are not in long supply. Among the causes are *(a)* the difficulty of knowing in advance who will turn out to be a good judge, *(b)* disagreement concerning the most effective means of selection, and *(c)* given our ambivalence on this as on other subjects, our lack of steady determination to do the things necessary—for example, to stop using judgeships for patronage—to select the people most likely to be most suitable.

While we fail too regularly to people the bench ideally, the ideal is not itself very uncertain. We can state with a substantial consensus the qualities we desire in our trial judges. The trial judge ought to be neutral, detached, kindly, benign, reasonably learned in the law, firm but fair, wise, knowledgeable about human behavior, and, in lesser respects as well, somewhat superhuman. Here and throughout, especially as the discussion grows more concrete and specific, the vision I have in mind is the judge presiding over the trial by jury of serious criminal cases, which is perhaps the crucible model and the one in which our failures are most frequent and notable. Responding to our tradition of judges as variable individuals—contrasting with the European continental goal of the standard, uniform, more predictable but perhaps less colorful judge —Judge Bernard L. Shientag, in a well-known lecture, defined the qualities in terms of "the personality" of the trial judge. He listed, and enlarged upon, the eight "virtues" of independence, courtesy and patience, dignity (but not excluding humor), open-mindedness, impartiality, thoroughness and decisiveness, an understanding heart, and social consciousness.[1] Others, judges and more objective observers, have compiled similar lists.[2] The consensus is not complete; both the list of requisites and the ranking of agreed qualities vary among people seemingly qualified to address the subject.[3]

Whatever the variations, a central core of agreed standards defines the trial judge as the neutral, impartial, calm, noncontentious umpire standing between the adversary parties, seeing that they observe the rules of the adversary game. The bedrock premise is that the adversary contest is the ideal way to achieve truth and a just result rested upon the truth.[4]

The idea of the judge solely, or even primarily, as "umpire" is not universally accepted. August pronouncements define the role more grandly. It is said that the trial judge—perhaps most especially in the federal court—has a more robust part. He may comment upon the evidence, perhaps direct somewhat, or at least guide, the course of the proceedings. I have given elsewhere my opinion that the judge as director or commentator, in a criminal case tried [by] a jury, is likely to be either ineffectual or dangerous.[5] But the disagreements about that are not vitally important at the moment.

What should go without saying is that the essence of the judicial role, active or passive, is impartiality and detachment, both felt and exhibited. In the quest for truth through the clash of contradictions, which is, of course, the only reason in theory for having trials, the judge does not care where the chips may fall. Concerned only that the right is done, the judge "should be patient, dignified, and courteous to litigants, jurors, witnesses, lawyers, and others"[6] as he presides over the contentious strivings toward that end.

These are banalities. Like many fundamental propositions, they are thought to be self-evident. Nevertheless, the fact is that these professed ideals, like others, seem not to be designed, under our practice, for consistently effective pursuit. The tension between the ideals and some insistent realities triggers the conflicts, or potentials for conflict, that constitute my central theme.

The Adversary Performance

Much of the time, the script, cues, and setting of the courtroom drama support the judge in performing his role as impartial arbiter between the parties and faithful guide of the jury toward the truth. The prescribed role has been learned by the judge during a (usually) long course of training and observation in the lists. The professed expectations of all the other participants, which are basic determinants of the role to begin with, support the prescription. The standard doctrine, respected for its own sake and as a weapon in the hands of higher courts, is a potent force. The ceremonial business is also a congruent pressure. The two sides, in the well, are physically equal. The judge sits between them, usually on a raised bench, and is called upon to reaffirm more than once the equality of the contestants before the law. The jurors are enjoined, over and over again, to be impartial, and the judge is both their mentor and their colleague in this effort. The usual pressures to conform encourage and drive the judge to be neutral.

But there are contradictions, powerful pressures in a different direction, that constitute the focus of this essay. The pressures may be of several kinds. I mean to consider only those that may be called systemic, inherent in the trial process as we conduct it. This excludes, among other things, an array of possible obstacles to impartiality that vary with cases, litigants, and judges — matters like legal or ideological preconceptions, biases touching people or groups, and things still more sinister and, it is hoped, more rare. The exclusions leave enough, I think, to warrant our concern.

The very nature of our accepted trial procedures generates forces that work against the judge's efforts to be neutral and detached. All of the several conditions and circumstances I plan to identify under this heading have in common a tendency to embroil the judge in the battle, to enlist him as an ally or to identify him as an enemy. Upon some reflection, however, I find these factors subdividing into two categories: those that cause the judge to take on combative qualities and those that serve to frustrate or impede or visibly depreciate his duty of leadership toward the truth. It seems convenient at any rate to divide the topic in this way.

The Judge Embattled

The supreme concern of the parties on trial, and therefore of counsel, is to win. Of course, the battle should be fought by the rules, but the goal is victory — not the triumph of "justice" viewed in detachment, but triumph. The high objective of the defense lawyer on trial is acquittal — not an acquittal because the client is innocent, just an acquittal. To be reminded of the cliché about criminal defense lawyers who say they could not bear the responsibility of representing an innocent man is amusing, not startling. We know that the great (and desired, and expensive) defense lawyers are those believed to be most likely to achieve vindication for clients who are not innocent. The following passage exaggerates somewhat, but makes the point:

> Because trial lawyers identify closely with their clients, they enjoy their practice only when they win, and nobody wins all the time. Recalling his own days as Steuer's assistant, a now prominent New York lawyer said recently that "there's grown to be a legend that none of Steuer's clients was convicted. That's nonsense, and no honor to Max. A good half of them were convicted — but nearly all of them were guilty. . . ."[7]

The preeminence of the concern for victory is less total for the prosecutor, but it is not a subordinate matter either. Prosecutors seek convictions. Under the rules, which seem increasingly to be obeyed, they have other, broader obligations. But their goal on trial is a guilty verdict, and their behavior in court is oriented accordingly.

With partisan counsel fighting to win, and with the judge as umpire to enforce the rules of the fight, there might seem a priori no reason in the nature of the contest why the judge should himself be, or seem to be, or perceive himself as being, drawn into the fray. The trial judge, likely to have moved to the bench from the ranks of advocates, may not start out wholly indisposed or unused to combat, but that progression is not unusual; all kinds of umpires are former contestants. The adversary trial, however, happens to be a game in which the role of umpire includes unorthodox features. Although it has no instant replays of particular events, its participants have a large stake in increasing the probability that the whole game may have to be replayed. This possibility depends largely, of course, on whether the judicial umpire himself commits fouls—"errors," as we say—in the regulating of the contest. And this element is liable to cause the detachment of the trial judge to be tested, threatened, and sometimes impaired, if not entirely lost.

The "big cases," heavily populated with lawyers, heighten the tension. When the crucial question has been asked, or almost asked, the courtroom explodes as people spring up at the several tables shouting objections, usually loudly because they are in some haste and heat to cut off forbidden answers. All perhaps look somehow menacing from combined effects of tension, hostility to the questioner, and anticipated conflict. Viewed from the bench, the rising warriors sometimes have an assaultive look, which is surely a fantasy, but a palpable one to be not, I think, experienced exclusively by judicial paranoids. Whatever the individual emotional impact, the occasion is a testing time for the judge. It may be an easy chance or a hard one. If the latter, the sense of being challenged and opposed by the demand for a ruling is a recurrent experience.

Nobody doubts the range of adversary implications in our description of the judge as being "on trial." Among the more explicit references to trying the judge are the usually proper things lawyers must do or say "for the record." But propriety or no, the statement may have a cutting edge. When the lawyer says, "Just for the record, judge," depending upon the degree of the judge's self-confidence, the phrase may seem to mean simply "to preserve our rights." Or, perhaps it means "This is too much for you, judge, but it is to be your undoing up above." And the lawyer may in fact intend that it be heard either way. Judge-baiting, if not one of the approved techniques, is, after all, not an utter rarity, although perhaps less common than some judges perceive it to be.

In viewing the judge as a probable adversary, the defendant manifests an attitude, and continues a tradition, that is ancient and far from dishonorable with us. Along with the prestige often attached to the office, along with the rituals of deference, we view trial judges with a deep strain of mistrust and hostility. We remember more trial judges in history as notorious than as notable. The hardy survival of the jury with us, as distinguished from its tendency to atrophy elsewhere, reflects a fundamental skepticism about judges. The Constitution itself teaches the lesson, commanding in effect that the fact findings of a jury be less vulnerable than a judge's.[8] The low pay of judges, in a society prone to estimate people in dollars, is part of the same story.

The Judge Discomforted

Apart from the threats to his detachment and neutrality, the adversary battle before the jury is frequently conducted under conditions that entail a potential sense of frustration, even stultification, for the presiding judge. Each of the contestants seeks to win. For either or both, in part or in whole, the goal of victory may be inconsistent with the quest for truth, which represents the public goal the judge is commissioned to pursue. "The very premise of our adversary system of criminal justice is that partisan advocacy on both sides of a case will best promote the ultimate objective that the guilty be convicted and the innocent go free."[9] If premises could be vindicated by reiteration, that one would by now have overwhelmed the skepticism it tends on its face to inspire. Whatever the case, the trial judge spends a good deal of his time solemnly watching clear, deliberate, entirely proper efforts by skilled professionals to block the attainment of "the ultimate objective."

When I say efforts are "clear" and "deliberate," I mean nothing less. This is not a jaundiced hunch; it is an open and shared professional understanding, concealed only from the jury. Often, the judge has been made explicitly aware before trial that the prosecution's assertions, though they will be contested at every step, are true. Less often, but often enough, the concession is made after trial, at sentencing or some other point when confession seems prudent or advantageous.

A whole class of examples arises in courts where plea bargaining is practiced. The bargaining, in which the judge frequently participates, starts from an understanding that the defendant has done approximately the wrong with which he is charged. In many cases, however, no deal is made. The defendant goes to trial. In the trial, the defense, by cross-examination and otherwise, fights to prevent demonstration of facts that were conceded before trial and are thus, in a sufficient and meaningful sense, known by the judge and counsel to be true.

Every trial judge could add illustrations from his own experience. I tender one here, perhaps more dramatic than routine, but apposite, I think, for our theme. A trial about two years ago involved a group of defendants charged with major dealings (multi-kilogram, hundreds of thousands of dollars) in heroin and cocaine. Important for both conspiracy and substantive counts was a suitcase that had been opened in a Toledo railroad baggage room and found to contain over five kilograms of heroin and a kilogram of cocaine.

Three of the defendants moved before trial to suppress this evidence as the product of an unlawful search and seizure. Their claim of a possessory interest giving them standing to seek suppression was resisted by the prosecution. It was concluded that the issue should go to an evidentiary hearing. The three defendant-movants took the stand for this purpose, protected by the prohibition against later use of their testimony as evidence at their trial, and proceeded to recount how they were indeed in the narcotics business, how they had bought the suitcase and packaged the heroin and cocaine for shipment to a Toledo customer, how their emissary had carried it from New York to the Toledo baggage room, delivering the claim check to the customer, and how they had retained "title" to the shipment pending receipt of payment in full.

The motion was eventually denied, both because the quaint claim of retained title proved defective and because the Toledo search was held in any event to have been reasonable.[10] But the points of particular interest here came later.

After other evidentiary hearings on pretrial motions adding to a total of 11 court days, we proceeded to a 19-day trial. While defendants did not take the stand, the considerable talents of numerous defense counsel were bent for four weeks on destroying any suggestion by any witness that would place their clients within miles at any time of any narcotics, including, of course, the Toledo shipment. Counsel for one of the erstwhile movants opened with the observation to the jury that there would "not be a shred of credible evidence," but only incredible assertions from "individuals who are the scum of the earth." A chemist who offered the opinion, novel only to the jury, that the substances in the Toledo suitcase were heroin and cocaine was raked by cross-examination for some three hours, his experience tested, his veracity and motives questioned, the modesty of his academic rank (and the fact that he was a mere Ph.D., not an M.D.) being duly brought to his attention when it became apparent he had a tendency to irascibility.[11]

Altogether, a total of 49 witnesses appeared. The jury heard over six hours of summation and a charge requiring (or at least lasting) nearly two hours. In deliberations extending over three days, including two nights of sequestration in a hotel, the jury called for testimony and exhibits reflecting questions, *inter alia,* that the movant-defendants had answered adversely to themselves, under oath, many weeks before. In the end, the defendants were convicted.

The purposes of and justifications for that four-week trial are familiar and (mostly) precious. The prosecution bears the burden of proof. Only lawful evidence is allowed. Defendants are presumed to be innocent. Jurors are to search out the truth, but doubts are to be resolved in favor of the defense. Granted all that and more, our immediate subject is role strain. How does it all look and feel to the impartial judge, regulating the contest, waiting to see whether the jury arrives at findings he knows to be correct or is successfully kept from doing so? Judges vary, of course, so there is no single answer, not even for any single judge.

My own survey—much self-analysis plus amateur polling—discloses several:

1. Trial judges are, preponderantly, ex-trial lawyers. The game is still fascinating. Participating, even as referee, is still fun.

2. The broad interests protected by the trial process are vital in themselves, and their furtherance day in and day out is a worthy form of service. The result in any single case is a matter of relatively lesser consequence.

3. It is galling to stand by helplessly while facts are obscured and distorted as part of the professional contribution to truth-seeking. The judicial role in such an enterprise is a sterile kind of umpiring. A quality of unreality haunts a process of bitterly contesting assertions that have been admitted (or sworn) to be true by the contestant in the very courtroom where the conflict now rages.

The satisfactions of the cases involving genuine, good-faith contests are nullified by such travesties.

4. The judge's role as teacher, along with the citizen-juror's role in the administration of justice, is warped and diminished when the jurors become the unwitting butt of a joke, launched on a chancy hunt after answers known to all the participants except themselves. Every trial is a drama. "Each case [is] a work of art,"[12] and it is entirely acceptable that there be felt in the courtroom the "faint magic of the theater. . . ."[13] But the play alone cannot be sufficient when the question is the doing of justice in real life. The jurors, who should leave the courthouse more appreciative than they were of themselves and the laws they helped vindicate, too often receive an unedifying demonstration that trickery and low cunning may be permitted to defeat the ends of justice.

NOTES

1. B. Sheintag, *The Personality of the Judge* (New York: The Association of the Bar of the City of New York, 1944).

2. See, e.g., B. Botein, *Trial Judge* (New York: Simon and Schuster, 1952); H. Jones, "The Trial Judge—Role Analysis and Profile," in *The Courts, the Public, and the Law Explosion* 124 (Englewood Cliffs, N.J.: Prentice-Hall, 1965); H. Lummus, *The Trial Judge* (Chicago: Foundation Press, 1937); C. Wyzanski, "A Trial Judge's Freedom and Responsibility," 65 *Harvard Law Review* 1281 (1952).

3. See M. Rosenberg, "The Qualities of Justices—Are They Sustainable?" 44 *Texas Law Review* 1063 (1966).

4. See, e.g., *Herring v. New York*, 422 U.S. 853 (1975).

5. See M. Frankel, "The Search for Truth: An Umperial View," 123 *University of Pennsylvania Law Review* 1031, 1041-1045 (1975).

6. The quoted words are from the *Code of Judicial Conduct*, Canon 3, Rule A(3). See also Canon 2, Rule A.

7. M. Mayer, *The Lawyers* 34 (New York: Harper & Row, 1967).

8. "In Suits at common law, where the value in controversy shall exceed twenty dollars, the right of trial by jury shall be preserved, and no fact tried by a jury, shall otherwise be reexamined in any Court of the United States, than according to the rules of the common law." U.S. Constitution, Amendment VII.

9. *Herring v. New York*, 422 U.S. 853, 862 (1975).

10. *United States v. Capra*, 372 F. Supp. 603 (S.D.N.Y., 1973), *aff'd*. in part, *rev'd*. in part, 501 F.2d 267 (2d Cir. 1974), *cert. denied*, 420 U.S. 990 (1975).

11. Consider for edifying cross-examination:

Q. And what was the title of your professorship?
A. It is assistant professor in pediatrics.
Q. You were an assistant professor, right?
A. Right, at Children's Hospital.
Q. And the next grade above that is what, associate professor?
A. That's right.

Q. And then there is another grade above that?

A. That's right.

Q. And that is called professor?

A. That's right. That's right.

Q. So that the lowest form of professorship is assistant professor?

A. That is not true.

Q. Is there something below that?

A. Yes. Instructor, research associate, there are teaching assistants that are involved with teaching. Now, we are getting into the definition of professor. This addition to professor is teacher—

Q. Doctor, if I may cut you off for a second, my question to you is that the lowest grade of professor is assistant professor, is that correct?

A. And my answer is: not correct.

Q. Oh, you say that instructor is a lower grade of professor?

A. Yes, and you also have a research—

Q. Do they call these instructors professors or instructors?

A. Yes, they can call them instructor professor, they could also be called—there are other forms called research assistant professor.

Q. Now, down in Washington, D.C., at the Children's Hospital, you worked presumably with children, is that correct?

A. Would you like to define what is children?

Transcript of trial testimony at 1956-57, *United States v. Capra,* 372 F. Supp. 603 (S.D.N.Y. 1973).

12. C. Bok, *I, Too, Nicodemus* 329 (New York: Knopf, 1946).

13. Ibid., at 324.

4

Reflections from the Appellate Bench: Deciding Appeals, Work Cycle, and Collaborating with Law Clerks

FRANK M. COFFIN
Judge, Court of Appeals, First Circuit

Deciding Appeals

Deciding an appeal is not a matter of approaching a problem as if for the first time. It is determining whether another, earlier, carefully structured decision should be upheld. That earlier decision, if by a court, is already the full-bodied product of a formal adversary hearing, held with all the garnishments of due process; if by an agency, it is the product of either such an adversary hearing or a rule-making proceeding in which the responsible official must invite and respond to public comments. Such a decision ought to be more likely to be just than the great mass of decisions that govern us in our everyday living, because the latter are made unilaterally, spontaneously, and perhaps emotionally by someone temporarily in charge of our fate, without organized forethought, testing, standards, or apprehension of review.

Even a structured lower court decision, however, can be in error. A jury can be carried away by passion or prejudice. A judge can make mistakes in rulings. (I hasten to confess that the fact that we rely on appellate judges to correct error carries no implication that they are wiser. Higher courts are "right" because they are "superior," not superior because they are right.) Apart from presenting an opportunity to correct mistakes, an appeal frequently provides an occasion for a desired change in legal doctrine. In such a case, one cannot say that the trial court has erred in applying conventional law; the appellate court's action in reversing is in pursuance not of its error-correcting function but of its lawmaking function.

At the same time, so much has been invested in the first decision that intuition tells us it should not be too easily discounted. There is no public policy for preferring a second decision that differs from the first only because the second decider weighs the evidence differently. Nor does what hindsight reveals to be a mistake by the trial judge, but one that has not significantly infected the final result, count enough in the scales of justice to warrant a second trial.

There must, therefore, be conscious and controlled deference to the decision of the lower court. By the same token, both sense and fairness dictate that the same ground rules govern the decision-making process in both arenas. Unlike a congressional committee, a government department head, or a business executive, an appellate court may not consider every last piece of information that comes to its attention. It is restricted in two ways: it must confine itself to the factual record established in the trial court or administrative agency, and it must generally recognize only those legal issues which were raised in the trial court.

While being so limited may be thought to shackle a reviewing court, the limitations are a source of strength. The raw materials for appellate deliberation are already fixed, assembled, and focused. Unlike other decision makers, appellate courts cannot worry over whether there is a need for more or better information. There is some advantage in having a target that has stopped moving. . . .

Every important appellate court decision is made by a group of equals. This fact reflects the shrewd judgment of the architects of our state and federal judicial systems that an appellate judge is no wiser than a trial judge. His only claim to superior judgment lies in numbers; three, five, seven, or nine heads are usually better than one. . . .

There is intimacy, continuity, and dynamism in the relations among judges, at least on the smaller courts.* They do not come together just to vote. They interact with each other, influence each other, and have each other in mind almost from the time they first read briefs for the next session of court. In a sense, the relationship among judges who differ in their values and views is a bargaining one, yet it is a continuing negotiation, where each player lays his cards on the table just as soon as he discovers what cards he has. There is, on a serene court, no suggestion that anyone seeks to manipulate anyone else.

In short, there is a difference between arriving at a yes or no decision through majority vote and working up an opinion on a close case so that three or more judges of different sensitivities, values, and backgrounds can join not only in the result, but in the rationale, tone, nuances, and reservations. Although the task of building toward a unanimous opinion, or even of carpentering a majority, demands a certain amount of sacrifice of ego and substantive concession, collegiality has its solid satisfactions. One quickly realizes that he is not the only source of useful insights. He learns to rejoice when he sees an opinion he has written measurably strengthened by the suggestion of one of his colleagues. Then, too, decisions are sometimes unpleasant, hard, risky, controversial, when the public and the press are hot and quick in their criticism. On such occasions, the comfort of collegiality is a pearl of no little worth.

*I am sensitive to the fact that my portrayal of the workings of collegiality is informed and limited by my own happy experience in the First Circuit. I realize that relationships on some larger courts may be characterized by more distance, differences, and tension than those I describe. Nevertheless, if what I depict is more often aspiration than actuality, there is I think, some merit in holding up a goal for the kind of judicial collegiality we have experienced.

At the risk of overemphasis I would say that *the* genius of appellate decision making is this final quality: a prolonged, graduated, and incremental process of deciding. Here is yet another paradox: the quality of decision is enhanced by prolonged indecisiveness. . . .

Judges, particularly, are expected to "Know the law." It is true that establishing what the facts are may take some time and the help of a jury, yet once this is done, a judge should have little trouble and need less time in applying the law to the facts and reaching a decision. This expectation is, in fact, realized in large numbers of cases that are either not appealed or should not be. But by definition an "appeal" is a protest by a party after a full-scale hearing, with the assistance of lawyers, before a trial judge and jury or an administrative agency. One would not expect such tribunals and processes often to produce decisions that are blatantly wrong. Nor would one expect a prudent person to appeal a decision that is incontestably right. Most of the time these expectations are realized. This leaves as the grist for appeal those cases where the trial judge or agency head had difficulty in coming to a decision, where error, though it may be significant, is not egregious but hidden and subtle, and where appellate judges apply a different perspective from the trial judge in guiding the evolution of the law. . . .

I see decision making as neither a process that results in an early conviction based on instant exposure to competing briefs nor one in which the judge keeps an open mind through briefs, discussion in chambers, argument, and conference, and then summons up the will to decide. I see the process, rather, as a series of shifting biases. It is much like tracing the source of a river, following various minor tributaries, which are found to rise in swamps, returning to the channel, which narrows as one goes upstream.

One reads a good brief from the appellant; the position seems reasonable. But a good brief from appellee, bolstered perhaps by a trial judge's opinion, seems incontrovertible. Discussion with the law clerks in chambers casts doubt on any tentative position.

Any such doubt may be demolished by oral argument, only to give rise to a new bias, which in turn may be shaken by the postargument conference among the judges. As research and writing reveal new problems, the tentative disposition of the panel of judges may appear wrong.

The opinion is written and circulated, producing reactions from the other judges, which again change the thrust, the rationale, or even the result. Only when the process has ended can one say that the decision has been made, after as many as seven turns in the road. The guarantee of a judge's impartiality lies not in suspending judgment throughout the process but in recognizing that each successive judgment is tentative, fragile, and likely to be modified or set aside as a consequence of deepened insight.

The nonlawyer looks on the judge as a model of decisiveness. The truth is more likely that the appellate judge in a difficult case is committed to the unpleasant state of prolonged indecisiveness. . . .

The Cycle of Work

What I have called the most important element in appellate work ways, incremental or graduated decision making, is the inevitable product of the cyclical patterns that shape the contours of life for appellate judges. While others may think our activity to be very much of a sameness, the cycles of work give judges a frequent and refreshing change of pace and challenge. They enable us to do confining, solitary work, month after month, without becoming desiccated by boredom.

The starting point is the schedule for hearing arguments at court. Each panel of three judges can hear no more than five to seven cases a day, depending on their complexity. A week's total of 30 to 35 cases is more than enough to keep three judges and their clerks busy in research and writing for the next three weeks. Some courts hear arguments for more than one week, then recess for six weeks' work in chambers. For me, the cycle is monthly, beginning in September and ending in June, leaving July for catching up on the year's work and, I always hope, most of August for vacation. Some judges may well cut out one or even two stages in a typical cycle, but I have found it natural to think of six. Each gives me a chance to approach a case from a different direction. In each phase I am likely to gain some new insight, perhaps at odds with one I had earlier. Each phase involves a different intellectual process:

- I read (or scan) briefs alone, usually at night.
- I talk over each case with my clerks, one of whom has given particular attention to it. I make notes of our colloquy.
- I listen to oral argument in court and ask a few questions.
- I confer with my fellow judges late in the day after the argument.
- I research, discuss, and draft an opinion in chambers or discuss, edit, and redraft the first draft of a clerk.
- I circulate my draft to my colleagues and respond to their suggestions; when they circulate their drafts, I propose changes to which they respond.

These phases, I have come to realize, are not merely sequential, chronological steps. They involve changes of environment, focus, and intensity that call to mind the metallurgical process of tempering a sword blade, alternately heating and cooling or quenching it until it achieves precisely the right condition of strength and ability to retain an edge. This is the kind of process served by the six stages of my decision-making cycle, which regularly alternate between the coolness of solitary reflection and the heat of animated discourse with others. Not only do they alternate, but the variation in the temperature of deliberations increases with each alternation.

Collaborating with Law Clerks

The importance of law clerks to the work and life of a judge cannot be stressed too much, particularly since the contemporary role of law clerk is so little understood. Law clerks have existed for over a hundred years, since Chief Justice Horace Gray of the Supreme Judicial Court of Massachusetts began in 1875 the practice of annually choosing a fresh law school graduate to help in chambers. Justice Oliver Wendell Holmes, Jr., succeeding Gray, continued the practice. The future Justice Felix Frankfurter, while a professor at Harvard Law School, undertook to pick out bright young third-year students and send them on to Washington to serve as clerks to various justices. Karl Llewellyn, of the Columbia Law School, twenty years ago, wrote, "I should be inclined to rate it as Frankfurter's greatest contribution to our law that his vision, energy, and persuasiveness turned this two-judge idiosyncrasy into what shows high possibility of becoming a pervasive American legal institution."[1] Pervasive indeed has this institution become, there being over a thousand law clerks serving federal judges, and more in the state courts.

A century ago, it may well have been that law clerks were kept busy and useful by checking citations, correcting galley proofs of opinions, running errands, and preparing memoranda on specific questions of law. Even today, there are judges who largely confine clerks to this range of narrowly defined tasks. But I suspect that judges increasingly are reposing larger responsibilities in their clerks, expecting them not merely to draft a memorandum of law on the major legal issues in an appeal but, after discussions with the judge, to organize and present the facts and to discuss the issues in some sensible order. Under this broader charter, the clerk's contribution is not a disembodied analysis of a refined legal issue; it is a prototype or aspirant opinion that reflects a sifting of the raw facts in the record, an ordering of priorities, and a discussion of the controlling law in the factual context that gives it point and purpose.

This means that the judge, instead of laboriously poring over briefs and the record to compose a succinct narration of the essential facts, is able to devote his attention to such things as whether an essential fact is missing or has been under- or overstressed and whether too many facts have been included. Of course, he is able more quickly to come to grips with determining if the legal discussion is as he wishes.

In short, as a result of the preparatory work of clerks, the judge's critical and judgmental faculties are released for action at a stage when the development of the opinion has ripened and the issues needing decision have been pinpointed. This also means that those critical faculties can be brought to bear on more issues in more cases.

It is the need to cope with caseload pressures that leaves no alternative, in most instances, to the kind of intensive utilization of law clerks that I have described. As we have seen, the decade between the late 1960s and the late 1970s saw the appellate caseload in most federal and state courts at least doubled, with very few additional judges made available to deal with the increase. Moreover, the increase was not merely quantitative; it was qualitatively characterized by the variety, novelty, and difficulty of the new flood of appeals, partly because of the continuing development of constitutional doctrine and partly because of the proliferation of statutes, state and federal.

Some idea of the pressures of time begins to emerge when we realize that the typical federal appeals judge will return to his chambers after a week of hearing argument with from eight to 12 opinions to draft. Perhaps three or four will be insubstantial, easily disposed of. Four or five will be of middling difficulty, where, although the law may be clear, the application is in doubt. Lengthy agency proceedings or trial transcripts must be digested. There will also be several cases that will demand the judge's best thinking on a novel legal issue. Even when, with good fortune, the judge will have two uninterrupted weeks in chambers, during the third week he must read 30 or 40 sets of new briefs for the next sitting of his court. The week after that, he is once again back in the courtroom. During his time in chambers, in addition to doing the thinking, research, writing, and editing of his eight or 12 new opinions, he must also continue any unfinished business, write critiques of his colleagues' opinions, respond to their suggestions and criticisms, tend to the daily flow of administrative duties, and try to catch up on his professional reading. A yearly output of 90 or even more formal opinions by a judge, in addition to less formal memoranda opinions and orders, not by any means a rarity, is perhaps three times the output of most judges in the early 1960s.

I doubt that any appellate judge relishes either the extent of these pressures or the role these pressures have created for him — that of the opinion architect-editor. I suspect that each opinion-writing judge would prefer doing every step of the process himself. When every last word in an opinion is the judge's own, there is no doubt about his authorship. When, however, words, organization, and selection were initially another's words, the way one knows that he has made that opinion his own is more subtle and ineffable. It grows out of a near-total immersion in the briefs, record, choices to be made, nuances of tone to be delicately sounded. . . .

[C]ollaboration with my law clerks takes place at almost every step of the appellate decision process, excluding only the conference among the judges. Even at the opinion-writing stage, collaborating with a law clerk takes many forms. The clerk's participation ranges from a minimum of checking citations and minor editing to being responsible for parts of an opinion . . . to crafting short opinions and to the maximum participation, having initial responsibility for a complex and significant opinion.

In all these situations, the clerk commences his work on a case with the benefit of notes of his own research and discussions with his judge before argument. He has also received his marching orders based on the vote of the judges at their conference following oral argument. Sometimes . . . the court remains undecided. It will be the task of the writing judge and his clerks to try to find a solution. The judge will frequently indicate on what issues research should be concentrated, and constant discussions between judge and clerk, and with fellow clerks, will take place as options become more sharply identified. As the clerk becomes more familiar with the judge's thought processes, style, and values, these become powerful if subtle sources of direction. The judge's careful review is, of course, the final and definitive control. The duty of exercising this control to the extent that a case warrants it is one of the judge's most demanding obligations. He must so immerse himself in the briefs and record and draft opinion that he is attuned to issues great and small, to both substance and style. He must then work over the draft until he can conscientiously say that it represents him with complete fidelity, not only as to the outcome, but as to approach, order of presentation, emphasis, length, and tone. Sometimes this point will have been reached after only a few word changes; sometimes not until the draft has been wholly rewritten. . . .

When my clerk and I—or sometimes in major cases all three clerks and I—work in tandem, each taking a distinct part of an opinion, I become the general editor and rewrite person. I must attain the same depth of familiarity with the parts initially written by others as I have with my own portion in order to be able to decide on sequence of discussion, transitions, tone, and emphasis. In a sense, this is not so difficult a task as that of reviewing a draft opinion wholly written by another, for I will have gotten into the record and the cases on one or more significant issues and inevitably will have familiarized myself with the remaining ones. My own work way is to read the draft rapidly to try to introduce it as soon as possible into my consciousness to plumb the depth at will. I note or check words that make me feel uncomfortable, awkward clauses or ponderous paragraphing, expressions that I think may grate on my colleagues. Then I reread the briefs, giving most attention to the losing party, noting arguments made that have not been dealt with in the draft.

Perhaps there is a good reason for the clerk's not dealing with them; perhaps not. If the opinion depends on the existence and significance of facts, my next step is most important—going back to the record, reading all of the relevant testimony, seeing how objections were made and how the judge's whole charge to the jury reads. This done, I am now in a position to work with my clerk in developing his draft into a finished opinion.

In one case I tried to identify how the process works. This was a criminal case involving eight or ten different issues, some of which were extremely close, arising out of a several-week trial of a number of defendants. It was the occasion for a particularly fruitful collaboration in the creation of an opinion with one of my law clerks. The lawyers for both the government and the defendants were unusually able. Such a combination of factors required two or three solid weeks of clerk time before the first rough draft appeared.

During its preparation the clerk saw to it that I became involved in specific issues and was aware of some of the close questions. Then came my reading, incubation, and more discussion. After several days of more intensive working together, discussing changes, trying out different language, and redrafting entire sections, both my clerk and I were satisfied that we had done as well as we could. The collaboration had proceeded somewhat as follows:

- The opening paragraph my clerk had drafted might have qualified as a one-act play, but not as a serious opinion where criminal convictions were at stake. (He really did not think this would survive but probably had to get it out of his system before he could settle down and write humble prose.) I substituted my own introduction to set the tone I thought was missing.
- My notes of the oral argument revealed a few significant facts being conceded that were not found in the briefs. We added these.
- My clerk had worked so closely with each issue from the very beginning that he tended to see each one as finely balanced, even though some of the issues no longer appeared at all close. I toned down some of the agonizing introductions to various issues, leaving them out and making them more neutral.
- Surgery was called for on some footnotes. For example, one footnote made a sound response to a very sophisticated argument that might have been, but was not, made. Another distinguished a case that could have been, but was not, cited. Similarly, I found some discussion in the text only marginally pertinent; we dropped this to a footnote.
- There were inevitable numerous, minor editing changes in paragraphing, sentence structure, split infinitives, unnecessary words.
- My major substantive contribution was to eliminate discussion of three issues that both sides had briefed but that were simply not part of the appeal; no objection to the allegedly improper evidence or jury instruction had been called to the trial judge's attention. As we have noted several times in these pages, part of the premise of appellate review is that the lower court has already had a chance to act on an issue. If we did not require points to be raised at trial, lawyers could play games, lulling the trial court by their apparent acquiescence with a ruling, then belatedly claiming error on appeal.

The result of this kind of collaboration is that two to three weeks of clerk time and two to three days or a week of judge time together produced a major opinion. Was it my opinion? In the case we have just reviewed, I had left enough traceable footprints to prove that I was familiar with the record, every nook and cranny of legal argument, and had made the opinion my own in many visible ways. The question would be less convincingly answered if I had made but a few changes in a draft opinion. Here, the challenge to the judge is a subtle one. If the issues are straightforward, if the draft is well organized, diligently researched, economically written, it makes little sense for the judge to make changes just to acquire a spurious feeling of authorship. On the other hand, the judge must somehow know that he has not been seduced into delegating his judgment by the blandishment of a most presentable, polished, and persuasive draft. To arrive at the point where the judge knows that he has done his duty may take, as in the case just summarized, days; it may take hours;

sometimes it may take only the fraction of an hour. I suppose that when and how a judge arrives at that point in a given case remains an uncommunicable mystery, the product of accumulated experience, wisdom, intuition, and integrity.

NOTE

1. Karl Llewellyn, *The Common Law Tradition: Deciding Appeals* 321 (Boston: Little, Brown, 1960).

5

Bureaucratization of the Federal Courts: The Tension Between Justice and Efficiency

ALVIN B. RUBIN

Judge, Court of Appeals, Fifth Circuit

During the two decades when I practiced and taught law, I thought of federal judges as magisterial if not regal. The district judge sat in black robes at a walnut bench in a paneled courtroom and presided at trials. If he—and at that time it was only "he"—did anything else, he was not judging. Circuit judges were even more august; they sat in stately triumvirates and, after listening to the oratory of argument, retired to their chambers where, in coat and vest, they studied law books and whence they issued opinions in phrases redolent of, if not equal to, those of Learned Hand and Benjamin Cardozo. This indeed was judging. All else was as incidental and unimportant as who held the judge's robe when he donned it.

Perhaps long ago that image was an accurate one. It is now fantasy. Today's federal judge is far busier than his predecessors, devotes a majority of his time to work in chambers and has much less time, if any at all, for reflection. The change is not due merely to an increase in the number of cases. Indeed, although total filings have increased dramatically, the number of annual filings per judgeship in district courts has not changed drastically in the last 40 years.[1] For the trial judge, management problems are due in great part to the mutation in the character of federal cases. Gone are most of the simple trials. Instead both civil and criminal litigation have evolved into complex proceedings, full of discovery and pretrial problems and culminating in lengthy trials.

Appellate judges are confronted not only with the same vast increase in intricacy of cases but, in addition, with a staggering increase in the volume of their work.[2] The annual appeals commenced per circuit panel in 1940 were 184. By 1978 the number had jumped to 585.[3] Our 1940 cases were largely one or two issue matters. Today, appeals involve records of thousands of pages and briefs arguing dozens of issues.

In testifying before the Commission on Revision of the Federal Court Appellate System, commonly called the Hruska Commission, Judge Ben Cushing Duniway stated:

When I came on the court [in 1961], I had time to not only read all of the briefs in every case I heard myself, which I still do, and all the motion papers . . . , which I still do, but I could also go back to the record and I could take the time as I went along to pull books off the shelves and look at them. And then I had time, when I was assigned a case, to write. And occasionally I could do what I call "thinking," which was to put my feet on the desk and look at the ceiling and scratch my head and say, "How should this thing be handled?"

. . .

Today the situation is quite different.

I have a strong feeling and I know many of my brothers and sisters on the Court have the same feeling—that we are no longer able to give to the cases that ought to have careful attention the time and attention that they deserve.[4]

As a result of changes both in the character and quantity of cases, much of the judge's work in 1980, a highly important part, will not be done on the bench. The average trial judge completed 47 trials last year, with an average duration of three days each. This means he spent about 141 days on the bench in open court. The rest of his time was not spent fishing; he considered motions, conducted pretrial conferences, assisted in the negotiated disposition of cases, prepared jury charges, wrote findings of fact and frequently ate lunch at his desk.

No appellate court works harder than the Fifth Circuit. Our judges handle about 25 percent of the total of all the federal appellate cases submitted for decision. Yet each of us spends only 40 to 60 days a year on the bench. The rest of our work is in chambers—studying briefs, writing opinions and doing myriad other judicial tasks.

Our courts continue to work furiously, but they are unable to cope with the torrent of cases without resorting to measures adopted primarily as time-savers. District courts delegate more and more of their work to magistrates, who handled 292,179 matters in 1978-79 alone. Appellate courts reduce time for oral argument. My own court, the Fifth Circuit, is compelled to decide 50 percent of its cases without any oral argument.

These changes have a hidden adverse impact. As more judges are appointed and as judges become busier, they have less time to communicate with each other. Their ability to harmonize opinions and reach collegial decisions diminishes. More conflicting opinions are rendered and the law becomes less predictable and less effective as a guide to behavior.

This is not the preamble, however, to a suggestion for more judgeships or more staff. Inundated by our case load, we of the judiciary have sought, and Congress has provided, palliatives: more judges, more magistrates, and larger staffs.[5] Magistrates and staff cost less per capita than judgeships. Accordingly, while the number of judgeships has grown, the size of supporting staffs has waxed even more. For example, our judges are now assisted by 1612 law clerks and 136 staff attorneys, a body the size of an army regiment. Let us take a look at the total size of our judicial branch: The 648 authorized federal judge-ships are supplemented by 181 retired judges, 444 U.S. magistrates, 236 bankruptcy judges, and a total complement of 11,857 other persons. The ratio of staff to federal judges (including retired judges) is 17 to one. (In 1954 it was 11 to one, so in 25 years the ratio itself has increased over 50 percent.)

Four decades ago district judges had a bailiff but no law clerk; each circuit judge had one clerk. Judge Charles Wyzanski has told me that, when he clerked for Learned Hand in 1932, he never prepared a draft opinion; indeed, Judge Hand told him never to write anything other than personal notes to prepare for discussing the case with the judge. His primary function was, in Judge Hand's words, to serve as a wall against whom the judge bounced balls. When Judge Hand was ready to discuss a case, he would summon his clerk and talk for an hour or so with feet on desk and hands behind his head. Then, having reached his decision, he wrote the entire opinion in longhand.

We are no longer able to work in this manner. To meet his responsibilities, the federal district judge today has, in addition to a secretary and two law clerks, a docket clerk assigned by the clerk's office, a court reporter, the services of a probation staff and the assistance of a magistrate and the magistrate's staff. He hears appeals from matters handled by bankruptcy judges and reviews the work of the magistrate. In effect, he runs a small law firm.

Each circuit judge now has three law clerks, two secretaries and the services of staff law clerks, the staff of the circuit clerk's office and the circuit executive. He has a small appellate enterprise.

So far as I can perceive, none of the 13,395 persons in the judicial branch is idle. I can truly say that I personally know of no one who does not work hard and for long hours. However, working hard and being efficient are not necessarily the same. Our judiciary now consists of a galaxy of judicial organizations. In work, as in judging, each is autonomous.

Fortunately, the quality of decision making is far superior to the methods used to bring issues to decision. At best, however, our operation is unwieldy and frequently ill-managed. Law clerks and secretaries work directly under the judge's supervision. Magistrates and their staffs, staff attorneys, clerks, probation staffs and other staff positions serve the court as a whole. Together they impose requirements on the practicing bar whose efforts to some degree supplement their own. When our orders or rules impose unnecessary or unproductive work on the bar, the result is to multiply the wasted effort prodigiously and increase the expense of litigation for clients.

Nominally the chief judge of each circuit and district is responsible for such management as the courts receive. He may, as is the case in our court, serve as the executive to implement policy made by the court as a body. He may, as is the case in our circuit, be assisted by committees. However, the policies embodied in court rules are frequently adopted with more regard to other considerations than good judging or efficient management. Moreover, the chief judge cannot be a chief executive because the time he can devote to administration is limited and he may or may not have managerial skills. He certainly has little time for or experience in supervising staff workers. As a result, no one appears to be in a position adequately to monitor the work being done by our staffs.

If these staffs are really competent to assist the judge, they do not act only ministerially. They do not merely run errands or perform chores; they assume responsibility. Responsibility is delegated throughout the system but the principal delegation lies at the hub, in the judge's relationship with his law clerks.

However hard a judge tries, he cannot completely review everything that his law clerks do or learn all that they know. Inevitably they assist him not only in routine tasks but in the work of judging. They read briefs, study precedents, prepare proposed jury charges and findings, and in some instances draft opinions for the judge's review. Of necessity the judge must rely to some degree on their work.

As a result, I fear we are approaching a kind of institutional judging in our courts. If each appellate judge today is reading every record and every brief that is filed with him, studying every authority cited as precedent and writing every word of every opinion he renders, he has more staff than is necessary. However, the fact is that each appellate judge does need every bit of assistance that he has because he cannot personally do each task in the way Learned Hand did—not if, as the average national appellate judge did in 1978, he is going to participate in the disposition of 585 cases, a total of 12 per working week or two per working day.

Last year, the average workload of a Fifth Circuit appellate judge included:

Opinions and participation in opinions	381
Considered petitions for rehearing en banc	285
Handled administrative and other interim matters	193
	859

If we assume a 48-week workyear, the average judge on our court wrote or participated in eight opinions each week, over one and a half per day. If he read each brief and each record, he read one and a half records and three or more briefs every working day, in addition to doing research and writing opinions. He also read one and a half briefs every day in connection with re-hearing applications, and read the briefs and decided one administrative matter every working day.

Nationally, the average judge was responsible for writing 75 opinions and for reading 287 records and over 600 briefs. I do not have the data for the additional work he did but I am certain that, like the judges of the Fifth Circuit, his duties that did not result in writing opinions required him to consider a vast number of other matters.

Why do we not have more great judges like the mighty jurists of yesteryear? To some degree, perhaps, we are lesser people today. But perhaps another reason is that, to produce great decisions, a judge must have time to think, ponder and write in pencil in longhand. In 1937 when Judge Hand was sixty-five years old, only a little above the average age of our present appellate judge, he wrote 60 opinions. Last year the average Fifth Circuit judge wrote 46 opinions, participated in 56 per curiam opinions and read briefs in and disposed of 23 cases without a written opinion—a total of 125 cases, more than twice as many as Judge Hand wrote. I have little doubt that in volume almost every federal appellate judge in the nation is required to perform more work every year than Justice Cardozo did when he was on the New York Court of Appeals.

It is obvious that we did not do this alone and that our regiment of law clerks had something to do with the decisional process. Those who apply for positions as law clerks are among the brightest and ablest graduates of our law schools. They seek a federal clerkship not merely to learn about how judgment is reached and rendered but also to participate in the process.

What are they doing in the judges' chambers? Surely not merely shelving books and running citations in *Shepard's*. They are in many situations para-judges. In some instances it is to be feared that they will become invisible judges as some of our colleagues succumb to the temptation of letting clerks' drafts form a major part of their opinions. Indeed, many observers have noted that opinions appear to grow longer in direct ratio to the growth of the judge's staff.

Even those of us who write every word of our opinions must be depending on these clerks to do something important. And who would not? The work is there to be done. It looms like a glacier before us, advancing inexorably. The short-term solution is to get more staff, delegate more work, accept the inevitable. But that surely means dilution of judicial responsibility as we have come to know it. In the long run it will lead to less respect for judicial decisions.

Here, then, is one aspect of our management problem: too much work, too little time to do it, the necessity for delegation, inefficient management and, ultimately, the dilution of responsibility for decision making. As the Department of Justice observed in its 1977 report on the needs of the federal courts, "[w]e are . . . creating a workload that is even now changing the very nature of courts, threatening to convert them from deliberative institutions to processing institutions, from a judiciary to a bureaucracy."

There are no panaceas. If, however, we are to prevent the conversion of federal judges from individual decision makers to spokesmen for a faceless bureaucracy, we must attack the problem on two fronts: We must manage our staffs better and we must halt the dilution of judicial responsibility. Let us first discuss the matter of management.

Justice Brandeis once said of the Supreme Court, "We are respected because we do our own work." It was likely for this reason that, when the Chief Justice of the Supreme Court was first authorized to employ three law clerks, Judge Hand said of Fred Vinson, then the Chief Justice, "I see that the Chief Justice has now become Vinson, Inc." His law clerk responded, "I fear he may have become Vinson, Ltd." For even as our assistants enable us to do more work, they narrow what we are able to do ourselves. Whatever part of our work is done by others, however urgently we need them to do it, is not our own work.

If we want judging to be done by judges and only by judges, then we need to institute other changes in addition to increased efficiency. However efficient the judicial branch may become, it cannot mass-produce justice. Wise decisions cannot be made if cases come in vast numbers on a judicial assembly line. . . .

NOTES

1. *1979 Administrative Office of the U.S. Courts, Annual Report of the Director,* tables 4 and 7, at 4.

District Court Filings

	Total Civil and Criminal	Per Judgeship
1940	68,135	359
1950	92,382	429
1960	89,112	364
1970	127,280	318
1978	174,753	438

2. *1979 Administrative Office of the U.S. Courts, Annual Report of the Director,* table 1.

Circuit Court Appeals Commenced

	Total	Per 3-Judge Panel
1940	3,466	184
1950	2,830	131
1960	3,899	172
1970	11,662	361
1978	18,918	585

3. The alert reader may note that this is based on the number of appellate judgeships in 1978. That number has been increased. However, the number of district judgeships has also been increased. Filings in district courts are not a measure of appeals. A filing does not result per se in an appeal. Appeals arise from final judgments and a few types of interlocutory orders by judges. Our experience in the Fifth Circuit is that the number of appeals per district judgeship, year in and year out, is forty. Therefore, we expect no decrease in the appeals per panel in the Fifth Circuit despite the addition of eleven new judgeships.

4. Quoted in R. Hruska, *The Commission on Revision of the Federal Court Appellate System: A Legislative History,* 1974 Ariz. St. L.J. 579, 583 n.14.

5. Most of the data is from *1979 Administrative Office of the U.S. Courts, Annual Report of the Director,* tables 20, 21 and 22 at 19-23.

	Total
Circuit Court Authorized Judgeships (increased by 35 in 1978)	132
District Court Authorized Judgeships (increased by 117 in 1978)	516
Special Court Judges	20
Territorial Court Judges	3
Retired Judges	181
Resigned Judges	6
U.S. Magistrates	444
Bankruptcy Judges	236
TOTAL JUDGES AND MAGISTRATES	1538
Law clerks (including those expected to be employed as a result of 1978 legislation: calculated on the basis of 3 per circuit judge, 2 per district judge, 1 per territorial court judge, and 1 per retired judge).	1,612
Circuit executives (10) and their staffs (18)	28
Secretaries to judges (calculated on basis of 2 per circuit judge in the Fifth and Ninth circuits, 1 for each other circuit judge, district judge, special court judge, and territorial court judge)	720
Secretaries to retired judges	139
Staff secretaries	126
Staff attorneys: 11 seniors, 125 others	136
Clerk's office personnel	2,717
Probation staffs	2,886
Bankruptcy staffs	1,333
Magistrates' staffs	358
Court criers	411
Court reporters	461
Supporting personnel of special courts	223
Librarians	51
Miscellaneous personnel	40
District of Columbia	10
Messengers	5
Nurses	3
Interpreters	14
Temporary Emergency Court of Appeals	8
Individual Panel on Multidistrict litigation	10
Jury Commissioner's staff	4
Staff of Administrative Office	473
Staff of Federal Judicial Center	129
TOTAL STAFFS	11,857
TOTAL JUDGES, MAGISTRATES, AND STAFFS	13,395

6

What Really Goes On at the Supreme Court

Lewis F. Powell, Jr.

Justice, Supreme Court of the United States

The Court is a place where Justices, and their small staffs, work extremely long hours; where the work is sometimes tedious, though always intellectually demanding; where we take our responsibility with the utmost seriousness; and where there is little or no time for socializing.

The constitutional duty of the Court, as John Marshall said in *Marbury v. Madison,* is to "say what the law is." In discharging this function, the Court is the final arbiter, and therefore its role in our system of government is powerful and unique. But it is remote from the mainstream of government.

It is natural, however, to be curious about secrets. For years — perhaps throughout the history of the Court — there have been stories and gossip about secret goings-on behind the Court's closed doors. I recall an article in the *New York Times Magazine* of 16 March 1975 that described the Supreme Court as probably the most "secret society in America."

The fact is that the extent of our secrecy is greatly exaggerated. The doors of the Court are open to the public. Both the press and the public are welcome at all of our argument sessions. Our decisions in the argued cases are printed and widely disseminated.

The charge of secrecy relates only to the discussions, exchanges of views by memoranda, and the drafting that precede our judgments and published opinions. As lawyers know, we get together almost every Friday to discuss petitions by litigants who wish us to hear their cases, and to debate and vote tentatively on the argued cases. Only Justices attend these conferences. There are no law clerks, no secretaries, and no tape recorders — at least none of which we have knowledge.

The Chief Justice, and the most junior Justice, have the responsibility of recording our votes. These votes always are tentative until the cases are finally decided and brought down. Each Justice may — and usually does — keep his own notes at Conference.

We rarely discuss cases with each other before going to Conference. After a tentative vote has been taken, the drafting of opinions is assigned to the individual Justices. When a Justice is satisfied with his draft, he circulates it to the other Chambers. Comments usually are made by exchanges of memoranda, although we feel free to visit Justices and discuss differences. There is less of this than one would like, primarily because of our heavy caseload and the logistical difficulties of talking individually to eight other Justices.

The process that I have described actually may take months after a case is argued. The preparation of an opinion often requires painstaking research, drafting, and revising, and additional efforts to resolve differences among Justices to the extent this is feasible.

It is this unstructured and informal process—the making of the decision itself, from the first conference until it is handed down in open Court—that simply cannot take place in public.

The integrity of judicial decision making would be impaired seriously if we had to reach our judgments in the atmosphere of an ongoing town meeting. There must be candid discussion, a willingness to consider arguments advanced by other Justices, and a continuing examination and re-examination of one's own views. The confidentiality of this process assures that we will review carefully the soundness of our judgments. It also improves the quality of our written opinions.[1]

Our decisions concern the liberty, property, and even the lives of litigants. There can be no posturing among us, and no thought of tomorrow's headlines.

I now wish to address two of the current myths about the Court. These have been repeated so often that they have attained a life of their own. One is simply untrue; the other reflects a fundamental misconception of the Court's role.

The nine Justices often are portrayed as fighting and feuding with each other.

This is a wholly inaccurate picture of the relationships at the Court. At the personal level, there is genuine cordiality. No Justice will deny this. We lunch together frequently, visit in each other's homes, celebrate birthdays, and enjoy kidding each other during our long and demanding conferences.

It is true that over the years there have been some fascinating examples of personal animosity on the Court. There are three Justices on the present Court who were law clerks during periods when some notable rivalries existed. Justice John Paul Stevens, one of these former clerks, recently told the Richmond Bar that he had been pleasantly surprised to find no such animosity on the present Court. "Reports to the contrary," he stated, are "simply not true."[2]

The media's erroneous perception of discord on the Court perhaps is based on a failure to distinguish between personal and professional disagreement.[3] Many cases present extremely close and difficult questions of law. Often these questions are intertwined with sensitive collateral judgments or morality and social policy. Examples of such cases include those involving capital punishment, abortions, obscenity, and the vast ramifications of equal protection and civil rights.

We do indeed have strong professional differences about many of our cases. These are exposed for the public to see. Unlike, for example, the Executive Branch, we record fully our disagreements in dissenting opinions. Frequently the language of a dissent is not a model of temperate discourse. We fight hard for our professional views. But, contrary to what one may read, these differences reflect no lack of respect for the Members of the Court with whom we disagree. In the course of a given Term, I find myself more than once in sharp disagreement with every other Justice.

It is fortunate that our system, unlike that in many other countries, invites and respects the function of dissenting opinions. The very process of dissent assures a rigorous testing of the majority view within the Court itself, and reduces the chance of arbitrary decision making. Moreover, as "Court-watchers" know, the forceful dissent of today may attract a majority vote in some future year.

A more substantive misconception concerns the role of the Supreme Court and the way it functions. A national magazine, in an article last July, described the Court as "rudderless, its nine Justices still searching for a theme."[4] Other commentators have said that the Court lacks strong leadership, and has no consistent judicial or ideological philosophy. Those who write this nonsense simply do not understand the responsibilities either of the Supreme Court or of the Chief Justice.[5] In the early years of what is called the Burger Court, one often read that the new Justices would vote consistently as a conservative bloc (the "Nixon bloc") to dismantle the great decisions of the Warren Court.[6] Now that this woeful expectation has not been realized, the criticism is that we are leaderless and unpredictable.

I have wondered whether those who decry the "rudderless Court" would like to be judged by a different kind of court. If, for example, one's liberty were at stake, would he like to be judged by a Court whose members were dominated by a willful Chief Justice? And what confidence could a litigant have in a Court that decided cases according to some consistently applied philosophy or "theme," rather than on the facts of his case and the applicable law?

To be sure, sweeping constitutional phrases such as "due process" and "equal protection of the law" cannot be applied with the exactitude of the rule against perpetuities. And in cases involving these and like phrases, Justices may tend to adhere to what often are called their own "liberal" or "conservative" interpretations. But in the application of these views, judgments are made on a case-by-case basis in light of relevant precedents.

Each of us has an equal vote, and though we endeavor to harmonize our views to reach a Court judgment,[7] the members of this Court vote independently. I do not suggest, however, that we differ in this respect from our predecessors. There is a long tradition at the Court of independent decision making. Indeed, this is the sworn duty of each Justice. . . .

NOTES

1. Both litigants and the public could be harmed if total "openness" were to prevail. For example, the decision in an antitrust case may affect the market prices of securities. Unless our initial Conference votes were final, the weeks or months of the opinion-writing process would be a continuous sideshow, with investors uncertain as to what to do. Or in a capital case that involved the death penalty, the condemned defendant would agonize over each memorandum circulated among the Justices.

2. *Richmond Times Dispatch* C-14 (31 January 1980).

3. Misconception as to differences among the Justices is not confined to the media. Law clerks, who are at the Court only for a year and usually have not practiced, may take personally the professional disagreements among us. A clerk's loyalty to his or her Justice tends to be high. This sometimes may cause a clerk—disappointed by the outcome of a particular case—to think harshly of Justices who have disagreed with his or her "boss."

4. *Newsweek* 67 (23 July 1979).

5. They seem to want a court that would take every opportunity to advance some preferred moral, philosophic, or political viewpoint. This would not be a court of law. It would be a supreme legislature—appointed for life. See *Younger v. Harris,* 401 U.S. 37, 52-53 (1971).

6. There was never justification for the alarm about a monolithic "Nixon bloc." The long history of the Court happily makes clear that Justices recognize no obligation to reflect the views of the President who appointed them. Life tenure, and the strong tradition of an independent federal judiciary, have assured this.

7. The Court fairly may be criticized for the increasing number of dissenting and concurring opinions. The diversity of views expressed in some cases reflects not only independence but more often the complexity of the type of cases that now come before us. See Gerald Gunther's "The Highest Court, the Toughest Issues," *Stanford Magazine* 34, 38 (Fall/Winter 1978).

7

The Supreme Court's Conference

William H. Rehnquist
Justice, Supreme Court of the United States

What I would like to do is to describe in some detail how the Conference of the Supreme Court of the United States operates.

It has been pointed out that the Conference of the Supreme Court is "secret." It is indeed secret, or closed, since only the nine members of the Court are permitted to be present while it is in session. But in order to put the matter in perspective, I would like to point out that a good part of the Court's work is done in public sessions, and that every single case, petition, or application presented to the Court is disposed of by an order entered in the public records of the Court. Let me present a synopsis of our Court's judicial year so that it can be seen how all of this fits together.

Beginning the first week of October in each year, we commence a new Term; we begin the Term by having three days of oral arguments before the full bench, sitting in the public Court Room in the Supreme Court building in Washington. On days of oral argument, the Court generally sits from ten o'clock in the morning until noon, takes an hour for lunch, and returns to the bench at one o'clock in the afternoon and sits until three or a little after. Generally each case which we hear argued is allocated one hour of time, so that in three days we will have heard 12 cases argued. These sessions of oral argument are held in the courtroom and are completely open to the press and to the public.

As soon as we come off the bench Wednesday afternoon around three o'clock, we go into "conference" in a room adjoining the chambers of the Chief Justice. This Conference is attended only by members of the Court, and at our Wednesday afternoon meeting we deliberate and vote on the four cases which we heard argued the preceding Monday. The Chief Justice begins the discussion of each case with a summary of the facts, his analysis of the law, and an announcement of his proposed vote (that is, whether to affirm, reverse, modify, etc.). The discussion then passes to the senior Associate Justice, who does likewise. It then goes on down the line to the junior Associate Justice. When the discussion of one case is concluded, the discussion of the next one is immediately taken up, until all the argued cases on the agenda for that particular Conference have been disposed of.

On Thursday during a week of oral argument we have neither oral arguments nor Conferences scheduled, but on the Friday of that week we begin a Conference at 9:30 in the morning, go until 12:30 in the afternoon, take 45 minutes for lunch, and return and continue our deliberations until the middle or late part of the afternoon. At this Conference we dispose of the eight cases which we heard argued on the preceding Tuesday and Wednesday, and we likewise dispose of all the petitions for certiorari (a writ from a higher court to a lower one, requesting the record of a case for review) and appeals which are before us that particular week.

Our jurisdiction to hear and decide cases on the merits is largely a discretionary one, rather than an obligatory one, and therefore the fact that we are asked to review many more cases during a particular year in the 1970s than we were in a particular year in the 1950s does not mean that we will necessarily hear and decide more cases on their merits in the more recent years. Our Friday Conference thus serves two separate purposes. First, as I have indicated, we vote and dispose of eight cases on the merits which we have heard orally argued earlier in the week. But at the same Conference we pass on what may be anywhere from 80 to 100 petitions for certiorari or appeals, usually not to decide them on their merits, but simply to decide whether we will grant plenary review and hear them argued at some later time. And while it requires a majority of the Court to dispose of a case one way or the other that has been argued on the merits, it requires only the votes of four of the nine members of the Court in order to grant a petition for certiorari in order that a case may be argued on the merits.

Thus a week of oral argument is composed of three public sessions, each lasting for about four hours, together with two closed Conferences which may together occupy anywhere from six to eight or nine hours. The Court's calendar usually puts two weeks of oral arguments such as this in a row, and at the end of such a two-week period we will have by our Conference votes tentatively decided somewhere between 20 and 24 cases on the merits. At the beginning of the week following the two-week sessions of oral arguments, the Chief Justice circulates to the other members of the Court an Assignment List, in which he assigns for the writing of a Court opinion all of the cases in which he voted with the Conference majority. Where the Chief Justice was in the minority, the senior Associate Justice voting with the majority assigns the case. This means that at the end of each two-week argument session, each member of the Court will have either two or possibly three Court opinions to write. In addition, he may well have to plan to write a dissenting or separate concurring opinion expressing the view of the minority or his own views in a particular case.

During the Recess following the two weeks of oral argument, a part of the time of the Justices and the law clerks and secretaries is devoted to preparation of the opinions which are to be written for the Court, preparation of dissenting opinions, and study of opinions circulated by other Justices. But a large amount of time during each Recess must likewise be spent in preparation for the next round of oral arguments, as well as preparation for the continued weekly Conferences dealing with the petitions for certiorari and appeals. Typically, during each Term of the Court, we schedule roughly 14 weeks of oral argument, beginning the first week in October and ending the last week in April. As the opinions in the cases heard early in the Term are written, circulated, and obtain a majority within the Court, and whatever dissenting views respecting them are likewise circulated, the Friday Conference will decide that such a case is ready to "come down." This means that immediately after we go on the bench at ten o'clock in the morning for a day of oral argument, the Justice who has written the opinion will briefly summarize the holding of the case and the Clerk of the Court will make copies of the Court opinion and dissenting opinions available to the public. Before this particular moment, all of the drafting, changing, and circularizing within the Court are regarded as absolutely confidential; the minute the opinion is handed down, it is available to the public and subscribers to a publication such as *Law Week* may obtain its full text in a matter of days.

A fair summary of the process I have described, it seems to me, is that in all of the 150 or so cases which the Court decides on the merits each Term the public is furnished not only the result reached, but each member of the Court joins one or another opinion in the case expressing his views on the questions raised. What is not available to the public is the internal deliberations which have taken place within the Court, or within each Justice's chambers, which have led to the reaching of this particular result. With respect to the decisions to grant or deny certiorari, or to summarily affirm or dismiss appeals, the result but not the reasoning is available to the public. The reason for the difference is essentially, I think, not a desire to conceal from the public the reasons for these latter dispositions, but rather the fact that because there are around 4000 of them, as opposed to 150 decisions on the merits, there simply is not the time available to formulate statements of reasons why review is denied or appeals are affirmed or dismissed without argument.

On the basis of my experience in sitting in on these deliberations, I have no hesitation in saying that the Court's Conference is a somewhat fragile institution. It is virtually unique in my experience in government in that the nine principals whose commissions authorize them to decide the cases before them are the only persons in attendance; no law clerks, no secretaries, no marshals, clerks, messengers, or pages, are present. The result of this fact is twofold. First, it permits a remarkably candid exchange of views among the members of the Conference. This candor undoubtedly advances the purpose of the Conference in resolving the cases before it. No one feels at all inhibited by the possibility that any of his remarks will be quoted outside of the Conference Room, or that any of his half formed or ill conceived ideas, which all of us have at times, will be later held up to public ridicule. I think this fact is generally recognized, and it is, I believe a consideration of some importance.

But the second equally important aspect of the nature of the Conference is that it forces each member of the Court to prepare himself for the Conference deliberation. All of us discuss the matters which will be coming up at Conference with our law clerks, and in the best tradition of our profession try to find good counsel from briefs, arguments, and research in the course of making up our minds. But the knowledge that once in the Conference it is our own presentation, and not that of one of our staff, which must be depended on, does make a difference in the way the Conference functions.

On a typical Friday, we will spend anywhere from five to seven hours arguing, exhorting, and at least figuratively gnashing our teeth over a series of cases that must be decided that day. As is evident from the written opinions which emanate from the Court, there are within the Court the most serious disagreements as to important constitutional principles. Yet day in and day out, week in and week out, year in and year out, a cordiality prevails among the individual members of the Court which transcends any differences there may be with respect to the decision in any particular case or group of cases.

Our ultimate dispositions of the cases we decide, and the divisions among us in making those dispositions, are of course a matter of record in the opinions which are filed. But there we have had the benefit of more careful deliberation and fine tuning, and an opportunity for second thoughts about what might have been hasty reactions to the views of our colleagues.

8

Deciding What to Decide:
The Docket and the Rule of Four

John Paul Stevens
Justice, Supreme Court of the United States

Whenever four justices of the United States Supreme Court vote to grant a petition for a writ of certiorari, the petition is granted even though a majority of the Court votes to deny. Although the origins of this so-called Rule of Four are somewhat obscure, it was first publicly described by the justices who testified in support of the judges' bill that became the Judiciary Act of 1925.[1] That Act enabled the Supreme Court to cope with the "utterly impossible" task of deciding the merits of every case on its crowded docket.[2] The Act alleviated the Court's problem by giving it the power to refuse to hear most of the cases on its docket.[3] Since 1925, most of the cases brought to the Supreme Court have been by way of a petition for a writ of certiorari—a petition which requests the Court to exercise its discretion to hear the case on the merits—rather than by a writ of error or an appeal requiring the Court to decide the merits.

In their testimony in support of the judges' bill, members of the Court explained that they had exercised discretionary jurisdiction in a limited number of federal cases since 1891 when the Circuit Courts of Appeals were created,[4] and also in a limited number of cases arising in the state courts since 1914.[5] They described in some detail the procedures they had followed in processing their discretionary docket, and made it clear that they intended to continue to follow those practices in managing the enlarged certiorari jurisdiction that would be created by the enactment of the judges' bill.

Several features of the Court's practice were emphasized in order to demonstrate that the discretionary docket was being processed in a responsible, nonarbitrary way.[6] These four are particularly worthy of note: (1) Copies of the printed record, as well as the briefs, were distributed to every justice;[7] (2) every justice personally examined the papers and prepared a memorandum or note indicating his view of what should be done;[8] (3) each petition was discussed by each justice at conference;[9] and (4) a vote was taken, and if four, or sometimes just three, justices thought the case should be heard on its merits, the petition was granted.[10] In his testimony, Justice Van Devanter pointed out that in the 1922 and 1923 Terms the Court had acted on 398 and 370 petitions respectively.[11] Since these figures indicate that the Court was processing only a handful of certiorari petitions each week, it is fair to infer that the practice of making an individual review and having a full conference discussion of every petition was not particularly burdensome. Indeed, at that time the number was so small that the Court was then contemplating the possibility of granting an oral hearing on every petition for certiorari.[12] Times have changed and so have the Court's practices.

In the 1947 Term, when I served as a law clerk to Justice Rutledge, the practice of discussing every certiorari petition at conference had been discontinued. It was then the practice for the Chief Justice to circulate a so-called dead list identifying the cases deemed unworthy of conference discussion. Any member of the Court could remove a case from the dead list, but unless such action was taken, the petition would be denied without even being mentioned at conference.

In the 1975 Term, when I joined the Court, I found that other significant procedural changes had occurred. The "dead list" had been replaced by a "discuss list"; now the Chief Justice circulates a list of cases that he deems worthy of discussion and each of the other members of the Court may add cases to that list. In a sense, the discuss list practice is the functional equivalent of the dead list practice, but there is a symbolic difference. In 1925, every case was discussed; in 1947, every case was discussed unless it was on the dead list; today, no case is discussed unless it is placed on a special list.

Other changes have also occurred. It is no longer true that the record in the court below is routinely filed with the certiorari petition. It is no longer true that every justice personally examines the original papers in every case. Published dissents from denials of certiorari were unknown in 1925 but are now a regular occurrence.[13] Today law clerks prepare so-called pool memos that are used by several justices in evaluating certiorari petitions. The pool memo practice may be an entirely proper response to an increase in the volume of certiorari petitions from seven or eight per week when the judges' bill was passed in 1925 to approximately 100 per week at the present time. It is nevertheless noteworthy that it is a significant departure from the practice that was explained to the Congress in 1924.

The rule that four affirmative votes are sufficient to grant certiorari has, however, survived without change. Indeed, its wisdom has seldom, if ever, been questioned.

During most of the period in which the Rule of Four was developed, the Court had more capacity than it needed to dispose of its argument docket. The existence of the rule in 1924 provided a persuasive response to the concern — expressed before the judge's bill was enacted — that the Court might not accept enough cases for review if its discretionary docket were enlarged. In my judgment, it is the opposite concern that is now dominant. For I think it is clear that the Court now takes far too many cases. Indeed, I am persuaded that throughout its history since the enactment of the judges' bill in 1925, any mismanagement of the Court's docket has been in the direction of taking too many, rather than too few, cases.

In his talk on *stare decisis* in 1944, Justice Jackson noted that the substitution of discretionary in place of mandatory jurisdiction had failed to cure the problem of overloading because judges found it so difficult to resist the temptation to correct perceived error or to take on an interesting question despite its lack of general importance.[14] In a letter written to Senator Wheeler in 1937 describing the workload of the Supreme Court, Chief Justice Hughes, after noting that less than 20 percent of the certiorari petitions raised substantial questions stated: "I think that it is the view of the members of the Court that if any error is made in dealing with these applications it is on the side of liberality."[15] In a recent letter Paul Freund, who served as Justice Brandeis's law clerk in 1932, advised me that the Justice "believed the Court was granting review in too many cases—not only because of their relative unimportance for the development or clarification of the law but because they deprived the Court of time to pursue the really significant cases with adequate reflection and in sufficient depth."[16]

It can be demonstrated that the Rule of Four has had a significant impact on the number of cases that the Court has reviewed on their merits. A study of Justice Burton's docket book for the 1946 and 1947 Terms reveals that in each of those Terms the decision to grant certiorari was supported by no more than four votes in over 25 percent of the granted cases.[17] It is, of course, possible that in some of those cases a justice who voted to deny might have voted otherwise under a Rule of Five, but it does seem fair to infer that the Rule of Four had significant impact on the aggregate number of cases granted.

A review of my own docket sheets for the 1979, 1980, and 1981 Terms confirms this conclusion. No more than four affirmative votes resulted in granting over 23 percent of the petitions granted in the 1979 Term, over 30 percent of those granted in the 1980 Term, and about 29 percent of those granted in the 1981 Term.[18] In my judgment, these are significant percentages. If all—or even most—of those petitions had been denied, the number of cases scheduled for argument on the merits this Term would be well within the range that all justices consider acceptable.

Mere numbers, however, provide an inadequate measure of the significance of the cases that were heard because of the rule. For I am sure that some Court opinions in cases that were granted by only four votes have made a valuable contribution to the development of our jurisprudence. My experience has persuaded me, however, that such cases are exceptionally rare. I am convinced that a careful study of all of the cases that have been granted on the basis of only four votes would indicate that in a surprisingly large number the law would have fared just as well if the decision of the court of appeals or the state court had been allowed to stand.[19] To enable interested scholars to consider the validity of this judgment, I have prepared footnotes listing 26 cases granted by a mere four votes in the 1946 Term[20] and 36 such cases granted in the 1979 Term.[21]

The rule is sometimes justified by the suggestion that if four justices of the Supreme Court consider a case important enough to warrant full briefing and argument on the merits, that should be sufficient evidence of the significance of the question presented.[22] But a countervailing argument has at least equal force. Every case that is granted on the basis of four votes is a case that five members of the Court thought should not be granted.[23] For the most significant work of the Court, it is assumed that the collective judgment of its majority is more reliable than the views of the minority.[24] Arguably, therefore, deference to the minority's desire to add additional cases to the argument docket may rest on an assumption that whether the Court hears a few more or a few less cases in any term is not a matter of first importance.[25]

NOTES

1. 43 Stat. 936.

2. On 18 December 1924, Justice McReynolds testified before the Committee on the Judiciary of the House of Representatives as follows: "Every year now Congress is passing many acts and every act that is passed probably sooner or later will come to us in some one or other of its aspects. The more Federal acts there are the more opportunities there are of bringing cases to us, and it has been growing and growing until it is utterly impossible for us to try every case in which there is a Federal question involved. So it must be determined whether the court will slip behind and delays will increase or whether the number of cases presented to the court shall be restricted." *Hearings on H.R. 8206 before the Committee on the Judiciary,* 68th Cong., 2d Sess., 20 (1924) (hereinafter "House Hearings").

3. "For the three terms preceding [the 1925 Act] eighty percent of the cases came to the Court as a matter of course, regardless of the Court's judgment as to the seriousness of the questions at issue. In less than twenty percent did the Court exercise discretion in assuming jurisdiction." F. Frankfurter and J. Landis, "The Supreme Court Under the Judiciary Act of 1925," 42 *Harvard Law Review* 10-11 (1928).

4. William Howard Taft described the background of the 1891 Act as follows: "At the centenary celebration of the launching of the Federal Constitution in Philadelphia, the addresses of the Justices of the Supreme Court and of the distinguished members of the Bar contained urgent appeals to Congress to relieve the Court, which was then considerably more than three years behind.

"Congress sought to remove the congestion by the Act of March 3d, 1891. [26 Stat. 826.] It created nine Circuit Courts of Appeals as intermediate courts of review. . . .

"In the Act of 1891, Congress for the first time conferred upon the Supreme Court, in extensive classes of litigation, discretion to decline to review cases if they did not seem to the Court to be worthy of further review. In this discretionary jurisdiction the most numerous class of cases was of those which depended upon the diverse citizenship of the parties as the basis of federal jurisdiction." W. Taft, "The Jurisdiction of the Supreme Court Under the Act of February 13, 1925," 35 *Yale Law Journal* 2 (1925).

5. Justice Van Devanter testified: "Then, we have the cases coming from the State courts. For a great many years cases came from the State courts on writ of error only

to the Supreme Court, the cases being those in which there were Federal questions which were decided adversely to the litigant asserting the Federal right. The statute was changed about 1914 so as to permit the Supreme Court to take cases on petitions for certiorari where the Federal question was decided in favor of the Federal right. That situation continued until 1916, when a statute was enacted which enlarged the number of cases that could come on petition for certiorari from State courts, and decreased accordingly the number that could come on writ of error." *Hearings on S. 2060 and 2061 before a Subcomm. of the Committee on the Judiciary,* 68th Cong., 1st Sess., 34 (1924) (hereinafter "Senate Hearings").

The Evarts Act, enacted in 1916, 39 Stat. 726, removed cases arising under the Federal Employers Liability Act from those which the Court was statutorily required to hear and thereby made a substantial enlargement in the Court's discretionary docket. Nevertheless, it remained true that over 80 percent of the Court's docket was obligatory rather than discretionary.

6. For example, Chief Justice Taft testified: "I heard the late Philander Knox, with whom I was on intimate terms, say either to me or to some one in my hearing, a word or two indicating that he thought the question of whether a case got in by certiorari or not was governed by the temperament, the digestion, and the good nature of the particular person in the court to whom the question was referred, that it was distributed in some way so that each member of the court had two or three certioraris that it could let in.

"Now, the truth is, and I want to emphasize that because I think perhaps I have more to do with certioraris in one way than any other member of the court, because I have to make the first statement of the case when a certiorari comes up for disposition; I write out every case that comes up for certiorari and I read it to the court. I think the members of the court are a little impatient sometimes because I give too much detail. Perhaps that is because I am a new member or was a new member. And then having stated the case I go around and ask each member of the court, who has his memorandum, as to what view he takes. Then having discussed the case we vote on it." House Hearings, supra note 2, at 26-27.

7. Justice Van Devanter testified: "The petition and brief are required to be served on the other party, and time is given for the presentation of an opposing brief. When this has been done copies of the printed record as it came from the circuit court of appeals and of the petition and briefs are distributed among the members of the Supreme Court. . . ." House Hearings, supra note 2, at 8.

8. Justice Van Devanter unequivocally stated that "each judge examines them and prepares a memorandum or note indicating his view of what should be done." Ibid.

9. "In conference these cases are called, each in its turn, and each judge states his views *in extenso* or briefly as he thinks proper; and when all have spoken any difference in opinion is discussed and then a vote is taken. I explain this at some length because it seems to be thought outside that the cases are referred to particular judges, as, for instance, that those coming from a particular circuit are referred to the justice assigned to that circuit, and that he reports on them, and the others accept his report. That impression is wholly at variance with what actually occurs." Chief Justice Taft elaborated on the procedure (see supra note 6).

10. Reading the legislative history in its entirety, I gain the impression that the principal emphasis in the presentation made by the justices concentrated on the individual attention given to every petition by every justice and the full discussion of every petition

at conference, and that significantly less emphasis was placed on the Rule of Four. House Hearings, supra note 2, at 8.

11. House Hearings, supra note 2, at 13. In *Southern Power Co. v. North Carolina Public Service Co.,* 263 U.S. 508, 509, the Court noted that 420 petitions for certiorari had been filed during the 1922 Term. However the difference between this figure and the figures mentioned by Justice Van Devanter may be explained (possibly by a difference between filings and dispositions), it is plain that the Court was required to deal with relatively few petitions each week.

12. Shortly after the enactment of the 1925 Act, Chief Justice Taft wrote: "A question has been under consideration by the Court as to whether it would be practical to give oral hearings to applications for certioraris. The changes in the new Act will doubtless increase the number of these applications, and if the Court could be relieved by short oral statements of the burden of close examination of briefs and records, it might help its disposition of the business and at the same time give assurance to counsel of the fact, which seems sometimes to have been doubted, that the full Court seriously considers every application for a certiorari and votes upon it as a real issue to be judicially determined. If there are to be five hundred applications for certiorari a year (a conservative estimate), and ten minutes should be allowed to a side, this would consume, if all the applications were orally presented and opposed, eight weeks of the oral sessions of the Court. The Court gives about eighteen weeks to oral sessions during an annual term, so that it would take a little less than one-half of the oral sessions devoted by the Court to argument. Of course it is suggested that even if argument were permitted, advantage would not be taken in many cases in which briefs would be solely relied on. An experiment of a week or two at the beginning of the term might possibly enable the Court to judge more safely as to this. I fear, however, that the experiment would show to be true what Senator Cummins said upon the floor of the Senate, when it was proposed to require oral hearings of certiorari applications, that we might just as well not pass the law at all." Taft, supra note 4, at 12.

13. I have previously commented on this use of the Court's scarce resources. See *Singleton v. Commissioner,* 439 U.S. 942 (Opinion of Stevens, J., respecting the denial of the petition for writ of certiorari).

14. "We once thought that substitution of discretionary in place of mandatory jurisdiction would cure overloading. It has helped greatly. But the burden of passing on petitions invoking discretion is considerable, and the temptation to judges is great to take hold of any result that strikes them as wrong or any question that is interesting, even if not of general importance. The fact is that neither the judges nor the profession have wholeheartedly and consistently accepted the implications of discretionary jurisdiction in courts of last resort." R. Jackson, "Decisional Law and Stare Decisis," 30 *American Bar Association Journal* 334 (1945).

15. Letter from Chief Justice Charles Evans Hughes to Senator Burton K. Wheeler (21 March 1937).

16. Letter from Paul A. Freund to John Paul Stevens (24 August 1982). I found that comment of particular interest because one of the points made in Justice Brandeis's criticism of the *Jensen* rule in his dissent in *Washington v. Dawson Co.,* 264 U.S., at 237—an opinion that was written while the judges' bill was under consideration—was that adherence to the *Jensen* rule would "make a serious addition to the classes of cases which this Court is required to review."

17. Harold Burton Papers, Manuscript Division, Library of Congress.

18. I am indebted to my law clerks, Carol Lee and Jeffrey Lehman, for assembling this data from Justice Burton's records and from my docket sheets, for identifying the cases listed in notes 20 and 21, infra, and for making a number of valuable criticisms of the text of these remarks. I am also indebted to my former law clerk Matthew Verschelden for valuable research assistance concerning the doctrine of *stare decisis*.

19. "It is interesting to note that the impression gained by Judge Henry J. Friendly from thumbing the volumes of 'a generation ago' is that the Court was deciding a good many cases not meriting its attention—as several Justices thought." H.J. Friendly, *Federal Jurisdiction: A General View* 51 (New York: Columbia University Press, 1973).

20. *Confederated Bands of Ute Indians v. United States*, aff'd., 330 U.S. 169; *Albrecht v. United States*, aff'd., 329 U.S. 599; *Land v. Dollar*, aff'd. unanimously, 330 U.S. 731; *Transparent-Wrap Mach. Corp. v. Stokes & Smith Co.*, rev'd. 5-4, 329 U.S. 637; *Adams v. Commissioner*, aff'd., 332 U.S. 752; *United States v. Standard Oil*, aff'd., 332 U.S. 301; *Bazley v. Commissioner*, aff'd., 331 U.S. 737; *Ellis v. Union Pacific R.R.*, rev'd. 8-1, 329 U.S. 649; *Fay v. New York*, aff'd., 332 U.S. 261; *Mexican Light & Power v. Texas Mexican R.R.*, aff'd., 331 U.S. 731; *NLRB v. Jones & Laughlin Steel*, rev'd., 331 U.S. 416; *Penfield Co. v. SEC*, aff'd., in part, 330 U.S. 585; *Foster v. Illinois*, aff'd., 332 U.S. 134; *Rutherford Food v. McComb*, aff'd. 8-1, 331 U.S. 722; *United States v. Bayer*, rev'd., 331 U.S. 532; *Champion Spark Plug v. Sanders*, aff'd. 9-0, 331 U.S. 125; *Oklahoma v. United States*, aff'd. per curiam, 331 U.S. 788; *Interstate Natural Gas v. FPC*, aff'd. 6-2, 331 U.S. 682; *McCullough v. Krammerer Corp.*, rev'd. 5-4, 331 U.S. 96; *Wade v. Mayo* (IFP), rev'd., 334 U.S. 672; *Oyama v. California*, rev'd., 332 U.S. 633; *Haley v. Ohio*, rev'd., 332 U.S. 596; *Local 2880 v. NLRB*, dismissed voluntarily on motion; *Blumenthal v. United States*, aff'd., 332 U.S. 539; *United States v. Fried*, dismissed voluntarily on motion; *Price v. Johnson*, rev'd., 334 U.S. 266.

21. *Sears v. County of Los Angeles*, aff'd. by eq. div. ct.; *Walker v. Armco Steel*, 446 U.S. 740; *Nachman v. Pension Benefit Guaranty Corp.*, 446 U.S. 359; *United States v. Clarke*, 445 U.S. 253; *Roberts v. United States*, 445 U.S. 552; *Thomas v. Washington Gas Light*, 448 U.S. 261; *NY Gaslight Club v. Carey*, 447 U.S. 54; *EPA v. National Crushed Stone Assn.*, 449 U.S. 64; *Fedorenko v. United States*, 449 U.S. 490; *Firestone v. Risjord*, 449 U.S. 368; *Cuyler v. Adams*, 449 U.S. 433; *Massachusetts v. Meehan*, 445 U.S. 39; *Larocca v. United States*, 446 U.S. 398; *Andrus v. Glover*, 446 U.S. 608; *Walter v. United States*, 447 U.S. 649; *California Retail Liquor v. Midcal Alum.*, 449 U.S. 97; *Diamond v. Chakrabarty*, 447 U.S. 303; *Standefer v. United States*, 447 U.S. 10; *United States v. Sioux Nation*, 448 U.S. 371; *Dawson Chemical v. Rohm and Haas*, 448 U.S. 176; *Reeves v. Stake*, 447 U.S. 429; *Maine v. Thiboutot*, 448 U.S. 1; *Northwest Airlines v. Transport Workers Union*, 451 U.S. 77; *Minnick v. Cal. Dept. of Corrections*, 452 U.S. 105; *Michael M. v. Sup. Ct. of Sonoma Cty.*, 450 U.S. 464; *Rawlings v. Kentucky*, 448 U.S. 98; *United States v. Cortez*, 449 U.S. 411; *Memphis v. Greene*, 451 U.S. 100; *Republic Steel v. OSHA*, (dismissed pursuant to Rule 53); *Andrus v. Utah*, 446 U.S. 500; *Andrus v. Shell Oil*, 446 US. 657; *Cuyler v. Sullivan*, 446 U.S. 335; *Maher v. Gagne*, 448 U.S. 122; *United States v. Henry*, 447 U.S. 264; *Roadway Express v. Piper*, 447 U.S. 752; *Watkins v. Sowders*, 449 U.S. 341.

The fact that there may be significant cases listed above and in note 20 does not necessarily demonstrate the value of the Rule of Four, because the significant issues decided in these cases might well have come before the Court in other litigation in due course. The frequency with which an issue arises is one measure of its significance.

22. See House Hearings, supra note 2, at 8.

23. It is of interest to note that another distinguished tribunal with a comparable volume of business and comparable discretionary control over its docket follows a majority vote case selection rule. Over 5000 petitions for review are filed in the California Supreme Court each year. I am told that that court follows a selection process of dividing the petitions into an "A" list and a "B" list, and that only the cases on one of those lists are discussed in conference. They also follow a Rule of Four, but since there are only seven justices on that court, that number represents a majority.

24. In an uncharacteristic slip during the interval between his service as an Associate Justice and his service as Chief Justice, Charles Evans Hughes inadvertently "observed that in the routine, every action of the Court is taken on the concurrence of a majority of its members." C. Hughes, *The Supreme Court of the United States* 56-57 (New York: Columbia University Press, 1928). I wonder if subconsciously the Chief Justice regarded the processing of certiorari petitions as a form of "second class work." Cf. Stevens, "Some Thoughts on Judicial Restraint," 66 *Judicature* 172 (1982).

25. A question raised in 1959 by Professor Henry M. Hart, Jr. puts the problem of numbers in proper perspective: "Does a nation of 165 million realize any significant gain merely because its highest judicial tribunal succeeds in deciding 127 cases by full opinion instead of 117? 137 cases? 147 cases? Or even 157 cases? The hard fact must be faced that the Justices of the Supreme Court of the United States can at best put their full minds to no more than a tiny handful of the trouble cases which year by year are tossed up to them out of the great sea of millions and even billions of concrete situations to which their opinions relate. When this fact is fully apprehended, it will be seen that the question whether this handful includes or excludes a dozen or so more cases is unimportant. It will be seen that what matters about Supreme Court opinions is not their quantity but their quality." H. Hart, Foreword: "The Time Chart of the Justices," 73 *Harvard Law Review* 73 (1958).

9

The Role of Oral Argument

John M. Harlan, Jr.
Justice, Supreme Court of the United States

I think that there is some tendency . . . to regard the oral argument as little more than a traditionally tolerated part of the appellate process. The view is widespread that when a court comes to the hard business of decision, it is the briefs, and not the oral argument, which count. I think that view is a greatly mistaken one. . . .

First of all, judges have different work habits. There are judges who listen better than they read and who are more receptive to the spoken word than the written word.

Secondly, the first impressions that a judge gets of a case are very tenacious. They frequently persist into the conference room. And those impressions are usually gained from the oral argument, if it is an effective job. While I was on the court of appeals, I kept a sort of informal scoreboard of the cases in which I sat, so as to match up the initial reactions which I had to the cases after the close of the oral argument with the final conclusions that I had reached when it came time to vote at the conferences on the decision of those cases. I was astonished to find during the year I sat on that court how frequently—in fact, more times than not—the views which I had at the end of the day's session jibed with the final views that I formed after the more careful study of the briefs which, under our system in the Second Circuit, came in the period between the closing of the arguments and the voting at the conference.

Thirdly, the decisional process in many courts places a special burden on the oral argument. I am giving away no secrets, I am sure, when I say that in one of the courts of appeals where I was assigned to sit temporarily the voting on the cases took place each day following the close of the arguments. In the Supreme Court, our practice, as is well known, has been to hold our conferences at the end of each week of arguments. They have been on Saturdays up until now, but under a more enlightened schedule they will be on Fridays next term, because beginning October we are going to sit four days a week. Under either of those systems you can see the importance which the oral argument assumes.

Fourth, and to me this is one of the most important things, the job of courts is not merely one of an umpire in disputes between litigants. Their job is to search out the truth, both as to the facts and the law, and that is ultimately the job of the lawyers, too. And in that joint effort, the oral argument gives an opportunity for interchange between court and counsel which the briefs do not give. For my part, there is no substitute, even within the time limits afforded by the busy calendars of modern appellate courts, for the Socratic method of procedure in getting at the real heart of an issue and in finding out where the truth lies.

Now, let me turn for a moment to some of the factors which seem to me to make for effective oral arguments. The art of advocacy—and it is an art—is a purely personal effort, and as such, any oral argument is an individualistic performance. Each lawyer must proceed according to his own lights, and if he tries to cast himself in the image of another, he is likely to become uneasy, artificial, and unpersuasive. But after you make allowance for the special talents of individuals, their different methods of handling arguments, their different techniques, it seems to me that there are four characteristics which will be found in every effective oral argument, and they are these: *first,* what I would call "selectivity"; *second,* what I would designate as "simplicity"; *third,* "candor"; and *fourth,* what I would term "resiliency." Let me address myself briefly to each.

By "selectivity," I mean a lawyer's selection of the issues to be argued. There is rarely a case which lends itself to argument of all of the issues within the normal time limitations upon oral argument. On the other hand, there is hardly a case, however complicated, where, by some selection of the issues to be argued, one hour is not enough. I am not talking about the unusual type of case, which we have from time to time in all courts, where in the nature of things extra time is essential. But in most cases, I think, the skillful advocate would not want more time for oral argument than the ordinary rules of court permit. However, it often happens that lawyers who attempt to cover *all* of the issues in the case find themselves left with the uncomfortable feeling that they have failed to deal with any of the issues adequately. You will find that thoughtful selection of the issues to be argued orally is a basic technique of every good appellate advocate.

Most cases have one or only a few master issues. In planning his oral argument the wise lawyer will ferret out and limit himself to the issues which are really controlling, and will leave the less important or subordinate issues to the court's own study of the briefs. Otherwise, one is apt to get tanglefoot, and the court is left pretty much where it began.

The next thing I refer to is "simplicity." Simplicity of presentation and expression, you will find, is a characteristic of every effective oral argument. In the instances where that quality is lacking, it is usually attributable to one of two reasons—lack of preparation or poor selection of the issues to be argued. There are some issues that do not lend themselves to oral argument as well as they do to written presentation. The preparation of an oral argument is a good deal more than merely making a short form summary of the briefs. An oral argument which is no more than that really adds nothing to a lawyer's cause.

The process of preparation that the appellate advocate undergoes involves, *first,* the selection of the issues he will argue; *second,* a marshaling of the premises on which those issues depend; *third,* planning the structure of his argument; and, *fourth,* deciding how he shall express his argument. It is sometimes forgotten by a lawyer who is full of his case, that the court comes to it without the background that he has. And it is important to bear this in mind in carrying out the preparation for argument in each of its phases. Otherwise the force of some point which may seem so clear to the lawyer may be lost upon the court.

The third thing which is of the essence of good advocacy is "candor." There is rarely a case, however strong, that does not have its weak points. And I do not know any way of meeting a weak point except to face up to it. It is extraordinary the number of instances one sees where through a question from the court or the argument of one's adversary a vulnerable point is laid bare, and the wounded lawyer ducks, dodges, and twists, instead of facing up to the point four square. Attempted evasion in an oral argument is a cardinal sin. No answer to an embarrassing point is better than an evasive one. With a court, lack of candor in meeting a difficult issue of fact or of law goes far to destroying the effectiveness of a lawyer's argument, not merely as to the point of embarrassment, but often as to other points on which he should have the better of it. For if a lawyer loses the confidence of the court, he is apt to end up almost anywhere.

The fourth and final thing which I have suggested goes to the root of a good oral argument is "resiliency." For some reason that I have never been able to understand, many lawyers regard questioning by the court as a kind of subversive intrusion. And yet, when one comes to sit on the other side of the bar, he finds very quickly that the answer made to a vital question may be more persuasive in leading the court to the right result than the most eloquent of oral arguments. I think that a lawyer, instead of shunning questions by the court, should welcome them. If a court sits through an oral argument without asking any questions, it is often a pretty fair indication that the argument has been either dull or unconvincing.

I am mindful, of course, that the court's privilege of asking questions is sometimes abused, and that often the price a lawyer has to pay is some interruption in the continuity of his argument, and perhaps some discomfiture — and in extreme instances perhaps never getting through with what he had planned to say. And yet, I think that the price is well worth what the lawyer may have to pay in the loss of the smooth-flowing quality he would like his argument to have. A lawyer can make no greater mistake, I can assure you, in answering questions by the court than to attempt to preserve the continuity of his argument by saying: "Judge, I have dealt with that in my brief" or by telling the judge who asks the question that he will come to it "later"— usually he never does. Even if the lawyer does come back to the question later on, the force of his answer, if it is a good one, and often also of his argument in other aspects where he perhaps is in a stronger position, is usually lost—at least upon the judge who has asked the question.

No doubt some judges ask too many questions, and I hasten to say, again as one freshly from the trial bar, that I am one of those who believe that competent lawyers ought to be allowed to try their cases and argue their appeals in their own fashion. Where an over-enthusiastic judge exceeds the bounds of what the lawyer might consider fair interruption, the lawyer will have to handle that problem for himself. I can tell you, however, how two lawyers, one a freshman and the other a seasoned barrister, dealt with such a situation. The freshman lawyer was trying his first case, a negligence case in which his client, the plaintiff, was a lovely young lady. Of course, he called her as the first witness. After the young man had gotten his client's name, age, and address on the record, the court interrupted and started to ask questions. The young lawyer stood first on one foot and then on the other as the court's questioning continued. He finally sat down, and in due course the court came to the end of his questioning and said: "Counselor, you may now continue with the witness. Proceed." The young man arose and said: "If your Honor please, I have no more questions to ask because I think the court has covered my case very thoroughly. But," he added, "I would like to make a statement. If your Honor please, this is my first case, my first client. I have prepared my case thoroughly. I have gone back to the Year Books on the law; I have questioned all eye witnesses to the accident with the greatest care; but if your Honor wants to try this case, it is all right with me, except, for goodness' sake, don't lose it!"

The examination of the more seasoned barrister was interrupted at a sensitive point by a question which the lawyer did not care for. "Have you an objection, counselor?" said the court as the lawyer put on a remonstrative look. "Perhaps, your Honor," replied the lawyer, "but I would first like to inquire on whose behalf your Honor put that question." "What difference would that make, counselor?" asked the court. "All the difference in the world," said the lawyer, "for if your Honor is asking the question on behalf of my opponent, then of course I must object to it, but if your Honor asks the question on my behalf, then I simply withdraw it." . . .

10

Precedent and Policy:
Judicial Opinions and Decision Making

WALTER V. SCHAEFER
Chief Justice, Supreme Court of Illinois

In the main, lawyers tend to treat all judicial opinions as currency of equal value. Exceptions must be made, of course, for the opinions of the acknowledged masters and for those opinions which carry dissents or special concurrences. But the masters are quickly numbered, and the discounted value of the opinion which carries a dissent or concurrence shows upon its face. When allowance has been made for the exceptions, there emerges the working thesis of the bar and perhaps even of the courts: "A case is a case is a case." To the working profession there is no such thing as an opinion which is just "a little bit" precedent or a precedent *pianissimo.* All of them carry the same weight.

Yet, when the judicial process is viewed from the inside, nothing is clearer than that all decisions are not of equivalent value to the court which renders them. There are hidden factors of unreliability in judicial opinions, whether or not there is dissent or special concurrence. Many an opinion, fair upon its face and ringing in its phrases, fails by a wide margin to reflect accurately the state of mind of the court which delivered it.

Several ingredients combine against complete certainty, even at the moment of decision. For a reviewing court the common denominator of all cases is that they must be decided, and must be disposed of, ordinarily by opinion. There are no intermediates. Judgment must go for one party or for the other. There are many cases in which complete conviction comes rather quickly. But there are many others in which conviction to a degree comes hard, and complete conviction never. Uncertainty, however, will not justify a failure to dispose of the case. So some opinions get written because the case must be disposed of rather than because the judge is satisfied with the abiding truth of what he writes.

That process is repeated with the other members of the court who are not directly charged with the preparation of the opinion. Indeed, with them it is likely to be aggravated. As a renowned jurist once said, or should have said, the judge who writes an opinion must be at least 51 percent convinced in the direction of the result he reaches. But with the other judges of the court conviction may be less than 50 percent, and the doubt will still go without expression. For that statement I can vouchsafe high authority to support my own observation. The constitutionality of the Adamson law, which provided an eight-hour day for railroad employees, was sustained by a divided Court. Chief Justice White wrote the opinion of the Court. Justice McKenna wrote a concurring opinion. Justices Day, Pitney, and McReynolds each wrote a dissenting opinion, and Justice Van Devanter concurred in Justice Pitney's dissent.[1] One might assume that this array of opinions fully expressed the views of members of the Court. But then we find Mr. Justice Holmes, who filed no opinion, writing this to Laski: "I send the Adamson opinions by this mail. They are all together. I thought Day's dissent wrong but the most rational. My own opinion goes the whole hog with none of the C.J.'s squeams."[2] And on another occasion Holmes tells Laski of an opinion he wrote "at high pressure in a short time, and with our Court very evenly balanced, though only Pitney and Clarke dissented."[3]

There is more unexpressed doubt of that sort than the bar is aware of. Dissents do not remove these lurking doubts, for dissents are born not of doubt but of firm convictions. The fighting spirit which spells dissent appears in another letter from Justice Holmes to Laski:

> I had last Monday the recrudescence of an old problem. Whether to dissent as to the judge's salaries being included in the income tax, was the occasion and the problem whether to allow other considerations than those of the detached intellect to count. The subject didn't interest me particularly. I wasn't at all in love with what I had written and I hadn't got the blood of controversy in my neck.[4]

And on another occasion:

> After all I succumbed and have written a short dissent in a case which still hangs fire. I do not expect to convince anyone as it is rather a statement of my convictions than an argument, although it indicates my grounds. Brandeis is with me, but I had written a note to him saying that I did not intend to write when the opinion came and stirred my fighting blood.[5]

Here is the stuff dissents are made of. Here, too, is additional evidence that there may be disagreement without dissent. Whether or not to express publicly his disagreement with the prevailing opinion by a dissent is not a novel problem to Holmes but an old, familiar one.

Writing of Justice Brandeis, Paul Freund says: "Not infrequently the preparation of a dissenting opinion was foregone because the demands of other items of work prevented an adequate treatment, but with the promise to himself that another occasion would be taken when circumstances were more propitious."[6]

The case of the specially concurring opinion is not quite so clear. Typically it would rest the result upon grounds other than those asserted in the prevailing opinion. Sometimes the choice of grounds may be the result of doubt as to that chosen by the majority. More often, I suspect, it, too, is the result of fighting conviction on the part of the concurring judge as to the ground which he selects.

The older practice of filing separate opinions helped considerably to eliminate the inherent element of unreliability in judicial decisions. But the working bar does not like multiple opinions. Paradoxically, the dislike seems to be based upon a desire for certainty. Moreover, only those courts whose jurisdiction is largely discretionary, or whose volume of work is small for other reasons, can indulge in the luxury of separate opinions in every case. . . .

It seems to me that the style of judicial opinions contributes its share to their latent uncertainties. Although an opinion may be born only after deep travail and may be the result of a very modest degree of conviction, it is usually written in terms of ultimate certainty. Learned Hand has referred to the tendency of some judges to reach their result by sweeping "all the chessmen off the board."[7] The contentions which caused deep concern at one stage have a way of becoming "clearly inapplicable" or "completely unsound" when they do not prevail. Perhaps opinions are written in that positive vein so that they may carry conviction, both within the court and within the profession; I suspect however, that the positive style is more apt to be due to the psychological fact that when the judge has made up his mind and begins to write an opinion, he becomes an advocate.

The fact that reviewing courts are multijudge courts influences the reliability of precedent in ways too numerous to mention. Opinions are read under the microscope. Particularly in the more esoteric reaches of property law, they are read with an eye to subtle nuances of meaning. The subtleties may, and often do, express the meaning of the judge who wrote the opinion. They do not in any realistic sense express the view of the court as a whole. On a multijudge court no man can or should have every opinion expressed in words which he chooses. Of course every judge can and should make suggestions to his colleagues. But the relationship among the judges is a personal one and a continuing one, and effectiveness can be blunted by excessive suggestions. The balance between complacent acquiescence and overassertiveness is delicate indeed.

The late Mr. Justice Jackson, speaking of decisional law and *stare decisis* some years ago, made an observation upon which I should like to comment. He said:

> The first essential of a lasting precedent is that the court or the majority that promulgates it be fully committed to its principle. That means such individual study of its background and antecedents, its draftsmanship and effects that at least when it is announced it represents not a mere acquiescence but a conviction of those who support it. When that thoroughness and conviction are lacking, a new case, presenting a different aspect or throwing new light, results in overruling or in some other escape from it that is equally unsettling to the law.[8]

With the ideal that doubt should be eliminated and with the suggestion that every opinion should express, so far as conscientious effort can make it possible, the conviction of every member of the court, I agree wholeheartedly. But

I venture to doubt that the ideal of full commitment of every member of the court can be realized in every case, regardless of the amount of effort expended.

At this point I can hear the practicing lawyers say, somewhat irritably: "What you say is all very well, but it is the published opinion of the court with which we must deal. For our purposes a hidden reservation is unimportant." I am certainly not proposing that they poll the court, if that were possible. What I have said perhaps has practical value only as a counsel of caution.

There are additional respects, and more perceptible ones, however, in which opinions, and hence precedents, differ.

The intrinsic quality of the precedent relied upon is significant in determining its fate. Judges in the act of overruling a prior decision have often reconciled their action with the general requirements of *stare decisis* by stating that there is no duty to follow decisions which are absurd or manifestly in error. That formula may obscure the fact that a decision is often overruled, not because of inherent error, but because it has become obsolete. Yet it remains true that an opinion which does not within its own confines exhibit an awareness of relevant considerations, whose premises are concealed, or whose logic is faulty, is not likely to enjoy either a long life or the capacity to generate offspring. There are exceptions. The decision that a corporation could claim equal protection of the laws was made by a court which simply announced from the bench that it did not wish to hear argument on the point inasmuch as all the members of the court were agreed on it.[9] The point so decided has successfully resisted attack. But, by and large, the appearance of full consideration is important. Beyond the appearance there lies the question of actual consideration. Hardly a term of court goes by but that we send for and examine the briefs in an earlier case which is relied upon as decisive to see just what was argued in the earlier case and the quality of the argument made. And I may say parenthetically that the results of our examination make it clear to me that the advocates who present the cases to us do not follow the same practice.

Dissenting and specially concurring opinions have their weight at this point, for they detract from the intrinsic value of the precedent. The therapeutic value of a dissenting opinion is important to the dissenting judge, but that is not its only value. Consider what our constitutional law might be today had there been no dissents. Nor is their value restricted to the field of public law.

Along with quality, quantity too is significant. A settled course of decision is more compelling than an isolated precedent, particularly when the latter, though never formally expelled from the books, has been vigorously ignored by the court which brought it into being.

This is not to say that a great volume of decisions upon a point of law necessarily commands respect. In some areas of the law decisions have proliferated without forming recognizable patterns. As examples I would cite the federal decisions on state taxation of interstate commerce or our own decisions in will-contest cases and zoning cases. The result is that although general principles are always stated in the opinions, decision actually turns on the court's subjective appraisal of the facts. Under such circumstances a court, unless it is bold enough to wipe the slate clean, is forced, despite Holmes's injunction, to join the lawyers in a search for cases on a pots-and-pans basis.[10]

So much, then, for the reported decisions and opinions on their face. What use will be made of them? Baldly stated, I suppose that whether a precedent will be modified depends on whether the policies which underlie the proposed rule are strong enough to outweigh both the policies which support the existing rule and the disadvantages of making a change. The problem is not different in kind from that which is involved in the decisions of other regulatory organs, private or public. In the case of any one decision we may be able to explain why this or that consideration has prevailed, but it is hardly possible to state a general formula which will describe the process in its totality.

A court does not select the materials with which it works. It is not self-starting. It must be moved to action, and it is moved to action by the record and the advocate. The role of the advocate is more significant, I think, than has been suspected. The record must be adequate to raise the issue. But even a record which is technically correct may not cast light on all the aspects of the problem. It was to supply this kind of deficiency that the technique of the Brandeis brief was evolved. More recently, I think, the kind of information contained in the Brandeis brief has been finding its way into the actual record before the court.

Much depends upon the extent to which the court feels sure that it can see the ultimate results which will flow from a departure from precedent. Its willingness to depart will, I think, vary in inverse ratio to the complexity of the problem. Mr. Justice Brandeis expressed the thought in the *Associated Press* case:[11]

> The unwritten law possesses capacity for growth; and has often satisfied new demands for justice by invoking analogies or by expanding a rule or principle. This process has been in the main wisely applied and should not be discontinued. Where the problem is relatively simple, as it is apt to be when private interests only are involved, it generally proves adequate. . . . Courts are ill-equipped to make the investigations which should precede a determination of the limitations which should be set upon any property right in news or of the circumstances under which news gathered by a private agency should be deemed affected with a public interest. Courts would be powerless to prescribe the detailed regulations essential to full enjoyment of the rights conferred or to introduce the machinery required for enforcement of such regulations. Considerations such as these should lead us to decline to establish a new rule of law in the effort to redress a newly-disclosed wrong, although the propriety of some remedy appears to be clear.[12] . . .

It remains to consider the factor of change itself. In part this involves matters of a tactical quality. In deciding whether to translate its dissatisfaction with a former decision into action, a court takes into account the likelihood of cure from some other source. So there is general agreement, I think, that, because constitutions are difficult to change, courts exercise a greater freedom in dealing with constitutional precedents than with others. The expectation of prompt legislative action militates against judicial change.

The frequency with which the court will have an opportunity to deal with the problem has a bearing. If the problem is recurrent, a more suitable case may soon come. The countering consideration, of course, is that with each repetition the unsatisfactory ruling becomes more firmly riveted. . . .

More basic, of course, than tactical considerations is the magnitude of the change involved. Courts may legislate, said Holmes, but they do so interstitially.[13] They are restricted from movement of the mass and confined to movement of the particles. In a sense this is an aspect of the difference I have referred to between the isolated precedent and the settled course of decision. To quote again: "A common law judge could not say I think the doctrine of consideration a bit of historical nonsense, and shall not enforce it in my court."[14]

In another, and perhaps deeper sense, this factor is expressed in another remark of Holmes: "As law embodies beliefs that have triumphed in the battle of ideas and then have translated themselves into action, while there still is doubt, while opposite convictions still keep a battle-front against each other, the time for law has not come; the notion destined to prevail is not yet entitled to the field."[15]

The merit and magnitude of a particular change are not determined by a court on the basis of its own subjective appraisal. It does not measure competing doctrines solely on its own determination of their intrinsic value without reference to the status of those doctrines among those who are informed on the subject and who are particularly affected. One informed class whose opinion carries weight is the legal profession. Its comments, expressed in treatises, law reviews, and other legal publications, always affect the attitude of a court toward a precedent. Of course the class of persons who are informed and who are concerned with the question can vary widely. When it becomes so large as to include the public generally, its attitude becomes more difficult to ascertain and, I think, less significant. But where the class is small, and its informed status apparent, as with Lord Mansfield's reliance upon special juries and the extra-judicial statements of merchants in the development of commercial law, informed opinion becomes significant. The state of medical knowledge as to the capacity of an unborn child to sustain life apart from its mother influences the right to recover for injuries suffered *en ventre sa mere*.[16] And the attitude of psychiatrists toward the rule in the *M'Naghten* case goes far to determine whether the common-law test for determining sanity in criminal cases will be reconsidered.[17]

In addition to the state of mind and the expectancy of the informed public is the state of mind and the expectancy of the parties immediately concerned. The most frequent, and perhaps the most substantial, argument made against a court's departure from precedent is that a sudden shift in the law will frustrate past transactions made in reliance on existing law. It is easy to overstate the objection, for in many fields of human action there is no reliance on past decisions and in many others no knowledge of the existing law. "The picture of the bewildered litigant lured into a course of action by the false light of a decision, only to meet ruin when the light is extinguished and the decision overruled, is for the most part a figment of excited brains."[18] But some reliance there undoubtedly is, and how much a court can only guess, so it is a consideration which cannot properly be disregarded. . . .

I have spoken for precedents and of some of the factors which move a court to adhere to a precedent or to depart from it. Having gone so far, I am unable to go further and indicate what weight is to be assigned to each of these factors in a particular case. Not only that—I must mention another pervasive ingredient which further complicates the problem.

The forces and factors which I have mentioned are not weighed in objective scales. Each judge will have his individual reaction to the value of a particular precedent. Each will respond in his own degree to the pressure of the facts of the case. And each will make his own appraisal of the weight to be given to the other considerations I have mentioned.

There is nothing new in the notion that the personality of the judge plays a part in the decision of cases. Cardozo pointed out that on the Court of Appeals in his day there were ten judges, of whom only seven sat at a time. "It happens again and again," he says. "where the question is a close one, that a case which one week is decided one way might be decided another way the next if it were then heard for the first time."[19]

And, again, in speaking of the subconscious forces that shape judgments, he says: "There has been a certain lack of candor in much of the discussion of the theme, or rather perhaps in the refusal to discuss it, as if judges must lose respect and confidence by the reminder that they are subject to human limitations."[20]

Perhaps there has been a lack of candor. I do not think so. Rather it seems to me that we lack the ability to describe what happens. I have tried to analyze my own reactions to particular cases. When I have tried in retrospect, I have doubted somewhat the result, for the tendency is strong to reconstruct along the lines of an assumed ideal process. William James said, "When the conclusion is there we have already forgotten most of the steps preceding its attainment."[21] And, when I have tried to carry on simultaneously the process of decision and of self-analysis, the process of decision has not been natural. I suspect that what is lacking is not candor but techniques and tools which are sensitive enough to explore the mind of a man and report accurately its conscious and subconscious operations.

So far as I am aware, decision with me has not turned upon the state of my digestion. And, if I have reached decision by means of a hunch, it has been a hunch with a long-delayed fuse, for often I have started confidently toward one conclusion, only to be checked and turned about by further study.

Cardozo has described an experience which I think is familiar to every judge:

I have gone through periods of uncertainty so great, that I have sometimes said to myself, "I shall never be able to vote in this case either one way or the other." Then, suddenly the fog has lifted. I have reached a stage of mental peace. I know in a vague way that there is doubt whether my conclusion is right. I must needs admit the doubt in view of the travail that I suffered before landing at the haven. I cannot quarrel with anyone who refuses to go along with me; and yet, for me, however it may be for others, the judgment reached with so much pain has become the only possible conclusion, the antecedent doubts merged, and finally extinguished, in the calmness of conviction.[22]

It was actually this experience, I am confident, that was intended to be compressed into the phrase "judicial hunch."

If I were to attempt to generalize, as indeed I should not, I should say that most depends upon the judge's unspoken notion as to the function of his court. If he views the role of the court as a passive one, he will be willing to delegate the responsibility for change, and he will not greatly care whether the delegated authority is exercised or not. If he views the court as an instrument of society designed to reflect in its decisions the morality of the community, he will be more likely to look precedent in the teeth and to measure it against the ideals and the aspirations of his time.

I do not feel that because it is impossible to place a precise value upon each of the elements which enter into the process of decision it is therefore futile to attempt to enumerate them. It is important that advocates be aware of them, so that cases can be brought more sharply into focus. And it is even more important that judges be conscious of them. If it is true, as I think it is, that in many cases the law stands at a crossroads, the men who choose the path for the future should make the choice, so far as they can, with an awareness of the elements that determine their decision.

Precedent speaks for the past; policy for the present and the future. The goal which we seek is a blend which takes into account in due proportion the wisdom of the past and the needs of the present. Two agencies of government are responsible for the proper blend, but each has other responsibilities as well. The legislature must deal with the ever increasing details of governmental operations. It has little time and little taste for the job of keeping the common law current. The courts are busy with the adjudication of individual controversies. Inertia and the innate conservatism of lawyers and the law work against judicial change.

I think that no one can look closely at the field on which precedent and policy meet without sensing the need for a closer liaison between the two agencies which are charged with the task of making the adjustments.

NOTES

1. *Wilson v. New et al., Receivers of the Missouri, Oklahoma and Gulf Railroad Co.,* 243 U.S. 332 (1916).

2. Oliver W. Holmes, *The Holmes-Laski Letters,* ed. by M. DeWolfe Howe, Vol. I, at 68 (Cambridge: Harvard University Press, 1953).

3. Ibid., at 85.

4. Ibid., at 266.

5. Ibid., at 560.

6. Paul Freund, *On Understanding the Supreme Court* 71 (Boston: Little, Brown, 1949).

7. Learned Hand, *The Spirit of Liberty* 131 (New York: Knopf, 1952).

8. Robert Jackson, "Decisional Law and Stare Decisis," 30 *American Bar Association Journal* 334, 335 (1944).

9. *Santa Clara County v. Southern Pacific Railroad,* 118 U.S. 394, 396 (1885).

10. Oliver E. Holmes, "The Path of the Law," 10 *Harvard Law Review* 457 (1897).

11. *International News Service v. Associated Press,* 248 U.S. 215 (1918).

12. Ibid., at 262, 267.

13. *Southern Pacific Co. v. Jensen,* 249 U.S. 203, 221 (1918) (dis.op.).

14. Ibid.

15. Oliver W. Holmes, "Law and the Court," in *Collected Legal Papers* 294-295 (New York: Peter Smith, 1952).

16. See *Amann v. Faidy,* 415 Ill. 422 (1953).

17. See *Durham v. United States,* 214 F.2d 862 (1954).

18. Benjamin Cardozo, *The Growth of Law* 122 (New Haven: Yale University Press, 1924).

19. Benjamin Cardozo, *The Nature of the Judicial Process* 150 (New Haven: Yale University Press, 1921).

20. Ibid., at 167-168.

21. Quoted by Benjamin Cardozo, *The Paradoxes of Legal Science* 61 (New York: Columbia University Press, 1945).

22. Ibid., at 80-81.

11

The Office of the Chief Justice: Warren E. Burger and the Administration of Justice

EDWARD A. TAMM

Judge, Court of Appeals, District of Columbia Circuit

PAUL C. REARDON

Retired Justice, Supreme Judicial Court of Massachusetts

The Office of the Chief Justice

To many, the Chief Justice symbolizes the Court during the years in which he presides; to some, he personifies American justice. Each year the Chief Justice must, like his colleagues, sift through thousands of petitions for review, decide cases on the merits, write opinions, and act on emergency motions from one or more circuits. In addition, he presides over all public sessions and conferences of the Court. He is responsible, when he is in the majority, for assigning the writing of Court opinions. He must see to it that the Court's work gets out, and he is responsible for a variety of "housekeeping" duties connected with the flow of cases. A variety of statutes require that he approve the hiring, termination, and setting of compensation of the Supreme Court's employees, and he is also ultimately responsible for office building security.[1] A Regent of the Smithsonian Institution by statute,[2] the Chief Justice is by tradition its Chancellor; he is also a trustee of the National Gallery of Art[3] and by tradition is a trustee of the National Geographic Society.[4]

However, what most clearly differentiates the Chief Justice from his colleagues on the Court are his duties as head of the federal court system, which numbers 648 active and 194 senior judges and 2836 supporting staff. By statute, he is Chairman of the Judicial Conference of the United States[5] and Chairman of the Board of the Federal Judicial Center.[6] Although the entire Court has the authority to appoint and remove the Director of the Administrative Office of United States Courts,[7] traditionally the Chief Justice alone appoints and removes the Director and oversees that office. The Chief Justice is frequently required to appoint representatives of the judicial branch to statutory tripartite and other commissions.[8] He makes hundreds of assignments, designates judges for temporary service outside their own courts, and is responsible for certifying the disability of judges who receive medical retirement.[9] When Congress creates a temporary or special court, such as the Temporary Emergency Court of Appeals, the "Wiretap" Panel, or the multidistrict litigation panels, the authority to designate the judges is vested in the Chief Justice.[10] Thus, the Office of Chief Justice entails much more than merely being a member of the Supreme Court.

It was William Howard Taft who gave content to the modern Office of Chief Justice, bringing to it the strong leadership qualities, prestige, and status of a former President. In his day, however, there were only 114 federal judges—fewer than were in either the Fifth or Ninth Circuits in 1980—and the administrative "housekeeping" functions of the federal courts were conducted by the Department of Justice. Taft openly and effectively "lobbied" for legislation such as that creating the Conference of Senior Judges and the bill to give the Supreme Court certiorari jurisdiction. He advised Presidents and Attorneys General about a variety of matters affecting the judiciary, including the appointment of judges and justices. In differing aspects and degrees, each of Taft's successors—Charles Evans Hughes, Harlan Fiske Stone, Fred M. Vinson, and Earl Warren—has lived up to the expectations set by Taft that the Chief Justice take some notable role in the leadership of the federal judiciary.[11]

Perhaps only once in a generation does a person "fit" a position as well as Warren Burger fit the position of Chief Justice in 1969. When he took office, the time was ripe for vigorous leadership. The litigation explosion and the growing public impatience with various aspects of the American court system indicated the general need for reform. At the same time, Burger's multifarious experiences had alerted him to many of the specific problems that needed to be addressed. As a practitioner for 23 years, he had observed flaws in court operations; as an appellate judge reviewing the trial records of thousands of cases and sitting occasionally by assignment as a trial judge, he had related theory to practice, observing, for example, the waste of juror time, the costly, cumbersome business of repeated continuances, pretrial motions made seriatim for purpose of delay, and time wastage caused by lawyers unprepared or inadequately trained for advocacy; and as an adjunct law teacher, he had sensed the deficiencies of legal education in relating theory to practical life. The times required a resourceful Chief Justice like Burger who was prepared to carry on Chief Justice Taft's tradition of actively seeking to improve the administration of justice.

Although Burger has interacted less directly with the executive and legislative branches than Taft did, in other respects he had expanded upon Taft's role by increasing the range of his activities. Not only has he actively headed the federal court system; he has also led the campaign for changing and strengthening state courts and legal systems. He has spurred the bar to raise its ethical standards and has called on both law schools and the bar to improve their training of lawyers.

The Chief Justice has remained true to his initial pledge to lead the fight to improve and reshape the administration of justice in the United States.[12] Immediately upon taking office he rejected any thought of assuming a cloistered role.[13] At the first meeting of the American Bar Association (ABA) that he attended as Chief Justice in August 1969, Burger spoke out on behalf of introducing more modern court management methods, urging that an Institute for Court Management be created to train court administrators. He also took steps to promote a reexamination of the American penal system. He even chastised law schools for doing an inadequate job of preparing their students for the realities of litigation. Justice Clark described the result: "In my 22 years of attending the [ABA] conventions, I've never seen anyone who so quickly and effectively built a fire under this group as Burger."[14] Similar responses appeared in a *Time* magazine story headlined *A Highly Visible Chief.*[15]

The years since that August 1969 speech have been what Burger himself has called the third period of ferment in judicial administration of this century. The first period was dominated by Roscoe Pound and later Arthur Vanderbilt. The second period, in the 1920s and 1930s, was the work of men like Moley, Vanderbilt, Parker, Taft, and Hughes, with Felix Frankfurter and Charles Clark advocating procedural change. The third period can be dated from around 1968, the year in which the federal magistrate system and the judicial panel on multidistrict litigation were created, and the year the Federal Judicial Center began operations. While Chief Justice Earl Warren deserves credit for those particular institutions, other names are associated with the changes that have occurred since then—Justice Tom Clark, Attorney General Griffin Bell, Chief Judges Irving Kaufman and Henry Friendly, State Chief Justice William O'Neill (Ohio), Senator Howell Heflin (Alabama), Edward McConnell (Director, National Center for State Courts), and professors and government officials such as Professors Daniel Meador, Maurice Rosenberg, and A. Leo Levin. It is against this general backdrop, and also mindful of our present circumstances, that we assess the results of Chief Justice Burger's work in the area of judicial administration.

Court Management and Efficiency

The Chief Justice has brought new dimensions to the concept of court "management." He has spoken out and worked for professional management, the streamlining of court practices on calendaring and pretrial proceedings, and the use of modern technology. Arguing that "there is nothing incompatible between efficiency and justice," and that efficiency need not lead to dehumanization,[16] Burger has stressed the values of productivity:

> Why are we concerned about productivity? A more productive judicial system is essential for justice . . . giving litigants their relief promptly, rather than forcing them to wait endlessly while memories grow dim and witnesses move or die. . . . [T]he more efficiently we operate the courts, the faster we terminate cases and

the less we tie up lawyers and witnesses in litigation. By making the judicial system more productive, we are making the federal courts accessible to all Americans at less personal financial expense and less emotional expense—all in addition to saving citizens' taxes.[17]

As a result of a wide range of programs, the average federal judge increased the disposition rate by more than 30 percent during the first eight years of Warren Burger's tenure as Chief Justice. He emphasized that this has come about for several reasons: judges have worked harder and have received special training in new techniques, senior (retired) judges have continued working, new procedures have been employed, chief judges have administered better, para-judicial personnel have been employed, and they and other personnel have received better training than before.[18] These developments grew from constant emphasis on management concepts in seminars and judicial meetings.

Professional Court Managers

When Burger came into office, he considered the question of why American justice takes so long. He attributed the delays in part to "the lack of up-to-date, effective procedures and standards for administration or management, and the lack of trained managers."[19]

One of his speeches given at the ABA meetings in Dallas in 1969—less than two months after he became Chief Justice—was entitled "Court Administrators: Where Would We Find Them?" He called for a "corps of trained administrators or managers . . . to manage and direct the machinery so that judges can concentrate on their primary professional duty of judging."[20] Looking for "a place where court administrators can be trained just as hospital administrators have long been trained,"[21] Burger urged that an institute for court management be created at once. . . .[22]

The idea was vigorously supported by ABA President Bernard G. Segal. Two months after Burger's speech an ABA task force had met. When the Board for the new structure was set up, members included James Webb (National Aeronautics and Space Administration), John Macy (Civil Service Chairman), Edward McConnell (long-time administrator of New Jersey courts), and, as Chairman, former Attorney General Herbert Brownell. By 14 January 1970, Burger and ABA President Bernard Segal announced a two-year pilot project to train court executives.[23] Ernest C. Friesen, Jr., Director of the Administrative Office of the United States Courts, was recruited to head the new institute.

Thus, the Institute for Court Management (ICM) had been created within four months of Burger's speech; within six months it was in operation. It was the result of a joint effort by the ABA, the Institute of Judicial Administration, and the American Judicature Society. The ICM was initially funded by a grant of $750,000 from the Ford Foundation. Its first training course—a full-time, intensive, six-month program at the University of Denver—began on 15 June 1970, just over ten months after the Dallas speech. The first certificates were presented by the Chief Justice to a class of 31 in December 1970.[24] The *Balti-*

more Sun editorialized, "Quietly, as was fitting, there was a ceremony at the Supreme Court on Saturday which marks a real leap ahead in the history of the federal judiciary."[25]

The past 12 years have been marked by an explosion of training programs for court managers and by a vast increase in the use of court administrators.[26] In 1969 there were trained court administrators in only four states.[27] By May 1980, 350 persons had completed both phases of the ICM Court Executive program. As of 1980, seven of ten circuit executives in the federal courts of appeals were graduates of the ICM, as were 14 state court administrators.[28]

Circuit Executives

The first reference to the idea of circuit managerial officers can be traced to a suggestion by Chief Justice Charles Evans Hughes in 1938 that each circuit council have an administrative officer.[29] That suggestion was revived in 1968 with a proposal in an American Bar Foundation Report that each court of appeals should have an administrative officer responsible for administering the court's business.[30] By the time the then new Chief Justice spoke to the ABA in August 1969, legislation to provide administrators for the federal courts had been introduced and was under study by the Subcommittee on Judicial Machinery of the Senate Committee on the Judiciary.

Concerning the pending legislation, Burger made the point that if it were enacted there would be virtually no qualified persons available for appointment. Noting that we had 38 trained astronauts, he pointed out: "If that legislation were passed at once we would not begin to fill the positions. We should indeed pass the legislation but we must also take immediate steps to ensure a supply of administrators. We cannot legislate court administrators any more than we can legislate astronauts; they must be trained."[31] Burger vigorously pressed for enactment of the legislation, and his support for an academy to train court administrators probably speeded up the bill's passage.

The Chief Justice's support for circuit executives rested on his belief that "[t]he management of busy courts calls for careful planning and definite systems and organization with supervision by trained administrator-managers."[32] He believed that the new position would spare judges the burden of performing many administrative tasks, thus saving money: "We should not use 'judge time' to accomplish tasks that others with less [legal] training can do at less expense to the public."[33] He also believed that the legislation would "provide a person who [would], in time, be able to develop new methods and new processes, which busy judges could not do in the past."[34]

In 1970, Congress passed the Circuit Court Executive Act in the closing hours of the 91st Congress.[35] The law authorized, but did not require, each judicial circuit to appoint a circuit executive from among persons certified by a statutory board of certification.

The chief judges of the circuits have reacted favorably to the circuit executives, who have alleviated administrative burdens, expedited new procedures, helped to increase communication among judges, and assisted the district courts. The new positions are not a panacea, however, for all ailments. Burger himself cautioned: "It will take time—perhaps several years—before these circuit executives develop their role and function. More than that, it will take patience and understanding and tolerance among judges and the Bar to make this concept productive."[36] Nevertheless, Burger has supported expansion of the program to the district courts, and in 1981 Congress appropriated funds for five district executive positions on an experimental basis.[37] Burger has also strongly endorsed the use of trained court administrators for state courts: "The time must come when every state will have one of its most qualified judges as overseer of administration backed by a staff of trained court administrators."[38] . . .

The Office of Administrative Assistant to the Chief Justice

In 1972 Congress and the President officially recognized the need of the Chief Justice to have an administrative assistant. As Chief Justice, Earl Warren used three law clerks, one secretary, and two messengers.[39] Warren Burger realized that the demands upon the Office of the Chief Justice were so considerable that he could not effectively exercise his office to full capacity without assistance. Burger remarked in an interview, "One more thing: The Office of the Chief Justice desperately needs a high-level administrative deputy or assistant. I devote four to six hours a day on administrative matters apart from my judicial work, and it is not possible—not physically possible—to continue this schedule very long."[40]

A bill authorizing the Chief Justice to appoint an administrative assistant at a salary of up to that earned by a district judge, then $40,000, became law in March 1972.[41] Burger called the creation of the position an important breakthrough.[42] It was filled shortly thereafter by Dr. Mark W. Cannon, then director of the private, nonprofit Institute of Public Administration in New York City.

The duties of the Administrative Assistant to the Chief Justice include supplying the Chief Justice with background research, serving as liaison with organizations dealing with judicial administration, fostering public education about the judicial system, and assisting the Chief Justice with internal management of the Supreme Court.[43] In appointing the first incumbent, the Chief Justice deliberately sought a nonlawyer with extensive governmental experience. Cannon, a Ph.D. in political science, had worked in Congress and as a consultant to state and foreign governments.

Judicial Fellows Program

The 1973 creation of the Judicial Fellows Program, paralleling similar programs in the executive and legislative branches, brought younger talent and interdisciplinary perspectives into the federal court system. The program was proposed by Mark Cannon and strongly supported by Burger. It was established to provide added creative staff assistance to the Office of the Administrative Assistant to the Chief Justice, the Directors of the Federal Judicial Center, and the

Administrative Office of the United States Courts; to interest scholars of other disciplines in the problems of judicial administration; to assist scholars' teaching and writing by giving them first-hand experience in the field of judicial administration; and, in a pioneering way, to expose those serving in judicial capacities to the insights of persons trained in other disciplines. . . .

Conference of Metropolitan Chief Judges

The Conference of Metropolitan Chief Judges (METCHIEFS), consisting of the chief judges of the largest federal district courts (currently 29 courts whose dockets comprise more than 60 percent of the federal court's business),[44] was convened by the Chief Justice in Denver, Colorado. Its function is to act as a clearinghouse for new ideas and concepts in organizing the work flow among the judges themselves, to facilitate communications between the judges and the Federal Judicial Center, to pool experience, and to develop strategies to attack common problems. . . .

Magistrates

Under the Federal Magistrates Act of 17 October 1968,[45] the old system of United States Commissioners (whose duties were limited to issuing warrants, holding preliminary hearings, and trying petty offenses) was replaced by a magistrate system with broader jurisdiction. This change was praised by the Chief Justice: "Congress wisely created the new office of United States magistrate . . . to relieve judges of some of their duties so that judges can devote more time to presiding over trials and other purely judicial work."[46]

Nearly half the federal district courts now regularly delegate a substantial portion of their civil pretrial duties to federal magistrates, while another quarter do so occasionally. Magistrates, who have proven invaluable in improving pretrial procedures and moving cases through discovery, are conducting an increasing number of trials. They provide the practical advantage to litigants of being more conveniently located geographically and more accessible than district court judges.[47]

At the Chief Justice's urging, the jurisdiction of magistrates has been enlarged.[48] Specific functions delegated to magistrates vary from district to district, ranging from ministerial and advisory functions to full, substantive roles. In criminal cases this latter role encompasses issuing warrants, fixing bail, holding preliminary hearings, and conducting trials for petty offenses. In civil cases it includes conducting pretrial discovery and acting as special masters.[49]

Innovative Procedures in the Federal Courts

As caseloads have increased in the federal courts, the Chief Justice has advocated a variety of new devices to attempt to meet the demands. These devices, coupled with the contributions of senior judges and the extra effort by all federal judges, have improved output. Chief Justice Burger has encouraged courts to employ these new techniques and has publicized successful procedures worthy of adoption. A number of devices have been employed by district courts and judges.

The Individual Calendar. Under the individual calendar all aspects of a case are assigned to a particular judge promptly after the case is filed. The individual calendar system discourages judge-shopping, focuses responsibility on a specific judge, and enables that judge to become familiar with the problems of a case before trial. It reduces lawyer time in explaining (both orally and in writing) the background of a case on each pretrial motion. For example, Chief Judge George Hart of the United States District Court for the District of Columbia credited the individual calendar with reducing that court's pending civil caseload after three years from 307 cases per judge to 149, and the criminal caseload from 101 per judge to 33.[50] Virtually all large federal courts have adopted the individual calendar.

The Omnibus Pretrial Hearing. The omnibus (or single) pretrial hearing procedure in criminal cases requires that all pretrial motions be submitted by an early, fixed date. The procedure was pioneered by the late Chief Judge James Carter in San Diego (when he was a district judge) and by Chief Judge Adrian Spears of San Antonio. It was also endorsed by the ABA Committee on Standards for Criminal Justice as part of the Standard on Discovery and Pre-Trial Procedure. Judge Spears has stated, "Use of the omnibus [hearing] has virtually eliminated the written motion practices; saved counsel and court time and effort; exposed latent procedural and constitutional problems; provided discovery for an informed plea; and substantially reduced the congestion of the trial calendar."[51]

The omnibus hearing clearly discourages spacing out pretrial motions for dilatory purposes. The Chief Justice has praised this procedure and has urged all federal judges to employ it.[52] Its use is now widespread.

Other Innovative Techniques. Other new techniques credited with improving productivity at the district court level include court reporter management and the use of video-taped depositions.[53] . . .

The Results—Improved Productivity
The emphasis on modern management principles, on new devices and techniques, and on increased innovation and effort by all federal judges[54] has contributed to an increased rate of case disposition per judge,[55] even though under the range of new statutes review of cases has become more difficult and time-consuming.[56]

Table 11.1 on page 108 demonstrates the sharp increase in case terminations from 1968 to 1978. That period was followed by a transitional decrease which resulted from an increased vacancy rate and the appointment of many new judges with the passage of the Omnibus Judgeship Bill in 1978.[57]

Table 11.1. Net Productivity 1968-80[58]

Terminations per Judgeship

	District Court	Court of Appeals
1968	285.4	85.2
1969	304.3	92.9
1970	285.8	110.3
1971	309.7	127.5
1972	352.8	142.6
1973	349.0	155.8
1974	347.3	158.9
1975	370.8	165.0
1976	385.5	169.3
1977	405.1	183.3
1978	409.5	182.6
1979	342.8	143.4
1980	367.8	158.2

Interbranch Communication and Legislation Affecting the Courts

Throughout American history congressional concern with judicial problems has been sporadic at best, with needs often remaining unremedied until they have gathered compelling momentum for action. Until recent years, the judicial branch did little to move Congress to action. Although in some instances unusually dramatic litigation aroused widespread general interest in reforms,[59] it was not until Chief Justice Taft's tenure that the judicial branch began to exhibit interest in changing the procedure or administration of the work of the courts.[60]

The occasional remark deriding the judiciary for "lobbying" overlooks the Judicial Code of 1949, which requires the Judicial Conference to comment upon pending legislation affecting the courts, but not upon police issues or substantive law. In addition, the 1949 Code authorizes the Conference to develop proposals for legislative activity.[61] Little else by way of communication exists between Judicial Conference committees and the Congress. Thus, the Conference has not always had an effective voice. Meeting only twice annually and lacking permanent staff, it often seemed unable to communicate its views to the Congress at an early enough stage to have meaning or impact. In 1976, for the first time, a legislative affairs officer was added to the staff. . . .

A profound need has existed for better channels of communication to bridge the gap among the branches. To improve communication, Chief Justice Burger has made himself visible, attempting to develop congressional interest in the problems of the courts through speeches, magazine interviews,[62] letters, and occasional meetings with key members of Congress. Gradually, communication with the judiciary committees has improved. Burger has also worked with the executive branch through the Attorney General and has delivered speeches to influence public and bar opinion.[63]

The Chief Justice has been critical of congressional inertia in providing the courts with the "tools to do the job," including provision for more judges where needed. He has also pressed Congress to make needed jurisdictional changes, such as the abolition of diversity jurisdiction and the elimination of three-judge district courts (which was largely accomplished in 1976); he has made similar efforts concerning the termination of the Supreme Court's mandatory jurisdiction and the restructuring of the circuits. Additionally, he has urged Congress to weigh the effect upon the federal courts of new legislation, proposing that "impact statements" be made by any comittee that recommends legislation having a direct impact on the judiciary, so that flawed legislation, like the Speedy Trial Act, will not be thrust on the courts. He has likewise proposed a continuing tripartite commission on the judiciary to advise Congress on the needs of the court. . . .

Meetings among those leaders of the three branches concerned with questions of the administration of justice have been held annually since 1978,[64] sponsored by the Brookings Institution (which also holds seminars for freshmen Congressmen). The conferences were conceived by Mark W. Cannon, Administrative Assistant to the Chief Justice, and Warren Cikins, a senior staff member at Brookings, to provide the channel of communication Burger had complained was absent. They have made a most significant contribution to better communication between the branches. . . .

These meetings signify a departure from the compartmentalization, inertia, and drift which have dominated the treatment of court problems at the federal level for almost two centuries. The meetings have established new channels of communication for the informal exchange of information, ideas, and differing perspectives. They have helped to break down extra-constitutional barriers between the branches, barrriers arising out of misunderstanding and lack of information. After the meetings, these new lines of communication have been employed to facilitate formulation and implementation of policy.

The value of the effort to achieve closer cooperation among branches is suggested by table 11.2.

Table 11.2. *Legislation Affecting the Courts,*
June 1969-December 1980
(91st through 96th Congresses)

Year	Law Number	Topic
1970	Pub. L. No. 97-271	Customs Court Amendments
	Pub. L. No. 91-272	U.S. District Court Judgeship Appointments
	Pub. L. No. 91-358	District of Columbia Court Reform and Criminal Procedure Act
	Pub. L. No. 91-644	Omnibus Crime Control Act
	Pub. L. No. 91-647	Circuit Executive Act

Table 11.2. Legislation Affecting the Courts (Continued)

Year	Law Number	Topic
1972	Pub. L. No. 92-238	Creation of Administrative Assistant to the Chief Justice
	Pub. L. No. 92-239	Amendments to the Federal Magistrates Act of 1968
	Pub. L. No. 92-269	Lowering minimum age of Jurors to 18
	Pub. L. No. 92-375	Temporary recall of senior commissioners, Court of Claims
	Pub. L. No. 92-397	Supreme Court Justices—Widow's Annuities
	Pub. L. No. 92-428	Magistrate's Salaries
	Pub. L. No. 92-489	Creation of Hruska Commission
1973	Pub. L. No. 93-83	Amendments to the Omnibus Crime Act of 1970
1974	Pub. L. No. 93-420	Hruska Commission Extension
	Pub. L. No. 93-512	Judicial Disqualification
	Pub. L. No. 93-595	Uniform Rules of Evidence
	Pub. L. No. 93-619	Speedy Trial Act
1975	Pub. L. No. 93-584	Eliminate direct appeal of ICC cases
	Pub. L. No. 94-64	Amendments to the Rules of Criminal Procedure
	Pub. L. No. 94-82	Salary Adjustments
1976	Pub. L. No. 94-233	Revamping of Federal parole practices
	Pub. L. No. 94-381	Elimination of three-judge courts
	Pub. L. No. 94-503	Amendments to Omnibus Crime Act of 1970
	Pub. L. No. 94-577	U.S. Magistrates' jurisdiction
1977	Pub. L. No. 95-19	Salaries
	Pub. L. No. 95-78	Federal Rules of Criminal Procedure
1978	Pub. L. No. 95-408	District Court Reorganization Bill (1)
	Pub. L. No. 95-486	Omnibus Judgeship Act
	Pub. L. No. 95-511	Foreign Intelligence Surveillance Act
	Pub. L. No. 95-521	Financial Disclosure Act
	Pub. L. No. 95-535	Witness Fee Bill
	Pub. L. No. 95-539	Court Interpreters Act
	Pub. L. No. 95-572	Jury Reform Act
	Pub. L. No. 95-573	District Court Reorganization Bill (2)
	Pub. L. No. 95-582	Nationwide Subpoena Service
	Pub. L. No. 95-598	Bankruptcy Reform Act
1979	Pub. L. No. 96-43	Amendments to Speedy Trial Act of 1974
	Pub. L. No. 96-82	Federal Magistrates Act
	Pub. L. No. 96-86	Continuing Appropriations Act
	Pub. L. No. 96-157	Justice System Improvement Act
1980	Pub. L. No. 96-190	Dispute Resolution Act
	Pub. L. No. 96-417	Customs Court Act
	Pub. L. No. 96-452	Fifth Circuit Reorganization Act
	Pub. L. No. 96-458	Judicial Councils Reform and Judicial Conduct and Disability Act

Strengthening State Courts and Reducing Friction
Between State and Federal Courts

Chief Justice Burger has been deeply committed to strengthening state court systems and to reducing friction between state and federal courts. He was instrumental in the founding of the National Center for State Courts and has devoted considerable effort to the Center's nurturing. Likewise, he has taken a leadership role in proposing a National Institute of Justice as a vehicle for aiding state courts. To strengthen state courts, Burger has also advocated carefully structured merit-based selection of state judges, higher compensation, and continuing training of state judges. He has been a leader in efforts to consider forms of dispute resolution other than litigation.

The Chief Justice believes that the problems of justice are indivisible: "I have felt an obligation to be concerned with problems of state courts as well as the federal courts because the problems of justice are indivisible and if we do not have strong and effective courts in both the state and federal systems, we have a failure of justice."[65] He views the state courts as important because they deal with over ninety percent of all litigation: "[The federal courts] are more visible but the state courts in all reality and candor are far more important. And so my concern is to have the state courts healthy."[66] Although state courts are able to handle the vast majority of problems they face, Burger is concerned because they remain "overburdened, understaffed, often poorly structured and administered and subject to undue political influence, particularly with respect to the process of selection and retention of judges and key court support personnel."[67] . . .

The Chief Justice has attempted to strengthen the quality of justice in the state courts by supporting the idea of continuing education for judges and those institutions providing this education. Since 1969 there has been a great expansion in the richness and variety of programs for judicial education.[68] . . .

The Proper Role of State and Federal Courts
Accepting the constitutional pronouncement that federal courts are courts of special and limited jurisdiction,[69] and the corollary that state courts are the basic and primary system of justice,[70] Chief Justice Burger has consistently opposed uncontrolled expansion of federal jurisdiction. He has invoked traditional principles of federalism to protect the federal courts from having even greater demands placed upon them. Expressing concern over signs that state and federal dockets are becoming more and more alike, he questions whether the federal system may be evolving toward a *de facto* merger with the state court system.[71]

Burger has emphasized that "federalism is not just a matter of pleasant historical nostalgia" but "a valid, constitutionally rooted doctrine appropriate to meet the needs of our country, now and for the future."[72] He has indicated his strong disapproval of the implicit disparagement of state courts that comes from the continuing expansion of federal jurisdiction.

Some few seem prepared to sacrifice our concepts of federalism for instant gratification of their own views, based on an assumption that state courts are either incapable, inadequate, or unwilling to enforce claims and rights which we would all agree were proper. This unarticulated disparagement of state jurisdiction and state courts is something I reject.[73]

His concern about the heavy demands upon the federal court system and his sense of federalism interact. He has noted that new federal statutes and court decisions expanding federal jurisdiction have brought pressures on the courts and delays to the litigants.[74] Although the courts can satisfy these demands to some extent with additional judgeships, this too has a serious cost: "Neither assembly-line justice, nor a rapid expansion of the size of the federal judiciary beyond anything presently contemplated, with the concomitant dilution of prestige and, I fear, quality, can be the answer."[75]

Felix Frankfurter warned decades ago that "inflation of the number of the district judges" will "in turn . . . result, by its own Gresham's law, in a depreciation of the judicial currency and the consequent impairment of the prestige and of the efficacy of the federal courts."[76]

Burger shares Frankfurter's concern that an expanding body of federal judges could reduce the historic attraction to become one. If the federal bench is unable to attract the best lawyers, its effectiveness will ultimately be diluted. This explains why Burger, acting on behalf of the Judicial Conference, strongly — and successfully—opposed the transmutation of bankruptcy referees into federal judges. It explains why he has asked that lawyers, Congress, and the public examine carefully each demand they make on the federal court system.[77] He has asked that legislation proposed to accomplish piecemeal shifts of jurisdiction away from state courts be examined carefully. He has forcefully emphasized the need to reexamine the allocation of the workload between federal and state courts, finding support in a prestigious and massive study of the American Law Institute.[78] In particular, Burger has suggested that federal diversity jurisdiction be abolished and that alternative means of dispute resolution be developed.

Conclusion

At the time of his appointment, some pundits paid little attention to the role Warren Burger might perform in the administration of justice. What they noted then were his moderate to conservative views on criminal justice and judicial restraint. Time has shown that the principal characteristic distinguishing Burger's tenure from the tenures of his predecessors has been his attempt to improve the administration of justice in the United States—"to try," as he promised during his nomination hearing, "to see that the judicial system functions more efficiently."[79] Beyond the full load of his judicial work, Burger has also expended an extraordinary amount of time and energy on these broader duties of the Office of Chief Justice of the United States.

Burger's record for making changes in the administration of justice can be attributed to his willingness to commit his efforts and the prestige of his office to the demands of the judicial system. Because he is Chief Justice, he naturally has access to groups and podiums that others do not. Because he is Chief Justice, he has an influential audience for his annual state of the judiciary message to the ABA. Because he is Chief Justice, he can reach out to dozens of organizations.

The Chief Justice has not hesitated to avail himself of these opportunities. For example, from July through September 1971 Burger attended 14 legal and judicial gatherings, including ABA meetings in New York and London, circuit judicial conferences, meetings of the Judicial Conference Committee on Court Administration, and meetings for the Board of Directors of the National Center for State Courts and the Federal Judicial Center Board. He usually pursued these objectives during periods after those he reserves for his strictly judicial duties. The result is a heavy work schedule. The magnitude of the work assumed by the Chief Justice evidences the depth of his commitment to the administration of justice. Of course, one of the reasons why Burger has been able to extend his activities has been the creation of the Office of Administrative Assistant to the Chief Justice. He has publicly paid tribute to Mark Cannon for his drive, zeal, and imaginative approach to judicial administration since his appointment in 1972.

Burger has indeed been a highly visible Chief Justice. He has succeeded in developing coalitions to spawn needed public awareness and in developing public support for his programs. He has sought support from lawyers' groups but has not limited himself to that audience. Generally he gives three or four formal speeches per year, including a *U.S. News & World Report* interview every two or three years, and occasionally writes articles on judicial subjects.

Burger has not hesitated to establish key personal relationships. He meets with all newly appointed federal judges in Washington when they attend Federal Judicial Center seminars. His attendance at ceremonial occasions is not only a duty of his office, but also a useful way to exchange ideas.

He remains in touch, often through Mark Cannon, with numerous groups in the judicial administration field. Like his predecessors, the Chief Justice speaks annually to the American Law Institute, usually advocating a program or releasing a "trial balloon." His working relations with the ABA have been quite salutary. He attends meetings of the Institute of Judicial Administration and the Conference of (State) Chief Justices. He visits regularly the National Center for State Courts and the National Judicial College.

Burger has continued to be an activist Chief Justice of the United States on questions of the improved administration of justice.[80] Burger does not believe that judges should suffer in silence: "Someone must make these problems of the courts known to the public and Congress, if intelligent choices are to be made. . . . This is, very clearly, one of the obligations of the office I occupy."[81]

Some have been concerned that, with this view of his role, Burger might slight his other duties, compromise his judicial independence, give the appearance of bias, become too political, or act contrary to the separation of powers.[82] Nevertheless, both Burger's conception of his office and his practice in that office suggest otherwise.

The late Alexander M. Bickel urged the Chief Justice to embark upon just such a course:

> As Chief Justice Burger takes up the task, it is not enough to hope that he will equal Taft's success, and stand with him among the Chief Justices as a great administrative reformer. . . . The problems are worse, the needs greater. Chief Justice Burger will have to outdo Taft, and he will need the help of Congress and the bar.[83]

Changes in the administration of justice have historically been difficult to achieve because of the inertia of the bar and the difficulty of activating the interest of legislators in issues lacking political allure. In the federal court system there are only two officials properly positioned to give dynamic leadership — the Attorney General and the Chief Justice.[84] The modern Attorney General, with rare exceptions, is something of a "transient"[85] who may have given little thought to judicial administration problems prior to taking office, and who is quickly overwhelmed with other issues upon taking office. (Attorney General Griffin Bell was the first notable exception to this since Herbert Brownell.)

The body designated by statute for involvement in these matters, the Judicial Conference of the United States, is not well equipped to give leadership. It is a body of members which meets twice a year, for two to three days each time, and lacks a permanent staff of its own. Therefore, without vigorous leadership from the Chief Justice, reform efforts will drift.

As Arthur Landever has written: "[W]e must understand the need and accept the fact that the chief judge — whether of the United States Supreme Court, the federal circuit court, or the state court panel — must wear two hats. If we are to have fairness and efficiency, he must be both judge and administrator."[86]

Burger has made his position clear. In October 1978 he summarized his stand:

> The problems of the courts do not have high visibility. They reach the attention of other branches and the public only if they are pressed forward by someone — and often not even then. The good citizen or the busy Congressman can be excused if he is not very familiar with the need to expand United States Magistrates' jurisdiction, for example, or to abolish diversity jurisdiction, the need for court administrators, or the need for more judges or changes in the court structure or rules of procedure. Someone must make the problems of the courts known to the public and Congress, if intelligent choices are to be made. Someone must make these problems real to the busy members of the Congress, overwhelmed as they are with a host of other, more visible problems. . . .

Continuing, the Chief Justice stressed:

This is, very clearly, one of the obligations of the office I occupy. The ultimate responsibility rests with the Congress—especially if questions of statutory change or rules of procedure, jurisdiction or appropriations are involved. And when Congress enacts laws, the President must sign or veto them. But given all the burdens and distractions of the political process, the Judiciary would fail dismally to perform its duty if it stood mute in this process. If a Chief Justice, as spokesman for the Judicial Conference, failed to participate in the process, he would be shirking his obligations.[87]

The speeches and articles of Chief Justice Burger in the 12 years of his present office and the 25 years as a United States Judge do not reveal his innermost thinking, but they clearly state his objectives. He may or may not know of the account from judicial lore of a conversation between two men he admires greatly—Charles Evans Hughes and Arthur Vanderbilt. Vanderbilt once expressed a sense of despair when he spoke to Hughes of the frustrations he felt in his efforts to overcome the die-hard opposition to the use of modern methods in the judiciary. Hughes, who had experienced some of this, is reported to have said, "Arthur, when people no longer remember a single opinion either of us ever wrote, they will remember what we tried to do to make justice work better."

NOTES

1. See, e.g., 28 U.S.C. §§ 671-677 (1976). See also 40 U.S.C. § 131 (1976).

2. 20 U.S.C. §§ 41-44 (1976).

3. He is a trustee of the National Gallery of Art, National Portrait Gallery, and Hirschorn Museum. See, e.g., 20 U.S.C. § 72 (1976 & Supp. III 1979); 20 U.S.C. § 76cc(b) (1976). For ten years, Burger served as chairman of the National Gallery.

4. Burger is also honorary chairman of the Institute of Judicial Administration (at New York University), the National Judicial College (at the University of Nevada), the Supreme Court Historical Society, and the Advisory Board of Project '87. He serves as chairman of the Visiting Committee of the Institute of Court Management, which he founded in 1969.

5. 28 U.S.C. § 331 (1976 and Supp. III 1979).

6. 28 U.S.C. § 621 (1976 and Supp. III 1979).

7. 28 U.S.C. § 601 (1976).

8. See, e.g., 44 U.S.C. § 3318(a)(1)(E) (1976) (authorizing the Chief Justice to appoint one member to the National Study Commission on Records and Documents of Federal Officials).

9. See, e.g., 28 U.S.C. §§ 291-295, 372 (1976 and Supp. III 1979).

10. 28 U.S.C. § 1407 (1976).

11. See, generally, P. Fish, *The Politics of Federal Judicial Administration* (Princeton: Princeton University Press, 1973).

12. *New York Times* A1, col. 7 (2 July 1969).

13. *New York Times* A17, col. 1 (20 June 1969).

14. *Time* A58 (22 August 1969).

15. Ibid.

16. Address by Warren E. Burger, "National Conference on the Causes of Popular Dissatisfaction with the Administration of Justice" (Pound Conference, 9 April 1976), reprinted in *The Pound Conference* 23, 32, ed. by A. Levin and R. Wheeler (St. Paul: West, 1979).

17. Press release by Warren E. Burger, "Thirty Percent Increase in Case Handling per Federal Judgeship" (October 1973). For the purposes of this and a number of the following footnote references, it should be noted that the Information Service of the Federal Judicial Center (Washington, D.C.) includes in its collection various published and unpublished speeches and addresses by federal judges, including the Chief Justice.

18. Address by Warren E. Burger, American Bar Association Mid-Year Convention, "1977 Report to the American Bar Association" (13 February 1977), reprinted in 63 *American Bar Association Journal* 504, 508 n. 5 (1977).

19. Address by Warren E. Burger, American Bar Association Convention, "Court Administrators: Where Would We Find Them?" (12 August 1969), reprinted in 5 *Lincoln Law Review* 1, 2 (1969).

20. Ibid., at 1.

21. Address by Warren E. Burger, American Bar Association Annual Meeting, "The State of the Federal Judiciary—1970" (10 August 1970), reprinted in 56 *American Bar Association Journal* 929 (1970).

22. Earl Warren and others had favored incorporating the training of court administrators into law school training, but little has been done about it. See Address by Earl Warren, Harvard Law School Sesquicentennial Banquet, "The Administration of the Courts" (23 September 1967), reprinted in 51 *Judicature* 196, 200-201 (1968). In 1968 Edward C. Gallas had emphasized the need for professional managerial training; see Gallas, "The Profession of Court Management," 51 *Judicature* 334 (1968). James A. Gazell stated: "The seeds of this development were implicit in the public remarks of Earl Warren while he was Chief Justice of the United States Supreme Court, the publications of prestigious national commissions, the slow emergence of the field as a profession, and the availability of extensive employment opportunities. However, the birth of ICM resulted directly from an American Bar Association address made . . . by . . . Warren E. Burger." See James A. Gazell, "University and Law School Education in Judicial Administration: A Case of National Proliferation," 1976 *Detroit Central Law Review* 423, 437-438 (footnotes omitted).

23. *New York Times* A16, col. 4 (15 January 1970).

24. *Third Branch,* January 1971, at 1.

25. *Baltimore Sun* A29, col. 1 (15 December 1970).

26. See Remarks by Warren E. Burger, Economic Club of New York Dinner Meeting (23 January 1974) (unpublished material collected in *Speeches of Chief Justice Warren Burger* in Brigham Young University Law Library).

27. New York, New Jersey, California, and Colorado.

28. Telephone interview with Harvey Solomon, executive director of the Institute for Court Management, Denver, Colorado (18 March 1981).

29. Ibid.

30. See J. Gazell, "Developmental Syndromes in Judicial Management," 38 *Brooklyn Law Review* 587, 612-617 (1972); Gazell, "University and Law School Education in Judicial Administration: A Case of National Proliferation," 1976 *Detroit Central Law Review* 423, 440-453; Dwayne L. Oglesby and Geoffrey S. Gallas, "Court Administration—A

New Profession: A Role for Universities," 10 *American Business Law Journal* 1, 11-15 (1972); Robert B. Yegge, "Professional Training for the Court Administrator," 60 *Judicature* 123 (1976).

31. Address by Warren E. Burger, supra note 19, at 4. "The very existence of this facility [the ICM] aided substantially in securing the passage by Congress of the Court Executives Act. . . ." Address by Warren E. Burger, American Bar Association, "State of the Federal Judiciary—1971 (5 July 1971)," reprinted in 57 *American Bar Association Journal* 885 (1971).

32. Address by Warren E. Burger, supra note 21, at 932.

33. Address by Warren E. Burger, supra note 19, at 3.

34. Address by Warren E. Burger, National Conference on the Judiciary, "Deferred Maintenance" (12 March 1971), reprinted in 57 *American Bar Association Journal* 425, 428 (1971).

35. Act of 5 January 1971, Pub. L. No. 91-647, 84 Stat. 1907 (codified at 28 U.S.C. § 332(e)-(f) (1976)).

36. Address by Warren E. Burger, American Bar Association Annual Meeting, "Report on the Federal Judicial Branch—1973 (6 August 1973)," reprinted in 59 *American Bar Association Journal* 1125 (1973).

37. The following five districts have been offered funding for this position: Northern District of Illinois, Central District of California, Eastern District of Michigan, Southern District of New York, and Southern District of Florida. By April 1981, none of this funding had been formally accepted and utilized by any of these districts.

38. Remarks by Warren E. Burger, supra note 26.

39. Mark W. Cannon, "An Administrator's View of the Supreme Court," 22 *Federal Bar News* 109-111 (1975). Chief Justice Warren also received part-time assistance from the law clerk assigned to retired Justice Stanley Reed.

40. Interview with Chief Justice Warren E. Burger, *U.S. News & World Report* 42 (14 December 1970).

41. Act of 1 March 1972, Pub. L. No. 92-238, 86 Stat. 46 (codified at 28 U.S.C. § 677 (1976)). See Congressional Quarterly Service, *Congress and the Nation* 304 (Washington, D.C.: Congressional Quarterly Press, 1973).

42. Remarks by Warren E. Burger, supra note 26.

43. The Office of Administrative Assistant to the Chief Justice (15 December 1976) (unpublished leaflet).

44. The chief judges of the federal district courts designated under title 28, section 133, of the U.S. Code to have six or more judges are invited to participate in the METCHIEFS.

45. Pub. L. No. 90-578, 82 Stat. 1107 (codified in scattered sections of 18, 28 U.S.C.).

46. Address by Warren E. Burger, supra note 36, at 1126.

47. In the year ending 30 June 1977, one-quarter of a million proceedings were handled by magistrates, including the trial of 85,880 petty offenses and 17,000 misdemeanors. There were only 148 appeals from these trials to the district judges.

48. 28 U.S.C. § 636 (1976 and Supp. III 1979). See *Third Branch* (November 1976).

49. See memorandum from William E. Foley to all Circuit Judges and District Judges (12 October 1979) (unpublished). See also C. McCabe, "The Federal Magistrate Act of 1979," 16 *Harvard Journal Legislation* 343 (1979).

50. *Third Branch* 6 (May 1973) (discussing report of Judge George Hart). See also *Third Branch* 1 (September 1969).

51. *Third Branch* 7 (April 1973).

52. Address by Warren E. Burger, American Bar Association Meeting, "Report on the Problems of the Judiciary," (11 August 1972), reprinted in 58 *American Bar Association Journal* 1049, 1050 (1972).

53. See, e.g., *Third Branch* 2 (September 1972).

54. The Chief Justice has commended highly the work of senior judges: "Were it not for the continued work of these Senior Judges, the Federal Court system would have collapsed during the past five or six years." W. Burger, "Year-End Report" (2 January 1977) (unpublished).

55. Address by Warren E. Burger, supra note 18.

56. See, e.g., Press Release by Warren E. Burger, supra note 17.

57. See Letter from Warren E. Burger to Peter Rodino (11 July 1978) (unpublished).

58. Administrative Office of the U.S. Courts, *Annual Report of the Director* 43, 58 (Washington, D.C.: Administration Office of the U.S. Courts, 1980).

59. See, generally, F. Frankfurter and J. Landis, *The Business of the Supreme Court* (Cambridge: Harvard University Press, 1928).

60. See, generally, W. Swindler, "Fifty-one Chief Justices," 60 *Kentucky Law Journal* 89 (1972).

61. The Judicial Code of 1949 states that "[t]he Chief Justice shall submit to Congress an annual report of the proceedings of the Judicial Conference and its recommendations for legislation." 28 U.S.C. § 331 (1976 and Supp. III 1979).

62. In a 1975 interview, the Chief Justice stated that communication between the judiciary and Congress "qualifie(d) as an overriding problem." He emphasized that "[t]he three branches can't function in complete isolation . . . [P]roblems can be solved only by active co-operation among the three branches." Interview with Warren E. Burger, "Why Courts Are in Trouble," *U.S. News & World Report* 28 (31 March 1975). In a 1977 interview, the Chief Justice again addressed the communication problem. He indicated, however, that "there has been a marked improvement. . . . On the whole, I think our communication with relevant committees is much better now than it was a few years ago." Interview with Warren E. Burger, "How to Break Logic in Courts," *U.S. News & World Report* 12 (19 December 1977).

63. The Chief Justice has not indicated great enthusiasm for the idea of delivering a State of the Judiciary Address to Congress. A bill authorizing such an address, sponsored by Senator Howell Heflin, passed the Senate in 1980. Some observers believe that such a speech might alter separation-of-powers relationships or affect internal relationships among the Justices of the Supreme Court. Others feel that such an address would give the Chief Justice an excellent forum to dramatize his concerns and give added importance to the judicial branch. Burger has not pressed the idea but suggests as an alternative a series of joint executive sessions with the judiciary committees to explore problems in depth on an agreed agenda.

64. The conferences have occurred in March 1978, March 1979, January 1980, and March 1981. For information on the Brookings Conference, see M. Cannon and W. Cikins, "Interbranch Cooperation in Improving The Administration of Justice: A Major Innovation," 38 *Washington & Lee Law Review* 1 (1981).

65. Address by Warren E. Burger, "State of the Federal Judiciary—1971," supra note 31, at 856.

66. Remarks by Warren E. Burger, Virginia Bar Association (10 February 1976) (unpublished).

67. Draft of speech prepared by Warren E. Burger, "What Bar Associations Can Do for State Courts" (4 August 1976) (unpublished).

68. Among the milestones on the road of judicial education are the ABA's Traffic Court Program (1942), the Institute for Judicial Administration's Appellate Judges' Seminar at NYU Law School (1956), the first seminars for federal trial judges (1957), and the National College of State Trial Judges (1964). See Philip M. Fairbanks, "Educating Judges for Courts of the Poor," *Trial* 43 (April-May 1970). See also R. Wheeler, "Orientation Techniques for Newly-Appointed Federal District Judges, Report to the Federal Judicial Center" (March 1975) (unpublished).

69. "State of the Judiciary and Access to the Courts: Hearings Before the Subcommittee on Courts, Civil Liberties, and the Administration of Justice, House Committee on the Judiciary," 95th Cong., 1st Sess., 6 (1977) (Letter from Warren E. Burger to Robert W. Kastenmeier).

70. Remarks by Warren E. Burger, Conference to Commemorate Dedication of National Center for State Courts (19 March 1978) (unpublished).

71. Remarks by Warren E. Burger, American Law Institute (10 June 1980) (unpublished).

72. Remarks by Warren E. Burger, supra note 70.

73. Ibid.

74. Address by Warren E. Burger, American Law Institute, "Has the Time Come?" (6 May 1972) (unpublished).

75. Letter to Kastenmeier, supra note 69, at 9 (quoting *Lumberman's Casualty Co. v. Elbert,* 348 U.S. 48, 59 [1954]).

76. *Lumberman's Casualty Co. v. Elbert,* 348 U.S. 48, 59 (1954) (Frankfurter, J., con. op.).

77. Remarks by Warren E. Burger, supra note 70.

78. Interview with Warren E. Burger, "New Ways to Speed Up Justice," *U.S. News & World Report* 40, 41 (21 August 1972).

79. *Nomination of Warren E. Burger, Hearings Before the Senate Committee on the Judiciary,* 91st Cong., 1st Sess., 5 (Washington, D.C.: Government Printing Office, 1969).

80. R. Kohlmeier, "Chief Justice Burger Is Expected to Push Administrative Reform," *Wall Street Journal* 1, col. 1 (28 October 1971).

81. Remarks by Warren E. Burger, accepting the Fordham Stein Award (25 October 1978) (unpublished).

82. See P. Kurland, "The Lord Chancellor of the United States," *Trial* 11 (November-December 1971); and R. Landever, "Chief Justice Burger and Extra-Case Activism," 20 *Journal of Public Law* 523 (1971).

83. A. Bickel, "The Courts: The Need for Change," *New York Times* 47, col. 1 (22 October 1971).

84. See W. Swindler, "The Chief Justice and Law Reform, 1921-1971," 1971 *Supreme Court Review* 241 (Chicago: University of Chicago Press, 1971).

85. The average tenure of the last 12 Attorneys General is just under two years.

86. Landever, supra note 82.

87. Remarks by Warren E. Burger, supra note 81.

PART III

The Judiciary and the Constitution

"WE ARE under a Constitution," Chief Justice Charles Evans Hughes declared, "but the Constitution is what the judges say it is."[1] The traditionally held view, in Chief Justice John Marshall's words, is that "[c]ourts are the mere instruments of law, and can will nothing."[2] Chief Justice Roger Taney similarly held that the Constitution "speaks not only in the same words, but with the same meaning and intent with which it spoke when it came from the hands of its framers. . . . Any other rule of construction would abrogate the judicial character of this Court, and make it the mere reflex of popular opinion or passion of the day."[3]

The power to declare the law, however, Justice Benjamin Cardozo maintained, "carries with it the power, within limits the duty, to make law when none exists."[4] Not all provisions of the Constitution are unambiguous. Interpretation is necessary because the nature of the Constitution, Chief Justice Marshall noted, "requires, that only its great outlines should be marked, its important objects designated, and the minor ingredients which compose those objects, be deduced from the nature of the objects themselves."[5] In constitutional interpretation the intent of the founding fathers provides a guide, but it is often difficult if not impossible to determine the extent of agreement among those who drafted and those who ratified the document in the various state constitutional conventions. Changing political circumstances, furthermore, present new problems that require judicial creativity in constitutional interpretation. Chief Justice William Howard Taft, for one, considered this the Court's "highest and most useful function." That "judges should interpret the exact intention of those who established the Constitution," he said, was a "theory of one who does not understand the proper administration of justice." Frequently, he continued, "new conditions arise which those who were responsible for the written law could not have had in view." Rather than "the exercise of legislative power . . . [this] is the exercise of a sound judicial discretion in supplementing the provisions . . . which are necessarily incomplete or lacking in detail essential to their proper application."[6]

The Supreme Court's dilemma, Chief Justice Marshall understood so well, lies in "never forget[ting] that it is *a constitution* we are expounding . . . [but] a constitution intended to endure for ages to come, and, consequently, to be adapted to the various *crises* of human affairs."[7] Central to the Court's dilemma and the problems of constitutional interpretation is the notion of a living Constitution: whether the Constitution should be construed to meet changing political circumstances, or whether the burden of the Court lies in bringing political controversies within the language, structure, and spirit of the Constitution. The notion of a living Constitution is examined by Justice William Rehnquist and from a different perspective by Chief Judge William Wayne Justice in chapters 12 and 13. The exchange between Justice Rehnquist and Judge Justice illuminates the relationship between the Court and the Constitution, including some of the perennial issues in constitutional interpretation.

"Do judges make law? Course they do. Made some myself," proclaimed Justice Jeremiah Smith of the New Hampshire Supreme Court.[8] "All judges exercise discretion, individualize abstract rules, make law," Judge Jerome Frank declared.[9] Judicial lawmaking on a case-by-case basis, Justice Dallin Oaks points out in chapter 14, is necessary in common law—law composed of rulings on matters not expressly treated in legislation. Interpretation of federal or state statutes may require judicial legislation as well; for example, when two statutes must be reconciled or when statutory language needs clarification to guide administrative action or the application of law to particular circumstances. In such instances, Justice Oliver Wendell Holmes said, "judges do and must legislate, but they can do so only interstitially; they are confined from the molar to molecular motions."[10]

Judicial legislation in constitutional law is another matter, as Justice Oaks explains in discussing the Supreme Court's 1965 decision in *Griswold v. Connecticut* in which the Court created out of whole constitutional cloth a right of privacy.[11] Judicial creativity is essential to constitutional interpretation, but as Justice Hugo Black, dissenting in *Griswold,* warned, "unbounded judicial [creativity] would make of this Court's members a day-to-day constitutional convention."[12] The threshold of permissible judicial creativity is crossed, Justices Oaks and Black argue, when the Court discovers and enforces values that are neither specifically enumerated in, nor fairly traceable to, some provision in the text of the Constitution. Likewise, in 1905 Justice Holmes criticized the majority in *Lochner v. New York* for becoming a superlegislature by inventing a "liberty of contract," thereby enforcing the majority's particular laissez-faire economic philosophy.[13] Although advocating that the judiciary has a special role in protecting discrete and insular minorities and ensuring access to the political process, Chief Justice Harlan Fiske Stone also lamented: "My more conservative brethren in the old days enacted their own economic prejudice into law. What they did placed in jeopardy a great and useful institution of government. The pendulum has now swung to the other extreme, and history is repeating itself. The Court is now in as much danger of becoming a legislative Constitution-making body, enacting into law its own predilections, as it was then."[14] Similarly, Justice Black cautioned, "when a 'political theory' embodied in our Constitution becomes outdated, it seems to me that a majority of the nine members of this Court are not only without constitutional power but are far less qualified to choose a new constitutional political theory than the people of this country."[15]

"Every Justice has been accused of legislating," Justice Robert Jackson commented, "and every one has joined in that accusation of others."[16] What nevertheless remains essential, Justice William Brennan points out, is that "[t]he Justices are charged with deciding according to law. . . . And while the Justices may and do consult history and the other disciplines as aids to constitutional decision, the text of the Constitution and relevant precedents dealing with that text are their primary tools."[17] Recalling the views of two other leading jurists, Judge Irving Kaufman also characterizes the role of the judge in constitutional interpretation: "Judge Learned Hand recognized that a judge is forever bound to remain detached and almost aloof from, and must, therefore, resist, all temptations to implement his personal vision of the just society—except, of course, to the extent that his vision is consonant with the law as it evolves in response to social change. Justice Benjamin Cardozo stated the principle with his customary eloquence: 'the judge . . . is not a knight-errant, roaming at will in pursuit of his own ideal of beauty or of goodness. His is to draw his inspiration from consecrated principles.' "[18]

In exercising judicial review and in approaching constitutional interpretation, the justices have a good deal of flexibility and may delay or avoid deciding constitutional questions. As Justice Felix Frankfurter opined: "This Court reaches constitutional issues last, not first."[19] Justice Oaks discusses five self-imposed rules—the actual case or controversy rule, the political questions doctrine, the standing requirements, and the ripeness and mootness limitations—that the justices usually consider before reaching constitutional questions. Justice Louis Brandeis provided a similar list of rules by which the Court might avoid "passing upon a large part of all constitutional questions pressed upon it for decision."[20] Both Justices Oaks and Brandeis underscore the view that the Court generally does not reach constitutional questions unless they are unavoidable, instead deciding cases on the basis of statutes or some other grounds.

When the justices do reach a constitutional question, they typically try to base their decision on the narrowest possible principle and in accord with *stare decisis* (prior decisions, precedent). The principle of a case, or the *ratio decidendi,* however, may not always be explicitly stated in the reasons given in an opinion for the Court's decision. The principle must be distinguished from *dicta,* that is, statements in an opinion that are unnecessary to the decision reached because they relate to factual situations other than that presented in the case at hand, or simply express a justice's personal philosophy. The principle of a case emerges from the facts that the Court treats as material *and* as immaterial to a decision as well as the reasons given in its opinion. The principle of a case depends as much on what is excluded as it does on what is included. Sometimes the Court will announce a *per se* rule. For example, Justice Black, in chapter 20, argues that the First Amendment per se forbids Congress from enacting any law abridging freedom of speech or press. More often, in line drawing the Court balances ad hoc competing interests and claims with different results turning on different factual circumstances. The principle of a case and its precedential value thus frequently emerge incrementally from a series of cases with the Court's consideration of a principle's application to various factual situations. If the decision is unanimous, its precedential value is stronger than when the justices are divided 5 to 4, for example, or when the Court's opinion is supported only by two or three justices with the others concurring in the result but not with the reasons given in the opinion of the Court. The incremental nature of constitutional interpretation, furthermore, provides numerous opportunities for distinguishing, extending or limiting, or overturning prior decisions, particularly when there are shifting alliances or the composition of the Court changes. Precedent and *stare decisis* are important, therefore, but not insurmountable. On constitutional questions, Justice William Douglas, among others, found "that *stare decisis* — that is, established law — was really no sure guideline because what did . . . the judges who sat there in 1875 know about, say, electronic surveillance? They didn't know anything about it."[21] Constitutional precedents, Justice Jackson in half-jest quipped, "are accepted only at their current valuation and have a mortality rate as high as their authors."[22]

In a political system based on a written constitution and with an independent judiciary, constitutional interpretation is necessary, judicial creativity important, and judicial lawmaking to some degree inevitable. But, in the second Justice John Marshall Harlan's words, "the Constitution does not confer on courts blanket authority to step into every situation where the political branch may be thought to have fallen short."[23] Given the role of the judiciary in a system of free government, and the difficulty of overriding by constitutional amendment a decision of the Court, Judge J. Clifford Wallace, in chapter 15, argues that the letter and spirit of the Constitution must serve as the Court's principal guide. That guide and the self-imposed restraints on judicial review are crucial to the functioning of an independent judiciary and a system of free government. For as Justice Felix Frankfurter once observed, "constitutional law is not at all a science, but applied politics."[24] Judge Robert Bork in chapter 16 presents his view of the role of political philosophy, tradition, and morality in constitutional law.

NOTES

1. C.E. Hughes, *Addresses of Charles Evans Hughes* 185-186 (New York: Putnam's, 1916).

2. *Osborn v. Bank of the United States,* 27 U.S. (9 Wheat.) 738, 866 (1824).

3. *Dred Scott v. Sandford,* 60 U.S. 393, 426 (1857).

4. B. Cardozo, *The Nature of the Judicial Process* 124 (New Haven: Yale University Press, 1921).

5. *McCulloch v. Maryland,* 17 U.S. (4 Wheat.) 316, 407 (1819).

6. W.H. Taft, *Popular Government* 222-223 (New Haven: Yale University Press, 1913).

7. *McCulloch v. Maryland,* 17 U.S. (4 Wheat.) 316, 407, 415 (1819).

8. Quoted by P. Freund, *On Understanding the Supreme Court* 3 (Boston: Little, Brown, 1949).

9. J. Frank, *Law and the Modern Mind* 137-138 (New York: Brentano's, 1930).

10. *Southern Pacific Co. v. Jensen,* 244 U.S. 205, 220 (1917).

11. For a further discussion, see D.M. O'Brien, *Privacy, Law, and Public Policy* (New York: Praeger, 1979).

12. *Griswold v. Connecticut,* 381 U.S. 479, 520 (1965) (Black, J., dis. op.).

13. *Lochner v. New York,* 198 U.S. 45 (1905) (Holmes, J., dis. op.).

14. H.F. Stone, Letter to Irving Brant (25 August 1945), quoted by A.T. Mason, *The Supreme Court from Taft to Burger* 168 (Baton Rouge: Louisiana State University Press, 3d ed., 1979).

15. *Harper v. Virginia State Board of Elections,* 383 U.S. 663, 678 (1966) (Black, J., dis. op.).

16. R. Jackson, *The Struggle Over Judicial Supremacy* 80 (New York: Knopf, 1949).

17. W.J. Brennan, Jr., "Inside View of the High Court," *New York Times Magazine* 35 (6 October 1963).

18. I. Kaufman, Remarks, "The Courts in Peril," The Palm Beach Round Table, 3-4 (10 February 1983).

19. Reported in 23 *U.S. Law Week* 265 (1955).

20. See *Ashwander v. TVA,* 297 U.S. 288, 341-356 (1936) (Brandeis, J., con. op.).

21. W.O. Douglas, Interview, *CBS Reports,* Transcript 13 (New York: CBS Reports, 6 September 1972).

22. R. Jackson, "The Task of Maintaining Our Liberties: The Role of the Judiciary," 39 *American Bar Association Journal* 962 (1953).

23. J.M. Harlan, Jr., Address, American Bar Center (Chicago, Ill.: 13 August 1963).

24. F. Frankfurter, "The Zeitgeist and the Judiciary," in *Law and Politics* 6, ed. by A. MacLeish and E. Prichard (New York: Harcourt, Brace, 1939).

12

The Notion of a Living Constitution

WILLIAM H. REHNQUIST
Justice, Supreme Court of the United States

At least one of the more than half-dozen persons nominated during the past decade to be an Associate Justice of the Supreme Court of the United States has been asked by the Senate Judiciary Committee at his confirmation hearings whether he believed in a living Constitution.[1] It is not an easy question to answer; the phrase "living Constitution" has about it a teasing imprecision that makes it a coat of many colors.

One's first reaction tends to be along the lines of public relations or ideological sex appeal, I suppose. At first blush it seems certain that a *living* Constitution is better than what must be its counterpart, a *dead* Constitution. It would seem that only a necrophile could disagree. If we could get one of the major public opinion research firms in the country to sample public opinion concerning whether the United States Constitution should be *living* or *dead*, the overwhelming majority of the responses doubtless would favor a *living* Constitution.

The phrase is really a shorthand expression that is susceptible of at least two quite different meanings. The first meaning was expressed over a half-century ago by Mr. Justice Holmes in *Missouri v. Holland*[2] with his customary felicity when he said:

> ... When we are dealing with words that also are a constituent act, like the Constitution of the United States, we must realize that they have called into life a being the development of which could not have been foreseen completely by the most gifted of its begetters. It was enough for them to realize or to hope that they had created an organism; it has taken a century and has cost their successors much sweat and blood to prove that they created a nation.[3]

I shall refer to this interpretation of the phrase "living Constitution," with which scarcely anyone would disagree, as the Holmes version.

The framers of the Constitution wisely spoke in general language and left to succeeding generations the task of applying that language to the unceasingly changing environment in which they would live. Those who framed, adopted, and ratified the Civil War amendments[4] to the Constitution likewise used what have been aptly described as "majestic generalities"[5] in composing the

Fourteenth Amendment. Merely because a particular activity may not have existed when the Constitution was adopted, or because the framers could not have conceived of a particular method of transacting affairs, cannot mean that general language in the Constitution may not be applied to such a course of conduct. Where the framers of the Constitution have used general language, they have given latitude to those who would later interpret the instrument to make that language applicable to cases that the framers might not have foreseen.

In my reading and travels I have sensed a second connotation of the phrase "living Constitution," however, one quite different from what I have described as the Holmes version, but which certainly has gained acceptance among some parts of the legal profession. Embodied in its most naked form, it recently came to my attention in some language from a brief that had been filed in a United States District Court on behalf of state prisoners asserting that the conditions of their confinement offended the United States Constitution.

The brief urged:

> We are asking a great deal of the Court because other branches of government have abdicated their responsibility. . . . Prisoners are like other "discrete and insular" minorities for whom the Court must spread its protective umbrella because no other branch of government will do so. . . . This Court, as the voice and conscience of contemporary society, as the measure of the modern conception of human dignity, must declare that the [named prison] and all it represents offends the Constitution of the United States and will not be tolerated.

Here we have a living Constitution with a vengeance. Although the substitution of some other set of values for those which may be derived from the language and intent of the framers is not urged in so many words, that is surely the thrust of the message. Under this brief writer's version of the living Constitution, nonelected members of the federal judiciary may address themselves to a social problem simply because other branches of government have failed or refused to do so. These same judges, responsible to no constituency whatever, are nonetheless acclaimed as "the voice and conscience of contemporary society."

If we were merely talking about a slogan that was being used to elect some candidate to office or to persuade the voters to ratify a constitutional amendment, elaborate dissection of a phrase such as "living Constitution" would probably not be warranted. What we are talking about, however, is a suggested philosophical approach to be used by the federal judiciary, and perhaps state judiciaries, in exercising the very delicate responsibility of judicial review. Under the familiar principle of judicial review, the courts in construing the Constitution are, of course, authorized to invalidate laws that have been enacted by Congress or by a state legislature but that those courts find to violate some provision of the Constitution. Nevertheless, those who have pondered the matter have always recognized that the ideal of judicial review has basically antidemocratic and antimajoritarian facets that require some justification in this Nation, which prides itself on being a self-governing representative democracy.

All who have studied law, and many who have not, are familiar with John Marshall's classic defense of judicial review in his opinion for the Court in *Marbury v. Madison.*[6] I will summarize very briefly the thrust of that answer, with which I fully agreee, because while it supports the Holmes version of the phrase "living Constitution," it also suggests some outer limits for the brief writer's version.

The ultimate source of authority in this Nation, Marshall said, is not Congress, not the states, not for that matter the Supreme Court of the United States. The people are the ultimate source of authority; they have parceled out the authority that originally resided entirely with them by adopting the original Constitution and by later amending it. They have granted some authority to the federal government and have reserved authority not granted it to the states or to the people individually. As between the branches of the federal government, the people have given certain authority to the President, certain authority to Congress, and certain authority to the federal judiciary. In the Bill of Rights they have erected protections for specified individual rights against the actions of the federal government. From today's perspective we might add that they have placed restrictions on the authority of the state governments in the Thirteenth, Fourteenth, and Fifteenth amendments.

In addition, Marshall said that if the popular branches of government—state legislatures, the Congress, and the Presidency—are operating within the authority granted to them by the Constitution, their judgment and not that of the Court must obviously prevail. When these branches overstep the authority given them by the Constitution, in the case of the President and the Congress, or invade protected individual rights, and a constitutional challenge to their action is raised in a lawsuit brought in federal court, the Court must prefer the Constitution to the government acts.

John Marshall's justification for judicial review makes the provision for an independent federal judiciary not only understandable but also thoroughly desirable. Since the judges will be merely interpreting an instrument framed by the people, they should be detached and objective. A mere change in public opinion since the adoption of the Constitution, unaccompanied by a constitutional amendment, should not change the meaning of the Constitution. A merely temporary majoritarian groundswell should not abrogate some individual liberty truly protected by the Constitution.

Clearly Marshall's explanation contains certain elements of either ingenuousness or ingeniousness, which tend to grow larger as our constitutional history extends over a longer period of time. The Constitution is in many of its parts obviously not a specifically worded document but one couched in general phraseology. There is obviously wide room for honest difference of opinion over the meaning of general phrases in the Constitution; any particular Justice's decision when a question arises under one of these general phrases will depend to some extent on his own philosophy of constitutional law. One may nevertheless concede all of these problems that inhere in Marshall's justification of judicial review, yet feel that his justification for nonelected judges exercising the power of judicial review is the only one consistent with democratic philosophy of representative government.

Marshall was writing at a time when the governing generation remembered well not only the deliberations of the framers of the Constitution at Philadelphia in the summer of 1787 but also the debates over the ratification of the Constitution in the 13 colonies. The often heated discussions that took place from 1787, when Delaware became the first state to ratify the Constitution,[7] until 1790, when recalcitrant Rhode Island finally joined the Union,[8] were themselves far more representative of the give-and-take of public decision making by a constituent assembly than is the ordinary enactment of a law by Congress or by a state legislature. Patrick Henry had done all he could to block ratification in Virginia,[9] and the opposition of the Clinton faction in New York had provoked Jay, Hamilton, and Madison to their brilliant effort in defense of the Constitution, the *Federalist Papers*.[10] For Marshall, writing the *Marbury v. Madison* opinion in 1803, the memory of the debates in which the people of the 13 colonies had participated only a few years before could well have fortified his conviction that the Constitution was, not merely in theory but in fact as well, a fundamental charter that had emanated from the people.

One senses no similar connection with a popularly adopted constituent act in what I have referred to as the brief writer's version of the living Constitution. The brief writer's version seems instead to be based upon the proposition that federal judges, perhaps judges as a whole, have a role of their own, quite independent of popular will, to play in solving society's problems. Once we have abandoned the idea that the authority of the courts to declare laws unconstitutional is somehow tied to the language of the Constitution that the people adopted, a judiciary exercising the power of judicial review appears in a quite different light. Judges then are no longer the keepers of the covenant; instead they are a small group of fortunately situated people with a roving commission to second-guess Congress, state legislatures, and state and federal administrative officers concerning what is best for the country. Surely there is no justification for a third legislative branch in the federal government, and there is even less justification for a federal legislative branch's reviewing on a policy basis the laws enacted by the legislatures of the 50 states. Even if one were to disagree with me on this point, the members of a third branch of the federal legislature at least ought to be elected by and responsible to constituencies, just as in the case of the other two branches of Congress. If there is going to be a council of revision, it ought to have at least some connection with popular feeling. Its members either ought to stand for reelection on occasion, or their terms should expire and they should be allowed to continue serving only if reappointed by a popularly elected Chief Executive and confirmed by a popularly elected Senate.

The brief writer's version of the living Constitution is seldom presented in its most naked form, but is instead usually dressed in more attractive garb. The argument in favor of this approach generally begins with a sophisticated wink—why pretend that there is any ascertainable content to the general phrases of the Constitution as they are written since, after all, judges constantly disagree about their meaning? We are all familiar with Chief Justice Hughes's famous aphorism that "We are under a Constitution, but the Constitution is what the judges say it is."[11] We all know the basis of Marshall's justification for judicial review, the argument runs, but it is necessary only to keep the window dressing in place. Any sophisticated student of the subject knows that judges need not limit themselves to the intent of the framers, which is very difficult to determine in any event. Because of the general language used in the Constitution, judges should not hesitate to use their authority to make the Constitution relevant and useful in solving the problems of modern society. The brief writer's version of the living Constitution envisions all of the above conclusions.

At least three serious difficulties flaw the brief writer's version of the living Constitution. First, it misconceives the nature of the Constitution, which was designed to enable the popularly elected branches of government, not the judicial branch, to keep the country abreast of the times. Second, the brief writer's version ignores the Supreme Court's disastrous experiences when in the past it embraced contemporary, fashionable notions of what a living Constitution should contain. Third, however socially desirable the goals sought to be advanced by the brief writer's version, advancing them through a freewheeling, nonelected judiciary is quite unacceptable in a democratic society.

It seems to me that it is almost impossible, after reading the record of the Founding Fathers' debates in Philadelphia, to conclude that they intended the Constitution itself to suggest answers to the manifold problems that they knew would confront succeeding generations. The Constitution that they drafted was indeed intended to endure indefinitely, but the reason for this very well-founded hope was the general language by which national authority was granted to Congress and the Presidency. These two branches were to furnish the motive power within the federal system, which was in turn to coexist with the state governments; the elements of government having a popular constituency were looked to for the solution of the numerous and varied problems that the future would bring. Limitations were indeed placed upon both federal and state governments in the form of both a division of powers and express protection for individual rights. These limitations, however, were not themselves designed to solve the problems of the future, but were instead designed to make certain that the constituent branches, when *they* attempted to solve those problems, should not transgress these fundamental limitations.

Although the Civil War Amendments were designed more as broad limitations on the authority of state governments, they too were enacted in response to practices that the lately seceded states engaged in to discriminate against and mistreat the newly emancipated freed men. To the extent that the language of these amendments is general, the courts are of course warranted in giving them an application coextensive with their language. Nevertheless, I greatly doubt that even men like Thad Stevens and John Bingham, leaders of the radical Republicans in Congress, would have thought any portion of the Civil War Amendments, except section five of the Fourteenth Amendment,[12] was designed to solve problems that society might confront a century later. I think they would have said that those amendments were designed to prevent abuses from ever recurring in which the states had engaged prior to that time.

The second difficulty with the brief writer's version of the living Constitution lies in its inattention to or rejection of the Supreme Court's historical experience gleaned from similar forays into problem solving.

Although the phrase "living Constitution" may not have been used during the nineteenth century and the first half of this century, the idea represented by the brief writer's version was very much in evidence during both periods. The apogee of the living Constitution doctrine during the nineteenth century was the Supreme Court's decision in *Dred Scott v. Sandford*.[13] In that case the question at issue was the status of a Negro who had been carried by his master from a slave state into a territory made free by the Missouri Compromise. Although thereafter taken back to a slave state, Dred Scott claimed that upon previously reaching free soil he had been forever emancipated. The Court, speaking through Chief Justice Taney, held that Congress was without power to legislate upon the issue of slavery even in a territory governed by it, and that therefore Dred Scott had never become free. Congress, the Court held, was virtually powerless to check or limit the spread of the institution of slavery.

The history of this country for some 30 years before the *Dred Scott* decision demonstrates the bitter frustration which that decision brought to large elements of the population who opposed any expansion of slavery. In 1820 when Maine was seeking admission as a free state and Missouri as a slave state, a fight over the expansion of slavery engulfed the national legislative halls and resulted in the Missouri Compromise,[14] which forever banned slavery from those territories lying north of a line drawn through the southern boundary of Missouri.[15] This was a victory for the antislavery forces in the North, but the Southerners were prepared to live with it. At the time of the Mexican War in 1846, Representative David Wilmot of Pennsylvania introduced a bill, later known as the Wilmot Proviso,[16] that would have precluded the opening to slavery of any territory acquired as a result of the Mexican War.[17] This proposed amendment to the Missouri Compromise was hotly debated for years both in and out of Congress.[18] Finally in 1854 Senator Stephen A. Douglas shepherded through Congress the Kansas-Nebraska Act,[19] which in effect repealed the Missouri Compromise and enacted into law the principle of "squatter sovereignty": the people in each of the new territories would decide whether or not to permit slavery.[20] The enactment of this bill was, of course, a victory for the proslavery forces in Congress and a defeat for those opposed to the expansion of slavery.

The great majority of the antislavery groups, as strongly as they felt about the matter, were still willing to live with the decision of Congress.[21] They were not willing, however, to live with the *Dred Scott* decision.

The Court in *Dred Scott* decided that all of the agitation and debate in Congress over the Missouri Compromise in 1820, over the Wilmot Proviso a generation later, and over the Kansas-Nebraska Act in 1854 had amounted to absolutely nothing. It was, in the words of Macbeth, "A tale told by an idiot, full of sound and fury, signifying nothing."[22] According to the Court, the decision had never been one that Congress was entitled to make; it was one that the Court alone, in construing the Constitution, was empowered to make.

The frustration of the citizenry, who had thought themselves charged with the responsibility for making such decisions, is well expressed in Abraham Lincoln's First Inaugural Address:

> [T]he candid citizen must confess that if the policy of the government, upon vital questions affecting the whole people, is to be irrevocably fixed by decisions of the Supreme Court, the instant they are made, in ordinary litigation between parties in personal actions, the people will have ceased to be their own rulers, having to that extent practically resigned their government into the hands of that eminent tribunal.[23]

The *Dred Scott* decision, of course, was repealed in fact as a result of the Civil War and in law by the Civil War Amendments. The injury to the reputation of the Supreme Court that resulted from the *Dred Scott* decision, however, took more than a generation to heal. Indeed, newspaper accounts long after the *Dred Scott* decision bristled with attacks on the Court, and particularly on Chief Justice Taney, unequalled in their bitterness even to this day.

The brief writer's version of the living Constitution made its next appearance, almost as dramatically as its first, shortly after the turn of the century in *Lochner v. New York*.[24] The name of the case is a household word to those who have studied constitutional law, and it is one of the handful of cases in which a dissenting opinion has been overwhelmingly vindicated by the passage of time. In *Lochner* a New York law that limited to ten the maximum number of hours per day that could be worked by bakery employees was assailed on the ground that it deprived the bakery employer of liberty without due process of law. A majority of the Court held the New York maximum hour law unconstitutional, saying, "Statutes of the nature of that under review, limiting the hours in which grown and intelligent men may labor to earn their living, are mere meddlesome interferences with the rights of the individual. . . ."[25]

The Fourteenth Amendment, of course, said nothing about any freedom to make contracts upon terms that one thought best, but there was a very substantial body of opinion outside the Constitution at the time of *Lochner* that subscribed to the general philosophy of social Darwinism as embodied in the writing of Herbert Spencer in England and William Graham Sumner in this country. It may have occurred to some of the Justices who made up a majority in *Lochner,* hopefully subconsciously rather than consciously, that since this philosophy appeared eminently sound and since the language in the due process clause was sufficiently general not to rule out its inclusion, why not strike a blow for the cause? The answer, which has been vindicated by time, came in the dissent of Mr. Justice Holmes:

> [A] constitution is not intended to embody a particular economic theory, whether of paternalism and the organic relation of the citizen to the state or of *laissez faire.* It is made for people of fundamentally differing views, and the accident of our finding certain opinions natural and familiar or novel and even shocking ought not to conclude our judgment upon the question whether statutes embodying them conflict with the Constitution of the United States.[26]

One reads the history of these episodes in the Supreme Court to little purpose if he does not conclude that prior experimentation with the brief writer's expansive notion of a living Constitution has done the Court little credit. There remain today those, such as wrote the brief from which I quoted, who appear to cleave nevertheless to the view that the experiments of the Taney Court before the Civil War, and of the Fuller and Taft Courts in the first part of this century, ended in failure not because they sought to bring into the Constitution a principle that the great majority of objective scholars would have to conclude was not there but because they sought to bring into the Constitution the *wrong* extraconstitutional principle. This school of thought appears to feel that while added protection for slave owners was clearly unacceptable and safeguards for businessmen threatened with ever-expanding state regulation were not desirable, expansion of the protection accorded to individual liberties against the state or to the interest of "discrete and insular" minorities,[27] such as prisoners, must stand on a quite different, more favored footing. To the extent, of course, that such a distinction may legitimately be derived from the Constitution itself, these latter principles do indeed stand on an entirely different footing. To the extent that one must, however, go beyond even a generously fair reading of the language and intent of that document in order to subsume these principles, it seems to me that they are not really distinguishable from those espoused in *Dred Scott* and *Lochner.*

The third difficulty with the brief writer's notion of the living Constitution is that it seems to ignore totally the nature of political value judgments in a democratic society. If such a society adopts a constitution and incorporates in that constitution safeguards for individual liberty, these safeguards indeed do take on a generalized moral rightness or goodness. They assume a general social acceptance neither because of any intrinsic worth nor because of any unique origins in someone's idea of natural justice but instead simply because they have been incorporated in a constitution by the people. Within the limits of our Constitution, the representatives of the people in the executive branches of the state and national governments enact laws. The laws that emerge after a typical political struggle in which various individual value judgments are debated likewise take on a form of moral goodness because they have been enacted into positive law. It is the fact of their enactment that gives them whatever moral claim they have upon us as a society, however, and not any independent virtue they may have in any particular citizen's own scale of values.

Beyond the Constitution and the laws in our society, there simply is no basis other than the individual conscience of the citizen that may serve as a platform for the launching of moral judgments. There is no conceivable way in which I can logically demonstrate to you that the judgments of my conscience are superior to the judgments of your conscience, and vice versa. Many of us necessarily feel strongly and deeply about our own moral judgments, but they remain only personal moral judgments until in some way given the sanction of law.

As Mr. Justice Holmes said in his famous essay on natural law:

> Certitude is not the test of certainty. We have been cocksure of many things that were not so. . . . One cannot be wrenched from the rocky crevices into which one is thrown for many years without feeling that one is attacked in one's life. What we most love and revere generally is determined by early associations. I love granite rocks and barberry bushes, no doubt because with them were my earliest joys that reach back through the past eternity of my life. But while one's experience thus makes certain preferences dogmatic for oneself, recognition of how they came to be so leaves one able to see that others, poor souls, may be equally dogmatic about something else. And this again means skepticism.[28]

This is not to say that individual moral judgments ought not to afford a springboard for action in society, for indeed they are without doubt the most common and most powerful wellsprings for action when one believes that questions of right and wrong are involved. Representative government is predicated upon the idea that one who feels deeply upon a question as a matter of concience will seek out others of like view or will attempt to persuade others who do not initially share that view. When adherents to the belief become sufficiently numerous, he will have the necessary armaments required in a democratic society to press his views upon the elected representatives of the people, and to have them embodied into positive law.

Should a person fail to persuade the legislature, or should he feel that a legislative victory would be insufficient because of its potential for future reversal, he may seek to run the more difficult gauntlet of amending the Constitution to embody the view that he espouses. Success in amending the Constitution would, of course, preclude succeeding transient majorities in the legislature from tampering with the principle formerly added to the Constitution.

The brief writer's version of the living Constitution, in the last analysis, is a formula for an end run around popular government. To the extent that it makes possible an individual's persuading one or more appointed federal judges to impose on other individuals a rule of conduct that the popularly elected branches of government would not have enacted and the voters have not and would not have embodied in the Constitution, the brief writer's version of the living Constitution is genuinely corrosive of the fundamental values of our democratic society.

NOTES

1. See *Hearings on Nominations of William H. Rehnquist and Lewis F. Powell, Jr., Before the Senate Committee on the Judiciary,* 92d Cong., 1st Sess., 87 (1971).

2. 252 U.S. 416 (1920).

3. Ibid., at 433.

4. U.S. Constitution, Amendents XIII, XIV, and XV.

5. *Fay v. New York,* 332 U.S. 261, 282 (1947) (Jackson, J.).

6. 5 U.S. (1 Cranch) 137 (1803).

7. F. Thorpe, *A Constitutional History of the American People,* Vol. 2, 18 (New York: Harper & Bros., 1898).

8. Ibid., at 191.

9. Ibid., at 81, 91-95.

10. Ibid., at 134-139.

11. C. Hughes, *Addresses and Papers of Charles Evans Hughes* 139 (New York: Putman's, 1908).

12. "The Congress shall have power to enforce, by appropriate legislation, the provisions of this article." U.S. Constitution, Amendment XIV, 5.

13. 60 U.S. (19 How.) 393 (1857).

14. Act of 6 March 1820, ch. 22, 3 Stat. 545.

15. See Thorpe, supra note 7, at 366-377 and 433.

16. Act of 19 June 1862, ch. 111, 12 Stat. 432.

17. Thorpe, supra note 7, at 430.

18. Ibid., at 430-432.

19. Act of 30 May 1854, ch. 59, 10 Stat. 277.

20. See Thorpe, supra note 7, at 518-521.

21. Ibid., at 536-542.

22. Shakespeare, *Macbeth,* V.v. 19.

23. First Inaugural Address by Abraham Lincoln, 4 March 1861, in A. Lincoln, *Complete Works of Abraham Lincoln* 171-172, ed. by J. Nicolay (1894).

24. 198 U.S. 45 (1905).

25. Ibid., at 61.

26. Ibid., at 75-76 (Holmes, J., dis. op.).

27. *United States v. Carolene Products Co.,* 304 U.S. 144, 152 n.4 (1938).

28. Oliver W. Holmes, "Natural Law," in *Collected Legal Papers* 310, 311 (New York: Peter Smith, 1920).

13

A Relativistic Constitution

WILLIAM WAYNE JUSTICE
Chief Judge, District Court, Eastern District of Texas

After a debate of nearly 200 years, a debate which has never lacked for participants, it may well be that all that can be said about judicial review and its legitimacy has already been said.

But it would be a mistake to assume that modern debate on the subject, however intense, has brought us any closer to a resolution of the problems that a federal judiciary and the institution of judicial review have posed for our contemporary society.

A relatively recent contribution to this debate concerning judicial review was an address by Mr. Justice Rehnquist, entitled "The Notion of a Living Constitution."[1] Justice Rehnquist focused upon a passage from a brief filed in a federal district court on behalf of state prisoners which complained of the conditions of their confinement. The brief writer urged relief from the district court, as "the voice and conscience of contemporary society,"[2] on the ground that the other branches of government had failed to act. Justice Rehnquist criticized this formulation by pointing out that the American form of government is a democratic one, founded on the principle of government by the consent of the governed. Within this framework, the only legitimate justification for judicial review is the one so eloquently propounded by Chief Justice Marshall in *Marbury v. Madison*[3]: that courts, when they strike down an act of a legislative body, do so by the command of the people as embodied in the Constitution. It is therefore not within the constitutional power of a federal judge to remedy every condition which he views as a social evil. Rather, values in a democratic society are best identified through the democratic branches of government.

At first glance, there seems little to disagree with in this formulation. On closer reading, however, I discerned three areas which may warrant a response: first, Justice Rehnquist's view of the place of judicial review in a democracy; second, his emphasis on, indeed, his exaltation of, relativism as a constitutional principle; and last, his quick derision of the brief writer's position.

Justice Rehnquist looked first to Marshall's defense of judicial review in *Marbury v. Madison,* according to which the Constitution, as the authoritative voice of the people, must prevail over any legislative acts which conflict with it. This explanation, in Justice Rehnquist's opinion, is "the only one consistent with [a] democratic philosophy of representative government."[4] My problem with it is twofold: First, as Alexander Bickel has convincingly pointed out,[5] the opinion in *Marbury v. Madison* not only begs the question, it begs the wrong question. Obviously, the Constitution is the supreme authority to which all governmental acts must conform; the difficult question is, why should the courts rather than the other two branches be the arbiters of the Constitution? In other words, the necessity for review goes without saying; the real question is, why *judicial* review?

My second objection goes to Justice Rehnquist's expressed desire to find a theory of review that is consistent with a democratic philosophy of government. This is the first instance in the speech of what develops into a recurring tendency, that is, to criticize judicial review, not according to the Constitution, but rather according to some extraconstitutional notion of democracy. The Constitution unquestionably contains some distinctly nonmajoritarian elements. The whole notion of binding future majorities to values they may, from time to time, desire to reject hardly represents adherence to pure majoritarianism. And most noteworthy, Article III withdraws one of the three key governmental functions from popular control. I do not mean that our Constitution is inconsistent with the principles of a self-governing, representative democracy, but I do insist that, rather than judging our Constitution by some abstract, personal, and perhaps arbitrary theory of "democracy," we should judge such a theory by the light of our venerated, and justly venerated, Constitution.

These two objections are intimately related. The answer to the question, why the judiciary should be the guardian of the Constitution, tells us something also about the kind of democracy that our Constitution guarantees. *Marbury v. Madison* takes the easy way out and avoids these questions. Chief Justice Marshall chose to cast the first judicial establishment of judicial review in terms that would least offend the People: he credited the People with superiority over their representatives, rather than according judges, in enforcing the commands of the Constitution, the power to override the representatives of the People.

A far more probing and contemporary justification of judicial review than Justice Marshall's intentional sleight of hand is to be found in Alexander Hamilton's *Federalist No. 78*,[6] published in 1788. The main point of *Federalist No. 78* is to explain the importance of an independent judiciary. Independent means independent of the *People;* precisely, that judges are not elected. Hamilton did not apologize for this feature; he celebrated it and extolled its virtues. And in meeting head-on the difficult and politically sensitive question why judicial review rather than Congressional or executive review, Hamilton answered, because *judges are independent.*

> The complete independence of the courts of justice is peculiarly essential in a limited [C]onstitution, . . . one which contains specified exceptions to the legislative authority. . . . Limitations of this kind can be preserved in practice no other way than through the medium of courts of justice, whose duty it must be to declare

all acts contrary to the manifest tenor of the [C]onstitution void. Without this, all the reservations of particular rights or privileges would amount to nothing.[7]

This is the justification of judicial review, in Hamilton's words the "bulwark," the "excellent barrier to the encroachments and oppressions of the representative body."[8]

I have come to believe that Hamilton's argument for what might seem to be the most undemocratic aspect of judicial review turns on the distinction between what the People adopt as a "solemn and authoritative act," as he characterized it; and what they might be tempted to decide, equally authoritatively —but less solemnly—later on. A great many of the individual rights set out in the Constitution were a restatement of English principles: the principles of Magna Carta, the Petition of Rights, the Commonwealth Parliament, and the Revolution of 1688. Others came as the result of our own experience. Nearly all, whether of English or American derivation, were the aftermath of wars, revolutions, insurrections, and civil disturbances. At such times, it appears that those involved are invested with a sense of urgency to memorialize the rights they have so painfully obtained in the form of a "solemn and authoritative act," as though they realize that they may later desire to modify the principles and be tempted to retract them in practice.

A very early and eloquent formulation of this view was suggested by a man of no mean democratic credentials, Thomas Jefferson. Writing in 1781 in his "Notes on the State of Virginia," Jefferson defended the importance of a bill of rights:

> Even in a government which fully reflects the "spirit of the People" . . . is the spirit of the times an infallible, a permanent reliance? . . . . The spirit of the times may alter, will alter. Our rulers will become corrupt, our people careless . . . It can never be too often represented, that the time for *fixing* every essential right on a legal basis is while our rulers are honest, and ourselves united. From the conclusion of this war, we shall be going downhill.[9]

The often-made comparison between the Bill of Rights and contemporary public opinion polls reflecting adverse views as to certain of the enumerated rights seems to support Jefferson's point; perhaps we have indeed gone "downhill." But I would suggest that Jefferson's statement applies even more strongly to those constitutional amendments adopted in the afterglow of the Civil War. In the wake of decades of debate and years of blood, the nation solemnly and authoritatively adopted certain essential principles. Slavery was forbidden, and also outlawed were whatever modified forms of oppression that were substituted for it. The nation committed itself to "equal protection of the laws." The theretofore important principle of relative autonomy for the individual states in their internal affairs was sacrificed to the ideal of the equal application of laws to all citizens.

The generosity of the language chosen reflects the largeness of spirit that prevailed at the time. I feel that the decision to preserve that breadth of spirit represented a hedge against what those who adopted the amendments were afraid they might feel in a less exalted moment. There can certainly be no doubt that the history of Reconstruction and of the first half of the twentieth century show a significant backsliding from the authoritative principles solemnly adopted as a result of our most severe national crisis.

To return to Justice Rehnquist, I wholeheartedly agree with him that judicial review must be confined to the application of the Constitution which the people have adopted. A "generously fair reading of the language and intent of that document,"[10] as he put it, is the only basis for a justifiable judicial decision. But the Justice argued for what amounts to a very minimal judicial review. He derived his views at least in part from what I regard as his rather extreme view of democracy, rather than the more complicated and differentiated governmental structure which the Constitution creates. In several instances, he made deprecatory comments concerning the nonelective status of federal judges. It is, of course, easy to understand that a member of the judiciary who feels compelled to apologize for his nonelected position might feel more uncomfortable in marshaling the Constitution against the will of the majority than would a judge not similarly disposed.

However, the address revealed a second, related, source of his argument for judicial impotence, one that I feel is alien to the Constitution—Justice Rehnquist's attachment to moral relativism. He argued that, since no value can be demonstrated to be intrinsically better or worse than any others, a particular value is *authoritative* only when it can claim majority support. I will seek to show that this sort of uncritical deference to the will of the majority goes far beyond judicial restraint and the intention of the Framers, toward judicial abdication. The key to this understanding I perceive in the decisions of Justice Oliver Wendell Holmes.

Justice Rehnquist began his discussion by identifying two "quite different" meanings to which the phrase "a living Constitution" is susceptible. One he attributed to an anonymous brief writer and the other to Justice Holmes. The Holmes version comes from his famous decision in *Missouri v. Holland,*[11] and reads as follows:

> [W]hen we are dealing with words that also are a constituent act, like the Constitution of the United States, we must realize that they have called into life a being the development of which could not have been foreseen completely by the most gifted of its begetters. It was enough for them to realize or to hope that they had created an organism; it has taken a century and has cost their successors much sweat and blood to prove that they created a nation.

A closer look at the context of this passage casts a rather curious light on what Justice Rehnquist called the Holmesian view of a "living Constitution," and with which, he stated, one could hardly disagree.

Missouri v. Holland involved a suit by the state of Missouri seeking to enjoin federal game wardens from enforcing the Migratory Bird Treaty Act of

1918, as an unconstitutional interference with the rights reserved to the states by the Tenth Amendment. The federal government, concerned with the imminent extinction of several species of migratory birds, had entered into a treaty with Great Britain which prohibited the killing, capturing, or selling of these birds except under regulations to be issued by the Secretary of Agriculture. Injunctive relief was denied by the Supreme Court. The language quoted by Justice Rehnquist, though vague in the extreme, acquires a very specific meaning in this context. First of all, the "being," the "organism" referred to in the passage, is not the Constitution at all; it is, rather, the nation that the Constitution created and, specifically, the federal legislative power. This power is what is living, and hence growing and developing. The Constitution is alive, in this sense, only insofar as it expands to give scope to governmental powers. Far from acting as any kind of limit on government action, the Constitution permits virtually anything Congress decides to do.

As a model of a living Constitution, this view has one distinctive limitation: it provides only for living governmental powers; it says nothing about whether the constitutional *limits* on governmental powers are alive as well. In terms of judicial review, this version of the living Constitution recommends restraint to the point of abdication.

Indeed, Holmes's entire body of work on the Court documents this tendency toward abdication. As Professor Walter Berns has pointed out,[12] we tend to view Holmes's decisions uncritically, even admiringly, because his theory of judicial review happened to correspond to the political views of New Deal reformers, much of whose handiwork has since been vindicated. What we tend to forget, although it is necessarily the other side of the relativist coin, is the number of Holmes's decisions which subsequent history has condemned. In *Bailey v. Alabama*,[13] a Negro plaintiff challenged a statutory system which maintained poor Negroes in a forced condition of peonage. Led by the conservative Justice Hughes, the Court held the system to violate the Thirteenth Amendment's prohibition of involuntary servitude. Holmes preferred to accept the legislature's characterization of the system as a voluntary contractual one and dissented. In *Patsone v. Pennsylvania*,[14] Holmes led the Court to uphold a statute making it unlawful for aliens to kill wild birds or animals or to possess guns. Once again, accepting the legislature's unsupported assumption that the "aliens were the peculiar source of evil,"[15] Holmes resorted to a degree of judicial review which was no review at all, and the law stood.

Finally, and most distressingly, Holmes wrote the infamous majority opinion in *Buck v. Bell*,[16] holding constitutionally valid a state's system of compulsory sterilization of the feebleminded. Although this program clearly intruded into the sacrosanct zone courts now know and respect as personal privacy, Holmes employed his habitually relaxed deference to legislative choice. Asking no questions about the effectiveness of the program, its even handedness, or necessity, he upheld the law. "The principle that sustains compulsory vaccination," he reasoned, "is broad enough to cover cutting the Fallopian tubes."[17]

Realizing the worst fears of all antirelativists, Holmes thus equated the elimination of smallpox with the elimination of children.

Holmes's relativism, which Justice Rehnquist professed to swallow whole, when revealed in this naked form, may shock us; but it is more relevant to us today in a different sense—in its relation to the Constitution, which I see as one of repugnancy. The main deficiency of philosophical relativism as a constitutional principle is that it is clearly a latter-day excrescence. The Framers gave no indication that they joined Justice Holmes is seeing "no reason for attributing to man a significance different in kind from that which belongs to a baboon or to a grain of sand."[18] They devoted their best efforts toward providing an environment in which men could achieve a happier existence, through the fullest exercise of their faculties.

This intense concern with the nature and quality of human existence is expressed in the Declaration of Independence, the Preamble to the Constitution, and throughout the *Federalist Papers*. And, although not spelled out in the body of the Constitution in so many words, its presence there is unmistakable, not only in its "majestic generalities,"[19] but in the very fact of the Constitution itself, whose Framers sought to bind future generations. My point is simply that if the relativism of Holmes and Justice Rehnquist had been conceived to be true by the Framers, there would have been no reason for any rights to have been written into a constitution. After all, those rights are only the preferences or "value judgments" of one set of men, and there would have been no reason for them to put on a "legal basis" which would make them difficult for later men, with differing opinions, to change. Following this reasoning, if the men of 1787 wanted religious freedom, they would have merely enacted a statute; why saddle us with their values? If the men of 1867 disliked slavery, a statute would have been sufficient, and would have left later majorities more free to change their minds.

This theory of relativism *implies* that any law more permanent than what a given majority favors is unwarranted. That view is attributable in part to our modern historical circumstance. As an historical observation, I cannot fault the notion that it is a lack of any common religious or moral order that leaves us with a system of law that receives its legitimacy largely from incarnating the focused energies of the body politic. But it is one thing to observe that popular will has become a substitute for any coherent moral vision, and quite another to celebrate this transition from principle to will. I cannot agree with Justice Rehnquist that, as a normative proposition, it is "the fact of their enactment that gives the law whatever moral claim they have upon us as a society."[20] This is a suggestion that consensus is, in itself, a sufficient principle of order. That proposition, under a constitutional system such as ours, cannot be true.

I have understood the source of our enduring and venerable ideals to be more than the *vox populi*. To vest the law with a purely systemic morality is to find in majority sentiment a degree of legitimacy that is simply undeserved.

Walter Lippmann urged, many years ago, that we dare not pretend that the principle of majority rule is anything more than a rule of practicality.[21] It is simply a mechanism for decision making, so that we may govern ourselves. The plain fact of the matter is that the majority is sometimes wrong. Lippmann warned that the rule of the majority

> may easily become an absurd tyranny if we regard it worshipfully, as though it were more than a political device. We have lost all sense of its true meaning when we imagine that the opinion of fifty-one percent is in some high fashion the true opinions of the whole hundred percent, or indulge in the sophistry that the rule of the majority is based upon the ultimate equality of man.[22]

Certainly the will of a transient majority should not lightly be permitted to overturn hard-won constitutional rights.

As I have sought to make clear, the inclination of the People to make certain laws more permanent than others must come from a belief that certain values are more important than others. In adopting a constitution, men voluntarily impose limitations on themselves and on future generations, because at that juncture they perceive that their best selves have triumphed. Justice Rehnquist and his mentor, Holmes, apparently do not share this understanding of the implicit reason for a constitution. Because their relativism can offer no real justification for the Constitution's power to bind, they tend to minimize that power, by discouraging its exercise.

But in so doing, they take great liberties with the Constitution. The "democratic theory" on which our Constitution is based is not indifferent to the substance of the People's rule. A complicated government with branches all derived from the People, some more and some less, was instituted in order to secure certain rights. Those rights are just as fundamental to our system as are the democratic principles that were also adopted. Judicial review may seem anomalous in the light of a "democratic theory" which dogmatically insists on popular choice but is dogmatically skeptical about what the people choose; it is not anomalous in a constitution which attempts to reconcile the principle of popular choice with inherent rights.

So far, I have tried to demonstrate that Justice Rehnquist began by adopting Marshall's appealing, popular justification for judicial review rather than the more intellectually candid one expressed by Hamilton in *Federalist No. 78*, and proceeded from this false beginning to a falsely restrictive sense of how judicial review should be exercised.

As my final point, I would like to offer a partial defense of the so-called brief writer's position, and in so doing complete the picture of how the Justice's version of judicial restraint, as set out in his speech, was derived not from a conservative or interpretivist view of the Constitution, with which I might differ only as a question of degree, but rather from the substitution of his own relativist majoritarian ideals for those embodied in the Constitution, a substitution which I cannot accept at all.

Justice Rehnquist criticized two main points in the brief writer's position: first, that "the federal judiciary may address themselves to a social problem simply because other branches of government have failed or refused to do so"; and second, that "[t]hese same judges, responsible to no constituency whatever," are expected to speak as "the voice and conscience of contemporary society" and as "the measure of the modern conception of human dignity."[23] Certainly the language here is a bit inflated; after all, the writer was seeking to persuade. But are the points made so contemptible as Justice Rehnquist made them out to be? My "generously fair" reading of the words convinces me that, on the contrary, they represent quite traditional constitutional thought.

The first point was made as part of the brief writer's argument that, as a discrete and insular minority, prisoners are entitled to heightened judicial solicitude. The language of "discrete and insular" minority is, of course, Justice Stone's from the famous footnote 4 of the *Carolene Products*[24] case. Justice Stone, in urging general judicial restraint when reviewing legislative acts, excepted those laws disadvantaging classes whose access to the representative processes was practically nonexistent. This seems to me perfectly consistent with Hamilton's description of the judiciary as a bulwark against majoritarian excesses, and with the language of the equal protection clause. It must have seemed so to others as well, since footnote 4 has become the source and mainstay of the Supreme Court's equal protection doctrine. While it would be premature to form an opinion about whether prisoners in fact constitute a discrete and insular minority, it would have been odd had their counsel neglected to urge it, and certainly not contemptible that he did.

The brief writer's second point is equally arguable. Like all other suits of this nature, the prisoner's complaint must necessarily have included a claim under the Eighth Amendment, which prohibits "cruel and unusual punishments." Justice Rehnquist never quoted, or even referred to, the constitutional provisions invoked. Yet any mode of judicial review must at least begin with the language of the Constitution. "Cruel and unusual" are subjective words; they are not susceptible of fixed, qualitative meanings. "Cruel" is a word of emotional charge; "unusual" requires comparison. Both take on meaning in the context of the facts. It is virtually uncontroverted that the Framers of the Constitution and their constituents contemplated judicial review to enforce the Bill of Rights. Knowing this, they refrained from prohibiting only dismemberment and other punishments frowned on at the time in favor of the more general language, just as after the Civil War the framers of the Fourteenth Amendment chose not to limit its protection only to freed slaves. Once again, I reserve judgment on the merits of the brief writer's argument that certain prison conditions conflict with the Eighth Amendment. Certainly, I interpret nothing in the Constitution as a "roving commission" inviting me to enforce my own personal values; but, directly confronting the Eighth Amendment, which Justice Rehnquist refrained from doing in his speech, I do not feel that the Constitution allows me to dismiss the argument out of hand. After all, it was in an

Eighth Amendment case, *Trop v. Dulles*,[25] that the Supreme Court said "the words of the Amendment are not precise, and . . . their scope is not static. The Amendment must draw its meaning from the evolving standards of decency that mark the progress of a maturing society."[26]

By paraphrasing these arguments and by ignoring the constitutional provisions behind them, the Justice appears to have distorted and obscured what is meritorious in them, and once again in the Holmesian mode, seems to have replaced judicial review with virtual abdication, calling it restraint. The brief writer suggested "that if the states' legislatures and governors, or Congress and the President, have not solved a particular social problem, then the federal court may act." Justice Rehnquist's answer was: "I do not believe that this argument will withstand rational analysis. Even in the face of a conceded social evil, a reasonably representative legislature may decide to do nothing."[27]

With this last statement I cannot disagree. But neither do I find it terribly useful to a judge trying to interpret the Constitution. Identifying something as a social evil does not advance a judge's task. There are all varieties of social evils. Some, like police policies of coercing confessions or making unreasonable searches, are unconstitutional. Others, like inadequate flood control and 7 percent unemployment, are not. Still others, concerning a state's administration of its welfare system or its prisons, may pose a close question. Justice Rehnquist's use of the phrase "social evil" perhaps emblematizes my main point of departure with the Justice. The phrase starts out with a political conclusion where a textual inquiry should begin. It blurs and obscures where there should be clarification and analysis. And it ends before any questions are asked, not with informed restraint, but with abdication.

In closing, I call your attention to the words of Professor Thayer: "The tendency of a common and easy resort to [judicial review], now lamentably too common, is to dwarf the political capacity of the people, and to deaden its sense of moral responsibility. It is not a light thing to do that."[28] I wholly agree with that sentiment. Let it be emphasized that I would prefer a regime in which the popular branches were sensitive to and respectful of constitutional restraints, so that judicial review would be unnecessary. I infinitely would favor legislative and administrative reform of prisons to attempts at reform by the judiciary. Similarly I would have preference for voluntary compliance with the Fourth Amendment to the exclusionary rule. I likewise would prefer that legislative encroachments and oppressions, against which the Framers intended Article III to be the bulwark, be few and far between, and that government by the People and respect for individual rights coexist.

But I also agree with the view of Justice Cardozo, who spoke to precisely this threat—the possibility that courts may come to oppress legislative initiative. This danger, according to Cardozo,

> must be balanced against those of independence from all restraint, independence on the part of public officers elected for brief terms, without the guiding force of a continuous tradition. On the whole, I believe the latter dangers to be the more

formidable of the two. Great maxims, if they may be violated with impunity, are honored often with lip service, which passes easily into irreverence. The restraining power of the judiciary does not manifest its chief worth in the few cases in which the legislature has gone beyond the lines that mark the limits of discretion. Rather shall we find its chief worth in making vocal and audible the ideals that might otherwise be silenced, in giving them continuity of life and of expression, in guiding and directing choice within the limits where choice ranges. This function should preserve to the courts the power that now belongs to them, if only the power is exercised with insight into social values, and with suppleness of adaptation to changing social needs.[29]

NOTES

1. W. Rehnquist, "The Notion of a Living Constitution," 54 *Texas Law Review* 693 (1976).

2. Ibid., at 695.

3. 5 U.S. (1 Cranch) 137 (1803).

4. Rehnquist, supra note 1, at 697.

5. A. Bickel, *The Least Dangerous Branch* 2 (Indianapolis: Bobbs-Merrill, 1962).

6. *The Federalist,* No. 78, ed. by J.C. Hamilton (Philadelphia: Lippincott, 1873).

7. Ibid., at 576-577.

8. Ibid., at 575.

9. T. Jefferson, *The Life and Selected Writings of Jefferson* 277, ed. by A. Koch and W. Peden (New York: Random House, 1944) (emphasis added).

10. Rehnquist, supra note 1, at 704.

11. 252 U.S. 416, 433 (1920).

12. W. Berns, *The First Amendment and the Future of American Democracy* 163 (New York: Basic Books, 1976).

13. 219 U.S. 219 (1911).

14. 232 U.S. 138 (1914).

15. Ibid., at 144.

16. 274 U.S. 200 (1927).

17. Ibid., at 207.

18. Oliver W. Holmes, *The Holmes-Pollock Letters,* Vol. 2, 252, ed. by M. DeWolfe Howe (Cambridge: Belknap Press, 1961).

19. *Fay v. New York,* 332 U.S. 261, 282 (1947) (Jackson, J.).

20. Rehnquist, supra note 1, at 704.

21. C. Rossiter and J. Lare, eds., *The Essential Lippmann* (New York: Random House, 1963).

22. Ibid., at 13.

23. Rehnquist, supra note 1, at 695.

24. *United States v. Carolene Products Co.,* 304 U.S. 144 (1938).

25. 356 U.S. 96 (1958).

26. Ibid., at 100.

27. Rehnquist, supra note 1, at 700.

28. J. Thayer, *John Marshall* 106-107 (Boston: Houghton, Mifflin, 1901).

29. B. Cardozo, *The Nature of the Judicial Process* 93-94 (New Haven: Yale University Press, 1921).

14

When Judges Legislate

DALLIN H. OAKS
Justice, Utah Supreme Court

Conventional wisdom holds that the legislature makes the law, the courts interpret it, and the executive enforces it. Like most conventional wisdom, this is only partly true. Judges also make law. They do so inevitably as they interpret statutes passed by the legislature, since interpretation can never be free from choices illuminated by the creative instinct and motivated by personal preference. Some judicial lawmaking is legitimate, and some is illegitimate. I propose to discuss which is which.

Traditional Forms of Judicial Legislation

In the closest application of the conventional wisdom the legislature passes a statute, and the courts interpret it. Sometimes this interpretation involves fitting the new statute into a structure of preexisting statutes, like a brickmason adding a few bricks to an existing wall. To make the new and old fit snugly together, he may need to chip the new or old bricks a little, or fill in some mortar.

The courts' lawmaking function through interpretation of statutes is very common. It is also comparatively noncontroversial. This is not surprising. If the legislature doesn't like the court's interpretation of its statute, it can pass another statute changing it.

Sometimes the ambiguity in a statute cannot be resolved by a single court decision. The ambiguity may even be part of a deliberate effort by the legislature to delegate to the courts a continuing interpretive function. In this circumstance, the courts make law on a larger scale and over a longer period than when they merely resolve a one-time ambiguity. Such circumstances are numerous and give rise to an important part of any court's business.

Thus, in the Sherman Antitrust Act of 1890, Congress outlawed business practices they called "monopolies" and "combinations in restraint of trade," but left it to the courts to define exactly what is meant by a monopoly and a restraint of trade. After almost a century, we have hundreds of judicial and administrative decisions on the meaning of those terms, all stemming from the enactment of a statute whose key terms were purposely general. In his fine book *A Lawyer Looks at the Constitution*, Solicitor General Rex E. Lee describes this type of judicial lawmaking and reminds us that in this area the executive branch also has important lawmaking functions, expressed through the interpretations it must make in fulfilling its responsibility to enforce the law.[1]

This lawmaking function, by which courts define the meaning of a statute on a case-by-case basis as specific lawsuits are brought before them, comprises a significant proportion of the business of an appellate court. And, it is important to note, these decisions are always subject to legislative oversight and correction by the enactment of specific contrary rules if the legislature disagrees with them.

Judges also make law as they define the common law. The common law is composed of the decisions of courts on matters that are not treated by the legislative branch. Some areas of law, such as those involving the law of crimes, taxation, or other powers of state and local governments, are almost entirely covered by statutes. Other areas of the law are affected to a limited extent by statutes, but consist mainly of governing principles drawn from the common law.

For example, if you want to know your rights under a contract (such as an employment contract), your chances of recovering damages from someone who has injured your person or property (such as in an auto accident), or the answer to a question about the ownership and transfer of property (such as a farm or home), you will have to look primarily at court decisions defining the common law. A modern court case resolves one controversy on the basis of the rule and reasoning in an earlier court opinion on a closely related question. The earlier case, in turn, had relied upon precedent from eastern states in colonial times, which themselves had relied on the decisions of the English courts, and so on back into the mists of antiquity.

I have now described three ways judges make law through the exercise of the judical function: (1) by interpreting an ambiguity or contradiction in a statute, (2) by gradually giving meaning to deliberately vague terms in statutes by a succession of interpretive decisions, and (3) by declaring the content of the common law.

All three of these instances of judicial lawmaking are subject to being overruled by the legislature, which can substitute its own rule by statute. To put it otherwise, the people of the state, who elect legislators periodically and who are free to influence them directly in the performance of their lawmaking duties, can, by that means, exercise supervisory control over the courts in each of these lawmaking activities.

This kind of judicial lawmaking is therefore subject to correction by popular sovereignty in the same manner as the laws contained in statutes passed by the legislature. Largely for this reason, court decisions interpreting statutes or declaring the meaning of the common law are rarely an occasion of popular dissatisfaction with the courts. When people accuse courts of "judicial legislation," they usually refer to the courts' vital function in interpreting the federal or state constitutions.

Constitutional Interpretation

When courts interpret the Constitution, their decisions cannot be reversed by statutes enacted by the legislature. The ultimate values protected by the written Constitution are deliberately placed beyond the powers of legislation. By this means, we are assured that the legislature cannot pass a law usurping the powers of another branch of government, authorizing the state to take private property without just compensation, or sending a person to prison without a trial to prove him guilty of a crime.

All of these examples involve rights the Constitution protects against official encroachment, even by the legislature. Once the courts decide that a right is protected by the state or federal Constitution, only the sovereign people can change the rule. Even the people's change can be made only by a constitutional amendment adopted through a process that is deliberately exacting and cumbersome to assure prolonged deliberation and a high degree of unanimity.

Because it is irreversible by the popularly elected lawmakers and cannot even be changed by the sovereign people except in the most unusual circumstances, a court decision resting on the Constitution is an extreme remedy. A constitutional ruling is therefore something a court should do only as a last resort. This principle of last resort is implemented by various rules. For example, if one interpretation of a statute would make it unconstitutional and another interpretation would make it constitutional, the court should always adopt the interpretation that makes the statute constitutional.[2] Similarly, if there is any basis upon which a case can be decided other than by finding a statute unconstitutional, that alternative basis of decision should always be employed.[3] Finally, the legal rules that confine courts strictly within the judicial function, which I discuss later, must be observed with special strictness in a case that involves a ruling based on the Constitution.

If all the prerequisites are met and it is clearly appropriate for a court to make a ruling on the Constitution, a statute should never be invalidated unless it is unconstitutional beyond a reasonable doubt.[4] A court must also be able to give a clear and persuasive explanation of why a statute or other government action is inconsistent with the Constitution. If a court relies on the Constitution to invalidate some government action and then is unable to give clear and persuasive reasons why it is in conflict with the Constitution, the legislators who enacted the law and the voters who elected them are likely to conclude that the judges have used the Constitution to legislate their own policy choices and preferences through the medium of a constitutional decision. The effects of that popular impression are very damaging to the judiciary.

Because most restraints on the exercise of judicial power are self-imposed by the courts, the other branches of government and the people are relatively powerless to prevent the courts from using the Constitution to impose their personal policy choices upon elected lawmakers and the sovereign people. The belief that judges do not restrain themselves from imposing their personal legislative policy choices through the medium of constitutional adjudication is a major cause of popular dissatisfaction with the courts. Various labels are attached to this abuse. They include judicial legislation, judicial activism, and noninterpretivism.

This last term — noninterpretivism — deserves an explanation. It is best defined by reference to its opposite. Under interpretivism, constitutional decisions are limited to interpretation of specific provisions of the Constitution. According to interpretivism, a statute or other act of government cannot be unconstitutional unless it is inconsistent with the express or clearly implied terms of specific words or phrases in the Constitution. Many hold that this is the only kind of constitutional interpretation that is legitimate.

The opposite point of view, noninterpretivism, has been defined as the determination of constitutionality through "the definition, elaboration, and enforcement of values beyond merely those constitutionalized by the Framers."[5] According to noninterpretivism, the Supreme Court must act as a "continuing constitutional convention" to update the original document by reinterpretation.[6] This point of view — that the courts must act as catalysts and engineers of social change — is so widespread that one respected observer, speaking to a foreign audience, referred to what he called "the sovereignty of the courts [in their] superintendence over a society," describing this as "perhaps the most important aspect of the present American form of governance."[7]

The contrast between interpretivism and noninterpretivism or judicial activism is boldly disclosed in the Supreme Court's 1965 decision in *Griswold v. Connecticut*.[8] Since 1879, Connecticut had a law making it a crime to use contraceptives. A doctor was convicted of aiding and abetting the violation of that law by providing information on contraceptives for a married couple who were his patients. His fine of $100 was affirmed by the state courts, but the United States Supreme Court reversed the conviction, voting 7 to 2.

Most observers cheered that result, but two dissenters pointed out some problems with the Court's reasoning. Although they said they thought this was, to use their words, "an uncommonly silly law,"[9] the dissenters challenged the majority to identify the precise provision of the Constitution with which Connecticut's law was in conflict. This is interpretivism. I quote from their opinion:

> At the oral argument in this case we were told that the Connecticut law does not "conform to current community standards." But it is not the function of this Court to decide cases on basis of community standards. We are here to decide cases "agreeably to the Constitution and laws of the United States." It is the essence of judicial duty to subordinate our own personal views, our own ideas of what legislation is wise and what is not.[10]

If the people of Connecticut thought this law was not in accord with their community standards, they could have had their legislators repeal it.

What did the majority offer as the basis for the Court's judgment that the Connecticut law was unconstitutional? Two justices said this anticontraceptive statute violated the due process clause, one because it violated basic values implicit in the concept of ordered liberty and the other because it deprived married couples of "liberty" without adequate justification.[11]

The opinion of the Court represented the views of five of the seven justices in the majority. Under that opinion, the Connecticut statute was invalid because it violated a "right of privacy" found in the "penumbras" that "emanat[ed]" from the specific guarantees of the First, Third, Fourth, Fifth, and Ninth amendments in the Bill of Rights.[12] Three of the five justices limited that holding to a "right of privacy in marriage," which was a fundamental personal right of "liberty" protected by the due process clause even though it was not specifically mentioned in the Bill of Rights.[13]

There were more cheers for the result in the *Griswold* case than for the reasoning the Court gave to explain it. Even those who believe in some judicial activism or some latitude for judicial legislation are wary of letting judges — especially those effectively insulated from direct responsibility to the people or their elected representatives by appointments for life — make constitutional decisions based on "penumbras" and "emanations" rather than from the specific language or clear implications of constitutional provisons. If constitutional decisions are not restrained by the specific language or clear implications of the written Constitution, what is to prevent judges from acting as a superlegislature to impose their personal policy preferences in the irreversible mold of constitutional adjudication?

Confining Courts to the Judicial Function

The controversy over judicial activism is essentially a controversy over the separation of powers. The question is whether the courts have exceeded their proper role. I will conclude by briefly describing several legal rules courts have fashioned to confine themselves to the judicial function.[14] If properly observed, these rules of "justiciability," as they are called, will minimize — though they cannot entirely eliminate — the occasions when courts would engage in judicial policy making beyond their constitutional function.

1. For example, judicial power only extends to real controversies. A court cannot act on its own initiative. A court has power to act only when real adverse parties submit a controversy for judicial resolution in a circumstance where the court can give suitable judicial relief, like money damages, or an order to do or refrain from doing a specific act. A court cannot give an "advisory opinion," which simply instructs some party on some legal question of interest.

2. The courts will also refrain from deciding constitutional cases which are essentially political questions. This principle forbids the courts from enforcing constitutional provisions that cannot readily be phrased in terms of guaranteed rights, especially where the Constitution specifically grants authority in such matters to the elected executive or legislative branches. Under this principle of self-restraint, courts have refused to give rulings on the adequacy of

training of a state national guard, the legality of the Vietnam War, and the legality of a particular form of state government.[15] Questions like these lie outside the competence of courts to decide, or the courts have no practical ability to enforce their decrees. When the courts identify such cases, they use the political question rule to stay out of them.

Three other limitations on the exercise of judicial power concern *who* can bring a case, *when* it can be brought, and when it is *no longer suitable for judicial action.* I will illustrate each of these by applying them to the familiar circumstances of a divorce case, at the same time pointing out ways in which these rules are also applied in the more complicated area of constitutional adjudication.

3. Suppose a husband and wife are having marital trouble, and the husband's mother brings suit to have the parties divorced. There may be grounds for divorce, but since the mother-in-law in not party to the marriage she cannot bring suit for the divorce. The law says that she lacks standing. If the court simply gave her its advisory opinion on whether there were grounds for divorce, it would not be resolving a real dispute between parties whose rights and duties would be affected by its order.

In a resounding reaffirmation of the standing requirement, the U.S. Supreme Court recently declared that the courts of the United States should not be used as "judicial versions of college debating forums" for the "ventilation of public grievances or the refinement of jurisprudential understanding. . . ."[16]

4. Suppose the wife desires a divorce, and her only ground is the husband's leaving the marital home to take employment in Alaska. The wife says this was willful desertion, which is grounds for divorce if continued for more than one year. The wife sues for divorce eight months after the husband leaves. The court should not entertain her suit at that point, even to advise her whether his departure under these circumstances would constitute willful desertion. The case currently lacks ripeness because it does not yet constitute an actual and present conflict of legal rights between the parties. As the Utah Supreme Court ruled in a recent case: "Where there exists no more than a difference of opinion regarding the hypothetical application of a piece of legislation to a situation in which the parties might, at some future time, find themselves, the question is unripe for adjudication."[17] That this is such a case is evident from the fact that if the husband returned to the marital home before the expiration of the 12-month period, no divorce could be granted for desertion, whatever the court had said on the legal effect of the original departure.

This principle of ripeness was the apparent basis for the U.S. Supreme Court's disposition of the appeal on the Equal Rights Amendment. A federal district court in Idaho ruled that several states could withdraw their previous ratification of the ERA and that Congress's attempted extension of the deadline for ratification of the Amendment was unconstitutional. Seeking to have this ruling reversed, supporters of the ERA argued in the Supreme Court that these important questions on the legality of certain states' ratifications were not ripe for decision since the questions would not need to be answered if the required number of states did not ratify by 1 July 1982, the revised deadline. In other words, the question posed by the case did not matter unless it was vital to a ratification count that would not be taken until a future date. The Supreme Court's order, which "stayed" the judgment of the district court—in effect putting the district court's opinion on the shelf for the present[18]—is an apparent acceptance of the argument that the case was not ripe for decision.

5. When a case is properly brought originally but some subsequent event makes it useless for the court to make a decision, the case is moot and a court will not rule on it. For example, suppose the husband in my example does not return, and after 12 months the wife brings suit for divorce for desertion. Then, while the case is pending, the husband is killed on the job in Alaska. The marriage having been severed by death, there is nothing the court can do to give any meaningful relief, and the divorce case will therefore be dismissed as moot.

These five self-imposed rules of justiciability—case or controversy, political question, standing, ripeness, and mootness—tend to keep courts within the judicial function, but they do not assure that result. All of these requirements were met in *Griswold v. Connecticut* and other cases that have been criticized as examples of judicial legislation. Something more is needed.

The best and only complete remedy is the self-imposed discipline of judicial restraint. The other branches of government can and should urge judicial restraint, and the people can demand it, but it is the courts themselves who must make it a reality. The same branch of government that has recognized the power and forged the tools of judicial activism must decline to exercise them. The rarest kind of power in our troubled world is a power recognized but unexercised. Yet that is the sort of example we have a right to expect from the branch of government that must define the limits of all the branches, including its own. In the end, the only completely effective remedy for judicial excess is judicial restraint.

NOTES

1. R. Lee, *A Lawyer Looks at the Constitution* 37 (Provo, Utah: Brigham Young University Press, 1981).

2. *Wagner v. Salt Lake City,* 29 Utah 2d 42, 49, 504 P.2d 1007, 1012 (1972).

3. *Hoyle v. Mousou,* 606 P.2d 240 (Utah, 1980).

4. *Greaves v. State,* 528 P.2d 805, 806-807.

5. M. Perry, "Noninterpretive Review in Human Rights Cases: A Functional Justification," 56 *New York University Law Review* 278, 282 (1981).

6. J. Beck, *The Constitution of the United States* (1922) and other sources cited in R. Berger, *Government by Judiciary* 2 (Cambridge: Harvard University Press, 1977).

7. E. Levi, "The Sovereignty of the Courts," in *Occasional Papers No. 17* (Chicago: University of Chicago Press, 1981).

8. 381 U.S. 479 (1965).

9. Ibid., at 527.

10. Ibid., at 530-531.

11. Ibid., at 500 and 502.

12. Ibid., at 484-486.

13. Ibid., at 491-492.

14. These rules are discussed in understandable terms in Lee, supra note 1, at 192-198.

15. L. Tribe, *American Constitutional Law* 71-79, 172-181 (Mineola: Foundation Press, 1978).

16. *Valley Forge Christian College v. Americans United for Separation of Church and State, Inc.,* 454 U.S. 464, 473 (1982).

17. *Redwood Gym v. Salt Lake County Commission,* 624 P.2d 1138, 1148 (Utah, 1981).

18. *National Organization for Women, Inc. v. Idaho,* 455 U.S. 918 (1982). On 4 October 1982 the Supreme Court of the United States vacated the district court's judgment and dismissed the complaints as moot. 103 S. Ct. 22 (1982).

15

The Jurisprudence of Judicial Restraint:
A Return to the Moorings

J. Clifford Wallace
Judge, Court of Appeals, Ninth Circuit

My purpose here is to sketch the theory and practice of, and argue for, a philosophy of judicial restraint. The opposite of judicial activism, judicial restraint has sometimes been referred to as "strict constructionism" or "interpretivism."[1] "Strict constructionism" or "interpretivism," in the natural meaning of those terms, is, as will emerge later, part, but only part, of judicial restraint.

Judicial restraint, as I will use the phrase, is not tied to any narrow sectarian politics, but rather is based upon concerns of legal predictability, uniformity, and judicial economy, and most importantly, upon values of liberty and democracy that are widely shared by our American citizens. Indeed, judicial restraint is dictated by the Constitution. My argument is that our Republic would be best served if the judiciary returned to those moorings.

The Constitution and the Theory of Judicial Restraint

Although the language of the Constitution is not as reminiscent of John Locke as is that of the Declaration of Independence, the substance of the Constitution shows the influence of Locke's theory that the central purpose of government is the protection of individual rights such as life, liberty, and private property. This purpose establishes one element of any judicial philosophy. The courts must protect constitutional rights against infringement, even infringement by the legally elected representatives of the majority. This, then, is one respect in which the Constitution is not entirely democratic. There are limits on what the majority may do.

For example, the representatives of the majority may not, without going through the amendment process, pass a bill of attainder, establish cruel and unusual punishment, or make race a condition of suffrage. In practice,[2] amendment requires a supermajority. Thus, although the Constitution imposes no absolute limits[3] on popular decision making, constitutional protections and structures do represent significant practical restraints on the scope of majoritarian democracy.

The Constitution includes a number of devices designed, at least in part, to protect the citizenry. The division of authority between the states and the federal government, for example, insures both that certain basic rights will be respected throughout the territory of the United States and that a wide range of decisions affecting rights will be made by a government less distant from the individual than is the federal government. Moreover, the danger that government will infringe rights is diminished whenever there is more than one center of power. The oppressive potential of a unified government is total. In a federal system, such total oppression is less likely because it requires the close cooperation of many different centers of power. Thus, our federal system wisely reserves all powers to the states except those delegated to the central government.

The Framers also designed the division of authority among three branches of the federal government to protect individual rights. The very separateness of the branches curtails the risk of oppression in the same fashion as does the division of power between federal and state governments. The more their separateness and relative equality are maintained, the less is the likelihood that the governmental branches will be united in undermining constitutional protections.

Beyond this, however, the Framers intended the judicial branch to have a special role in the protection of rights. One of the motivations for creating this unique role for the judicial branch may have been a distrust of the other branches. The Framers probably feared most the executive branch of government because they had fresh in their minds the oppressive potential of a king. Legislatures were, however, not free of suspicion. During the Confederation period the state legislatures had inspired widespread distrust. Many thought that democracy was getting out of hand by violating rights of citizens in an excessive zeal for equality. Oppression by the judicial branch was not feared as much by the Framers, presumably because in their experience the colonial and state courts had been relatively benign. As is well known, Hamilton considered the judiciary the "least dangerous" and "weakest" branch.[4] This perhaps explains why the Constitution neither expressly directs nor restrains the judiciary very much.

The partisans of both judicial activism and judicial restraint agree that government cannot act beyond the outer limits established by constitutional boundaries without becoming subject to judicial intervention. The controversial question is just where those limits are and thus how extensive the territory is within which government can function free of judicial intervention.

To answer this question we must look to a second aspect of our Constitution—its democratic side. The Constitution establishes the framework for a federal representative democracy and guarantees to the states a "republican form of government."[5]

The Founders structured the democracy of the federal government to ameliorate what some of them perceived as egalitarian excesses of democracy. The federal democracy, then, is a limited democracy. The Constitution imposes external limits, such as the Bill of Rights, and internal devices of indirect voting and representation. Most of the internal checks on the federal democracy remain. Similarly, the Founders intended the "republican form of government" clause to embrace a wide range of political forms of state governments. Regardless, however, of the built-in checks on the federal democracy and latitude afforded state governments, the Framers intended the basic form of both the federal government and state governments to be democratic in the broad sense. Citizens would make decisions, directly or indirectly. I wish now to focus upon this democratic aspect of our governmental enterprise.

Difficult cases concerning whether a decision by Congress, a state legislature, or elected officials falls within the permissible range of discretion afforded those bodies or officials often test one's belief in judicial restraint. An examination of the value of democracy can assist one in arriving at an answer in these controversial cases. If democracy is an intrinsic, fundamental value, then the area of legislative discretion is presumably larger than it would be if democracy were a minor or derivative value.

Democracy is, I believe, intrinsically and fundamentally valuable. Therefore, judges, mindful of the Constitution, must be extremely cautious in taking decisions away from elected representatives and elected officials.

The opposing theory is that democracy is simply an instrumental value. Under the instrumental theory, democracy is valuable only to the extent that it produces substantively "better" decisions than would any other available decision-making procedure. This view has the corollary that democracy should be replaced by a benevolent dictator or a computer if one can be found that will make better decisions.

If one believes that the value of democracy is only instrumental and if one runs across a congressional enactment that is clearly unwise, then one has a duty to correct the mistake, if possible. A democratic decision procedure that is corrected in an undemocratic fashion when clearly wrong is better, instrumentally speaking, than the same procedure without the correction.

We may fairly assume that no judge believes that he or she can correct any enactment that comes before the court solely because it is perceived to be unwise. At the least there must be some colorable argument for unconstitutionality or a rationale for interpreting the statute in a way that overrides legislative intent. If one believes in the instrumental theory of democracy, however, one is likely to find the required constitutional argument or statutory construction when faced with what one perceives to be a bad statute.

A noninstrumental theory of democracy, by contrast, places value in the democratic process even when decisions fall short of the best possible — indeed even when the majority makes a decision that is stupid, irrational, or completely wrong-headed. As a private citizen one may vote directly or indirectly against bad legislation while still believing that the majority, because it is the majority, has a right to be mistaken. The majority does not have a right to make just any sort of mistake, of course, because constitutional limits remain.

The noninstrumentalist, however, believes that, aside from the constitutional restraints, it is better that the majority make a wrong decision than that a judge make the decision, even if the judge would make a socially more beneficial decision. As a judge, he or she will be careful to allow only the legislature to develop social policy. Such a judge believes that, aside from what is proscribed by the Constitution, the legislature has a right to be wrong. A judge who believes in the intrinsic value of democracy will, then, shrink from abrogating legislative decisions and will look for ways to uphold legislation rather than to strike it down.

A corollary of the noninstrumental theory of democracy is that it is better for the majority to make a mistaken policy decision, within broad limits, than for a judge to make a correct one. That is, the process by which the decision is made may have greater value than the decision itself.

I hope that, on reflection, you will agree that democracy is intrinsically valuable. If you are not yet persuaded, let me give an argument for the proposition.

The starting assumption of my argument is that *liberty* is intrinsically valuable. This assumption is very nearly an article of faith of our American political philosophy. It is better to be free and hungry than to be a well-fed slave. We do think that, as a general rule, people make better decisions for themselves than others would make for them, but this instrumental advantage of liberty is secondary. Freedom is necesary for a realization of what makes human beings human. To take away a person's power to make decisions—his or her autonomy—is an extreme measure only slightly less severe than taking away the power to think.

My argument for the intrinsic value of democracy is that democracy is an extension of liberty into the realm of social decision making. One cannot consistently be an instrumentalist about democracy and believe that liberty is intrinsically valuable. This rather abstract-sounding philosophical claim can be illustrated by a homely example. Suppose that five co-owners of a building are in disagreement whether it should be painted white or blue. If there were only one owner, he would be free to paint the building as he chose. His choice would not be frustrated. With five persons of differing opinions, however, some choices will inevitably be frustrated. A majority decision minimizes the number of persons whose choices are frustrated. In this way, democracy most nearly approximates the liberty of a single free decision maker. In general, majoritarian democracy is more respectful of individual autonomy than is any other social decision-making procedure that guarantees a decision. Therefore, the same respect for human autonomy that underlies liberty underlies democracy as well and establishes its intrinsic value.

Liberty and democracy can, of course, come into conflict. The majority may vote to restrict liberty. To resolve this conflict between the two intrinsic values, one must answer this question: Which decisions are to be made individually and which collectively through the democratic process? The Constitution provides part of the answer to this question by establishing limits on the powers of Congress and the states. A great many issues, however, are not committed by the Constitution either to the democratic process or to individual decision.

Consider a decision that really should, as a matter of sound political philosophy or moral theory, be left to the individual, but that is not reserved to the individual by the Constitution. Suppose that Congress or a state legislature passes an act deciding the issue and thus takes it out of the hands of the individual. There are, I believe, federal and state statutes of this description. Possible examples include state laws requiring drivers to wear seat belts and federal laws removing cyclamates from the market. Alternatively, consider taxation. From a theoretical perspective, every tax dollar limits the individual taxpayer's effective freedom by restricting his or her capacity to make purchases or investments. Some of this loss of freedom through taxation is of course, well-justified by the federal or state programs supported by the revenues. Not every spending program, however, is sufficiently worthwhile to provide an adequate justification for taxation. I will leave you free to nominate your own candidates for the least worthwhile state and federal spending programs.

Certainly we can all agree that there are some laws that restrict individual liberty in ways that are unwise, though constitutionally permissible. Activists would argue that in at least some such cases, the judiciary should step in to vindicate liberty on the theory that the intrinsic value of liberty outweighs the intrinsic value of democracy.

The problem is in identifying an unwise, though constitutional, limitation on liberty. I may be confident that a particular statute is unwise. The legislature, however. may have been just as confident that the statute represented good social policy. Are judges, as a group, better at making judgments of social policy than are legislatures? Certainly legislatures, with their committees, staffs, and deliberative processes, are institutionally better-equipped to investigate the consequences of policy decisions than are the courts. I do not believe that one gains added wisdom or a keener perception of social value merely by becoming a judge. Indeed, because a judge is removed from the political process while a legislator is constantly immersed in it, the legislator is more closely exposed to the basic needs of society.

There undoubtedly remain cases in which an omniscient Being could verify that the judge's instincts are better than those of the legislature. But the judge does not have that perception, and his or her subjective confidence is a wholly inadequate substitute for objective omniscience. There is, in this instance, a process deficiency.

A judge cannot act on the belief that he or she knows better than the legislature on a question of policy, because the judge can never be justifiably certain that he or she is right even when the judge happens to be right. In this way, appropriate judicial humility weighs against judicial activism. Thus, even when the intrinsic value of liberty or other values outweigh the intrinsic value of democracy, there is no justification for judicial activism.

The intrinsic value of democracy thus provides a general theoretical underpinning for judicial restraint—an underpinning not undermined by the possibility that in a given case other values may be more important than democracy.

But the important value of democracy underlies only one aspect of judicial restraint. Other aspects I will describe only briefly, not because they are unimportant, but because they are easy to identify and analyze. Concern for legal predictability and for the coherence of the legal system as a whole also fosters judicial restraint. These values suggest following the natural interpretation of statutory language and case law. They also suggest a general caution towards legal innovation.

Legal economy further justifies judicial restraint. Many disputes are better resolved in a nonjudicial setting. Courts are cost-effective, for the most part, in settling disputes. They become cost-ineffective when asked to re-engineer social structures and reorganize social priorities.

Litigation does not produce wealth. On its civil side, it is primarily a means of redistributing wealth, and a very expensive means at that. One party wins; the other pays. Both incur litigation expenses. Society pays directly, in supporting the courts, and indirectly, through losses in productivity. No other nation devotes as much of its resources to litigation as ours does. In this era of international economic competition, we should hardly wish to excel in the category of litigation expense. Judicial restraint addresses this problem by being cautious about jurisdiction and the extension of causes of action.

Finally, judicial restraint is consistent with and complementary to the balance of power among the three independent branches. It accomplishes this in two ways. First, judicial restraint not only recognizes the equality of the other two branches with the judiciary, but also fosters that equality by minimizing interbranch interference by the judiciary. In this analysis, judicial restraint might better be called judicial respect; that is, respect by the judiciary for the other coequal branches. In contrast, judicial activism's unpredictable results make the judiciary a moving target and thus decrease the ability to maintain equality with the co-branches. Restraint stabilizes the judiciary so it may better function in a system of interbranch equality.

Second, judicial restraint tends to protect the independence of the judiciary. When courts become engaged in social legislation, almost inevitably voters, legislators, and other elected officials will conclude that the activities of judges should be closely monitored. If judges act like legislators, it follows that judges should be elected like legislators. This is counterproductive. The touchstone of an independent federal judiciary has been its removal from the political process. Even if this removal has sometimes been less than complete, it is an ideal worthy of support and one that has had valuable effects.

The constitutional trade-off for independence is that judges must restrain themselves from the areas reserved to the other, separate branches. Thus, judicial restraint complements the twin, overarching values of the independence of the judiciary and the separation of powers.

The Practical Application of Judicial Restraint

So much for the theory of judicial restraint. I would now like to say something about its practice. By way of summary, the overall and abstract conception of judicial restraint, as I understand it, is that to avoid usurping the policy-making role of democratically elected bodies and officials, a judge should always hesitate to declare statutes or governmental actions unconstitutional and cautious to supplement or modify statutes when construing them. Courts should make as little social policy as possible consistent with deciding properly presented controversies. As a corollary, judges should remain keenly aware of the possibility that a controversy is not, in fact, properly before them and should resist the temptation to decide an issue broader than the one actually before the court.

Constitutional law is perhaps the realm in which questions of judicial activism and judicial restraint are of most interest. Because constitutional law concerns the interpretation of a legal document in the light of prior case law, it combines the considerations involved in the statutory and common-law contexts. If there were no common-law legacy, judicial restraint would apply to constitutional interpretation just as it does to the interpretation of statutes. Drawing on the discussion of statutory interpretation, and temporarily assuming away the existence of case law, I would tentatively suggest the following principles:

1. Stand by the clear language of the Constitution unless doing so is manifestly counter to the Framers' intent.

2. Clarify unclear constitutional language in line with the Framers' intent if that intent is ascertainable with reasonable certainty.

3. If neither of the prior principles applies, clarify unclear constitutional language by selecting the alternative that least restricts the discretion of elected lawmakers and officials.

4. If none of the prior principles applies, clarify unclear constitutional language in line with the best estimate of the Framers' intent or in the manner most congruent with prior expectations.

This approach is at odds with the popular "living Constitution" or "growing Constitution" theory of interpretation, with its touchstone—current social attitudes. Conceivably, current social attitudes might be relevant to constitutional interpretation. I find no constitutional language, however, that explicitly builds current social attitudes into the Constitution. Still, the Framers possibly intended certain specific clauses of the Constitution or its amendments to be read as if they contained variables ranging over social attitudes. For example, one might argue that the Framers used the term "cruel and unusual punishment" in the Eighth Amendment to provide for a varying societal approach.

Although it is possible that the Framers intended to write this sort of flexibility into the Constitution, constitutional language to that effect is absent.

The burden of historical proof should therefore be on those who assert that the Framers intended a so-called living Constitution.

Some have argued that a constitution is by its very nature a growing document. The Framers could not have intended otherwise, the argument runs, because they could not have intended to put the future into a straitjacket.[6] This is an extremely tenuous historical hypothesis upon which to base an all-inclusive constitutional theory. More importantly, it is unlikely that the Framers, who made the Constitution so difficult to change by amendment, would have made it so easy to change by reference to sociological surveys.

In addition, squaring the belief held by the Framers' generation in self-evident truth and inalienable rights with the normative relativity of the "growing Constitution" theory is difficult. The relativity of truth and rights would have made no more sense to the Framers than it would have to John Locke, that is, no sense at all. In short, I strongly suspect that the "living" or "growing" Constitution is a twentieth-century theory anachronistically projected back onto the eighteenth and nineteenth centuries.

The living Constitution theory also displays a naive faith in consistent moral and social progress. The idea that the Constitution changes with shifting public opinion seems relatively benign if one expects public opinion to become more enlightened with the passage of time. If, however, one expects public opinion to become more enlightened with the passage of time, one may not want a constitution at all. Why not simply have a democratic body without any restrictions on its decisions—like the British Parliament? Why should a less enlightened past put *any* restrictions on a more enlightened future?

Constitution making apparently assumes a less than complete optimism about the consistency of future political progress. In this light, consider the possibility that due to various tragic circumstances our country is shaken by a wave of bigotry and racism. Are we to assume that drafters of the Fourteenth Amendment intended the meaning of the equal protection clause to change under these circumstances, losing its bite? Far more likely, they intended the Fourteenth Amendment not only to remedy the precise problem facing them, but to protect against possible future changes in the composition and racial views of the enfranchised electorate.

At this point, I may appear to be inconsistent. Earlier I argued in favor of judicial restraint by citing the intrinsic value of democracy. Now I argue against the "living Constitution" theory by citing the Framers' fears of future electorates. There is, however, no inconsistency. The Constitution, the Framers' intent, and our proper attitude towards the Constitution all have democratic as well as nondemocratic aspects. There can be no doubt that the Constitution establishes outer bounds on legislation and official conduct. What I have been arguing just now is that there is no good reason to believe that the Framers intended those bounds to change with time and public opinion, short of amendment. To conclude that the bounds are stationary, however, is not yet to establish their location. The democratic component of judicial restraint encourages placing those outer bounds as widely as the language of the Constitution permits in order to maximize the area of legislative discretion in solving social problems.

In fact, there is much less reason to think that the constitutional limits must change with time if they do not cover too broad a range of subjects to begin with. A constitution is properly a short document; like the Ten Commandments, it needs to say very little to be of great importance. It guards the most vital political structures and most fundamental human rights in an unyielding and changeless way. Exactly because it intrudes on future democratic decisions only in the most important respects, it deserves serious attention when it does speak. It should not be trivialized. A constitution interpreted so broadly that it plays the same role as social legislation must change as social conditions change. There is, however, no need for such a constitution. We have Congress and the state legislatures to write laws in the light of changing conditions. By accepting the Constitution as a brief set of fixed guiding principles, it may be applied to new situations, but not modified by ever-changing public opinion. Thus, the democratic aspect of judicial restraint is complementary to the view that the Framers intended the Constitution to "grow" only through amendment.

The "living Constitution" school and others that see the major role of the judiciary as a social instrument to effectuate change may be suspected of a certain historical one-sidedness. They favor a growing Constitution only when it grows their way. More generally, activism loses much of its appeal if one considers the possibility of a court composed of judges whose activism favored social positions diametrically opposed to one's own philosophy. I will discuss this problem in general in its historical setting in a few moments.

So far, in discussing constitutional interpretation, I have operated under the enormously simplifying assumption that there is no case law. For better and for worse, there is a great deal of case law. Much of it is sound in terms of the canons of judicial restraint. Some of it is not.

For a judge, and especially a judge below the Supreme Court, the case law of a higher court, and usually that of the judge's own court, is given, even when it is wrong. Judicial restraint that did not follow binding precedent would not be worthy of its name. There is a difference, however, between following precedent and extending it. Predictability and uniformity increase when a judge applies a precedent to an analogous set of facts. The closer the analogy, the more judicial restraint will tend to favor the application. This is only a tendency, however.

If the extension runs counter to the principles of judicial restraint regarding constitutional interpretation, this conflict will provide a reason for refusing to extend the precedent. Whether extending the precedent to new areas is the judicially restrained course of action, all things considered, depends upon the closeness of the precedent to the new area and its degree of perceived wrongness. In making the determination, the judge must take into account the rationale of the precedent because the rationale is relevant to considerations of predictability and uniformity.

Judicial Restraint's Response to Judicial Activism

The abstract theory of judicial restraint that I discussed earlier may in certain respects sound a little radical — although I would say it is radical only in the sense of returning to the origin, the fundamental moorings of the Constitution and our judicial heritage. The underlying values of judicial restraint are not those of any particular political party or ideology, but rather are the values of liberty, democracy, predictability, uniformity, and judicial economy. By the very nature of judicial restraint, there can be nothing radical, in the popular sense, about its practice. It requires that one play the game with strict attention to the rules. Its model of the judge is more that of neutral expounder of justice under law than that of a moral reformer. It recognizes that the judge is not the complete problem-solver, but one part of a team. It requires him or her to give proper deference to the other independent branches, even when he or she believes that they have made an incorrect choice of policy.

Judicial restraint only rarely permits one to overturn the law made by activist judges. This obviously gives such judges a certain advantage, because judges who deplore their innovations will nonetheless often retain, though rarely extend, them.

If left entirely unchecked, periodic activist inroads over the years could emasculate fundamental doctrines and undermine the separation of powers. Judges may therefore overturn judicial decisions in certain special circumstances: if the decisions are clearly wrong, have important effects, and would otherwise be difficult to negate.

A constitutional case will more often meet the third of these conditions than will a case concerning statutory construction. An incorrect interpretation of a statute can be set aside by Congress through a more explicit enactment. A constitutional misinterpretation, however, may do continuing damage because of the difficulty of the amendment process. Similarly, because of the institutional centrality of the Constitution and because of its unique role of protecting the citizenry, a constitutional case will very often meet the second condition — importance. Constitutional cases may also provide the best examples of the first condition — clear error. They will tend to be clearly wrong, for example, when judges, influenced by "living Constitution" jurisprudence, spin twentieth-century sociology out of the eighteenth- or nineteenth-century language.

The activist judge must not therefore assume, particularly in constitutional cases, that judicially restrained successors will let stand every activist misconstruction of the Constitution. Undoing an activist mistake does not offend the democratic values underlying restraint. Indeed, undoing antidemocratic forays supports those values. But such a course may offend predictability and perhaps uniformity. For these reasons, judges must approach the overturning process with the greatest care. These considerations, however, do not totally militate against the necessary overruling of precedent. Predictability and uniformity are important instrumental values, but they are outweighed when the great values of our Constitution are at stake.

Thus, even when, in overruling precedent, judicial restraint most nearly resembles activism, it maintains a general consistency with its underlying principles. Those principles demand the neutralization of activist judicial decisions that fundamentally distort the Constitution.

Judicial restraint is also consistent in its application to different historical periods. Its practice does not vary with changing political currents among legislators and judges. It adheres to a consistency of principle.

Judicial activism, by contrast, has no such consistency. Many who deplored the activism of the economic substantive due process era earlier in this century praised the activism of the Warren Court. Although one may try to draw subtle jurisprudential distinctions, I must be excused for suspecting that the only real difference was pure politics unattached to constitutional principles. Virtue seemed to be dictated by the result. In one era, these theorists found the legislatures more congenial to their political preferences than was the bench. In the later era, this relationship was reversed. A judicial doctrine that waxes and wanes with the political tides is unworthy of the name "philosophy." It is nothing more than a rationalization of a willingness to use whatever means are expedient to reach one's preferred results. Regardless of one's political or social view, one should reject such a judicial approach.

NOTES

1. E.g., J. Ely, *Democracy and Distrust* (Cambridge: Harvard University Press, 1980).

2. Even if the state legislatures accurately reflect their constituents, a majority can, in theory, amend the Constitution. This is because only a bare majority in each of three-fourths of the states need approve the amendment. The citizens of the remaining one-quarter of the states, which might be the most populous states, might unanimously disapprove.

3. There is one exception. Article v prohibits depriving a state of equal suffrage in the Senate without consent of the state. Presumably this clause of Article v and the relevant parts of Article I, Sec. 3, are unamendable.

4. *The Federalist*, No. 78, at 504, ed. by S. Miltell (Washington, D.C.: National Home Library Foundation, 1938).

5. U.S. Constitution, Art. IV, Sec. 4, cl. I.

6. E.g., M. Perry, "Abortion, Public Morals, and the Police Power," 23 *U.C.L.A. Law Review* 689, 713 (1977).

16

Tradition and Morality in Constitutional Law

ROBERT H. BORK

Judge, Court of Appeals, District of Columbia Circuit

When a judge undertakes to speak in public about any subject that might be of more interest than the law of incorporeal hereditaments he embarks upon a perilous enterprise. There is always, as I have learned with some pain, someone who will write a story finding it sensational that a judge should say anything. There is some sort of notion that judges have no general ideas about law or, if they do, that, like pornography, ideas are shameful and ought not to be displayed in public to shock the squeamish. For that reason, I come before you, metaphorically at least, clad in a plain brown wrapper.

One common style of speech on occasions such as this is that which paints a bleak picture, identifies even bleaker trends, and then ends on a note of strong and, from the evidence presented, wholly unwarranted optimism. I hope to avoid both extremes while talking about sharply divergent ideas that are struggling for dominance within the legal culture. While I think it serious and potentially of crisis proportions, I speak less to thrill you with the prospect of doom—which is always good fun—than to suggest to you that law is an arena of ideas that is too often ignored by intellectuals interested in public policy. Though it was not always so, legal thought has become something of an intellectual enclave. Too few people are aware of the trends there and the importance of those trends for public policy.

It is said that, at a dinner given in his honor, the English jurist Baron Parke was asked what gave him the greatest pleasure in the law. He answered that his greatest joy was to write a "strong opinion." Asked what that might be, the baron said, "It is an opinion in which, by reasoning with strictly legal concepts, I arrive at a result no layman could conceivably have anticipated."

That was an age of formalism in the law. We have come a long way since then. The law and its acolytes have since become steadily more ideological and more explicit about that fact. That is not necessarily a bad thing: there are ideologies suitable, indeed indispensable, for judges, just as there are ideologies that are subversive of the very idea of the rule of law. It is the sharp recent growth in the latter that is worrisome for the future.

We are entering, I believe, a period in which our legal culture and constitutional law may be transformed, with even more power accruing to judges than is presently the case. There are two reasons for that. One is that constitutional law has very little theory of its own and hence is almost pathologically lacking in immune defenses against the intellectual fevers of the larger society as well as against the disorders that were generated by its own internal organs.

The second is that the institutions of the law, in particular the schools, are becoming increasingly converted to an ideology of the Constitution that demands just such an infusion of extraconstitutional moral and political notions. A not untypical example of the first is the entry into the law of the First Amendment of the old, and incorrect, view that the only kinds of harm that a community is entitled to suppress are physical and economic injuries. Moral harms are not to be counted because to do so would interfere with the autonomy of the individual. That is an indefensible definition of what people are entitled to regard as harms.

The result of discounting moral harm is the privatization of morality, which requires the law of the community to practice moral relativism. It is thought that individuals are entitled to their moral beliefs but may not gather as a community to express those moral beliefs in law. Once an idea of that sort takes hold in the intellectual world, it is very likely to find lodgment in constitutional theory and then in constitutional law. The walls of the law have proved excessively permeable to intellectual osmosis. Out of prudence, I will give but one example of the many that might be cited.

A state attempted to apply its obscenity statute to a public display of an obscene word. The Supreme Court majority struck down the conviction on the grounds that regulation is a slippery slope and that moral relativism is a constitutional command. The opinion said, "The principle contended for by the State seems inherently boundless. How is one to distinguish this from any other offensive word?" One might as well say that the negligence standard of tort law is inherently boundless, for how is one to distinguish the reckless driver from the safe one? The answer in both cases is, by the common sense of the community. Almost all judgments in the law are ones of degree, and the law does not flinch from such judgments except when, as in the case of morals, it seriously doubts the community's right to define harms. Moral relativism was even more explicit in the majority opinion, however, for the Court observed, apparently thinking the observation decisive: "One man's vulgarity is another's lyric." On that ground, it is difficult to see how law on any subject can be permitted to exist.

But the Court immediately went further, reducing the whole question to one of private preference, saying: "We think it is largely because governmental officials cannot make principled distinctions in this area that the Constitution leaves matters of taste and style so largely to the individual." Thus, the community's moral and aesthetic judgments are reduced to questions of style and those are then said to be privatized by the Constitution. It testifies all the more clearly to the power of ideas floating in the general culture to alter the Constitution that this opinion was written by a justice generally regarded as moderate to conservative in his constitutional views.

George Orwell reminded us long ago about the power of language to corrupt thought and the consequent baleful effects upon politics. The same deterioration is certainly possible in morality. But I am not concerned about the constitutional protection cast about an obscene word. Of more concern is the constitutionalizing of the notion that moral harm is not harm legislators are entitled to consider. As Lord Devlin said, "What makes a society is a community of ideas, not political ideas alone but also ideas about the way its members should behave and govern their lives." A society that ceases to be a community increases the danger that weariness with turmoil and relativism may bring about an order in which many more, and more valuable, freedoms are lost than those we thought we were protecting.

I do not know the origin of the notion that moral harms are not properly legally cognizable harms, but it has certainly been given powerful impetus in our culture by John Stuart Mill's book *On Liberty*. Mill, however, was a man of two minds and, as Gertrude Himmelfarb has demonstrated, Mill himself usually knew better than this. Miss Himmelfarb traces the intellectual themes of *On Liberty* to Mill's wife. It would be ironic, to put it no higher, if we owed major features of modern American constitutional doctrine to Harriet Taylor Mill, who was not, as best I can remember, one of the framers at Philadelphia.

It is unlikely, of course, that a general constitutional doctrine of the impermissibility of legislating moral standards will ever be framed. So the development I have cited, though troubling, is really only an instance of a yet more worrisome phenomenon, and that is the capacity of ideas that originate outside the Constitution to influence judges, usually without their being aware of it, so that those ideas are elevated to constitutional doctrine. We have seen that repeatedly in our history. If one may complain today that the Constitution did not adopt John Stuart Mill's *On Liberty*, it was only a few judicial generations ago, when economic laissez faire somehow got into the Constitution, that Justice Holmes wrote in dissent that the Constitution "does not enact Mr. Herbert Spencer's *Social Statics*."

Why should this be so? Why should constitutional law constantly be catching colds from the intellectual fevers of the general society?

The fact is that the law has little intellectual or structural resistance to outside influences, influences that should properly remain outside. The striking, and peculiar, fact about a field of study so old and so intensively cultivated by men and women of first-rate intelligence is that the law possesses very little theory about itself. I once heard George Stigler remark with some astonishment: "You lawyers have nothing of your own. You borrow from the social sciences, but you have no discipline, no core, of your own." And, a few scattered insights here and there aside, he was right. This theoretical emptiness at its center makes law, particularly constitutional law, unstable, a ship with a great deal of sail but a very shallow keel, vulnerable to the winds of intellectual or moral fashion, which it then validates as the commands of our most basic compact.

This weakness in the law's intellectual structure may be exploited by new theories of moral relativism and egalitarianism now the dominant mode of constitutional thinking in a number of leading law schools. The attack of these theories upon older assumptions has been described by one Harvard law professor as a "battle of cultures," and so it is. It is fair to think, then, that the outcome of this confused battle may strongly affect the constitutional law of the future and hence the way in which we are governed.

The constitutional ideologies growing in the law schools display three worrisome characteristics. They are increasingly abstract and philosophical; they are sometimes nihilistic; they always lack what law requires, democratic legitimacy. These tendencies are new, much stronger now than they were even ten years ago, and certainly nothing like them appeared in our past.

Up to a few years ago most professors of constitutional law would probably have agreed with Joseph Story's dictum in 1833: "Upon subjects of government, it has always appeared to me, that metaphysical refinements are out of place. A constitution of government is addressed to the common-sense of the people, and never was designed for trials of logical skill or visionary speculation." But listen to how Nathan Glazer today perceives the lawyer's task, no doubt because of the professors he knows: "As a political philosopher or a lawyer, I would try to find basic principles of justice that can be defended and argued against all other principles. As a sociologist, I look at the concrete consequences, for concrete societies."

Glazer's perception of what more and more lawyers are doing is entirely accurate. That reality is disturbing. Academic lawyers are not going to solve the age-old problems of political and moral philosophy any time soon, but the articulated premise of their abstract enterprise is that judges may properly reason to constitutional decisions in that way. But judges have no mandate to govern in the name of contractarian or utilitarian or what-have-you philosophy rather than according to the historical Constitution. Judges of this generation, and much more, of the next generation, are being educated to engage in really heroic adventures in policy making.

The abstract, universalistic style of legal thought has a number of dangers. For one thing, it teaches disrespect for the actual institutions of the American polity. These institutions are designed to achieve compromise, to slow change, to dilute absolutisms. They embody wholesome inconsistencies. They are designed, in short, to do things that abstract generalizations about the just society tend to bring into contempt.

More than this, the attempt to define individual liberties by abstract reasoning, though intended to broaden liberties, is actually likely to make them more vulnerable. Our constitutional liberties arose out of historical experience and out of political, moral, and religious sentiment. They do not rest upon any general theory. Attempts to frame a theory that removes from democratic control areas of life the framers intended to leave there can only succeed if abstractions are regarded as overriding the constitutional text and structure, judicial precedent, and the history that gives our rights life, rootedness, and meaning. It is no small matter to discredit the foundations upon which our constitutional freedoms have always been sustained and substitute as a bulwark only abstractions of moral philosophy. The difference in approach parallels the difference between the American and French revolutions, and the outcome for liberty was much less happy under the regime of "the rights of man."

It is perhaps not surprising that abstract, philosophical approaches to law often produce constitutional nihilism. Some of the legal philosophers have begun to see that there is no overarching theory that can satisfy the criteria that are required. It may be, as Friedrich Hayek suggested, that nihilism naturally results from sudden disillusion when high expectations about the powers of abstract reasoning collapse. The theorists, unable to settle for practical wisdom, must have a single theoretical construct or nothing. In any event, one of the leading scholars has announced, in a widely admired article, that all normative constitutional theories, including the theory that judges must only interpret the law, are necessarily incoherent. The apparently necessary conclusion—that judicial review is, in that case, illegitimate—is never drawn. Instead, it is proposed that judges simply enforce good values, or rather the values that seem to the professor good. The desire for results appears to be stronger than the respect for legitimacy, and, when theory fails, the desire to use judicial power remains.

This brings into the open the fundamental antipathy to democracy to be seen in much of the new legal scholarship. The original Constitution was devoted primarily to the mechanisms of democratic choice. Constitutional scholarship today is dominated by the creation of arguments that will encourage judges to thwart democratic choice. Though the arguments are, as you might suspect, cast in terms of expanding individual freedom, that is not their result. One of the freedoms, the major freedom, of our kind of society is the freedom to choose to have a public morality. As Chesterton put it, "What is the good of telling a community that it has every liberty except the liberty to make laws? The liberty to make laws is what constitutes a free people." The makers of our Constitution thought so too, for they provided wide powers to representative assemblies and ruled only a few subjects off limits by the Constitution.

The new legal view disagrees both with the historical Constitution and with the majority of living Americans about where the balance between individual freedom and social order lies.

Leading legal academics are increasingly absorbed with what they call "legal theory." That would be welcome, if it were real, but what is generally meant is not theory about the sources of law, or its capacities and limits, or the prerequisites for its vitality, but rather the endless exploration of abstract philosophical principles. One would suppose that we can decide nothing unless we first settle the ultimate questions of the basis of political obligation, the merits of contractarianism, rule or act utilitarianism, the nature of the just society, and the like. Nor surprisingly, the politics of the professors becomes the command of the Constitution. As Richard John Neuhaus puts it, "the theorists' quest for universality becomes simply the parochialism of a few intellectuals," and he notes "the limitations of theories of justice that cannot sustain a democratic consensus regarding the legitimacy of law."

Sometimes I am reminded of developments in another, perhaps parallel, field. I recall one evening listening to a rather traditional theologian bemoan the intellectual fads that were sweeping his field. Since I had a very unsophisticated view of theology, I remarked with some surprise that his church seemed to have remarkably little doctrine capable of resisting these trends. He was offended and said there had always been tradition. Both of our fields purport to rest upon sacred texts, and it seemed odd that in both the main bulwark against heresy should be only tradition. Law is certainly like that. We never elaborated much of a theory—as distinguished from mere attitudes—about the behavior proper to constitutional judges. As Alexander Bickel observed, all we ever had was a tradition, and in the last 30 years that has been shattered.

Now we need theory, theory that relates the framers' values to today's world. That is not an impossible task by any means, but it is a good deal more complex than slogans such as "strict construction" or "judicial restraint" might lead you to think. It is necessary to establish the proposition that the framers' intentions with respect to freedoms are the sole legitimate premise from which constitutional analysis may proceed. It is true that a willful judge can often clothe his legislation in sophistical argument and the misuse of history. But hypocrisy has its value. General acceptance of correct theory can force the judge to hypocrisy and, to that extent, curb his freedom. The theorists of moral abstraction are devoted precisely to removing the judge's guilt at legislating and so removing the necessity for hypocrisy. Worse still, they would free the intellectually honest judge from constraints he would otherwise recognize and honor.

It is well to be clear about the role moral discourse should play in law. Neuhaus is entirely correct in saying

> whatever else law may be, it is a human enterprise in response to human behavior, and human behavior is stubbornly entangled with beliefs about right and wrong. Law that is recognized as legitimate is therefore related to—even organically related to, if you will—the larger universe of moral discourse that helps shape human behavior. In short, if law is not also a moral enterprise, it is without legitimacy or binding force.

To that excellent statement I would add only that it is crucial to bear in mind what kind of law, and what legal institutions, we are talking about. In a constitutional democracy the moral content of law must be given by the morality of the framer or the legislator, never by the morality of the judge. The sole task of the latter—and it is a task quite large enough for anyone's wisdom, skill, and virtue—is to translate the framer's or the legislator's morality into a rule to govern unforeseen circumstances. That abstinence from giving his own desires free play, that continuing and self-conscious renunciation of power, that is the morality of the jurist.

PART IV

The Judiciary and Federal Regulation: Line Drawing and Statutory Interpretation

"IT IS in the courts and not the legislature that our citizens primarily feel the keen, cutting edge of the law."[1] Reiterating that view of New Jersey State Supreme Court Chief Justice Arthur T. Vanderbilt, Justice Tom Clark observed: "In a democracy the national welfare should be the primary objective of the legislature whose statutes may quickly pattern effective measures to that end. The courts, on the other hand, have the duty of interpreting and enforcing such legislation. Theirs' is the machinery through which law finds its teeth."[2]

Judicial participation in regulatory politics at the federal level has greatly increased since the New Deal, and particularly during the 1960s and 1970s, because of congressional creation of new administrative agencies and legislation aimed at ensuring civil rights and liberties, as well as promoting health, safety, and consumer and environmental protection. Appeals of administrative decisions, for instance, rose fivefold in the last 20 years; appeals climbed from 737 in 1960 to 1522 in 1970 and to 2290 by 1975, with a further rise to over 3800 cases in 1981.[3] Pointing out that ambiguous legislation often invites litigation, Chief Justice Warren Burger accordingly called on Congress to require "judicial impact statements" prior to enactment of new legislation.[4] The federal judiciary has indeed become a forum for challenging federal regulation and congressional legislation by those who are either denied access to or disagree with the outcome of the administrative and legislative process.

The growing importance of statutory interpretation, along with constitutional interpretation, is evident as well in the changing character of the business of the Supreme Court. In historical perspective, the Court gradually became a tribunal of constitutional and statutory interpretation. During roughly the first decade of the Court's history, over 40 percent of its business consisted in admiralty prize cases. Approximately 50 percent of the docketed cases raised questions of law—largely diversity actions (suits by citizens of different states) and other matters of common law—with the remaining 10 percent matters such as equity, including one probate case.[5] Litigation before the Court was not immune from socioeconomic changes after the Civil War brought by Reconstruction and the Industrial Revolution. In the 1882 term, for instance, the number of admiralty suits dropped to less than 4 percent. Almost 40 percent of the decisions handed down still dealt with either disputes at common law or questions of jurisdiction, practice, and procedure. Over 43 percent of the Court's business, however, resolved issues of statutory interpretation; less than 4 percent were matters of constitutional law.[6] The decline in admiralty and common-law adjudication, and the concomitant rise in cases over statutory and constitutional interpretation, reflects the impact in the late nineteenth century of changing socioeconomic conditions and increasing congressional legislation. In 1890, Justice Stephen Field observed:

> Thus by the new agencies of steam and electricity in the movement of machinery and transmission of intelligence, creating railways and steamboats, telegraphs and telephones, and adding almost without number to establishments for the manufacture of factories, transactions are carried on to an infinitely greater extent than before between different states, leading to innumerable controversies between their citizens, which have found their way to [the Supreme Court] for decision.[7]

In the twentieth century, particularly after the Judiciary Act of 1925 enlarged the Court's discretionary jurisdiction—the trend continued toward a Supreme Court that principally decides issues of constitutional and statutory interpretation. In the 1980 term, 47 percent of the cases disposed of by full or per curiam opinion involved matters of constitutional law, while 38 percent dealt with statutory interpretation. The remaining 15 percent of the cases resolved matters of administrative law or taxation, patents, and claims.[8]

The modern Supreme Court is therefore not primarily concerned, as it once was, with resolving disputes per se; but instead with providing uniformity, stability, and predictability to the law—principally by means of constitutional and statutory interpretation. "The legislature does not speak with finality as to the meaning of its own powers," Justice Benjamin Cardozo noted. "The final word is for the courts."[9] Invalidation of congressional legislation steadily increased throughout the twentieth century as the Supreme Court assumed a special role in safeguarding individual freedoms against encroachments by Congress. The Court, for example, developed doctrines such as "void for vagueness" and "statutory overbreadth" when striking down legislation that it viewed as impinging on First Amendment freedoms.[10] With the expansion of congressional legislation and the emergence of the so-called administrative state, the Court also assumed an important role in providing guidance to lower federal courts and administrative agencies by clarifying and supervising the implementation of congressional mandates. An appellate court, in Judge Jerome Frank's words, "is, vis-à-vis the Supreme Court, 'merely a reflector, serving as a judicial moon.' Judges on such a court usually must, as best they can, cautiously follow new 'doctrinal trends' . . . [a]s their duty is usually to learn, 'not the congressional intent, but the Supreme Court's intent.' "[11]

Statutory interpretation is no less vexatious than constitutional, and perhaps often more difficult due to the doctrine of *stare decisis*. "The Court has felt far freer," Justice Lewis Powell explains, "to reverse constitutional decisions than it has to reverse the interpretation of statutes"[12] because of the need for stability in the law and respect for the principle of separation of powers.

The starting point and first rule of statutory interpretation is strict adherence to the text, to the plain meaning of statutory language. As Justice Oliver Wendell Holmes put it: "We do not inquire what the legislature meant; we ask only what the statute means."[13] Statutory language, however, is often vague, ambiguous if not also esoteric, as in some areas of antitrust or health, safety, and environmental legislation. "Such is the character of human language," Chief Justice John Marshall recognized, "that no word conveys to the mind in all situations, one single definite idea."[14] The task of the judge, according to Justice Holmes, is "to work out, from what is expressly said and done, what would have been said with regard to events not definitely before the minds of the parties, if those events had been considered."[15]

Interpretation of statutes thus frequently moves beyond the text to the context of legislation—to congressional testimony, hearings, floor debate, and history—in a quest for "the intent" of Congress. Indeed, the Supreme Court increasingly cites legislative history to justify its interpretation of statutory language. In 1938, for instance, the Court cited items of legislative history only 19 times, whereas by the late 1970s such materials were cited at a rate of 300 to 400 per term.[16] Congressional history has become more important because legislation typically does not embody a clear intent; instead it is a mandate for federal agencies to regulate and implement policy. This is in part because congressmen rarely agree on the details of an enactment or anticipate all possible applications of a statute. Justice Cardozo put the problem this way:

> The difficulties of so-called interpretation arise when the legislature has had no meaning at all; when the question which is raised on the statute never occurred to it; when what the judges have to do is, not to determine what the legislature did mean on a point which was present to its mind, but to guess what it would have intended on a point not present to its mind, if the point had been present.[17]

Congressmen, moreover, are susceptible to lobbying of special-interest groups, "logrolling" on matters of little immediate concern to their particular constituents, and largely dependent on their staffs for drafting and negotiating statutory language. Issues that should be settled during the legislative process are left for courts to resolve; and judges confront deliberate ambiguities in statutory language or congressional silence and no certain, unambiguous congressional history.

The ambiguities of language and congressional silence or conflicting records render the task of statutory interpretation truly challenging, inviting considerable judicial creativity. Justice Felix Frankfurter, in chapter 17, further examines the problems of text, context, and congressional intent. He also contrasts the interpretative styles and approaches of Justices Holmes, Cardozo, and Louis Brandeis. His own insistence remains noteworthy: "There is a difference between reading what is and rewriting it."[18] That difference frequently appears elusive and may occasion a good deal of controversy. As a former congressman and now a federal court of appeals judge, Abner Mikva, observed:

> When I was in Congress I used to get irritated at the way I felt courts were misinterpreting what I considered the clear meaning of a piece of legislation. I am convinced now that, almost without exception, judges really are trying to do what Congress says but that the meanings just aren't as clear when you're looking at them in the isolation of a court case.[19]

Despite the problems of ambiguity and congressional silence, Justice Brandeis was wont to say, "to supply omissions transcends the judicial function."[20] Nonetheless, justices at times do supply omissions and rewrite statutory language. Justice William Brennan, in *United Steelworkers of America v. Weber,* over the forceful dissents of Chief Justice Burger and Justice Rehnquist, for example, argued that "a thing may be within the letter of the statute and yet not within the statute, because not within its spirit nor within the intention of its makers."[21]

When Congress delegates authority to an agency, but the enabling legislation and congressional history are challenged, the alternates to judicial rewriting of a statute are either to uphold the agency view of the legislation or to invoke the nondelegation doctrine—striking down the legislation as impermissibly broad, without clear standards for guiding agency action.

Historically, the Court has permitted agencies to "fill in the details"[22] of legislation in recognition of the fact that Congress cannot foresee all possible applications of a statute and that implementation of legislation often requires the expertise of administrative agencies. On that basis the Court upholds broad delegations of power to federal agencies and independent regulatory commissions. The Interstate Commerce Commission, for example, is authorized to fix "just and reasonable" rates; the Federal Trade Commission is empowered to eliminate "unfair methods of competition"; the Securities and Exchange Commission is charged with maintaining "a fair and orderly market" on "just and equitable principles of trade"; and the Federal Communications Commission is authorized to regulate radio and television licenses on a standard of "public convenience, interest, or necessity."

The nondelegation doctrine, though invoked during the heyday of the New Deal,[23] has been infrequently employed by the Supreme Court, although state courts continue to enforce the doctrine against state legislation. In Justice Thurgood Marshall's view, the nondelegation doctrine is "moribund"[24] and ought to be laid to rest. By contrast, Justice Rehnquist, among others, urges its merit and utility in preserving the separation of powers between Congress and the executive branch.[25] In chapter 18, Judge Carl McGowan of the Court of Appeals for the District of Columbia Circuit—the circuit court that because of its location and proximity to federal agencies reviews the overwhelming portion of challenges to regulatory actions—further discusses the nondelegation doctrine and the problems of reviewing congressional legislation and agency regulations. Judge McGowan concludes that reliance on the nondelegation doctrine in a few isolated cases will do little to curb the tide of congressional legislation and federal regulation, or the litigation that follows in the wake.

During the late 1960s and 1970s Congress and the Supreme Court in fact encouraged lower court supervision of regulatory politics, especially with regard to health, safety, and environmental regulation. Judicial oversight of the administration process grew in part because of the fear that new agencies—such as the Environmental Protection Agency, the Occupational Safety and Health Administration, and the Consumer Product Safety Commission—would be "captured" by special interest groups and in part because of a distrust of agency expertise and a demand for more public participation in the formulation of regulatory policies. Supervision of the regulatory process by generalist federal judges was encouraged by Congress and the judiciary in three ways: by "liberalizing" the law of standing and thus permitting more challenges to agency actions and inactions; by "judicializing" the process of administrative decision making and rule making in order to ensure public participation and open, adjudicative-type examination of all competing views of regulatory action; and by heightening the standards for judicial review of final agency decisions.[26] By the end of the 1970s there thus emerged, in Judge Harold Leventhal's words, "a new era in administrative law."[27] Judge Antonin Scalia of the Court of Appeals for the District of Columbia Circuit, in chapter 19 further examines the law of standing and its relation to the evolution in the so-called judicial/administrative partnership in regulatory politics and the trend toward greater judicial intervention in the administrative process.

The form and extent of judicial intervention in regulatory politics bears emphasizing, for it reflects basic differences in judicial self-perception. Federal judges differ in their perceptions of their role and capacity as "generalists" to scrutinize complex, science-policy regulations. The U.S. Court of Appeals for the District of Columbia was, for more than a decade, sharply divided over the kind of review that should be given to the procedural and scientific basis for regulatory action.

The complexity of the issues is not the problem, Judge David Bazelon maintained, since courts review no less vexing economic issues when reviewing Federal Communications Commission and Security and Exchange Commission decisions. Rather, science-policy disputes confront judges, who have no "knowledge and training to assess the merits of competing scientific arguments" with vexatious issues over which there frequently exists no scientific consensus. Even if there was agreement within the scientific community, basic moral-political choices remain—choices that in a constitutional democracy should be ventilated in public forum. For Judge Bazelon, lack of judicial competence implies judicial self-restraint. Courts should not substitute their judgments for those of scientific and administrative experts: "Courts are *not* the agency either to resolve the factual disputes, or to make the painful value choices."[28] Judges, however, are presumably experts on process, and adherence to judicial self-restraint on substantive matters need not preclude judicial activism on procedural grounds. According to Judge Bazelon:

> [I]n cases of great technological complexity, the best way for courts to guard against unreasonable or erroneous administrative decisions is not for judges themselves to scrutinize the technical merits of each decision. Rather, it is to establish a decision that can be held up to the scrutiny of the scientific community and the public.[29]

The federal judiciary thus should supervise the process of administrative decision making and, when necessary, impose procedural requirements in order to ensure public participation, open discussion, and the reasoned elaboration of the scientific basis for an agency's regulations.

By contrast, Judge Harold Leventhal argued that, although deference should be shown to administrative and scientific expertise, judges should engage in "enough steeping" in technical matters to permit informed, substantive review of administrative decisions. With searching review, a judge "becomes aware, especially from a combination of danger signals, that the agency has not really taken a 'hard look' at the salient problems, and has not genuinely engaged in reasoned decision making."[30]

The "hard look" approach requires judges to do more than, as Judge Henry Friendly said, simply look for "good faith efforts of agencies."[31] A court, according to Judge Leventhal, should "penetrate to the underlying decisions of an agency decision to satisfy itself that the agency has exercised a reasoned discretion with reasons that do not deviate from or ignore the ascertainable legislative intent."[32] Although courts should not innovate procedurally or substitute more rigorous processes for those adopted by agencies, judges are capable of informing themselves about scientific and technical matters and thus may scrutinize, criticize, and overturn the basis for administrative decisions.

The hard-look approach, which the Supreme Court endorsed in *Vermont Yankee Nuclear Power Corporation v. Natural Resources Defense Council, Inc.,*[33] demands a great deal of judges and may provide a pretense for judicial intervention in the regulatory process when reviewing agencies' final decisions. Not all federal judges share the ability or personal dedication of Judge Leventhal to master all the technical details of complex science-policy disputes. They typically find such litigation perplexing, taxing, and time-consuming. As one federal judge remarked with regard to the adjudication of science-policy disputes: "In environmental litigation we are constantly placed in a position of choosing between the lies told by the fisherman's experts and the lies told by [the] utility company's experts. The overwhelming temptation for an appellate court is to accept the original fact finder's conclusion as to which expert was telling the smallest lie."[34]

The difficulties of statutory interpretation and the role of federal courts in overseeing the administrative process are not likely to diminish. Ultimately, as Judge McGowan among others conclude, Congress itself must provide clearer, more detailed standards for delegating power and controlling agency implementation of congressional policy.

NOTES

1. A.T. Vanderbilt, *The Challenge of Law Reform* 4 (Princeton: Princeton University Press, 1955).

2. T. Clark, "Random Thoughts on the Court's Interpretation of Individual Rights," 1 *Houston Law Review* 75, 75 (1963).

3. See *Annual Reports of the Director of the Administrative Office of the United States Courts, 1975-1981* (Washington, D.C.: Administrative Office of the U.S. Courts, 1975-1981).

4. See W.E. Burger, "New Ways to Speed Up Justice: Interview with Chief Justice Warren E. Burger," *U.S. News & World Report* 38, 40 (21 August 1979); Remarks, American Bar Association Opening Assembly, at 11 (Atlanta, 9 August 1976).

5. Based on data in J. Goebel, Jr., Appendix: The Business of the Supreme Court, 1789-1801, in *History of the Supreme Court of the United States: Antecedents and Beginnings to 1801,* at 796-798 (New York: Macmillan, 1971).

6. Based on an analysis by the author.

7. S. Field, "The Centenary of the Supreme Court of the United States," 24 *American Law Review* 23 (1890).

8. Based on analysis by the author.

9. B. Cardozo, *The Paradoxes of Legal Science* 99 (New Haven: Yale University Press, 1929).

10. See, e.g., *Baggett v. Bullitt,* 377 U.S. 360 (1964).

11. J. Frank, *Courts on Trial* 307 (Princeton: Princeton University Press, 1959).

12. L. Powell, "Constitutional Interpretation: An Interview with Justice Lewis Powell," *Kenyon College Alumni Bulletin* 14, 15 (Summer 1979).

13. O.W. Holmes, "The Theory of Legal Interpretation," in *Collected Legal Papers* 207 (New York: Harcourt, Brace, 1920).

14. *McCulloch v. Maryland,* 17 U.S. (4 Wheat.) 316, 414 (1819).

15. O.W. Holmes, *The Common Law* 303 (Boston: Little, Brown, 1881).

16. See P. Wald, "Some Observations on the Use of Legislative History in the 1981 Term," 68 *Iowa Law Review* 195 (1983).

17. B. Cardozo, *The Nature of the Judicial Process* 15 (New Haven: Yale University Press, 1921).

18. *Shapiro v. United States,* 335 U.S. 1, 43 (19).

19. A.J. Mikva, Q. and A.: "On Leaving Capitol Hill for the Bench," *Washington Post* B8, col. 3 (12 May 1983).

20. *Iselin v. United States,* 270 U.S. 245, 251 (1926).

21. *United Steelworkers of America v. Weber,* 443 U.S. 193, 201 (1979), quoting *Holy Trinity Church v. United States,* 143 U.S. 457, 459 (1892).

22. *Wayman v. Southard,* 23 U.S. (10 Wheat.) 1 (1825).

23. See, e.g., *Schechter Poultry Co. v. United States,* 295 U.S. 495, 529 (1935).

24. *FPC v. New England Power Co.,* 415 U.S. 345, 353 (1974).

25. See *Industrial Union Department, AFL-CIO v. American Petroleum Institute,* 448 U.S. 607, 671-88 (1980) (Rehnquist, J., con. op.).

26. For a further discussion, see D.M. O'Brien, "Courts, Technology Assessment and Science-Policy Disputes," in D.M. O'Brien and D. Marchand, *The Politics of Technology Assessment: Politics, Institutions and Policy Disputes* 79-119 (Lexington, Mass.: Lexington Books, 1982).

27. H. Leventhal, "Environmental Decisionmaking and the Role of the Courts," 122 *University of Pennsylvania Law Review* 509 (1974).

28. D. Bazelon, "Coping with Technology Through the Legal Process," 62 *Cornell Law Review* 817, 822 (1977).

29. *International Harvester Co. v. Ruckelshaus,* 478 F.2d 615, 653 (D.C. Cir. 1973) (Bazelon, J., con. op.).

30. *Ethyl Corp. v. EPA,* 541 F.2d 1, 20 (D.C. Cir. 1976).

31. *New York City v. United States,* 344 F. Supp. 929 (E.D.N.Y. 1972). See also H. Friendly, "Some Kind of Hearing," 123 *University of Pennsylvania Law Review* 1267 (1975).

32. *Greater Boston Television Corp. v. FCC,* 444 F.2d 841, 850 (D.C. Cir. 1970).

33. *Vermont Yankee Nuclear Power Corp. v. Natural Resources Defense Council, Inc.,* 435 U.S. 519 (1978).

34. Quoted by M. Rosenberg, "Contemporary Litigation in the United States," in H. Jones, ed., *Legal Institutions Today* 152, 158 (New York: American Bar Association, 1977).

17

Some Reflections on the Reading of Statutes

FELIX FRANKFURTER
Justice, Supreme Court of the United States

Though it has its own preoccupations and its own mysteries, and above all its own jargon, judicial construction ought not to be torn from its wider, non-legal context. Anything that is written may present a problem of meaning, and that is the essence of the business of judges in construing legislation. The problem derives from the very nature of words. They are symbols of meaning. But unlike mathematical symbols, the phrasing of a document, especially a complicated enactment, seldom attains more than approximate precision. If individual words are inexact symbols, with shifting variables, their configuration can hardly achieve invariant meaning or assured definiteness. Apart from the ambiguity inherent in its symbols, a statute suffers from dubieties. It is not an equation or a formula representing a clearly marked process, nor is it an expression of individual thought to which is imparted the definiteness a single authorship can give. A statute is an instrument of government partaking of its practical purposes but also of its infirmities and limitations, of its awkward and groping efforts. With one of his flashes of insight, Mr. Justice Johnson called the science of government "the science of experiment." *Anderson v. Dunn,* 6 Wheat. 204, 226. The phrase, uttered 125 years ago, has a very modern ring, for time has only served to emphasize its accuracy. To be sure, laws can measurably be improved with improvement in the mechanics of legislation, and the need for interpretation is usually in inverse ratio to the care and imagination of draftsmen. The area for judicial construction may be contracted. A large area is bound to remain.

The difficulties are inherent not only in the nature of words, of composition, and of legislation generally. They are often intensified by the subject matter of an enactment. Moreover, government sometimes solves problems by shelving them temporarily. The legislative process reflects that attitude. Statutes as well as constitutional provisions at times embody purposeful ambiguity or are expressed with a generality for future unfolding. "The prohibition contained in the Fifth Amendment refers to infamous crimes—a term obviously inviting interpretation in harmony with conditions and opinions prevailing from time to time." Mr. Justice Brandeis in *United States v. Moreland,* 258 U.S. 433, 451. And Mr. Justice Cardozo once remarked, "a great principle of constitutional law is not susceptible of comprehensive statement in an adjective." *Carter v. Carter Coal Co., 298 U.S. 238, 327.*

The intrinsic difficulties of language and the emergence after enactment of situations not anticipated by the most gifted legislative imagination, reveal doubts and ambiguities in statutes that compel judicial construction. The process of construction, therefore, is not an exercise in logic or dialectic: The aids of formal reasoning are not irrelevant; they may simply be inadequate. The purpose of construction being the ascertainment of meaning, every consideration brought to bear for the solution of that problem must be devoted to that end alone. To speak of it as a practical problem is not to indulge a fashion in words. It must be that, not something else. Not, for instance, an opportunity for a judge to use words as "empty vessels into which he can pour anything he will"—his caprices, fixed notions, even statesmanlike beliefs in a particular policy. Nor, on the other hand, is the process a ritual to be observed by unimaginative adherence to well-worn professional phrases. To be sure, it is inescapably a problem in the keeping of the legal profession and subject to all the limitations of our adversary system of adjudication. When the judge, selected by society to give meaning to what the legislature has done, examines the statute, he does so not in a laboratory or in a classroom. Damage has been done or exactions made, interests are divided, passions have been aroused, sides have been taken. But the judge, if he is worth his salt, must be above the battle. We must assume in him not only personal impartiality but intellectual disinterestedness. In matters of statutory construction also it makes a great deal of difference whether you start with an answer or with a problem.

The Judge's Task

Everyone has his own way of phrasing the task confronting judges when the meaning of a statute is in controversy. Judge Learned Hand speaks of the art of interpretation as "the proliferation of purpose." Who am I not to be satisfied with Learned Hand's felicities? And yet that phrase might mislead judges intellectually less disciplined than Judge Hand. It might justify interpretations by judicial libertines, not merely judicial libertarians. My own rephrasing of what we are driving at is probably no more helpful, and is much longer than Judge Hand's epigram. I should say that the troublesome phase of construction is the determination of the extent to which extraneous documentation and external circumstances may be allowed to infiltrate the text on the theory that they were part of it, written in ink discernible to the judicial eye.

Chief Justice White was happily endowed with the gift of finding the answer to problems by merely stating them. Often have I envied him this faculty but never more than in recent years. No matter how one states the problem of statutory construction, for me, at least, it does not carry its own answer. Though my business throughout most of my professional life has been with statutes, I come to you empty-handed. I bring no answers. I suspect the answers to the problems of an art are in its exercise. Not that one does not inherit, if one is capable of receiving it, the wisdom of the wise. But I confess unashamedly that I do not get much nourishment from books on statutory construction, and I say this after freshly reexamining them all, scores of them.

When one wants to understand or at least get the feeling of great painting, one does not go to books on the art of painting. One goes to the great masters. And so I have gone to great masters to get a sense of their practice of the art of interpretation. However, the art of painting and the art of interpretation are very different arts. Law, Holmes told us, becomes civilized to the extent that it is self-conscious of what it is doing. And so the avowals of great judges regarding their process of interpretation and the considerations that enter into it are of vital importance, though that ultimate something called the judgment upon the avowed factors escapes formulation and often, I suspect, even awareness. Nevertheless, an examination of some 2000 cases, the bulk of which directly or indirectly involves matters of construction, ought to shed light on the encounter between the judicial and the legislative processes, whether that light be conveyed by hints, by explicit elucidation, or, to mix the metaphor, through the ancient test, by their fruits.

And so I have examined the opinions of Holmes, Brandeis, and Cardozo and sought to derive from their treatment of legislation what conclusions I could fairly draw, freed as much as I could be from impressions I had formed in the course of the years.

Holmes came to the Supreme Court before the great flood of recent legislation, while the other two, especially Cardozo, appeared at its full tide. The shift in the nature of the Court's business led to changes in its jurisdiction, resulting in a concentration of cases involving the legislative process. Proportionately to their length of service and the number of opinions, Brandeis and Cardozo had many more statutes to construe. And the statutes presented for their interpretation became increasingly complex, bringing in their train a quantitatively new role for administrative regulations. Nevertheless, the earliest opinions of Holmes on statutory construction, insofar as he reveals himself, cannot be distinguished from Cardozo's last opinion, though the latter's process is more explicit.

A judge of marked individuality stamps his individuality on what he writes, no matter what the subject. What is however striking about the opinions of the three Justices in this field is the essential similarity of their attitude and of their appraisal of the relevant. Their opinions do not disclose a private attitude for or against extension of governmental authority by legislation, or towards the policy of particular legislation, which consciously or imperceptibly affected their judicial function in construing laws. It would thus be a shallow judgment that found in Mr. Justice Holmes's dissent in the *Northern Securities* case (193 U.S. 197, 400) an expression of his disapproval of the policy behind the Sherman Law. His habit of mind—to be as accurate as one can—had a natural tendency to confine what seemed to him familiar language in a statute to its familiar scope. But the proof of the pudding is that his private feelings did not lead him to invoke the rule of indefiniteness to invalidate legislation of which he strongly disapproved (Compare *Nash v. United States,* 229 U.S. 373, and *International Harvester Co. v. Kentucky,* 234 U.S. 216), or to confine language in a constitution within the restrictions which he gave to the same language in a statute. (Compare *Towne v. Eisner,* 245 U.S. 418, and *Eisner v. Macomber,* 252 U.S. 189.)

The reservations I have just made indicate that such differences as emerge in the opinions of the three Justices on statutory construction are differences that characterize all of their opinions, whether they are concerned with interpretation or constitutionality, with admiralty or patent law. They are differences of style. In the case of each, the style is the man.

If it be suggested that Mr. Justice Holmes is often swift, if not cavalier, in his treatment of statutes, there are those who level the same criticism against his opinions generally. It is merited in the sense that he wrote, as he said, for those learned in the art. I need hardly add that for him "learned" was not a formal term comprehending the whole legal fraternity. When dealing with problems of statutory construction also he illumined whole areas of doubt and darkness with insights enduringly expressed, however briefly. To say, "We agree to all the generalities about not supplying criminal laws with what they omit, but there is no canon against using common sense in construing laws as saying what they obviously mean," *Roschen v. Ward,* 279 U.S. 337, 339, is worth more than most of the dreary writing on how to construe penal legislation. Again when he said that "the meaning of a sentence is to be felt rather than to be proved," *United States v. Johnson,* 221 U.S. 488, 496, he expressed the wholesome truth that the final rendering of the meaning of a statute is an act of judgment. He would shudder at the thought that by such a statement he was giving comfort to the school of visceral jurisprudence. Judgment is not drawn out of the void but is based on the correlation of imponderables all of which need not, because they cannot, be made explicit. He was expressing the humility of the intellectual that he was, whose standards of exactitude distrusted pretensions of certainty, believing that legal controversies that are not frivolous almost always involve matters of degree, and often degree of the nicest sort. Statutory construction implied the exercise of choice, but precluded the notion of capricious choice as much as choice based on private notions of policy. One gets the impression that in interpreting statutes Mr. Justice Holmes reached meaning easily, as was true of most of his results, with emphasis on the language in the totality of the enactment and the felt reasonableness of the chosen construction. He had a lively awareness that a statute was expressive of purpose and policy, but in his reading of it he tended to hug the shores of the statute itself, without much re-enforcement from without.

Mr. Justice Brandeis, on the other hand, in dealing with these problems as with others, would elucidate the judgment he was exercising by proof or detailed argument. In such instances, especially when in dissent, his opinions would draw on the whole arsenal of aids to construction. More often than either Holmes or Cardozo, Brandeis would invoke the additional weight of some "rule" of construction. But he never lost sight of the limited scope and function of such "rules." Occasionally, however, perhaps because of the nature of a particular statute, the minor importance of its incidence, the pressure of judicial business or even the temperament of his law clerk, whom he always treated as a co-worker, Brandeis disposed of a statute even more dogmatically, with less explicit elucidation, than did Holmes.

For Cardozo, statutory construction was an acquired taste. He preferred common law subtleties, having great skill in bending them to modern uses. But he came to realize that problems of statutory construction had their own exciting subtleties and gave ample employment to philosophic and literary talents. Cardozo's elucidation of how meaning is drawn out of a statute gives proof of the wisdom and balance which, combined with his learning, made him a great judge. While the austere style of Brandeis seldom mitigated the dry aspect of so many problems of statutory construction, Cardozo managed to endow even these with the glow and softness of his writing. The differences in the tone and color of their style as well as in the moral intensity of Brandeis and Cardozo made itself felt when they wrote full-dress opinions on problems of statutory construction. Brandeis almost compels by demonstration; Cardozo woos by persuasion.

Scope of the Judicial Function

From the hundreds of cases in which our three Justices construed statutes one thing clearly emerges. The area of free judicial movement is considerable. These three remembered that laws are not abstract propositions. They are expressions of policy arising out of specific situations and addressed to the attainment of particular ends. The difficulty is that the legislative ideas which laws embody are both explicit and immanent. And so the bottom problem is: What is below the surface of the words and yet fairly a part of them? Words in statutes are not unlike words in a foreign language in that they too have "associations, echoes, and overtones." Judges must retain the associations, hear the echoes, and capture the overtones. In one of his very last opinions, dealing with legislation taxing the husband on the basis of the combined income of husband and wife, Holmes wrote: "The statutes are the outcome of a thousand years of history. . . . They form a system with echoes of different moments, none of which is entitled to prevail over the other." *Hoeper v. Tax Commission,* 284 U.S. 206, 219.

Even within their area of choice the courts are not at large. They are confined by the nature and scope of the judicial function in its particular exercise in the field of interpretation. They are under the constraints imposed by the judicial function in our democratic society. As a matter of verbal recognition certainly, no one will gainsay that the function in construing a statute is to ascertain the meaning of words used by the legislature. To go beyond it is to usurp a power which our democracy has lodged in its elected legislature. The great judges have constantly admonished their brethren of the need for discipline in observing the limitations. A judge must not rewrite a statute, neither to enlarge nor contract it. Whatever temptations the statesmanship of policy making might wisely suggest, construction must eschew interpolation and evisceration. He must not read in by way of creation. He must not read out except to avoid patent nonsense of internal contradiction. "If there is no meaning in it," said Alice's King, "that saves a world of trouble, you know, as we needn't try to find any." Legislative words presumably have meaning and so we must try to find it.

This duty of restraint, this humility of function as merely the translator of another's command, is a constant theme of our Justices. It is on the lips of all judges, but seldom, I venture to believe, has the restraint which it expresses, or the duty which it enjoins, been observed with so consistent a realization that its observance depends on the self-conscious discipline. Cardozo put it this way: "We do not pause to consider whether a statute differently conceived and framed would yield results more consonant with fairness and reason. We take this statute as we find it." *Anderson v. Wilson*, 289 U.S. 20, 27. It was expressed more fully by Mr. Justice Brandeis when the temptation to give what might be called a more liberal interpretation could not have been wanting. "The particularization and detail with which the scope of each provision, the amount of the tax thereby imposed, and the incidence of the tax, were specified, preclude an extension of any provision by implication to any other subject. . . . What the Government asks is not a construction of a statute, but, in effect, an enlargement of it by the court, so that what was omitted, presumably by inadvertence, may be included within its scope." *Iselin v. United States,* 270 U.S. 245, 250-251. An omission, at the time of enactment, whether careless or calculated, cannot be judicially supplied however much later wisdom may recommend the inclusion.

The vital difference between initiating policy, often involving a decided break with the past, and merely carrying out a formulated policy, indicates the relatively narrow limits within which choice is fairly open to courts and the extent to which interpreting the law is inescapably making law. To say that, because of this restricted field of interpretive declaration, courts make law just as do legislatures is to deny essential features in the history of our democracy. It denies that legislation and adjudication have had different lines of growth, serve vitally different purposes, function under different conditions, and bear different responsibilities. The judicial process of dealing with words is not at all Alice in Wonderland's way of dealing with them. Even in matters legal some words and phrases, though very few, approach mathematical symbols and mean substantially the same to all who have occasion to use them. Other law terms like "police power" are not symbols at all but labels for the results of the whole process of adjudication. In between lies a gamut of words with different de-

notations as well as connotations. There are varying shades of compulsion for
judges behind different words, differences that are due to the words themselves,
their setting in a text, their setting in history. In short, judges are not unfet-
tered glossators. They are under a special duty not to overemphasize the episod-
ic aspects of life and not to undervalue its organic processes—its continuities
and relationships. For judges at least it is important to remember that continuity with the past is not only a necessity but even a duty.

The Process of Construction

Let me descend to some particulars.

The text.   Though we may not end with the words in construing a dis-
puted statute, one certainly begins there. You have a right to think that a hoary
platitude, but it is a platitude too often not observed at the bar. In any event,
it may not take you to the end of the road. The Court no doubt must listen
to the voice of Congress. But often Congress cannot be heard clearly because
its speech is muffled. Even when it has spoken, it is as true of Congress as of
others that what is said is what the listener hears. Like others, judges too listen
with what psychologists used to call the apperception mass, which I take it
means in plain English that one listens with what is already in one's head. One
more caution is relevant when one is admonished to listen attentively to what
a statute says. One must also listen attentively to what it does not say.

We must, no doubt, accord the words the sense in which Congress used
them. That is only another way of stating the central problem of decoding the
symbols. It will help to determine for whom they were meant. Statutes are not
archaeological documents to be studied in a library. They are written to guide
the actions of men. As Mr. Justice Holmes remarked upon some Indian legislation "The word was addressed to the Indian mind," *Fleming v. McCurtain,* 215
U.S. 56, 60. If a statute is written for ordinary folk, it would be arbitrary not
to assume that Congress intended its words to be read with the minds of ordinary men. If they are addressed to specialists, they must be read by judges with
the minds of the specialists.

The context.   Legislation is a form of literary composition. But construction is not an abstract process equally valid for every composition, not even
for every composition whose meaning must be judicially ascertained. The nature
of the composition demands awareness of certain pre-suppositions. For instance,
the words in a constitution may carry different meanings from the same words
in a statute precisely because "it is a constitution we are expounding." The reach
of this consideration was indicated by Mr. Justice Holmes in language that remains fresh no matter how often repeated:

> When we are dealing with words that also are a constituent act, like the Constitu-
> tion of the United States, we must realize that they have called into life a being

the development of which could not have been foreseen completely by the most gifted of its begetters. It was enough for them to realize or to hope that they had created an organism; it has taken a century and has cost their successors much sweat and blood to prove that they created a nation. The case before us must be considered in the light of our whole experience and not merely in that of what was said a hundred years ago. *Missouri v. Holland,* 252 U.S. 416, 433.

And so, the significance of an enactment, its antecedents as well as its later history, its relation to other enactments, all may be relevant to the construction of words for one purpose and in one setting but not for another. Some words are confined to their history; some are starting points for history. Words are intellectual and moral currency. They come from the legislative mint with some intrinsic meaning. Sometimes it remains unchanged. Like currency, words sometimes appreciate of depreciate in value.

"Proliferation of Purpose"

You may have observed that I have not yet used the word "intention." All these years I have avoided speaking of the "legislative intent," and I shall continue to be on my guard against using it. The objection to "intention" was indicated in a letter by Mr. Justice Holmes which the recipient kindly put at my disposal:

> Only a day or two ago—when counsel talked of the intention of a legislature, I was indiscreet enough to say I don't care what their intention was. I only want to know what the words mean. Of course the phrase often is used to express a conviction not exactly thought out—that you construe a particular clause or expression by considering the whole instrument and any dominant purposes that it may express. In fact intention is a residuary clause intended to gather up whatever other aids there may be to interpretation beside the particular words and the dictionary.

If that is what the term means, it is better to use a less beclouding characterization. Legislation has an aim; it seeks to obviate some mischief, to supply an inadequacy, to effect a change of policy, to formulate a plan of government. That aim, that policy is not drawn, like nitrogen, out of the air; it is evinced in the language of the statute, as read in the light of other external manifestations of purpose. That is what the judge must seek and effectuate, and he ought not be led off the trail by tests that have overtones of subjective design. We are not concerned with anything subjective. We do not delve into the mind of legislators or their draftsmen, or committee members.

Unhappily, there is no table of logarithms for statutory construction. No item of evidence has a fixed or even average weight. One or another may be decisive in one set of circumstances, while of little value elsewhere. A painstaking, detailed report by a Senate Committee bearing directly on the immediate question may settle the matter. A loose statement even by a chairman of a committee, made impromptu in the heat of debate, less informing in cold type than when heard on the floor, will hardly be accorded the weight of an encyclical.

Spurious use of legislative history must not swallow the legislation so as to give point to the quip that only when legislative history is doubtful do you go to the statute. While courts are no longer confined to the language, they are still confined by it. Violence must not be done to the words chosen by the legislature. Unless indeed no doubt can be left that the legislature has in fact used a private code, so that what appears to be violence to language is merely respect to special usage. In the end, language and external aids, each accorded the authority deserved in the circumstances, must be weighed in the balance of judicial judgment. Only if its premises are emptied of their human variables, can the process of statutory construction have the precision of a syllogism. We cannot avoid what Mr. Justice Cardozo deemed inherent in the problem of construction, making "a choice between uncertainties. We must be content to choose the lesser." *Burnet v. Guggenheim,* 288 U.S. 280, 288.

18

Congress, Court, and Control
of Delegated Power

CARL MCGOWAN
Judge, Court of Appeals, District of Columbia Circuit

The court on which I sit is one which, for a number of reasons including its location, is primarily concerned with civil litigation involving the federal government. That litigation derives in substantial part from Acts of Congress that broadly delegate power to the executive departments and to agencies and commissions of varying degrees of independence. With seemingly acute awareness of their breadth, Congress has, for some years now, been accompanying these delegations of power with express provisions for judicial review.[1] It is as if sensitivity to the fact that it has failed to define its grants of authority with precision has prompted Congress to rely on the courts to keep the delegatees within proper bounds in their execution of the trusts reposed in them.[2]

A case which heavily engaged the energies of our court not long ago provides a concrete example.[3] In 1970 Congress amended the Clean Air Act to empower the Administrator of the Environmental Protection Agency to regulate gasoline additives causing automobile exhaust emissions that, in the words of the statute, "will endanger the public health or welfare."[4] The Administrator initiated informal rulemaking to determine what limitations should be placed by him on the use of lead additives. He issued proposals upon which he invited comments from the public, which were forthcoming in extensive degree. Under the regulations as finally issued, the use of lead in all gasoline was directed to be phased down over a five-year period to a figure that represented a very substantial decline in the production by the chemical industry of lead additives.

The Clean Air Act provided that judicial review of regulations issued under this provision should be exclusively in the United States Court of Appeals for the District of Columbia Circuit.[5] Since the Administrator founded his regulation upon the informal rulemaking contemplated by the Administrative Procedure Act, the standard for our review was whether the action taken was "arbitrary, capricious, an abuse of discretion, or otherwise not in accordance with law."[6]

The industry challenged the action in two ways. First, it argued that the Administrator twice misinterpreted the Act by (1) insisting that an administrative conclusion that lead emissions "present a significant risk of harm to the health of urban populations, particularly to the health of city children,"[7] met the statute's "will endanger" requirement, and (2) asserting that the statutory language did not require a determination that the lead emissions, alone and of themselves, cause the risk. In other words, this first claim was that Congress meant that a showing must be made that the lead caused emissions *would* in fact cause harm, rather than that they, together with other sources of lead poisoning, might present a "significant risk" of harm. Second, the industry contended that the evidence compiled in the administrative proceeding did not make out the requisite proof under either interpretation.

I do not set forth these contentions with any thought of speaking to their merits. That was done both by a 2 to 1 panel decision in favor of the challengers, and later by a 5 to 4 decision of the court *en banc* going the other way, which the Supreme Court chose not to review. What I do wish to examine is the *nature* of the determinations which the court was compelled to make.

The statutory interpretation question was essentially whether Congress contemplated actual danger or merely possible danger as the condition precedent to the imposition of regulation. One might have thought that a Congress prepared to authorize the Administrator to eliminate a major industry which had existed since 1923 would have made itself crystal clear, one way or the other, on that vital question. Votes for or against the bill might well have turned on which approach was taken. In any event, it at least might be said that when the Administrator chose to put the interpretation he did upon the statutory language, Congress was in a better position than the court to say whether the regulation embodying that interpretation reflected the purposes of Congress. But, of course, the interpretation of statutes in the adversary context of a lawsuit is, under our legal tradition, for the courts.

In thinking about the second question posed to the court, that of whether the evidence compiled supported the Administrator's ruling, it is important to recall the procedural components of informal rulemaking: public notice of the proposed regulation, an opportunity to submit written comments about it, an opportunity to urge orally one's views upon the Administrator if, as was true in this case, he chooses to provide that opportunity, and the issuance by the Administrator of a "concise general statement" of the reasons why he had decided to issue the regulation in its final form.[8] There is no cross-examination of witnesses or of the sponsors of documentary material. The Administrator makes no findings of fact drawn from the record, as he would in formal rulemaking or adjudicatory proceedings.

Thus, the record in informal rulemaking typically consists of a mass of letters, memoranda of experts looking in different directions, research theses, magazine articles, newspaper clippings, and anything else anyone happens to mail in. This record tends to resemble nothing so much as the record made in a legislative committee hearing on a proposed bill. By the same token, it can be said with some plausibility that the vote of a judge scrutinizing that record resembles nothing so much as the vote for or against a bill by a conscientious legislator who has done his homework.[9]

In such circumstances, the conclusional labels to be affixed by the court—"arbitrary," "capricious," "an abuse of discretion," or "discriminatory"—can slide very easily into the same value judgments as are made by legislators in casting their votes, or by administrators in formulating their statements of reasons for doing what they are doing.

In the leaded gasoline case, the scientific evidence was conceded by all to fall short of conclusiveness; indeed, it was taken by both the Administrator and the majority of our court to fall within what we have, in another connection, called "the frontiers of scientific knowledge," that is to say, a zone where anything even approaching certainty is not possible in the present state of the art.[10] In such a case—and the Congress in recent years has been addressing itself to many such cases—the question inevitably recurs as to whether judicial review is an adequate protection against the abdication by Congress of substantive policy making in favor of broad delegation of what may essentially be the power to make laws and not merely to administer them. If it be concluded that it is not feasible for Congress to function without some broad delegation, should judicial review of agency action thereunder seek to do more than to assure that the procedures prescribed for implementing such delegated authority afford the fundamentals of procedural due process, and have been scrupulously followed?[11] If it does not do more, of course, the logical outcome of such review will be that, in the absence of procedural defect, the agency action, be it affirmative or negative, is left undisturbed.

Judicial Review of Delegative Legislation

Speculations of this nature have recently prompted suggestions that the times may be ripe for revival of the doctrine of unconstitutional delegation of legislative power.[12] This doctrine originally purported to prevent Congress from delegating any of its law-making authority to the executive.[13] Despite broad statements to this effect, however, the Supreme Court has never invalidated a congressional enactment on so sweeping a ground—nor could it today without, in Professor Davis's words, invalidating "approximately one hundred percent of federal legislation conferring rulemaking authority on federal agencies. . . ."[14]

In fact, until 1935, the Court had never invoked *any* form of the doctrine to strike down an Act of Congress, and it has not done so since that year of stormy confrontation between the Court and the two other branches. In the doctrine's several months of vibrancy in 1935, the Court required that Congress provide standards to channel and confine agency discretion.[15] As reformulated in later cases upholding broad delegations, however, this requirement of congressional standards has mandated merely that the statute and any legislation accompanying or related to it, its explicit or reasonably discernable implicit purposes, and its history, taken together, provide the Administrator with sufficiently clear guidance so that a court in reviewing the Administrator's action can "ascertain whether the will of Congress has been obeyed."[16]

Although the nondelegation principle continues to have greater utility at the state level,[17] this brief synopsis of its ambivalent history suggests why it is widely thought to be "moribund" with respect to Acts of Congress.[18] At the beginning of the oral argument to the *en banc* court in the leaded gasoline case,[19] I observed to one very able counsel for the industry that the issue of unconstitutional delegation had not been raised. His response was to say, in effect, that I knew as well as he how little chance that approach was likely to have in view of the Supreme Court's treatment of the doctrine over the past 40 years.[20] Of course, what lay behind his answer—and the Supreme Court cases to which he referred—was a recognition that Congress, in an increasingly complex and changing world, is called upon to deal with subject matter that is novel and imprecise, and for which it is frequently ill-equipped to do more than to paint with a broad brush, leaving the details to be filled in by less unwieldy and more technically expert administrative authority.[21]

Nonetheless, I believe that distinctions can be, and in fact have been, made by legislators and commentators between such situations and those in which Congress fixes upon broad delegation for reasons of internal political maneuver or as an escape from having to stand up and be counted.[22] Some of the state cases suggest that courts can distinguish in a principled manner between levels of constitutionally permissible delegation by referring to the amenability of the subject matter of the legislation to precise, lay-written standards.[23] This approach could do much to augment the quality—and effectiveness as a check against arbitrary or unauthorized administrative action—of judicial review in the occasional cases in which Congress debates alternative policy choices entirely feasible for it to make, but chooses instead to compromise the matter by delegation in order to get a bill enacted[24] or to avert the assumption of direct responsibility for a result in a controversial area.[25] In such cases, there would be a subversion of the democratic decision making contemplated by the Constitution, as well as an imposition upon both the administrative process and judicial review.[26] Just as the Supreme Court jolted the Congress in 1935 with its reminder that there are constitutional limitations upon the delegation of law-making powers, so it may be that a similar shock treatment will again be administered when the issue is raised in the right case.

Judicial invalidation in appropriate cases, although helpful in curbing legislative irresponsibility, is no answer for the growing number of subjects pressing for congressional attention in which breadth of discretion in administration is a legitimate aid to the law-making process. The prospect, however, of a delegated discretion that is wholly uncontrolled appears not to be acceptable to the public at large, since it would leave them, as John Adams thought, vulnerable in both mind and body. The question thus becomes one of the quarter from which control is to come, and the means by which it is to be exercised.

The pattern of the recent past has been that of a Congress largely content to rely upon the courts. It is true that some strong joint congressional committees, notably in the fields of taxation and atomic energy,[27] have closely and powerfully monitored the administration of statutes. These committees, however, represent the exception rather than the rule. In general, the courts have been left as the primary refuge for those complaining of unauthorized extensions of executive power or irrationality in its exercise.[28]

More recently, however, there have been signs of a reviving congressional desire to retain for itself a more direct control over the exercises of powers devolved by it upon the administrators.[29] Instead of advocating less delegation of power, this congressional interest in control of administrative action has been manifested primarily in the many legislative proposals, patterned after a practice long used in England, that would give either house of Congress a veto power over rules and regulations promulgated under authority already delegated.[30]

Looking in a different direction, although with similar motives, another school of thought in Congress favors not the one-house veto but legislation that would drastically enlarge the scope of review of administrative action by the courts.[31]

A final proposal, not emanating from Congress itself and perhaps therefore less likely to capture its support, would use a three-step procedure: first, the President would be given a role in reviewing, revising, and even rejecting administrative action — even that of the traditionally "independent" regulatory agencies; Congress would then be given commensurate powers to supervise the President in this endeavor; and, finally, the courts would afford expedited review of any action that results from this process.

The lessons of almost 200 years of a federal government founded upon the principle of the separation of powers are surely that it is both unwise and impracticable to depend too heavily upon any one of the branches for the total solution to the problem of administrative accountability. Rather, the solution should come from the individual efforts of all three, functioning within their appropriate constitutional spheres. A Congress genuinely concerned about delegated power has one effective contribution that it, and only it, can make — the identification and definition, as precisely as possible, of that power, and of the standards to be observed in its exercise.

NOTES

1. See, e.g., H.R. Rep. No. 1656, at 5, reprinted in [1976] *U.S. Code Cong. & Ad. News,* at 6125. ("For years almost every regulatory statute enacted by Congress has contained provisions authorizing Federal courts to review the legality of administrative action that has adversely affected private citizens.")

2. This legislative thought process may once have been largely subconscious. More recently, however, members of Congress have shown more awareness of the correlation between expansive delegation and a need for broad judicial review. Some of these members purport to perceive that the courts are themselves cutting back on the availability of such review (using, for example, the doctrine of standing); they have thereby felt compelled to advocate those new means of controlling the exercise of delegated powers that are the subject of this lecture. See, e.g., Letter from Rep. Levitas to Members of Congress (20 September 1976), reprinted in 122 *Cong. Rec.* 1110.678 (daily ed. 21 September 1976); *Congressional Review of Administrative Rulemaking: Hearings Before the Subcomm. on Administrative Law and Government Relations of the House Comm. on the Judiciary,* 94th Cong., 1st Sess. 387 (1975) (remarks of Rep. Mince). Hereinafter referred to as *Congressional Review Hearings.*

3. *Ethyl Corp. v. EPA,* 541 F.2d 1 (D.C. Cir.) (en banc), *cert. denied,* 426 U.S. 941.

4. Clean Air Act, § 211(c)(1)(A), 42 U.S.C. § 1875f-6c(c)(1)(a) (1970).

5. Ibid. § 307(b)(1), 42 U.S.C. § 1857h-5(b)(1) (1970).

6. Administrative Procedure Act, §§ 4, 10, 5 U.S.C. §§ 553, 706(2)(A) (1970).

7. 38 Fed. Reg. 33.734 (1973).

8. Administrative Procedure Act, § 4, 5 U.S.C. § 553 (1970).

9. Under one view, ably espoused on the District of Columbia Circuit by Judge Leventhal, broad congressional delegations to agencies accompanied by judicial review provisions, in a sense, also delegations of part of the legislative function of the courts: "In the case of legislative enactments, the sole responsibility of courts is constitutional due process review. In the case of agency decision making the courts have an additional responsibility set by Congress. Congress has been willing to delegate its legislative powers broadly — and courts have upheld such delegation — because there is court review to assure that the agency exercises the delegated power within statutory limits, and that it fleshes out objectives within those limits by an administration that is not irrational or discriminatory." See *Ethyl Corp. v. EPA,* 541 F.2d at 68 (separate statement of Leventhal, J.). Judge Leventhal has argued that to carry out its role a reviewing court should engage in "enough steeping in technical matters" to allow a modest substantive review of administrative action. *Portland Cement Ass'n. v. Ruckelshaus,* 486 F.2d 375, 402 (D.C. Cir. 1973), *cert. denied,* 417 U.S. 921 (1974). But see *Ethyl Corp. v. EPA,* 541 F.2d at 66 (Bazelon, C.J., concurring); *International Harvester Co. v. Ruckelshaus,* 478 F.2d 615, 652 (D.C. Cir. 1973) (Bazelon, C.J., concurring).

10. *Industrial Union Dep't. v. Hodgeson,* 499 F.2d 467, 474 (D.C. Cir. 1974), quoted in *Ethyl Corp. v. EPA,* 541 F.2d at 26-27, 47 n.97.

11. "[I]n cases of great technological complexity, the best way for courts to guard against unreasonable or erroneous administrative decisions is not for the judges themselves to scrutinize the technical merits of each decision. Rather, it is to establish a decision-making process which assures a reasoned decision that can be held up to the scrutiny of the scientific community and the public." See *International Harvester Co. v. Ruckelshaus,* 478 F.2d 615, 652 (D.C. Cir. 1973) (Bazelon, C.J., concurring). See also *Industrial Union Dep't. v. Hodgson,* 499 F.2d 467, 474-475 n.18 (D.C. Cir. 1974). ("Where existing methodology or research in a new area of regulation is deficient, the agency necessarily enjoys broad discretion to attempt to formulate a solution to the best of its ability on the basis of available information.")

12. E.g., Wright Book Review, 81 *Yale Law Journal* 575, 582-586 (1972). See sources cited in W. Gellhorn and C. Byse, *Administrative Law* 78 n.4 (6th ed., Mineola, N.Y.:

Foundation Press, 1974). But see K. Davis, *Administrative Law of the Seventies* § 2.17, at 38-39 (Rochester: Lawyer Cooperative, 1976); R. Stewart, "The Reformation of American Administrative Law," 88 *Harvard Law Review* 1667, 1695 (1975). Although Professors Davis and Stewart both oppose any efforts to revitalize the doctrine as a means of invalidating congressional enactments, both have proposed alternative legal rules aimed at accomplishing the goals ascribed to the unconstitutional-delegation doctrine. Under Professor Davis's proposal, the courts would require that the agencies, rather than Congress, devise standards to guide their decision making and would insist that the agencies adhere to those standards. See K. Davis, supra. § 2.00, at 20-21; Davis, "A New Approach to Delegation," 36 *University of Chicago Law Review* 713 (1969). Professor Stewart has advanced a more modest approach, which would require that a clear statement of legislative purpose accompany each delegation of congressional authority.

13. E.g., *Field v. Clark*, 143 U.S. 649, 692 (1982). ("That Congress cannot delegate legislative power to the President is a principle universally recognized as vital to the integrity and maintenance of the system of government ordained by the Constitution.") This formulation of the doctrine is still repeated in some state courts. E.g., *People v. Tibbitts*, 56 Ill.2d 56, 305 N.E.2d 152 (1973).

14. K. Davis, supra note 12, § 2.04, at 33.

15. Between January and May of 1935, the Court decided the only two cases that found delegations of power unconstitutionally broad. *Schecter Poultry Corp. v. United States*, 295 U.S. 495 (1935); *Panama Ref. Co. v. Ryan*, 293 U.S. 388 (1935). Both cases struck down provisions in the National Industrial Recovery Act, ch. 90, 48 Stat. 195 (1933), that gave the President certain powers to restrain what at the time was believed to be unhealthy competitive conditions in certain industries. Justice Cardozo alone dissented in *Panama*, but even he concurred with the unanimous court in *Schecter*, because "[t]he delegated power of legislation which has found expression in this code is not canalized within banks that keep it from overflowing." 295 U.S. at 551 (Cardozo, J., concurring).

16. *Yakus v. United States*, 321 U.S. 414, 425 (1944). See *Amalgamated Meat Cutters & Butcher Workmen v. Connolly*, 337 F.Supp. 737, 746-747 (D.D.C. 1971) (three-judge court).

Since 1935, the courts have been satisfied that the requisite guidance inheres in such phrases as "generally fair and equitable," *Yakus v. United States*, 321 U.S. 414, 427 (1944) (price controls), or "just and reasonable," *FPC v. Hope Natural Gas Co.*, 320 U.S. 591, 600 (1944) (natural gas rates), and even in statutes omitting any such terms because they, or similar ones, could be inferred from the events leading to the enactment of the facially standardless statutes in question. E.g., *Arizona v. California*, 373 U.S. 546 (1963) (standardless grant of authority to Secretary of Interior to determine rights to the waters of the Colorado River); *Amalgamated Meat Cutters & Butcher Workmen v. Connolly*, 337 F.Supp. 737 (D.D.C. 1971) (three-judge court) (grant of power to the President to establish wage controls omitted the phrase, usually buttressing such legislation, requiring that the controls be "fair and equitable").

17. See, e.g., cases discussed in J. Mashaw and R. Merrill, *Introduction to the American Public Law System* 213-223 (Indianapolis: Bobbs-Merrill, 1975).

18. *FPC v. New England Power Co.*, 415 U.S. 345, 353 (1974) (Marshall, J., concurring). ("This [nondelegation] doctrine is surely as moribound as the substantive due process approach of the same era . . . if not more so.") See *Congressional Review Hearings*, supra note 2, at 151, 152-154 (memorandum prepared by N. Gozansky and F. Sam-

ford). In fact, no more than seven years had elapsed after the modern doctrine of unconstitutional delegation was announced in 1935 before commentators purported to detect its almost total demise. See C. B. Nutting, "Congressional Delegations since the Schecter Case," 14 *Mississippi Law Journal* 350, 366-367 (1942).

19. *Ethyl Corp. v. EPA*, 541 F.2d 1 (D.C. Cir.) (en banc), *cert. denied*, 426 U.S. 941 (1976).

20. See *FPC v. New England Power Co.*, 415 U.S. 345, 353 n.1 (1974) (Marshall, J., dissenting), (quoting K. Davis, supra note 28, § 2.01). ("Lawyers who try to win cases by arguing that congressional delegations are unconstitutional almost invariably do more harm than good to their client's interests.")

21. See, e.g., L. Jaffe, *Judicial Control of Administrative Action* 37 (Boston: Little, Brown, 1965); Stewart, supra note 12, at 1695.

22. Recent statements by members of Congress themselves, remarking on the processes by which federal agencies are accorded such pervasive impact on the lives of most citizens, illustrate this distinction. Compare, for example, the statements of Congressmen Levitas and Flowers on the floor of the House of Representatives. Both were speaking in favor of the same legislation giving Congress the power to veto administrative regulations. Congressman Levitas noted that "Congress is far too lax in delegating authority broadly and without guidelines to administrative agencies. When hard decisions have to be made, we pass the buck to the agencies with vaguely worded statutes. Who can, or should, vote against safe cars, clean air, or nondiscrimination. But when the implementing regulations [are formulated] . . . , the actual benefit of safe cars, clean air, or nondiscrimination [may be] called into question." 122 *Cong. Rec.* H10.685 (daily ed. 1 September 1976). Congressman Flowers, on the other hand, supported congressional delegation when the "complexities of our day require that Government have the flexibility to meet varied demands and problems." Ibid., at H10.668.

Some commentators, while also suggesting the dichotomy suggested above, have argued that broad delegation is a positive necessity in both cases. E.g., R. Fuchs, "Introduction: Administrative Agencies and the Energy Problem," 47 *Indiana Law Journal* 606, 608 (1972); Stewart, supra note 12, at 1695-1696. Both Fuchs and Stewart feel that the political volatility and controversial nature of many issues would prevent the 535 members of Congress from ever reaching agreement on many major problems if specifically were required in their enactments.

23. E.g., *Clean Air Constituency v. California State Air Resources Bd.*, 11 Cal.3d 801, 518, 523 P.2d 617, 627, 114 Cal. Reptr. 577, 587 (1974). ("Although the breadth of the standard [guiding the delegation of authority] may vary with the subject matter of the legislation, it must not enable an administrative agency to exercise greater discretion than that which is necessary for the fulfillment of the Legislature's purpose.") See K. Davis, supra note 12, § 2.04, at 34 (cautiously approving this approach).

The federal courts are not strangers to this distinction between statutory subject matter imbued with technological or industrial complexities and that reflecting "common sense" policy decisions. Thus, the federal courts often use this deference to accord administrative interpretations of the same. E.g., *Addison v. Holly Hill Co.*, 322 U.S. 607, 618 (1944).

24. The delegation at issue in *Rodway v. United States Dep't. of Agriculture*, 514 F.2d 809 (D.C. Cir. 1975), provides an illustration. In that case, food stamp recipients asked the District of Columbia Circuit to decide whether the allotment system devised by the Department of Agriculture (DOA) fulfilled the statutory directive under 7 U.S.C.

§ 2013(a) (1970) that food stamp recipients be given "an opportunity to obtain a nutritionally adequate diet. . . ." 514 F.2d at 811.

The legislative history of this provision shows that the imprecise phrase, "nutritionally adequate," was chosen instead of several alternative and more specific proposals. These proposals would have fixed a month's allotment for a family of four at various points from $106 to $134 by focusing on one of two alternative allotment plans previously prepared by the DOA. The "nutritionally adequate" language was originally proposed by the Nixon Administration and was included in the bill passed by the House. There are some indications that the Administration and the House originally intended the phrase "nutritionally adequate" to be synonymous with the less generous of the two DOA plans—the so-called economy plan, which would have allotted $106 to a family of four. See, e.g., H.R. Rep. No. 1402, 91st Cong., 2d Sess. 31 (1970), reprinted in [1970] *U.S. Code Cong. & Ad. News* 6025, 6045 (dissenting views of Reps. Foley and Lowenstein). The Senate, however, precipitated a conference committee battle by adopting the DOA's so-called low-cost plan, which would have allotted $134 to a family of four. See *Conf. Rep. No.* 1793, 91st Cong., 2d Sess. 2 (1970), reprinted in [1970] *U.S. Code Cong. & Ad. News* 6051, 6052. At conference, the Senators proposed a compromise which would have "split the difference" between the two plans, allotting $120 for a family of four. 116 *Cong. Rec.* 44.441 (1970) (remarks of Sen. Miller). Although the House prevailed on the Senate to accept the "nutritionally adequate" language, by this time the phrase's meaning had become even less clear. The Senate agreed to the House language only after being assured that House supporters of the "nutritionally adequate" provision "did not care whether [the allotment for a family of four] cost $50, $100, or $150; whatever it cost [it] must provide for an adequate and nutritional diet." Ibid., at 44.440-441.

In light of the availability of the two DOA plans and other supporting data, see, e.g., Appendix to Appellant's Brief, *Rodway v. United States Dep't. of Agriculture,* 514 F.2d 809 (D.C. Cir. 1975), it can be seen that Congress itself had the ability to make an informed policy choice as to the exact amount of money the government should spend on upgrading the diets of the nation's low income citizens. The price of the Senate's hurried passage of the Conference Bill on the last day of 1971, however, was its decision to postpone that difficult political decision, leaving it for arguably less qualified (if only because not elected) administrators to make and judges to review.

25. See, e.g., 122 *Cong. Rec.* 1110.673 (daily ed. 21 September 1976) (remarks of Rep. Flowers): "We in the Congress pass myriad laws and pieces of legislation that go on the books, and we invest the agencies with all of this vast power to make rules and regulations, and then we stand back and say when our constituents are aggrieved or oppressed by various rules and regulations, 'Hey, it's not me. We didn't mean that. We passed this well-meaning legislation, and we intended for those people . . . to do exactly what we meant, and they did not do it.' "

26. "There are, of course, many regulatory issues which the President and Congress consider it politically safer not to address directly—issues on which they prefer to let the independent and politically unaccountable regulatory agencies take the inevitable political heat. This can hardly be claimed as a virtue of the present system, since an elected government ought not to be able to avoid responsibility for governing effectively." L. Cutler and D. Johnson, "Regulation and the Political Process," 84 *Yale Law Journal* 1315, 1380 (1975) (emphasis in original).

27. See, generally, W. Gellhorn and C. Byse, supra note 12 at 109-122.

28. See Stewart, supra note 12, at 1195. Some commentators have perceived a recent effort by the courts to replace strictly judicial and ad hoc control of administrative agencies with a system of judicially supervised and ongoing administrative self-control. Under this approach, agency action can be invalidated if the administrators have not established and followed procedural and substantive standards to guide and control their future decision making. Professor Davis has advanced this technique as a full-fledged alternative to the nondelegation doctrine. K. Davis, supra note 12, § 2.00, at 20-22; K. Davis, *Administrative Law Treatise* § 2.00-5 (Supp. 1970). For an application of this approach in a nondelegation doctrine case, see *Amalgamated Meat Cutters & Butcher Workmen v. Connolly*, 337 F.Supp. 737, 758 (D.D.C. 1971) (three-judge court).

Although this approach does achieve the nondelegation doctrine's goal of protecting citizens from arbitrary governmental action, it does less to accomplish the doctrine's other policies in aid both of the separation of powers and of principled judicial review of the accordance of agency action with the legislative will.

29. E.g., Congressional Review Hearings, supra note 18, at 162-163 (remarks of Rep. Blanchard) (arguing that Congress should "reassert power we have had all along in the Constitution and should have been exercising and really should never, never have relinquished").

30. See, e.g., H.R. 12.048, 94th Cong., 2d Sess. § 4a, 122 *Cong. Rec.* H10.667 (daily ed. 21 September 1976), reproduced. S. 1463, 95th Cong., 1st Sess., §§ 601-608 (1977).

31. E.g., S. 86, 95th Cong., 1st Sess. (1977). Senator Bumpers has championed this approach.

19

The Doctrine of Standing as an Element of the Separation of Powers

ANTONIN SCALIA
Judge, Court of Appeals, District of Columbia Circuit

The principle of separation of powers is not expressed in our Federal Constitution and yet appears throughout. It determined the very structure of the document, which successively describes where the legislative, executive, and judicial powers, respectively, shall reside.[1] Madison said of it, in *Federalist, No. 47,* that "no political truth is certainly of greater intrinsic value, or is stamped with the authority of more enlightened patrons of liberty."[2] And no less than five of the *Federalist Papers* were devoted to the demonstration that the principle was adequately observed in the proposed Constitution.[3]

The thesis of this chapter is that the judicial doctrine of standing is a crucial and inseparable element of that principle, whose disregard will inevitably produce — as it has during the past few decades — an overjudicialization of the processes of self-governance.[4] More specifically, I want to suggest that courts need not accord greater weight than they have in recent times to the traditional requirement that a plaintiff's alleged injury be a particularized one which sets him apart from the citizenry at large.

The Doctrine of Standing

The Supreme Court has described standing as "a sufficient stake in an otherwise justiciable controversy to obtain judicial resolution of that controversy."[5] In more pedestrian terms, it is an answer to the first question that is sometime rudely asked whenever one person complains of another's actions: "What's it to you?" The requirement of standing has been made part of American constitutional law through (for want of a better vehicle) the provision of Article III, sec. 2, which states that "the judicial Power shall extend" to certain "Cases" and "Controversies." There is no case or controversy, the reasoning has gone, when there are no adverse parties with personal interest in the matter.[6] Surely not a linguistically inevitable conclusion, but nonetheless an accurate description of the sort of business courts had traditionally entertained, and hence of the distinctive business to which they were presumably to be limited under the

Constitution. It is interesting how clear the proper role of the judiciary was thought to be. In *Federalist No. 48,* describing why the legislature is the most dangerous branch, Madison says the following:

> It is not unfrequently a question of real nicety in legislative bodies, whether the operation of a particular measure will, or will not, extend beyond the legislative sphere. On the other side, the executive power being restrained within a narrower compass, and being more simple in its nature, and the judiciary being described by landmarks still less uncertain, projects of usurpation by either of these departments would immediately betray and defeat themselves.[7]

Few modern commentators would find the landmarks delimiting the judicial role so clearly.[8] Indeed, by comparison, the limitations upon the mode and scope of operation of the legislative and executive branches are a model of definiteness.

The sea-change that has occurred in the judicial attitude toward the doctrine of standing—particularly as it affects judicial intrusion into the operations of the other two branches—is evident from comparing recent opinions with the first case in which the Supreme Court contemplated interference with high-level Executive activities, and avoided such interference only by interfering with a congressional enactment. In *Marbury v. Madison,*[9] the Court was concerned that its issuance of a *mandamus* to the Secretary of State, commanding delivery of Mr. Marbury's judicial commission, "should at first view be considered by some, as an attempt to intrude into the cabinet, and to intermeddle with the prerogatives of the executive."[10] The Court replied to that concern as follows:

> It is scarcely necessary for the court to disclaim all pretensions to such a jurisdiction. An extravagance, so absurd and excessive, could not have been entertained for a moment. The province of the court is, solely, to decide on the rights of individuals, not to inquire how the executive, or executive officers, perform duties in which they have a discretion.[11]

A not dissimilar attitude is reflected as late as 1944, in *Stark v. Wickard,* a Supreme Court standing decision (generous for its day) which permitted milk producers to challenge the lawfulness of a Department of Agriculture Milk Marketing Order:

> When . . . definite personal rights are created by federal statute, similar in kind to those customarily treated in courts of law, the silence of Congress as to judicial review is, at any rate, in the absence of an administrative remedy, not to be construed as a denial of authority to the aggrieved person to seek appropriate relief in the federal courts. . . . When Congress passes an act empowering administrative agencies to carry on governmental activities, the power of those agencies is circumscribed by the authority granted. This permits the courts to participate in law enforcement entrusted to administrative bodies *only to the extent necessary to protect justiciable individual rights against administrative action fairly beyond the granted powers.* . . . This is very far from assuming that the courts are the protec-

tion of the rights of the people. Congress and the Executive supervise the acts of administrative agents. . . . These branches have the resources and personnel to examine into the working of the various establishments to determine the necessary changes of function or management. But under Article III, Congress established courts to adjudicate cases and controversies as to claims of infringement of individual rights whether by unlawful action of private persons or by the exertion of unauthorized administrative power.[12]

Compare these descriptions of the "province of the court" with the opening paragraph of the 1971 Court of Appeals decision in the landmark *Calvert Cliffs* case, which was the beginning of the judiciary's long love affair with environmental litigation:

These cases are only the beginning of what promises to become a flood of new litigation—litigation seeking judicial assistance in protecting our natural environment. Several recently enacted statutes attest to the commitment of the government to control, at long last, the destructive engine of material "progress." But it remains to be seen whether the promise of this legislation will become a reality. Therein lies the judicial role. In these cases, we must for the first time interpret the broadest and perhaps most important of the recent statutes: the National Environmental Policy Act of 1969 (NEPA). We must assess claims that one of the agencies charged with its administration has failed to live up to the congressional mandate. Our duty, in short, is to see that important legislative purposes, heralded in the halls of Congress, are not lost or misdirected in the vast hallways of the federal bureaucracy.[13]

It would be a mistake to think that the difference between the first two opinions and the last represents merely the effect of legal realism—a healthy acknowledgement, after years of mind-clouding fiction, that the courts do indeed (in the 1980s as in 1803) assure the regularity of Executive action. It goes beyond that. The point is not whether they *do* it, but whether the doing of it is alone sufficient justification to invoke their powers; whether the doing of it is itself the "judicial role," or rather merely the incidental effect of what *Marbury v. Madison* took to be the judges' proper business—"solely, to decide on the rights of individuals." That there has been a change in function rather than merely in perception is suggested by comparing *Marbury v. Madison's* careful description of the individual interest of Mr. Marbury, and *Stark v. Wickard's* description of "what's in it" for the plaintiff milk producer, with *Calvert Cliffs'* description of the petitioners' interest. The last is easy to set forth, because it does not exist. From reading the opinion, one gets no idea whether the Calvert Cliffs' Coordinating Committee, which brought construction of the Calvert Cliffs nuclear generating plant to a halt, was composed of environmentalists or owners of land adjacent to the proposed plant of competing coal-generating power companies or was even, perish the thought, a front for the Corps of Engineers, which is reputed to prefer dams to atoms. For the 1971 court, the point was of no real consequence.

Recent Changes in the Doctrine

Having described the change, let me try to explain how and why it has occurred. At the outset, it is necessary to take note of a peculiar characteristic of standing: the fact that its existence or nonexistence is largely within the control of Congress. It is universally agreed, for what it is worth, that standing requires the assertion of a legal wrong. But legal injury is by definition no more than the violation of a legal right; and legal rights can be created by the legislature.

Thus, whether I have standing to complain of my neighbor's erection of a gas station in violation of zoning codes, depends upon whether the legislature has given *me personally* a right to be free of that action or has rather left zoning enforcement (like the enforcement of parking limitations on the street in front of my house) exclusively to public authorities.

The Supreme Court has chosen to take account of this element of legislative control over standing by splitting the doctrine into two separate parts. The first part consists of "prudential limitations of standing" allegedly imposed by the Court itself, subject to elimination by the Court or by Congress. This part explains those numerous situations, such as the zoning example just given, in which standing once denied will later be acknowledged, after passage of a statute, removing the prudential bar. The second part is the constitutional "core" of standing, that is, a minimum requirement of injury in fact which not even Congress can eliminate.[14] Personally, I find this distinction unsatisfying — not least because it leaves unexplained the Court's source of authority for simply granting or denying standing as its prudence might dictate. As I would prefer to view the matter, the Court must always hear the case of a litigant who asserts the violation of a legal right.

In some cases, the existence of such a right is, on the basis of our common law traditions, entirely clear — as is the case, for example, where the plaintiff asserts that a governmental benefit specifically directed to him by name is wrongfully withheld. (That was the sort of right asserted in *Marbury v. Madison*.)[15] In other cases, however, the legislative intent to create a legal right is much more problematic — for example, when Congress requires the Executive to implement a general program (e.g., environmental protection) which will enhance the welfare of many individuals.

In such cases (as I view the matter) the courts apply the various "prudential" factors, not by virtue of their own inherent authority to expand or constrict standing, but rather as a set of presumptions derived from common law tradition designed to determine whether a legal right exists. Thus, when the legislature explicitly *says* that a private right exists, this so-called prudential inquiry is precluded. Ultimately, however (as I have already indicated and will discuss in more detail shortly), there is a limit upon even the power of Congress to convert generalized benefits into legal rights — and that is the limitation imposed by the so-called core requirement of standing. It is a limitation,

I would assert, only upon the *congressional* power to confer standing, and not upon the courts—since the courts *have* no such power to begin with.

In any event, using the Supreme Court's own terminology for the moment, federal courts have displayed a great readiness in recent years to discern a congressional elimination of traditional "prudential" standing barriers with regard to challenges of federal executive action. First, existing judicial review provisions in substantive statutes were given a new breadth by interpretation. For example, in the famous *Scenic Hudson* case, involving the Federal Power Commission's approval of the Storm King hydroelectric project, the Court of Appeals for the Second Circuit found that the old Federal Power Act provision according a right of review of FPC action to "aggrieved" parties included "those who by their activities and conduct have exhibited a special interest" in "the aesthetic, conservational, and recreational aspects of power development."[16] Such a statement would have been unthinkable in the 1940s, much less when the Federal Power Act was passed.

An even more important development has been the interpretation of the Administrative Procedure Act to create liberalized judicial review provision where none existed before. It is worth a few moments to explain that development, which has been of enormous consequence. The judicial review provision of the 1947 Administrative Procedure Act stated that "any person suffering *legal* wrong because of any agency action, or adversely affected or aggrieved by such action *within the meaning of any relevant statute,* shall be entitled to judicial review thereof."[17] A "legal" wrong, of course, could only mean a wrong already cognizable in the courts—that is, one as to which standing already existed pursuant to traditional principles.[18] And the phrase "adversely affected or aggrieved . . . within the meaning of any relevant statute" was an obvious reference to various substantive statutes which permitted any person "adversely affected or aggrieved" to sue, and thereby broadened the traditional rules in those particular fields.[19] (Quite obviously, one cannot be "adversely affected or aggrieved within the meaning of a . . . statute" that does not contain those—or at least substantially similar—words.[20] Just as it would make no sense to speak of one "defamed within the meaning of the Constitution," since the Constitution does not contain the word "defamed.")

This evident meaning is supported by authoritative portions of the legislative history—notably, the statement of Attorney General Clark,[21] quoted in the floor debate by Senator McCarran, the Senate Floor manager and chief architect of the legislation,[22] to the effect that the review provision "reflects existing law." It is also supported by the Attorney General's *Manual on the Administrative Procedure Act* (1947), "a contemporaneous interpretation . . . given some deference by [the Supreme] Court because of the role played by the Department of Justice in drafting the legislation,"[23] which indicates that the provision was "a restatement of existing law."[24]

Through the 1960s, most of the cases adopted this plain interpretation of the statute.[25] They were repudiated by the Supreme Court's decisions, both issued the same day, in *Association of Data Processing Service Organizations, Inc. v. Camp*[26] and *Barlow v. Collins*.[27] These decisions read "adversely affected or aggrieved within the meaning of a relevant statute" to mean no more than "adversely affected or aggrieved in a respect which the statute sought to prevent." In other words, the reference to existing liberalized statutory review provisions was converted into merely a requirement that the plaintiff be within the "zone of interests" that the statute seeks to protect.[28] A grandfathering of existing standing was thus transmogrified into an affirmative grant of standing in (to use the words of the D.C. Circuit) "all situations in which a party who is in fact aggrieved seeks review, regardless of a lack of legal right or specific statutory language."[29]

It is difficult to exaggerate the effect which this interpretation of the "adversely affected or aggrieved" portion of the APA has had upon the ability of the courts to review administrative action. For these agency actions covered by the APA,[30] it effectively eliminated the difference in liberality of standing between so-called statutory review (i.e., review under generous standing provisions of particular substantive statutes such as the Federal Power Act) and so-called nonstatutory review (i.e., review on the basis of traditional, more restrictive notions of "legal wrong," through the use of common-law writs such as injunction and mandamus). In fact, the Court's interpretation of the APA had the weird effect of precisely *reversing* the preexisting scheme, causing many statutory review provisions to constrict, rather than expand, the ability to seek review that would otherwise be available. Thus, when the Surface Mining Control and Reclamation Act of 1977 says that review of regulations can be sought by "any person who participated in the administrative proceedings and who is aggrieved by the action of the Secretary,"[31] it is *denying* rather than *according* judicial review—that is, denying it to those "aggrieved persons" who did not participate in the administrative proceedings.

How diminutive the new APA requirements of standing may be is apparent from the famous *SCRAP* case,[32] which challenged the ICC's failure to prepare an environmental impact statement before it permitted a nationwide railroad freight surcharge to take effect. The suit was brought by a group of Georgetown Law School students, who assertedly used park and forest areas, which areas assertedly would be rendered less desirable by reason of increased litter, which increase assertedly would result from decline in the use of recyclable goods, which decline assertedly would follow from a rise in the cost of such goods, which rise assertedly would be produced by the freight surcharge. And if that were not harm enough, the aggrieved plaintiffs also averred that each of them "breathes the air within the Washington metropolitan area and the area of his legal residence and that this air has suffered increased pollution caused by the modified rate structure."[33] The Supreme Court held that these injuries were held adequate to support the suit. Indeed, the Court intimated, with respect to this governmental action "all who breathe [the country's] air"[34] could sue.

Standing and the Separation of Powers

Thus far I have addressed the Court's progressive elimination of the so-called prudential limitations upon standing. Inevitably, I suppose, the "core" element —the portion that not even Congress itself could eliminate—came to be narrowed as well. The major development in this regard was the Court's 1968 opinion in *Flast v. Cohen*,[35] which gave a federal taxpayer standing to challenge, on establishment clause grounds, federal expenditures that would assist denominational schools. Never before had an improper expenditure of federal funds been held to "injure" a federal taxpayer in such fashion as to confer standing to sue. And the reason, I would assert, is that never before had the doctrine of standing been severed from the principle of separation of powers. The Court wrote in *Flast* as follows:

> The "gist of the question of standing" is whether the party seeking relief has "alleged such a personal stake in the outcome of the controversy as to assure that concrete adverseness which sharpens the presentation of issues upon which the court so largely depends for illumination of difficult constitutional questions." *Baker v. Carr*, 369 U.S. 186, 204 (1962). . . . So stated, the standing requirement is closely related to, although more general than, the rule that federal courts will not entertain friendly suits, . . . or those which are feigned or collusive in nature. . . .
>
> The question whether a particular person is a proper party to maintain the action does not, by its own force, raise separation of powers problems related to judicial interference in areas committed to other branches of the Federal Government. Such problems arise, if at all, only from the substantive issues the individual seeks to have adjudicated. Thus, in terms of Article III limitations on federal court jurisdiction, the question of standing is related only to whether the dispute sought to be adjudicated will be presented in an adversary context and in a form historically viewed as capable of judicial resolution.[36]

Standing, in other words, is only meant to assure that the courts can do their work well, and not to assure that they keep out of affairs better left to the other branches.

I must note at the outset (although it has been said often before[37]) that if the purpose of standing is "to assure that concrete adverseness which sharpens the presentation of issues," the doctrine is remarkably ill designed for its end. Often the best adversaries are national organizations such as the NAACP or the American Civil Liberties Union that have a keen interest in the abstract question at issue in the case, but no "concrete injury in fact" whatever. Yet the doctrine of standing clearly excludes them, unless they can attach themselves to some particular individual who happens to have some personal interest (however minor) at stake.[38]

Nor is it true, as *Flast* suggests, that the doctrine cannot possibly have any bearing upon the allocation of power among the branches since it excludes only *persons* and not *issues* from the courts. This overlooks the fact that if all persons who could conceivably raise a particular issue are excluded, the issue is excluded as well. *Flast* itself demonstrates the point. If the determination of whether a particular federal expenditure constitutes an establishment of religion cannot be made the business of the courts at the instance of a federal taxpayer, it is difficult to imagine who else could possibly bring it there. The determination of compliance with that constitutional provision would be left entirely to the legislative and executive branches,[39] just as the denial of taxpayer standing has left to those branches the determination of compliance with the constitutional requirement that "a regular Statement and Account of the Receipts and Expenditures of all public Money . . . be published from time to time."[40]

Even if it were true, moreover, that the doctrine of standing never excludes issues entirely from the courts, it would still have an enormous effect upon the relationship among the branches. The degree to which the courts become converted into political forums depends not merely upon what issues they are permitted to address, but also upon *when* and *at whose instance* they are permitted to address them. As Tocqueville observed:

> It will be seen . . . that by leaving it to the private interest to censure the law, and by intimately uniting the trial of the law with the trial of an individual, legislation is protected from wanton assaults and from the daily aggressions of party spirit. The errors of the legislator are exposed only to meet a real want; and it is always a positive and appreciable fact that must serve as the basis of a prosecution.[41]

The great change that has occurred in the role of the courts in recent years results in part from their ability to address issues that were previously considered beyond their ken. But in at least equal measure, in my opinion, it results from their ability to address both new and old issues promptly at the behest of almost anyone who has an interest in the outcome. It is of no use to draw the courts into a public policy dispute after the battle is over, or after the enthusiasm that produced it has waned. The *sine qua non* for emergence of the courts as an equal player with the executive and legislative branches in the formulation of public policy was the assurance of prompt access to the courts by those interested in conducting the debate. The full-time public interest law firm, as permanently in place as the full-time congressional lobby, became a widespread phenomenon only in the last few decades, not because prior to that time the courts could not reach issues profoundly affecting public policy, but rather because prior to that time the ability to draw them into those issues at will (to make "wanton assaults," to use Tocqueville's pejorative characterization) was drastically circumscribed. The change has been effected by a number of means, including such apparently unrelated developments as the virtual elimination of restrictions against champerty and maintenance (so that the cause may now more readily seek a victim to represent), alteration in the doctrine of ripeness (so that suits once deemed premature can be entertained immediately), and—to return to the point—alteration in the doctrine of standing.

ANTONIN SCALIA

The Separation of Powers and
the Rights of Individuals

Having established, I hope, that the doctrine of standing does affect the separation of powers, I turn to the inquiry of the manner in which it does so and when it is most reasonable. Is standing functionally related to the distinctive role that we expect the courts to perform? The question is not of purely academic interest, because if there is a functional relationship it may have some bearing upon how issues of standing are decided in particular cases.

There is, I think, a functional relationship, which can best be described by saying that the law of standing roughly restricts courts to their traditional, undemocratic role of protecting individuals and minorities against impositions of the majority, and excludes them from the (even more undemocratic) role of prescribing how the other two branches should function in order to serve the interests *of the majority itself.* Thus, when an individual who is the very *object* of a law's requirement or prohibition seeks to challenge it, he always has standing. That is the classic case of the individual against the majority, and the court will not pause to inquire whether the grievance is a "generalized" one.

Contrast that classic form of court challenge with the increasingly frequent administrative law cases in which the plaintiff is complaining of an agency's unlawful *failure* to impose a requirement or prohibition upon *someone else.* Such a failure harms the plaintiff, by depriving him, as a citizen, of governmental acts which the Constitution and laws require. But that harm alone is, so to speak, a *majoritarian* one. The plaintiff may *care* more about it; he may be a more ardent proponent of constitutional regularity or of the necessity of the governmental act that has been wrongfully omitted. But that does not establish that he has been harmed distinctively—only that he assesses the harm as more grave, which is a fair subject for democratic debate in which he may persuade the rest of us. Unless the plaintiff can show some respect in which he is harmed *more* than the rest of us (for example, he is a worker in the particular plant where the Occupational Safety and Health Administration has wrongfully waived legal safety requirements) he has not established any basis for concern that the majority is suppressing or ignoring the rights of a minority that wants protection, and thus has not established the prerequisite for judicial intervention.

That explains, I think, why "concrete injury"—an injury apart from the mere breach of the social contract, so to speak, affected by the very fact of unlawful government action—is the indispensable prerequisite of standing. Only that injury can separate the plaintiff from all the rest of us who also claim benefit of the social contract, and can thus entitle him to some special protection from the democratic manner in which we ordinarily run our social-contractual affairs. Of course concrete injury is a necessary but not necessarily sufficient condition. The plaintiff must establish not merely minority status, but minority status relevant to the particular governmental transgression that he seeks to correct. If the concrete harm that he will suffer as a consequence of the government's failure to observe the law is purely fortuitous—in the sense that the law was not specifically designed to avoid that harm, but rather for some other (usually more general) purpose—then the majority's failure to require observance of the law cannot be said to be directed *against him,* and his entitlement to the special protection of the courts disappears. That is the essential inquiry conducted, in the old cases, under the heading of whether the plaintiff who claimed standing had suffered any "legal wrong"; or whether he comes within the definition of "adversely affected" or "aggrieved" under the various substantive statutes that employ such terms; or whether he is within a substantive statute's protected "zone of interests" under the post-*Data Processing* distortion of the APA.

If I am correct that the doctrine of standing, as applied to challenges to governmental action, is an essential means of restricting the courts to their assigned role of protecting minority rather than majority interests, several consequences follow. First of all, a consequence of some theoretical interest but of relatively small (if not entirely nonexistent) practical effect: It would follow that not *all* "concrete injury" indirectly flowing from governmental action or inaction would be capable of supporting a congressional conferral of standing. One can conceive of such a concrete injury so universal in its reach that a congressional specification that the statute at issue was meant to preclude precisely that injury would nevertheless not suffice to mark out a subgroup of the body politic requiring judicial protection. For example, allegedly wrongful governmental action that affects "all who breathe." There is surely no reason to think that an alleged governmental default of such general impact would not receive fair consideration in the normal political process.

A more practical consequence of my analysis pertains not to congressional power to confer standing, but to judicial interpretation of congressional intent in that regard. If the doctrine does serve the separation of powers function I have suggested, then in the process of answering the question whether a "legal wrong" has been committed, or whether a person is "adversely affected or aggrieved," so that standing does exist, the courts should bear in mind the *object* of the exercise, and should not be inclined to assume congressional designation of a "minority group" so broad that it embraces virtually the entire population. I have in mind a recent case which found a congressional intent to confer standing upon a group no less expansive than all consumers of milk. It is hard to believe that the democratic process, if it works at all, could not and should not have been relied upon to protect interests of such an almost all-inclusive group.

But that is the ultimate question: Even if the doctrine of standing was once meant to restrict judges "solely, to decide on the rights of individuals," what is wrong with having them protect the rights of the majority as well? They have done so well at one, why not promote them to the other? The answer is that there is no reason to believe they will be any good at it. In fact, they have in a way been specifically *designed* to be bad at it—selected from the aristocracy of the highly educated, instructed to be governed by a body of knowledge that values abstract principle above concrete result, and (just in case any connection with the man in the street might subsist) removed from all accountability to the electorate. That is just perfect for a body that is supposed to protect the individual against the masses; it is just terrible (unless you are a monarchist) for a group that is supposed to decide what is good for the masses. Where the courts do enforce upon the executive branch—in the supposed interest of all the people—adherence to legislative policies that the political process itself would not enforce, they are likely, (despite the best of intentions) to be enforcing the political prejudices of their own class. Their greatest success in such an enterprise—ensuring strict enforcement of the environmental laws, not to protect particular minorities but for the benefit of all the people—met with approval in the classrooms of Cambridge and New Haven, but not in the factories of Detroit and the mines of West Virginia. It may well be, of course, that the judges know what is good for the people better than the people themselves, or that democracy simply does not permit the *genuine* desires of the people to be given effect; but those are not the premises under which our system operates.

Does what I have suggested mean that, so long as no minority interests are affected, "important legislative purposes, heralded in the halls of Congress, [can be] lost or misdirected in the vast hallways of the federal bureaucracy"? Of *course* it does—and a good thing, too. Where no peculiar harm to particular individuals or minorities is in question, lots of once-heralded programs ought to get lost or misdirected, in vast hallways or elsewhere. Yesterday's herald is today's bore—although we judges, in the seclusion of our chambers, may not be *au courant* enough to realize it. The ability to lose or misdirect laws can be said to be one of the prime engines of social change, and the prohibition against such carelessness is (believe it or not) profoundly conservative. Sunday blue laws, for example, were widely unenforced long before they were widely repealed—and had the first not been possible, the second might never have occurred.

Return to the Original Understanding

In the early 1970s—after *Flast* had pronounced that the doctrine of standing "does not, by its own force, raise separation of powers problems related to judicial interference in areas committed to other branches of the Federal Government,[42] and after *Data Processing, Barlow v. Collins,* and *SCRAP* had demonstrated the Supreme Court's apparent intent to operate on that assumption—the subject addressed here would have been of merely historical interest. It might have been retitled "Former Relevance of Standing to the Separation of Powers." Since that time, however, the Supreme Court's theory has returned to earlier traditions, and there may be reason to believe that its practice will as well. The dictum of *Flast* has been disavowed by opinions that explicitly acknowledge that standing and separation of powers are intimately related.[43] And the essential element that links the two—the requirement of *distinctive* injury not shared by the entire body politic—has been resurrected. *Flast* was essentially a repudiation of the famous case of *Frothingham v. Mellon*,[44] where the Court had disallowed a taxpayer suit to prevent expenditures in violation of the Commerce Clause, because it was not enough to allege an injury suffered in "some indefinite way in common with people generally."[45] More recent cases, however, such as *United States v. Richardson* and *Schlesinger v. Reservists Committee to Stop the War*, not only restore *Frothingham* to a place of honor[46] but quote the following passage from the venerable case of *Ex parte Levitt:*

> It is an established principle that to entitle a private individual to invoke the judicial power to determine the validity of executive or legislative action he must show that he has sustained or is immediately in danger of sustaining a direct injury as the result of that action and it is not sufficient that he has merely a general interest common to all members of the public.[47]

It is unlikely that this reversion to former theory will not ultimately entail some degree of reversion to former practice. Apparently, *Flast* has already been limited strictly to its facts,[48] and I anticipate that the Court's *SCRAP*-era willingness to discern breathlessly broad congressional grants of standing will not endure. There is already indication of this in opinions demonstrating a reluctance to "imply" in federal statutes rights of action against private parties,[49] which opinions have been cited in the context of suits against executive officials as well. Though the APA's phrase "within the meaning of a relevant statute" will not likely be restored to its original meaning, the effectively substituted phrase "adversely affected or aggrieved" (involving application of the "zone of interests" test) leaves plenty of room for maneuvering. I expect the direction of that maneuvering to be in the direction of separation of powers.

NOTES

1. U.S. Constitution, Art. I, Sec. I; Art. II, Sec. I; and Art. III, Sec. I.

2. J. Madison, *The Federalist,* No. 47, at 313, ed. C. Rossiter (New York: Modern Library, 1945).

3. See ibid., Nos. 47 (J. Madison), 48 (J. Madison), 49 (A. Hamilton or J. Madison), 50 (A. Hamilton or J. Madison), and 51 (A. Hamilton or J. Madison).

4. See, e.g., D. Horowitz, *The Courts and Social Policy* 4-5 (Washington, D.C.: Brookings Institution, 1977).

5. *Sierra Club v. Morton,* 405 U.S. 727, 731 (1972).

6. See *Muskrat v. United States,* 219 U.S. 346 (1911); *United States v. Ferreira,* 54 U.S. (13 How.) 40, 46 (1851); and *Hayburn's Case,* 2 U.S. (2 Dall.) 309 (1972).

7. *The Federalist,* supra note 2, No. 48, at 323.

8. Compare, e.g., L. Fuller, "The Forms and Limits of Adjudication," 92 *Harvard Law Review* 353 (1978), with A. Chayes, "The Role of the Judge in Public Law Litigation," 89 *Harvard Law Review* 1281 (1976).

9. 5 U.S. (1 Cranch) 87 (1803).

10. Ibid., at 106.

11. Ibid., at 106-107.

12. *Stark v. Wickard*, 321 U.S. 288, 309-310 (1944) (emphasis added).

13. *Calvert Cliffs Coordinating Comm. v. AEC*, 449 F.2d 1109, 1111 (D.C. Cir. 1971).

14. *Warth v. Seldin*, 422 U.S. 490, 498-501 (1975).

15. Other cases exemplifying the same principle include *Decatur v. Pauling*, 39 U.S. (14 Pet.) 496 (1840) (suit against Secretary of the Navy for pension awarded by Congress to widow of Commodore Stephen Decatur); and *United States v. Schurz*, 102 U.S. 378 (1880) (suit against Secretary of the Interior for delivery of land patent issued in realtor's name).

16. *Scenic Hudson Preservation Conference v. FPC*, 354 F.2d 608, 616 (2d Cir., 1965).

17. 60 Stat. 237, 5 U.S.C. Sec. 702 (1982) (emphasis added).

18. A 1939 Supreme Court case discusses those traditional principles as follows: "The appellants invoke the doctrine that one threatened with direct and special injury by the act of an agent of the government which but for statutory authority for its performance, would be a violation of his legal rights, may challenge the validity of the statute in a suit against the agent. The principle is without application unless the right invaded is a legal right—one of property, one arising out of contract, one protected against tortious invasion, or one founded on a statute which confers a privilege." *Tennessee Power Co. v. TVA*, 306 U.S. 118, 137-138 (1939) (footnotes omitted). The Court went on to find that the Tennessee Power Company did not have standing as a competitor of the Tennessee Valley Authority to challenge the TVA's constitutionality, because it had no legal right to be free of competition. Ibid., at 137-147. Other cases exemplifying the stinginess of traditional "legal wrong" standing include *Perkins v. Lukins Steel Co.*, 310 U.S. 113, 125 (1940).

19. Compare with the cases described in note 20, supra, *FCC v. Sanders Bros. Radio Station*, 309 U.S. 470 (1940), interpreting § 402(b) of the Federal Communications Act, 47 U.S.C. § 402 (b)(6) (1982), conferring a right to review on "any . . . person aggrieved or whose interests are adversely affected," to allow a station to challenge the grant of a license to a competitor.

20. There were statutory review provisions that used terms other than "person adversely affected or aggrieved"—for example, "party in interest" (Interstate Commerce Act, 49 U.S.C. § 1(20) (1970) or "person disclosing a substantial interest" (Federal Aviation Act, 49 U.S.C. § 1486(a) (1970)). It would not do violence to the obvious intent of § 702 to consider the phrase "person adversely affected or aggrieved . . . within the meaning of relevant statute" to be a sort of synechdoche, designed to cover as well a "party in interest . . . within the meaning of a relevant statute." Such an interpretation would have the elegant effect of causing the two provisions of § 702 ("person suffering legal wrong" and "person adversely affected or aggrieved . . . within the meaning of a relevant statute") to coincide precisely with what have come to be known as "nonstatutory review" and "statutory review," respectively. See Scalia, "Sovereign Immunity and Nonstatutory Review of Federal Administrative Action: Some Conclusions from

the Public-Lands Cases," 68 *Michigan Law Review* 867, 870 (1970).

21. S. Rep. No. 752, 79th Cong., 1st Sess. 44 (1945), reprinted in APA, *Legislative History.*

22. *92 Cong. Rec.* 2153 (1946), APA, *Legislative History.*

23. *Vermont Yankee Nuclear Power Corp. v. Natural Resources Defense Council, Inc.,* 435 U.S. 519, 546 (1978).

24. Attorney General's Manual on the Administrative Procedure Act 96 (1947). Some portions of the floor debate, including formulations agreed to by Senator McCarran, display an intent to expand judicial review. See *Legislative History* at 308-311, 318-319, 325-326, 384. Since these statements, some of which have the flavor of contrived legislative history, contradict not only the statutory text but other portions of the legislative history that agree with the text, they cannot be regarded as governing. If they had represented a correct interpretation of the bill, it is inconceivable that the Justice Department would not have opposed it; and it is similarly inconceivable that they alone should form the basis for the historic transfer of power from the Executive to the judicial branch described below.

25. The leading case was *Kansas City Power & Light Co. v. McKay,* 225 F.2d 924, 932 (D.C. Cir.), *cert. denied,* 350 U.S. 884 (1955). Other cases taking this view of the APA were *Association of Data Processing Organizations, Inc. v. Camp,* 406 F.2d 837 (8th Cir. 1969), *rev'd.,* 397 U.S. 150 (1970); *Rural Electrification Administration v. Northern States Power Co.,* 373 F.2d 686, 692 and n.9 (8th Cir. 1967); *Braude v. Wirtz,* 350 F.2d 702, 706-708 (9th Cir. 1965); *Gonzalez v. Freeman,* 334 F.2d 570, 574-576 (D.C. Cir. 1964); *Duba v. Schuetzle,* 303 F.2d 570, 574-575 (8th Cir. 1962); *Copper Plumbing & Heating Co. v. Campbell,* 290 F.2d 368, 370-371 (D.C. Cir. 1961). But see *Road Review League v. Boyd,* 270 F. Supp. 650, 660-61 (S.D.N.Y. 1967) and *American President Lines v. FMC,* 112 F. Supp. 346, 349 (D.D.C. 1953), both adopting a view of APA standing similar to that ultimately embraced by the Supreme Court.

26. 397 U.S. 150, 154-155 (1970).

27. 397 U.S. 159, 164-165 (1970). See *Sierra Club v. Morton,* 405 U.S. 727, 733 (1972), where the Court describes *Data Processing* as having overruled the court of appeals cases cited supra note 27.

28. *Association of Data Processing Service Organizations v. Camp,* 397 U.S. 150, 153-154 (1970); and *Barlow v. Collins,* 397 U.S. 159, 164-165 (1970).

29. *Scanwell Laboratories, Inc. v. Shaffer,* 424 F.2d 859, 872 (D.C. Cir., 1970).

30. Not all actions by agencies are covered by the judicial review provisions of the APA. See 5 U.S.C. Sec. 701 (1982).

31. 30 U.S.C. Sec 1276 (Supp. III, 1979).

32. *United States v. Students Challenging Regulatory Agency Procedures,* 412 U.S. 669 (1973).

33. Ibid., at 678.

34. Ibid., at 682.

35. 392 U.S. 83 (1968).

36. Ibid., at 99-101.

37. See, e.g., L. Tribe, *American Constitutional Law* 3-21 (Mineola, N.Y.: Foundation Press, 1978); L. Jaffee, "The Citizen as Litigant in Public Actions: Non-Hofeldian or Ideological Plaintiff," 116 *University of Pennsylvania Law Review* 1033, 1037-1038 (1968); and Scott, "Standing in the Supreme Court—A Functional Analysis," 86 *Harvard Law Review* 645, 674 (1973).

38. *Sierra Club v. Morton,* 405 U.S. 727, 731 (1972).

39. Of course where the establishment had the effect of restricting or coercing individual religious belief, it could be challenged in the courts under the "freedom of religion" clause of the First Amendment, but that is quite a different issue. See, e.g., *McCollum v. Board of Education,* 333 U.S. 203 (1948).

40. U.S. Constitution, Art. 1, Sec. 9, cl. 7. See *United States v. Richardson,* 418 U.S. 166 (1974).

41. A. de Tocqueville, *Democracy in America,* Vol. 1, at 102, ed. Bradley (New York: Vintage, 1945).

42. *Flast v. Cohen,* 392 U.S. 68, 100-101 (1968).

43. *Valley Forge Christian College v. Americans United for Separation of Church and State,* 454 U.S. 464, 471-474 (1982); and *Warth v. Seldin,* 422 U.S. 490, 498 (1974).

44. 262 U.S. 447 (1923).

45. Ibid., at 486.

46. *United States v. Richardson,* 418 U.S. 166, 171-173 (1974); and *Schlesinger v. Reservists Committee to Stop the War,* 418 U.S. 208, 220 n.8 (1974).

47. *Ex parte Levitt,* 302 U.S. 633, 634 (1937), quoted in *United States v. Richardson,* 418 U.S. 166, at 177-178.

48. The Court refers to this as "the rigor with which the *Flast* exception . . . ought to be applied." *Valley Forge Christian College v. Americans United for Separation of Church and State,* 454 U.S. 464, at 479-480. The basis for distinguishing *Flast* in both seem utterly irrelevant to what *Flast* sought to accomplish. The Court seems to have adapted the suggestion by Justice Powell in *United States v. Richardson,* 418 U.S. 166, at 196 (con. op.) that it "limit the expansion of federal taxpayer and citizen standing to an outer boundary drawn by the *results* in *Flast* and *Baker v. Carr.*"

49. *California v. Sierra Club,* 451 U.S. 287 (1981); *Transamerica Mortgage Advisors, Inc. v. Lewis,* 444 U.S. 11 (1979) and *Touche Ross & Co. v. Redington,* 442 U.S. 560 (1974).

PART V

Our Dual Constitutional System: The Bill of Rights and the States

THE VERY purpose of a bill of rights, Justice Robert Jackson observed, "was to withdraw certain subjects from the vicissitudes of political controversy, to place them beyond the reach of majorities and officials and to establish them as legal principles to be applied by the Courts. One's right to life, liberty, and freedom of worship and assembly, and other fundamental rights may not be submitted to vote; they depend on the outcome of no election."[1]

The Bill of Rights, like the Constitution, emerged from considerable debate and numerous compromises. A bill of rights, Alexander Hamilton argued in *The Federalist,* was "not only unnecessary . . . but would even be dangerous." Any enumeration of rights was unnecessary because "the Constitution itself, in every rational sense, and to every useful purpose, is a bill of rights."[2] Parchment guarantees might also prove dangerous, he thought, by prohibiting the exercise of powers for which no express authority was granted to the national government. In our dual constitutional system, Hamilton reasoned, the national government possesses only limited, expressly delegated powers, and thus civil liberties are secure and subject to state constitutions enforced by state courts. By contrast, James Madison and Thomas Jefferson advanced libertarian arguments for adopting a federal bill of rights, but even they differed in their understanding of the rights to be secured. Madison, like Hamilton, worried about the potential problems arising from a declaration of rights. In a letter to Jefferson, he explained:

> My own opinion has always been in favor of a bill of rights; provided it be so framed not to imply powers not meant to be included in the enumeration. . . . I have not viewed it in an important light . . . [however, because] there is a great reason to fear that a positive declaration of some of the most essential rights could not be obtained in the requisite latitude.[3]

Jefferson agreed that any declaration of rights inevitably poses problems of inclusion and exclusion, yet contended that, "half a loaf is better than no bread.

If we cannot secure all our rights, let's secure what we can."[4] Responding to Madison's fears, he added:

> In the arguments in favor of a declaration of rights, you omit one which has great weight to me, the legal check which it puts into the hands of the judiciary. This is a body, which if rendered independent, and kept strictly to their own department, merits great confidence for their learning and integrity.[5]

Both Madison and Jefferson came to view a bill of rights as providing through the judiciary a check on a coercive national government and a way to ensure "the requisite latitude" of civil rights and liberties. Madison, nonetheless, was more libertarian than Jefferson, proposing that neither the states nor the national government "shall violate the equal rights of conscience" of any citizen.[6] Ratified on 15 December 1791, the Bill of Rights applied only to the national government and therefore was to Hamilton superfluous, though possibly dangerous. To Madison it was an insufficient safeguard for individual freedom, particularly with regard to the states. To Jefferson it was a reaffirmation both of the limits of the national government and of the reserved powers of the states.

"Bills of rights give assurance to the individual of the preservation of his liberty," Justice Benjamin Cardozo notes. "They do not define the liberty they promise."[7] The courts, as Madison and Jefferson foresaw, assumed a guardianship role in defining and protecting civil rights and liberties. As a guardian of the Bill of Rights, the Supreme Court forged a constitutional revolution with profound consequences for individual freedom and federalism. On the one hand, Justice Hugo Black explains in chapter 20, the Court assumed the vexatious task of defining the nature and scope of the enumerated guarantees, thereby limiting the coercive powers of the national government. On the other hand, as Justice William Brennan details in chapter 21, the court also extended guarantees of the Bill of Rights to the states under the Fourteenth Amendment due process clause, which prohibits any *state* from "depriving a person of life, liberty, or property without due process of law."

With notably few exceptions, the guarantees of the Bill of Rights have been enlarged and nationalized. On a selective, incremental, case-by-case basis the Court applied them to the states via incorporation into the due process clause of the Fourteenth Amendment. In addition, in *Griswold v. Connecticut* the Court interpreted various amendments—the First, Third, Fourth, Fifth, and Ninth amendments—to secure an unenumerated but enforceable constitutional right of privacy, which also applies to the states. Table V.1 on page 217 lists the guarantees enforceable against both the national government and the states.

Although the Supreme Court successfully nationalized the Bill of Rights, a majority of the justices failed to agree on a justification for incorporating those provisions into the Fourteenth Amendment. This was due to shifting alliances among the justices, different judicial philosophies, and the Court's changing composition. At one extreme, some justices, like Chief Justice John Marshall in *Barron v. Baltimore,* one of his last major decisions, maintained that

Table V.1
The Nationalization of the Bill of Rights:
A Process of Selective Incorporation-Plus[a]

Amendment	Year	Case
v. "Fair use" and "just compensation"	1896 1897	Missouri Pacific Railway Co. v. Nebraska; Chicago, B. and Q. Railway Co. v. Chicago
i. Freedom of speech	1927	Fiske v. Kansas; Gitlow v. New York (dictum, 1925)
i. Freedom of the press	1931	Near v. Minnesota
vi. Fair trial and right to counsel in capital cases	1932	Powell v. Alabama
i. Freedom of religion	1934	Hamilton v. Regents of the U. of California (dictum)
i. Freedom of assembly (and right to petition)	1937	DeJonge v. Oregon
i. Free exercise of religious belief	1940	Cantwell v. Connecticut
i. Separation of church and state	1947	Everson v. Board of Education
vi. Right to public trial	1948	In re Oliver
iv. Right against unreasonable search and seizures	1949	Wolf v. Colorado
i. Freedom of association	1958	NAACP v. Alabama
iv. Exclusionary rule	1961	Mapp v. Ohio
viii. Right against cruel and unusual punishment	1962	Robinson v. California
vi. Right to counsel in all felony cases	1963	Gideon v. Wainwright
v. Right against self-incrimination	1964	Malloy v. Hogan
vi. Right to confront witnesses	1965	Pointer v. Texas
i, iii, iv, v, and ix. Right of privacy	1965	Griswold v. Connecticut
vi. Right to impartial jury	1966	Parker v. Gladden
vi. Right to speedy trial	1967	Klopfer v. North Carolina
vi. Right to compulsory process for obtaining witnesses	1967	Washington v. Texas
vi. Right to jury trial in serious crime	1968	Duncan v. Louisiana
v. Right against double jeopardy	1969	Benton v. Maryland
vi. Right to counsel in all criminal cases entailing a jail term	1972	Argersinger v. Hamlin

a. The only provisions of the Bill of Rights that have not been extended to the States are the Second, Third, and Seventh amendments, as well as the Fifth Amendment's guarantee for indictment by a grand jury, and the Eighth Amendment's rights against excessive fines and bail.

the Bill of Rights as ratified applies only to the national government. After the adoption of the Fourteenth Amendment, however, some justices contend that congressional leaders intended the amendment to incorporate and apply the guarantees of the Bill of Rights to the states. Justice John Marshall Harlan, Sr., for one, thus urged the "total incorporation" of the Bill of Rights.[8] Drawing inspiration from Madison's libertarian precepts, as he explains in chapter 20, Justice Black similarly advocates total incorporation and an "absolutist" interpretation of enumerated guarantees. In recognition of the history of the Bill of Rights and our dual constitutional system, most justices nonetheless tend to view incorporation as a matter of balancing particular liberties against state police powers and interests in law enforcement. Justice Cardozo contended that some but not all of the provisions of the Bill of Rights have a "preferred position" because they are "implicit in the concept of ordered liberty." He therefore urged the "selective incorporation" and extension of the First Amendment, for example, but not the Fourth Amendment's guarantee against "unreasonable searches and seizures."[9] Justice Felix Frankfurter argued that only those rights required by "fundamental fairness," or whose violation "shocks the conscience," are enforceable against the states.[10] At the other extreme, Justices Frank Murphy, Wiley Rutledge, and William Douglas advanced a position of "total incorporation-plus" other unenumerated yet allegedly "fundamental rights."[11]

The Supreme Court's nationalization of the Bill of Rights profoundly altered our dual constitutional system and the relationship between federal and state courts. With the increasing prominence of the federal judiciary, the role of state courts tends to be overshadowed. Yet the work of the Supreme Court and the federal judiciary, Justice Brennan appropriately cautions, "must not divert attention from the vital importance of the work of the state courts in the administration of justice. Actually the composite work of the courts of the 50 states probably has greater significance in measuring how well America attains the ideal of equal justice for all."[12]

State courts continue to handle the overwhelming volume of all litigation — well over 90 percent of all filings. In 1980-81 alone, 180,576 civil and 31,287 criminal cases were filed in federal courts. By comparison, state courts faced over 26 million filings — 13,689,450 civil and 12,145,623 criminal cases.[13] The type of litigation in state courts also tends to diverge from that in federal courts. Apart from criminal cases, the largest portion of state supreme court litigation, for instance, involves economic issues — whether relating to state regulation of public utilities, zoning and small businesses, or labor relations and workers' compensation, natural resources, energy, and the environment. Litigation varies from state to state as well, depending on factors such as population size, urbanization, and socioeconomic conditions.[14]

The important role of state courts in the administration of justice is underscored, Justice Brennan notes, when we remind ourselves that the Supreme Court intrudes in state court policy making in only a very narrow class of litigation — the class of cases in which the state courts deal with federal questions. Federal questions rarely emerge from the grist of the state courts, Justice Brennan emphasizes: "If cases were grains of sand, federal question cases would be hard to find on the beach. The final and vital decisions of most controversies upon which depend life, liberty, and property are made by the state courts."[15] If a case does not raise a substantial federal question or was decided on independent state grounds — for example, a state constitution or bill of rights — then the Court declines review, respecting the principle of comity between federal and state judiciaries.

State courts thus continue to have a crucial role in the administration of justice, particularly as "guardians of our liberties" when interpreting and applying state constitutions and bills of rights. State bills of rights tend to be neglected due to the nationalization of the federal Bill of Rights. Yet Justices Brennan and Hans Linde of the Oregon Supreme Court, in chapters 21 and 22, argue that state courts should look first to their own bills of rights. This is so both because those guarantees historically precede the nationalization of the Bill of Rights, and because it is more appropriate to apply them first, given the logic of federalism and our dual constitutional system. Moreover, Justices Brennan and Linde suggest that state courts need not always follow the leadership of federal courts and that by interpreting their own state constitutions and bills of rights, state courts may chart their own boundaries for protected civil rights and liberties.

During the last 20 years the relationship between federal and state courts has evolved, with federal courts gaining more prominence and greater supervisory responsibilities. Still, no less than federal courts, as Justices Brennan and Linde point out, state courts are guardians of our liberties and important forums for fashioning public policies. Justice Sandra Day O'Connor further discusses, in chapter 23, the evolution and other trends in the relationship between federal and state courts in our increasingly litigious society.

NOTES

1. *West Virginia State Board of Education v. Barnette,* 319 U.S. 624, 638 (1943).

2. A. Hamilton, *The Federalist,* No. 84, ed. by C. Rossiter, at 513-514 (New York: Mentor Books, 1961).

3. T. Jefferson, Letter from James Madison to Thomas Jefferson (17 October 1788), *The Papers of Thomas Jefferson,* Vol. 14, at 16 and 18, ed. by J. Boyd (Princeton: Princeton University Press, 1955).

4. T. Jefferson, Letter to James Madison, in ibid., at 659.

5. Ibid.

6. *Annals of Congress,* Vol. 1, at 766 (Washington, D.C.: Gates and Seaton, 1834).

7. B.N. Cardozo, "Paradoxes of Legal Science," in *Selected Writings of Benjamin Nathan Cardozo* 311, ed. by M. Hall (New York: Fallon, 1947).

8. See *Hurtado v. California,* 110 U.S. 516 (1884).

9. See *Palko v. Connecticut,* 302 U.S. 319 (1937).

10. See *Adamson v. California,* 332 U.S. 46 (1947); and *Rochin v. California,* 342 U.S. 165 (1952).

11. See *Adamson v. California,* 332 U.S. 46 (1947) (Murphy, J., and Rutledge, J.); and *Griswold v. Connecticut,* 381 U.S. 479 (1965) (DOUGLAS, J.).

12. W.J. Brennan, Jr., Address, Pennsylvania Bar Association (3 February 1960), appearing in 31 *Pennsylvania Bar Association Quarterly* 393, 394 (1960).

13. These figures were provided by Robert Roper of the National Center for State Courts. See also V. Fango and M. Elsner, "Advance Report: The Latest State Caseload Data," *State Court Journal* 16 (Winter 1983).

14. See, e.g., H. Glick and K. Vines, *State Court Systems* (Englewood Cliffs, N.J.: Prentice-Hall, 1973); Project Report, "Toward an Activist Role for State Bills of Rights," 8 *Harvard Civil Rights-Civil Liberties Law Review* 271 (1973), and R. Kagan et al., "The Business of State Supreme Courts, 1870-1970," 30 *Stanford Law Review* 121 (1977).

15. Brennan, supra note 12, at 398.

20

The Bill of Rights

Hugo L. Black

Justice, Supreme Court of the United States

What is a bill of rights? In the popular sense it is any document setting forth the liberties of the people. I prefer to think of our Bill of Rights as including all provisions of the original Constitution and Amendments that protect individual liberty by barring government from acting in a particular area or from acting except under certain prescribed procedures. I have in mind such clauses in the body of the Constitution itself as those which safeguard the right of habeas corpus, forbid bills of attainder and ex post facto laws, guarantee trial by jury, and strictly define treason and limit the way it can be tried and punished. I would certainly add to this list the last constitutional prohibition in Article Six that "no religious Test shall ever be required as a Qualification to any Office or public Trust under the United States."

I shall speak to you about the Bill of Rights only as it bears on powers of the Federal Government. Originally, the first ten amendments were not intended to apply to the states but, as the Supreme Court held in 1833 in *Barron v. Baltimore,*[1] were adopted to quiet fears extensively entertained that the powers of the big new national government "might be exercised in a manner dangerous to liberty." I believe that by virtue of the Fourteenth Amendment, the first ten amendments are now applicable to the states, a view I stated in *Adamson v. California.*[2] I adhere to that view. In this talk, however, I want to discuss only the extent to which the Bill of Rights limits the Federal Government.

In applying the Bill of Rights to the Federal Government there is today a sharp difference of views as to how far its provisions should be held to limit the lawmaking power of Congress. How this difference is finally resolved will, in my judgment, have far-reaching consequences upon our liberties. I shall first summarize what those different views are.

Some people regard the prohibitions of the Constitution, even its most unequivocal commands, as mere admonitions which Congress need not always observe. This viewpoint finds many different verbal expressions. For example, it is sometimes said that Congress may abridge a constitutional right if there is a clear and present danger that the free exercise of the right will bring about a substantive evil that Congress has authority to prevent. Or it is said that a right may be abridged where its exercise would cause so much injury to the public that this injury would outweigh the injury to the individual who is deprived of the right. Again, it is sometimes said that the Bill of Rights' guarantees must "compete" for survival against general powers expressly granted to Congress and that the individual's right must, if outweighed by the public interest, be subordinated to the Government's competing interest in denying the right. All of these formulations, and more with which you are doubtless familiar, rest, at least in part, on the premise that there are no "absolute" prohibitions in the Constitution, and that all constitutional problems are questions of reasonableness, proximity, and degree. This view comes close to the English doctrine of legislative omnipotence, qualified only by the possibility of a judicial veto if the Supreme Court finds that a congressional choice between "competing" policies has no reasonable basis.

I cannot accept this approach to the Bill of Rights. It is my belief that there *are* "absolutes" in our Bill of Rights, and that they were put there on purpose by men who knew what words meant, and meant their prohibitions to be "absolutes." The whole history and background of the Constitution and Bill of Rights, as I understand it, belies the assumption or conclusion that our ultimate constitutional freedoms are no more than our English ancestors had when they came to this new land to get new freedoms. The historical and practical purposes of a Bill of Rights, the very use of a written constitution, indigenous to America, the language the Framers used, the kind of three-department government they took pains to set up, all point to the creation of a government which was denied all power to do some things under any and all circumstances, and all power to do other things except precisely in the manner prescribed.

The form of government which was ordained and established in 1789 contains certain unique features which reflected the Framers' fear of arbitrary government and which clearly indicate an intention absolutely to limit what Congress could do. The first of these features is that our Constitution is written in a single document. Such constitutions are familiar today and it is not always remembered that our country was the first to have one. Certainly one purpose of a written constitution is to define and therefore more specifically limit government powers. An all-powerful government that can act as it pleases wants no such constitution — unless to fool the people. England had no written constitution and this once proved a source of tyranny, as our ancestors well knew. Jefferson said about this departure from the English type of government: "Our peculiar security is in possession of a written Constitution. Let us not make it a blank paper by construction."[3]

A second unique feature of our Government is a Constitution supreme over the legislature. In England, statutes, Magna Charta, and later declarations of rights had for centuries limited the power of the King, but they did not limit the power of Parliament. Although commonly referred to as a constitution, they were never the "supreme law of the land" in the way in which our Constitution is, much to the regret of statesmen like Pitt the elder. Parliament could change this English "Constitution"; Congress cannot change ours. Ours can only be changed by amendments ratified by three-fourths of the states. It was one of the great achievements of our Constitution that it ended legislative omnipotence here and placed all departments and agencies of government under one supreme law.

A third feature of our Government expressly designed to limit its powers was the division of authority into three coordinate branches none of which was to have supremacy over the others. This separation of powers with the checks and balances which each branch was given over the others was designed to prevent any branch, including the legislative, from infringing individual liberties safeguarded by the Constitution.

Finally, our Constitution was the first to provide a really independent judiciary. Moreover, as the Supreme Court held in *Marbury v. Madison,*[4] correctly I believe, this judiciary has the power to hold legislative enactments void that are repugnant to the Constitution and the Bill of Rights. In this country the judiciary was made independent because it has, I believe, the primary responsibility and duty of giving force and effect to constitutional liberties and limitations upon the executive and legislative branches. Judges in England were not always independent and they could not hold Parliamentary acts void. Consequently, English courts could not be counted on to protect the liberties of the people against invasion by the Parliament, as many unfortunate Englishmen found out, such as Sir Walter Raleigh, who was executed as the result of an unfair trial, and a lawyer named William Prynne, whose ears were first cut off by court order and who subsequently, by another court order, had his remaining ear stumps gouged out while he was on a pillory. Prynne's offenses were writing books and pamphlets.

All of the unique features of our Constitution show an underlying purpose to create a new kind of limited government. Central to all of the Framers of the Bill of Rights was the idea that since government, particularly the national government newly created, is a powerful institution, its officials — all of them — must be compelled to exercise their powers within strictly defined boundaries. As Madison told Congress, the Bill of Rights' limitations point "sometimes against the abuse of the Executive power, sometimes against the Legislative, and in some cases against the community itself; or, in other words, against the majority in favor of the minority."[5] Madison also explained that his proposed amendments were intended "to limit and qualify the powers of Government, by excepting out of the grant of power those cases in which the Government ought not to act, or to act only in a particular mode."[6] In the light of this purpose let us now turn to the language of the first ten amendments to consider whether their provisions were written as mere admonitions to Congress or as absolute commands, proceeding for convenience from the last to the first.

The last two Amendments, the Ninth and Tenth, are general in character, but both emphasize the limited nature of the Federal Government. Number Ten restricts federal power to what the Constitution delegates to the central government, reserving all other powers to the states or to the people. Number Nine attempts to make certain that enumeration of some rights must "not be construed to deny or disparage others retained by the people." The use of the words, "the people," in both these Amendments strongly emphasizes the desire of the Framers to protect individual liberty.

The Seventh Amendment states that "in Suits at common law, where the value in controversy shall exceed twenty dollars, the right of trial by jury shall be preserved. . . ." This language clearly requires that jury trials must be afforded in the type of cases the Amendment describes. The Amendment goes on in equally unequivocal words to command that "no fact tried by a jury, shall be otherwise re-examined in any Court of the United States, than according to the rules of the common law."

Amendments Five, Six, and Eight relate chiefly to the procedures that government must follow when bringing its powers to bear against any person with a view to depriving him of his life, liberty, or property.

The Eighth Amendment forbids "excessive bail," "excessive fines," or the infliction of "cruel and unusual punishments." This is one of the less precise provisions. The courts are required to determine the meaning of such general terms as "excessive" and "unusual." But surely that does not mean that admittedly "excessive bail," "excessive fines," or "cruel punishments" could be justified on the ground of a "competing" public interest in carrying out some generally granted power like that given to Congress to regulate commerce.

Amendment Six provides that in a criminal prosecution an accused shall have a "speedy and public trial, by an impartial jury of the State and district wherein the crime shall have been committed, which district shall have been previously ascertained by law, and to be informed of the nature and cause of the accusation; to be confronted with the witnesses against him; to have compulsory process for obtaining witnesses in his favor, and have the Assistance of Counsel for his defence." All of these requirements are cast in terms both definite and absolute. Trial by jury was also guaranteed in the original Constitution. The additions here, doubtless prompted by English trials of Americans away from their homes, are that a trial must be "speedy and public," "by an impartial jury," and in a district which "shall have been previously ascertained by law." If there is any one thing that is certain it is that the Framers intended both in the original Constitution and in the Sixth Amendment that persons charged with crime by the Federal Government have a right to be tried by jury. Suppose juries began acquitting people Congress thought should be convicted. Could Congress then provide some other form of trial, say by an administrative agency, or the military, where convictions could be more readily and certainly obtained, if it thought the safety of the nation so required? How about secret trials? By *partial* juries? Can it be that these are not absolute prohibitions?

The Sixth Amendment requires notice of the cause of an accusation, confrontation by witnesses, compulsory process, and assistance of counsel. The experience of centuries has demonstrated the value of these procedures to one on trial for crime. And this Amendment purports to guarantee them by clear language. But if there are no absolutes in the Bill of Rights, these guarantees too can be taken away by Congress on findings that a competing public interest requires that defendants be tried without notice, without witnesses, without confrontation, and without counsel.

The Fifth Amendment provides:

> No person shall be held to answer for a capital, or otherwise infamous crime, unless on a presentment of indictment of a Grand Jury, except in cases arising in the land or naval forces, or in the Militia, when in actual service in time of War or public danger; nor shall any person be subject for the same offence to be twice put in jeopardy of life or limb; nor shall be compelled in any criminal case to be a witness against himself, nor be deprived of life, liberty, or property without due process of law; nor shall private property be taken for public use, without just compensation.

Most of these Fifth Amendment prohibitions are both definite and unequivocal. There has been much controversy about the meaning of "due process of law." Whatever its meaning, however, there can be no doubt that it must be granted. Moreover, few doubt that it has an historical meaning which denies Government the right to take away life, liberty, or property without trials properly conducted according to the Constitution and laws validly made in accordance with it. This, at least, was the meaning of "due process of law" when used in Magna Charta and other old English Statutes where it was referred to as "the law of the land."

The Fourth Amendment provides:

> The right of the people to be secure in their persons, houses, papers, and effects, against unreasonable searches and seizures, shall not be violated, and no Warrants shall issue, but upon probable cause, supported by Oath of affirmation, and particularly describing the place to be searched, and the persons or things to be seized.

The use of the word "unreasonable" in this Amendment means, of course, that not *all* searches and seizures are prohibited. Only those which are *unreasonable* are unlawful. There may be much difference of opinion about whether a particular search or seizure is unreasonable and therefore forbidden by this Amendment. But if it *is* unreasonable, it is absolutely prohibited.

Likewise, the provision which forbids warrants for arrest, search, or seizure without "probable cause" is itself an absolute prohibition.

The Third Amendment provides that:

> No Soldier shall, in time of peace be quartered in any house, without the consent of the Owner, nor in time of war, but in a manner to be prescribed by law.

Americans had recently suffered from the quartering of British troops in their homes, and so this Amendment is written in language that apparently no one has ever thought could be violated on the basis of an overweighing public interest.

Amendment Two provides that:

A well regulated Militia, being necessary to the security of a free State, the right of the people to keep and bear Arms, shall not be infringed.

Although the Supreme Court has held this Amendment to include only arms necessary to a well-regulated militia, as so construed, its prohibition is absolute.

This brings us to the First Amendment. It reads:

Congress shall make no law respecting an establishment of religion, or prohibiting the free exercise thereof; or abridging the freedom of speech, or of the press; or the right of the people peaceably to assemble, and to petition the Government for a redress of grievances.

The phrase "Congress shall make no law" is composed of plain words, easily understood. The Framers knew this. The language used by Madison in his proposal was different, but no less emphatic and unequivocal. That proposal is worth reading:

The civil rights of none shall be abridged on account of religious belief or worship, nor shall any national religion be established, nor shall the full and equal rights of conscience be in any manner, or on any pretext, infringed.

The people shall not be deprived or abridged of their right to speak, to write, or to publish their sentiments; and the freedom of the press, as one of the great bulwarks of liberty, shall be inviolable.

The people shall not be restrained from peaceably assembling and consulting for their common good; nor from applying to the Legislature by petitions, or remonstrances, for redress of their grievances.[7]

Neither as offered nor as adopted is the language of this Amendment anything less than absolute. Madison was emphatic about this. He told the Congress that under it "the right of freedom of speech is secured; the liberty of the press is expressly declared to be *beyond the reach of this Government.* . . ."[8] Some years later Madison wrote that "it would seem scarcely possible to doubt that *no power whatever* over the press was supposed to be delegated by the Constitution, as it originally stood, and that the amendment was intended as a *positive and absolute reservation of it.*"[9] With reference to the positive nature of the First Amendment's command against infringement of religious liberty, Madison later said that "there is not a shadow of right in the general government to intermeddle with religion,"[10] and that "this subject is, for the honor of America, perfectly free and unshackled. The *government has no jurisdiction over it.*"[11]

To my way of thinking, at least, the history and language of the Constitution and the Bill of Rights, which I have discussed with you, make it plain that one of the primary purposes of the Constitution with its amendments was to withdraw from the Government all power to act in certain areas—whatever the scope of those areas may be. If I am right in this then there is, at least in those areas, no justification whatever for "balancing" a particular right against some expressly granted power of Congress. If the Constitution withdraws from Government all power over subject matter in an area, such as religion, speech, press, assembly, and petition, there is nothing over which authority may be exerted.

For my own part, I believe that our Constitution, with its absolute guarantees of individual rights, is the best hope for the aspirations of freedom which men share everywhere. I cannot agree with those who think of the Bill of Rights as an eighteenth-century straitjacket, unsuited for this age. It is old but not all old things are bad. The evils it guards against are not only old, they are with us now, they exist today. Almost any morning you open your daily paper you can see where some person somewhere in the world is on trial or has just been convicted of supposed disloyalty to a new group controlling the government which has set out to purge its suspected enemies and all those who had dared to be against its successful march to power. Nearly always you see that these political heretics are being tried by military tribunals or some other summary and sure method for disposition of the accused. Now and then we even see the convicted victims as they march to their execution.

Experience all over the world has demonstrated, I fear, that the distance between stable, orderly government and one that has been taken over by force is not so great as we have assumed. Our own free system to live and progress has to have intelligent citizens, citizens who cannot only think and speak and write to influence people, but citizens who are free to do that without fear of governmental censorship or reprisal.

The provisions of the Bill of Rights that safeguard fair legal procedures came about largely to protect the weak and the oppressed from punishment by the strong and the powerful who wanted to stifle the voices of discontent raised in protest against oppression and injustice in public affairs. Nothing that I have read in the Congressional debates on the Bill of Rights indicates that there was any belief that the First Amendment contained any qualifications. The only arguments that tended to look in this direction at all were those that said "that all paper barriers against the power of the community are too weak to be worthy of attention."[12] Suggestions were also made in and out of Congress that a Bill of Rights would be a futile gesture since there would be no way to enforce the safeguards for freedom it provided. Mr. Madison answered this argument in these words:

> If they [the Bill of Rights amendments] are incorporated into the Constitution, independent tribunals of justice will consider themselves in a peculiar manner the guardians of those rights; they will be an impenetrable bulwark against any assumption of power in the Legislative or Executive; they will be naturally led to resist every encroachment upon rights expressly stipulated for in the Constitution by the declaration of rights.[13]

I fail to see how courts can escape this sacred trust.

NOTES

1. 32 U.S. (7 Pet.) 242, 249 (1833).
2. 332 U.S. 46, 71-72 (1947) (dis. op.)
3. T. Jefferson, *Writings,* Vol. 4, 506 (Washington ed., 1859).
4. 5 U.S. (1 Cranch) 137 (1803).
5. 1 *Annals of Cong.* 437 (1789).
6. Ibid.
7. 1 *Annals of Cong.* 434 (1789).
8. 1 *Annals of Cong.* 738 (1789) (emphases added in all quotations).
9. J. Madison, *Writings,* Vol. 6, 391 (Hunt ed., 1906).
10. J. Madison, *Writings,* Vol. 5, 176 (Hunt ed., 1904).
11. Ibid., at 132.
12. 1 *Annals of Cong.* 437 (1789).
13. 1 *Annals of Cong.* 439 (1789).

21

Guardians of Our Liberties—State Courts No Less Than Federal

WILLIAM J. BRENNAN, JR.
Justice, Supreme Court of the United States

Over the past two decades, decisions of the Supreme Court of the United States have returned to the fundamental promises wrought by the blood of those who fought our War between the States, promises which were thereafter embodied in our Fourteenth Amendment—that the citizens of all our States are also and no less citizens of our United States, that this birthright guarantees our federal constitutional liberties against encroachment by governmental action at any level of our federal system, and that each of us is entitled to due process of law and the equal protection of the laws from our state governments no less than our national one. Although courts do not today substitute their personal economic beliefs for the judgments of our democratically elected Legislatures, Supreme Court decisions under the Fourteenth Amendment have significantly affected virtually every other area, civil and criminal, of state action. And while these decisions have been accompanied by the enforcement of federal rights by federal courts they have significantly altered the work of state court judges as well. This is both necessary and desirable under our federal system—state courts no less than federal are and ought to be the guardians of our liberties.

The decisions of the Supreme Court enforcing the protections of the Fourteenth Amendment generally fall into one of three categories. The first concerns enforcement of the federal guarantee of equal protection of the laws. The best known of course are *Brown v. Board of Education,*[1] invalidating state laws requiring public schools to be racially segregated, and *Baker v. Carr,*[2] and its progeny,[3] which invalidated state laws diluting individual voting rights by legislative malapportionments. But perhaps even more the concern of state bench and bar, in terms of state court litigation, are decisions invalidating state legislative classifications that impermissibly impinge on the exercise of fundamental rights, such as the rights to vote,[4] and to travel interstate,[5] or to bear or beget a child,[6] and decisions that require exacting judicial scrutiny of classifications that operate to the peculiar disadvantage of politically powerless groups whose members have historically been subjected to purposeful discrimination—racial minorities[7] and aliens[8] are two examples.

The second category of decisions concern the Fourteenth Amendment's guarantee against the deprivation of life, liberty or property where that deprivation is without due process of law. The root requirement of due proces is that, except for some extraordinary situations, an individual be given an opportunity for a hearing before he is deprived of any significant "liberty" or "property" interest. Our decisions enforcing the guarantee of the Due Process Clause have elaborated the essence of "liberty" and "property" in light of conditions existing in contemporary society. For example, "property" has come to embrace such crucial expectations as a driver's license[9] and the statutory entitlement to minimal economic support, in the form of welfare, of those who by accident or birth or circumstance find themselves without the means of subsistence.[10] The due process safeguard against arbitrary deprivation of these entitlements, as well as of more traditional forms of property, such as a workingman's wages[11] and his continued possession and use of goods purchased under conditional sales contracts.[12] has been recognized as mandating prior notice and the opportunity to be heard. At the same time, conceptions of "liberty" have come to recognize the undeniable proposition that prisoners and parolees retain some vestiges of human dignity, so that prison regulations and parole procedures must provide some form of notice and hearing prior to confinement in solitary[13] or the revocation of parole.[14] Moreover, the concepts of liberty and property have combined in recognizing that under modern conditions tenured public employees may not have their reasonable expectation of continued employment,[15] and school children their right to a public education,[16] revoked without notice and opportunity to be heard.

I suppose, however, that it is mostly the third category of decisions by the United States Supreme Court during the last 20 years—enforcing the specific guarantees of the Bill of Rights against encroachment by state action—that has required the special consideration of state judges, particularly as those decisions affect the administration of the criminal justice system.

After his retirement, Chief Justice Earl Warren was asked what he regarded to be the decision during his tenure that would have the greatest consequence for all Americans. His choice was *Baker v. Carr,* because he believed that if each of us has an equal vote, we are equally armed with the indispensable means to make our views felt. I feel at least as good a case can be made that the series of decisions binding the States to almost all of the restraints of the Bill of Rights will be even more significant in preserving and furthering the ideals we have fashioned for our society. Before the Fourteenth Amendment was added to the Constitution, the Supreme Court held that the Bill of Rights did not restrict state, but only federal, action.[17] In the decades between 1868, when the Fourteenth Amendment was adopted, and 1897, the Court decided in case after case that the Fourteenth Amendment did not apply various specific restraints in the Bill of Rights to state action.[18] The breakthrough came in 1897 when prohibition against taking private property for public use without payment of just compensation was held embodied in the Fourteenth Amendment's proscription, "nor shall any state deprive any person of . . . property, without due process of law."[19] But extension of the rest of the specific restraints was slow in coming. It was 1925 before it was suggested that perhaps the restraints of the First Amendment applied to state action.[20] Then in 1949 the Fourth Amendment's prohibition of unreasonable searches and seizures was extended,[21] but the extension was virtually meaningless because the States were left free to decide for themselves whether any effective means of enforcement of the guarantee was to be made available. It was not until 1961 that the Court applied the exclusionary rule to state proceedings.[22]

But the years from 1962 to 1969 witnessed the extension of nine of the specifics of the Bill of Rights, and these decisions have had a profound impact on American life, requiring the deep involvement of state courts in the application of federal law. The Eighth Amendment's prohibition of cruel and unusual punishment was applied to state action in 1962,[23] and is the guarantee under which the death penalty as then administered was struck down in 1972.[24] The provision of the Sixth Amendment that in all prosecutions the accused shall have the assistance of counsel was applied in 1963 and in consequence counsel must be provided in every courtroom of every State of this land to secure the rights of those accused of crime.[25] In 1964, the Fifth Amendment privilege against compulsory self-incrimination was extended.[26] And after decades of police coercion, by means ranging from torture to trickery, the privilege against self-incrimination became the basis of *Miranda v. Arizona,* requiring police to give warnings to a suspect before custodial interrogation.[27]

The year 1965 saw the extension of the Sixth Amendment right of an accused to be confronted by the witnesses against him;[28] in 1967 three more guarantees of the Sixth Amendment—the right to a speedy and public trial, the right to a trial by an impartial jury, and the right to have compulsory process for obtaining witnesses were extended.[29] In 1969 the double jeopardy clause of the Fifth Amendment was applied.[30] Moreover, the decisions barring state-required prayers in public schools,[31] limiting the availability of state libel laws to public officials and public figures,[32] and confirming that a right of association is implicitly protected,[33] are significant restraints upon state action that resulted from the extension of the specifics of the First Amendment.

These descisions over the past two decades gave full effect to the principle of *Boyd v. United States,*[34] the case Mr. Justice Brandeis hailed as "a case that will be remembered so long as civil liberty lives in the United States."[35] It is a matter of pride to all of us from New Jersey that *Boyd* was written by Mr. Justice Bradley who was appointed to the Supreme Court from our State. The *Boyd* principle stated by Mr. Justice Bradley was: ". . . constitutional provisions for the security of person and property should be liberally construed. It is the duty of courts to be watchful for the constitutional rights of the citizen, and against any stealthy encroachment thereon."[36]

The thread of this series of holding that the Fourteenth Amendment guarantees citizens the protections of the Bill of Rights in confrontations with state action reflects a conclusion—arrived at only after a long series of decisions grappling with the pros and cons of the question—that there exists in modern America the necessity for protecting all of us from arbitrary action by governments more powerful and pervasive than in our ancestors' time, and that the protections must be construed to preserve their fundamental policies, and thereby the maintenance of our constitutional structure of government for a free society.

For the genius of our Constitution resides not in any static meaning that it had in a world that is dead and gone, but in the adaptability of its great principles to cope with the problems of a developing America. A principle to be vital must be of wider application than the mischief that gave it birth. Constitutions are not ephemeral documents, designed to meet passing occasions. The future is their care, and therefore, in their application, our contemplation cannot be only of what has been but of what may be.

Of late, however, more and more state courts are construing state constitutional counterparts of provisions of the Bill of Rights as guaranteeing citizens of their States even more protection than the federal provisions, even those identically phrased. This is surely an important and highly significant development for our constitutional jurisprudence and for our concept of federalism. I suppose it was only natural that when during the 1960s our rights and liberties were in the process of becoming increasingly federalized, state courts saw no reason to consider what protections, if any, were secured by state constitutions. It isn't easy to pinpoint why state courts are beginning to emphasize the protections of their States' own Bill of Rights. It may not be wide of the mark, however, to suppose that these state courts discern in recent opinions of the United States Supreme Court, and disagree with, a pulling back from, or at least, a suspension for the time being of the enforcement of the *Boyd* principle in respect of application of the federal Bill of Rights and the restraints of the Due Process and Equal Protection Clauses of the Fourteenth Amendment. Under the Equal Protection Clause, for example, the Court has found permissible laws that accord lesser protection to over half of the members of our society due to their susceptibility to the medical condition of pregnancy.[37] The Court has found uncompelling the claims of those barred from judicial forums due to their inability to pay access fees.[38]

Under the Due Process Clause, it has found no liberty interest in the reputation of an individual—never-tried and never-convicted—who is publicly branded as a criminal by the police without benefit of notice, let alone hearing.[39] The Court has recently indicated that tenured public employees might not be entitled to any more process before deprivation of their employment than the Government sees fit to give them.[40] It has approved the termination of payments to disabled individuals completely dependent upon those payments prior to an oral hearing, a form of hearing statistically shown to result in a huge rate of reversals of preliminary administrative determinations.[41]

In the category of the specific guarantees of the Bill of Rights, the Court has found the First Amendment insufficiently flexible to guarantee access to essential public forums when in our evolving society those traditional forums are under private ownership in the form of suburban shopping centers.[42] It has found that the warrant requirement plainly appearing on the face of the Fourth Amendment does not require the police to obtain a warrant before arrest, however easy it might have been to get an arrest warrant.[43] It has declined to read the Fourth Amendment to prohibit searches of an individual by police officers following a stop for a traffic violation, although there exists no probable cause to believe the individual has committed any other legal infraction.[44] The Court has found permissible police searches grounded upon consent regardless of whether the consent was a knowing and intelligent one.[45] The Court has found that none of us has a legitimate expectation of privacy in the contents of our bank records, thus permitting governmental seizure of those records without our knowledge or consent.[46]

Moreover, the Court has held, contrary to *Boyd v. United States,* that we may not interpose the privilege against self-incrimination to bar Government attempts to obtain our personal papers, no matter how private the nature of their contents.[47] The Court has held that the privilege against self-incrimination is not violated when statements unconstitutionally obtained from an individual are used for purposes of impeaching his testimony,[48] or securing his indictment by a grand jury.[49]

The Sixth Amendment guarantee of assistance of counsel has been held not available to an accused in custody when shuffled through pre-indictment identification procedures, no matter how essential counsel might be to the avoidance of prejudice to his rights at later stages of the criminal process.[50] And in the face of our requirement of proof of guilt beyond a reasonable doubt, the Court has upheld the permissibility of less than unanimous jury verdicts of guilty.[51]

Also a series of decisions have shaped the doctrines of jurisdiction, justiciability, and remedy, so as increasingly to bar the federal courthouse door in the absence of showings probably impossible to make.[52] It is true of course that there has been an increasing amount of litigation of all types filling the calendars of virtually every state and federal court. But a solution that shuts the courthouse door in the face of the litigant with a legitimate claim for relief, particularly a claim of deprivation of a constitutional right, seems to be not only the wrong tool but also a dangerous tool for solving the problem. The victims of the use of that tool are most often the litigants most in need of judicial protection of their rights — the poor, the underprivileged, the deprived minorities. The very life blood of courts is popular confidence that they mete out even-handed justice, and any discrimination that denies these groups access to the courts for resolution of their meritorious claims unnecessarily risks loss of that confidence.

Some state decisions have indeed suggested a connection between these recent decisions of the United States Supreme Court and the state court's reliance on the state's Bill of Rights. For example, the California Supreme Court, recently held that statements taken from suspects before first giving them *Miranda* warnings are inadmissible in California courts to impeach an accused who testifies in his own defense; and stated: "We declare that [the decision to the contrary of the U.S. Supreme Court] is not persuasive authority in any state prosecution in California. . . . We pause to reaffirm the independent nature of the California Constitution and our responsibility to separately define and protect the rights of California citizens despite conflicting decisions of the United States Supreme Court interpreting the federal Constitution."[53]

"Other examples abound where state courts have independently considered the merits of constitutional arguments and declined to follow opinions of the United States Supreme Court they find unconvincing, even where the state and federal constitutions are similarly or identically phrased. As the Supreme Court of Hawaii has observed, "while this results in a divergence of meaning between words which are the same in both federal and state constitutions, the system of federalism envisaged by the United States Constitution tolerates such divergence where the result is greater protection of individual rights under state law than under federal law. . . ."[54]

And of course state courts that rest their decisions wholly or even partly on state law need not apply federal principles of standing and justiciability that deny litigants access to the courts. Moreover, the state decisions not only cannot be overturned by, they indeed are not even reviewable by, the Supreme Court of the United States. We are utterly without jurisdiction to review such state decisions.[55]

Some state courts seem apparently even to be anticipating contrary rulings by the United States Supreme Court and are therefore resting decisions on state law grounds to avoid review. For example, the California Supreme Court held, as a matter of state constitutional law, that bank depositors have a sufficient expectation of privacy in their bank records to invalidate the voluntary disclosure of such records by a bank to the police without the knowledge or consent of the depositor;[56] thereafter the United States Supreme Court ruled that Federal law was to the contrary.[57]

This development puts to rest the notion that state constitutional provisions were adopted to mirror the federal Bill of Rights. The lesson of history is otherwise; indeed, the drafters of the federal Bill of Rights drew upon corresponding provisions in the various state constitutions. Prior to the adoption of the Federal Constitution, each of the rights eventually recognized in the federal Bill of Rights had previously been protected in one or more state constitutions.[58]

The essential point I am making, of course, is not that the United States Supreme Court is necessarily wrong in its interpretation of the Federal Constitution, or that ultimate constitutional truths invariably come prepackaged in the dissents, including my own, from decisions of the Court. It is simply that the decisions of the Court are not dispositive of questions regarding rights guaranteed by counterpart provisions of state law.

NOTES

1. *Brown v. Board of Education*, 437 U.S. 483 (1954).
2. *Baker v. Carr*, 269 U.S. 186 (1962).
3. *Reynolds v. Sims*, 377 U.S. 533 (1964).
4. *Harper v. Va. State Board*, 383 U.S. 663 (1966).
5. *Shapiro v. Thompson*, 394 U.S. 618 (1969).
6. *Eisenstadt v. Baird*, 405 U.S. 438 (1972); *Griswold v. Connecticut*, 381 U.S. 479 (1965).
7. *Brown v. Board of Education*, 347 U.S. 483 (1954).
8. *Sugarman v. Dougall*, 413 U.S. 634 (1973).
9. *Bell v. Burston*, 402 U.S. 535 (1971).
10. *Goldberg v. Kelly*, 397 U.S. 254 (1970).
11. *Sniadach v. Family Finance Corp.*, 395 U.S. 337 (1969).
12. *Fuentes v. Shevin*, 407 U.S. 67 (1972).
13. *Wolf v. McDonnell*, 418 U.S. 539 (1974).
14. *Morrissey v. Brewer*, 408 U.S. 471 (1972).
15. *Perry v. Sinderman*, 408 U.S. 593 (1972).
16. *Goss v. Lopez*, 419 U.S. 565 (1975).
17. *Barron v. Baltimore*, 32 U.S. (7 Pet.) 243 (1833).
18. See *Walker v. Sauvinet*, 92 U.S. 90 (1875); *United States v. Cruikshank*, 92 U.S. 542, 552-556 (1875); *Hurtado v. California*, 110 U.S. 516 (1884); *Presser v. Illinois*, 116 U.S. 252, 263-268 (1886); *In re Kemmler*, 136 U.S. 436, 448, (1890); *McElvaine v. Brush*, 142 U.S. 155, 158-159 (1891); *O'Neil v. Vermont*, 144 U.S. 323, 332 (1892).
19. *Chicago, B. & Q. R.R. v. Chicago*, 166 U.S. 226, 241 (1897).
20. *Gitlow v. New York*, 268 U.S. 652, 666 (1925); compare *Prudential Insurance Co. v. Cheek*, 259 U.S. 530, 543 (1922).
21. *Wolf v. Colorado*, 338 U.S. 25, 27-28 (1949).
22. *Mapp v. Ohio*, 367 U.S. 643 (1961).
23. *Robinson v. California*, 370 U.S. 660 (1962).
24. *Furman v. Georgia*, 408 U.S. 238 (1972).
25. *Gideon v. Wainwright*, 372 U.S. 335 (1963); *Argersinger v. Hamlin*, 407 U.S. 25 (1972).
26. *Malloy v. Hogan*, 378 U.S. 1 (1964).
27. *Miranda v. Arizona*, 384 U.S. 436 (1966).
28. *Pointer v. Texas*, 380 U.S. 400 (1965).
29. *Klopfer v. North Carolina*, 386 U.S. 213 (1967); *Parker v. Gladden*, 385 U.S. 363 (1966); *Washington v. Texas*, 388 U.S. 14 (1967).
30. *Benton v. Maryland*, 395 U.S. 784 (1969).
31. *School District of Abinton v. Schempp*, 374 U.S. 203 (1963).
32. *New York Times v. Sullivan*, 376 U.S. 254 (1964).
33. *NAACP v. Alabama*, 377 U.S. 288 (1964).
34. *Boyd v. United States*, 116 U.S. 616 (1886).
35. *Olmstead v. United States*, 277 U.S. 438, 474 (1928) (dis. op.).
36. *Boyd v. United States*, 116 U.S., at 635 (1886).
37. *Geduldig v. Aiello*, 417 U.S. 484 (1974).
38. *Ortwein v. Schwab*, 410 U.S. 656 (1973); *United States v. Kras*, 409 U.S. 434 (1973).

39. *Paul v. Davis*, 96 S. Ct. 1155 (1976).

40. *Arnett v. Kennedy*, 416 U.S. 134 (1974).

41. *Matthews v. Eldridge*, 424 U.S. 319 (1976).

42. *Hudgens v. NLRB*, 424 U.S. 507 (1976); *Lloyd Corp., Ltd. v. Tanner*, 407 U.S. 551 (1972).

43. *United States v. Watson*, 423 U.S. 411 (1976).

44. *United States v. Robinson*, 414 U.S. 218 (1973); *Gustafson v. Florida*, 414 U.S. 260 (1973).

45. *Schneckloth v. Bustamonte*, 412 U.S. 218 (1973); *United States v. Watson*, 423 U.S. 411 (1976).

46. *United States v. Miller*, 96 S. Ct. 1619 (1976).

47. *Fisher v. United States*, 96 S. Ct. 1569 (1976).

48. *Harris v. New York*, 401 U.S. 222 (1971).

49. *United States v. Calandra*, 414 U.S. 338 (1974).

50. *Kirby v. Illinois*, 406 U.S. 682 (1972).

51. *Apodaca v. Oregon*, 406 U.S. 404 (1972).

52. *Rizzo v. Goode*, 96 S. Ct. 598 (1976); *Warth v. Seldin*, 422 U.S. 490 (1975); *O'Shea v. Littleton*, 414 U.S. 488 (1974).

53. *People v. Disbrow*, 127 Cal. Rptr. 360, 545 P.2d 272 (1976).

54. *State v. Kaluna*, 520 P.2d 51, 58 n.6 (Hawaii 1974).

55. *Murdock v. City of Memphis*, 20 Wall. 590 (1875).

56. *Burrows v. Superior Court*, 13 Cal. 3d 238, 529 P.2d 590 (1974).

57. *United States v. Miller*, 96 S. Ct. 1619 (1976).

58. See generally W. Brennan, "The Bill of Rights and the States," in *The Great Rights*, ed. E. Cahn 71-72 (New York: Macmillan, 1963).

22

First Things First: Rediscovering the States' Bills of Rights

HANS A. LINDE

Justice, Oregon State Supreme Court

State bills of rights are first in two senses: first in time and first in logic.

History

It was not unheard of in 1776, long before the drafting of the Federal Constitution, for the revolutionaries of that day to declare in the charters of their new states that the liberty of the press should be inviolably preserved, or that warrants to search any place or to seize any person or property must be based on information under oath and describing the place or the person. Nor was it unusual in these charters to grant every criminal defendant a right to a speedy trial before an impartial jury, with the assistance of counsel, to confront and question the witnesses against him, not to be compelled to give evidence against himself, nor to be subjected to excessive bail or fines nor to cruel or unusual punishment.[1]

By 1783, 13 states, all but Rhode Island, had adopted written constitutions. The majority of them contained most of the catalogue of civil liberties included in Virginia's Declaration of Rights, and Maryland's, and Delaware's, and Pennsylvania's. But they were by no means identical.[2] That was no accident. During the months preceding independence, political leaders debated the case for having the Continental Congress prepare uniform constitutions for the states. They finally rejected this idea in favor of calling upon each state to write a constitution satisfactory to itself.[3]

Far from being the model for the states, the Federal Bill of Rights was added to the Constitution to meet demands for the same guarantees against the new central government that people had secured against their own local officials. Moreover, the states that adopted new constitutions during the following decades took their bills of rights from the preexisting state constitutions rather than from the federal amendments. For example, Oregon's constitution in 1859 adopted Indiana's copy of Ohio's version of sources found in Delaware and elsewhere.

The Federal Bill of Rights did not supersede those of the states. It was not interposed between the citizen and his state. When the Fifth Amendment was invoked against the City of Baltimore in 1833, John Marshall replied that its adoption "could never have occurred to any human being, as a mode of doing that which might be effected by the state itself."[4] Only the Civil War made it clear that it might sometimes be necessary to use federal law as a mode of doing that which a state could but did nor effect for itself—the protection of some of its citizens against those in control of its government.

It is the Fourteenth Amendment that has bound the states to observe the guarantees of the Federal Bill of Rights. I do not underestimate that crucial role of the Fourteenth Amendment. But the effect has gone beyond assuring that state officials respect the rights guaranteed by federal law. It has led many state courts and the lawyers who practice before them to ignore the state's law, enforcing only those personal rights guaranteed by federal law, or to assume that the state's own guarantees must reflect whatever the United States Supreme Court finds in their federal analogues.

We tend to forget how recently the application of the Federal Bill of Rights to the states developed. Throughout the nineteenth century and the first quarter of the twentieth, state courts decided questions of constitutional rights under their own state constitutions. In 1925, it was only a hypothesis that the states were bound by the First Amendment.[5] That was really settled only after 1937.[6] Fifth Amendment guarantees against compulsory self-incrimination and double jeopardy did not bind the states until 1964 and 1969, respectively.[7] I shall not go through the catalogue; most of the decisions binding the states to observe the procedures of the Fourth, Fifth, and Sixth amendments date from the same period.[8] Of course, the states had all these guarantees in their own laws long before the Federal Bill of Rights was applied to the states. State courts had been administering these laws, sometimes generously, more often not, for a century or more without awaiting an interpretation from the United States Supreme Court.

Historically, the states' commitment to individual rights came first. Restraints on the federal government were patterned upon the states' declarations of rights. Even in modern times the United States Supreme Court has sometimes looked to that original history to interpret a federal clause.[9] But today, most state courts look to interpretations of the Federal Bill of Rights for the meaning of their own state constitutions, in the rare cases when they consider them at all.

The Logic of Federalism

Just as rights under the state constitutions were first in time, they are first also in the logic of constitutional law. For lawyers, the point is quickly made. Whenever a person asserts a particular right, and a state court recognizes and protects that right under state law, then the state is not depriving the person of whatever federal claim he or she might otherwise assert. There is no federal question.

Every state supreme court, I suppose, has declared that it will not needlessly decide a case on a constitutional ground if other legal issues can dispose of the case. The identical principle applies when examining that part of the state's law which is in its own constitution. In my view, a state court should always consider its state constitution before the Federal Constitution. It owes its state the respect to consider the state constitutional question even when counsel does not raise it, which is most of the time. The same court probably would not let itself be pushed into striking down a state law before considering that law's proper interpretation. The principle is the same.

Let us avoid any misunderstanding. The United States Constitution is the supreme law of the land. Nothing in the state's law or constitution can diminish a federal right. But no state court needs or, in my view, ought to hold that the law of its state denies what the Federal Constitution demands, without at least discussing the guarantees provided in its own bill of rights. In fact, Justices of the Supreme Court frequently invite a state court to do just that, usually when those Justices disagree with the majority's decision of the federal issue presented. As Chief Justice Burger once observed, "for all we know, the state courts would find this statute invalid under the State Constitution, but no one on either side of the case thought to discuss this or exhibit any interest in the subject."[10] Justices Brennan and Marshall, disappointed at decisions that have reversed state courts when they protected a claim under the Fourteenth Amendment, have issued frequent reminders that the state courts could have reached the same decisions under the state constitution.[11]

Granted, a state court might often reach the opposite result under the state constitution and bend only to the external compulsion of the Fourteenth Amendment. A state constitution does not always protect whatever the Federal Constitution protects. But a state court should put things in their logical sequence and routinely examine its state law first, before reaching a federal issue.

Putting Principle Into Practice

Let us examine what putting first things first means in practice, both for courts and for the practitioner.

When a state court deals with constitutional claims that do not currently occupy the *United States Reports,* the state court is quite accustomed to making its own analysis under the state constitution. Commonplace examples are issues of the condemnation of property for public use or alleged disparities of assessments for taxation. But when the issue arises in an area in which the Supreme Court has been active, lawyers generally stop citing the state's own law and decisions of the state court, and the court abandons reference to the state constitution. Such reference to the state constitution reappears only when counsel and the state court wish to extend a constitutional right beyond the decisions of the Supreme Court and to do so without facing possible reversal on certiorari. In other words, the normal and logical sequence is reversed: counsel and court first determine whether the state has violated the Federal Constitution, and only when it has done so do they reach a question of state law. That practice stands the Constitution on its head.

The tactic of using the state constitution only selectively is best illustrated by two famous California cases concerning equal protection. In *Serrano v. Priest*,[12] the California Supreme Court held that the amount spent on public schools could not depend on the different tax bases available to rich and to poor local school districts. The opinion was written in the terminology of federal equal protection doctrine, with only a passing reference to California's own article I, section 21.[13] That section forbade laws granting to any citizen or class of citizens privileges or immunities which, upon the same terms, shall not equally belong to all citizens. This is a common provision which is older than the Fourteenth Amendment and independent of its context of race discrimination. Before the *Serrano* litigation was concluded, the United States Supreme Court rejected the same equal protection claim in *San Antonio Independent School District v. Rodriguez*.[14] Thereafter, the California court reaffirmed its original holding under the California clause.[15]

One might think that, having discovered the clause in the California Constitution prohibiting laws granting to any class of citizens privileges which are not equally open to all citizens on the same terms, the California court either would have found the clause relevant to Allan Bakke's attack on the preferential admissions system at the medical school in Davis,[16] or that the court would at least discuss why not.

Indeed, California amended its constitution in 1974 to provide expressly that the "rights guaranteed by this Constitution are not dependent on those guaranteed by the United States Constitution."[17] But that discussion of equality of privileges did not occur. In *Bakke v. Regents of the University of California*,[18] the California court studiously bypassed all preliminary issues of state law and placed its decision squarely on the Fourteenth Amendment, so as to invite Supreme Court review of this controversial issue. The court did not seem concerned about the implication that the law of California offered Mr. Bakke no protection for a right to which the court, rightly or wrongly, believed him to be entitled.[19]

From the lawyer's standpoint, the state's bill of rights may seem utterly irrelevant when the federal precedents are squarely in his favor. Nevertheless, it is a mistake to ignore the state guarantee. In the early 1970s, lawyers invariably took every civil liberties case to the federal district court. One very good lawyer did just that in *Tanner v. Lloyd Corp., Ltd.*[20] The plaintiffs in that case were denied the right to distribute anti-war leaflets in a large shopping center in Portland. On the basis of existing Supreme Court decisions, both the federal district court,[21] and the Court of Appeals for the Ninth Circuit[22] sustained the claim under the First Amendment; no one bothered with the Oregon Constitution. By the time the Supreme Court granted certiorari and reversed its prior direction,[23] it was of course too late.

I would guess that if the plaintiff from the outset had invoked the Oregon Constitution's free speech and assembly provisions, these provisions would have been interpreted consistently with the existing First Amendment precedents in the plaintiff's favor. After the reversal under the First Amendment, lawyers who had litigated a similar shopping center case in state court and had relied on the lower federal court's decision against the Lloyd Center tried belatedly to switch their argument to the Oregon Constitution, but they found that the Oregon court was reluctant to contradict the Supreme Court's *Lloyd Corp.* decision.[24] California, incidentally, has done so under its constitution.[25]

Many other cases show that what is sound in theory is also intensely practical. In recent years, state courts have often found themselves reversed by the Supreme Court when they decided in favor of some individual right on the basis of the United States Constitution.[26] An Alabama court, for instance, held that an employer could not be made to pay an employee while on jury duty.[27] The Pennsylvania Supreme Court held that a gross receipts tax on parking lots took the operator's property without due process.[28] The Idaho court thought that its unemployment benefit rules violated the equal protection clause.[29] These decisions indeed may not have been good Fourteenth Amendment law and deserved to be reversed. But I venture to say that in every case the court could have cited the state's own constitution for its holding. Some years ago, for example, in *Maryland Board of Pharmacy v. Save-A-Lot, Inc.,*[30] Judge Levine reaffirmed the doctrine that in Maryland due process requires statutes to have a substantial relation to some identified objective, notwithstanding what the Supreme Court might say. I have little enthusiasm for that doctrine,[31] but I am the first to say Maryland is entitled to it under its own constitution. Without the Maryland Constitution, the court might have found itself reversed, as the North Dakota court was when it thought it was following an old federal due process case that had escaped being expressly overruled in the 1940s.[32]

The lesson, I suggest, is that a claim under the state's own law must be more than a perfunctory afterthought. First things first. Indeed, when a court ties a state constitutional guarantee as a tail to the kite of the corresponding federal clause, it may simply find the state ground ignored on certiorari, as happened recently in *Delaware v. Prouse.*[33] But the habit that developed in the 1960s of making a federal case of every claim and looking for all law in Supreme Court opinions dies hard.

NOTES

1. See, e.g., Md. Const., Decl. of Rights arts. 19, 20, 22, 23, 38.
2. F. Green, *Constitutional Development in the South Atlantic States, 1776-1860,* at 52-56 (Chapel Hill: University of North Carolina Press, 1930).

3. *Barron v. Mayor of Baltimore,* 32 U.S. 242 (1833).

4. See *Gitlow v. New York,* 268 U.S. 652 (1925); cf. *Pierce v. Society of Sisters,* 268 U.S. 510 (1925) (First Amendment not used to invalidate Oregon statute which would effectively close religious primary schools).

5. See *Cantwell v. Connecticut,* 310 U.S. 296 (1940); *Thornhill v. Alabama,* 310 U.S. 88 (1940); *DeJonge v. Oregon,* 299 U.S. 353 (1937).

6. See *Benton v. Maryland,* 395 U.S. 784 (1969); *Mallory v. Hogan,* 378 U.S. 1 (1964).

7. E.g., *Duncan v. Louisiana,* 391 U.S. 145 (1968) (trial by jury); *Klopfer v. North Carolina,* 386 U.S. 213 (1967) (speedy trial); *Pointer v. Texas,* 380 U.S. 400 (1965) (right to confrontation); *Gideon v. Wainwright,* 372 U.S. 335 (1963) (right to counsel); *Mapp v. Ohio,* 367 U.S. 643 (1961) (the exclusionary rule).

8. See *Apodaca v. Oregon,* 406 U.S. 404 (1972); *Williams v. Florida,* 399 U.S. 78 (1970); *Duncan v. Louisiana,* 391 U.S. 145 (1968). An earlier, interesting example arising in Maryland was *In re Provoo,* 17 F.R.D. 183 (1955).

9. Justice Marshall has suggested that the United States Supreme Court refrain from reversing a state judgment in favor of a defendant relying on constitutional grounds "unless it is quite clear that the state court has resolved all applicable state law questions adversely to the defendant and that it feels compelled by its view of the federal constitutional issue to reverse the conviction at hand." *Oregon v. Haas,* 420 U.S. 714, 729 (1975) (dissenting opinion); see P. Galie and L. Galie, "State Constitutional Guarantees and Supreme Court Review: Justice Marshall's Proposal in *Oregon v. Haas,*" 82 *Dickinson Law Review* 273 (1978). I have stated elsewhere that lower federal courts also should inquire into state constitutional guarantees when plaintiffs attack state action on federal constitutional grounds. See Linde, "Book Review," 52 *Ohio Law Review* 325 (1973).

10. *Wisconsin v. Constantineau,* 400 U.S. 440 (1971) (Burger, C.J., dissenting).

11. E.g., *Idaho Dept. of Employment v. Smith,* 434 U.S. 100 (1977); *Michigan v. Mosley,* 423 U.S. 96 (1975); *Texas v. White,* 423 U.S. 67 (1975). See also *New Jersey v. Portash,* 440 U.S. 450 (1979).

12. 5 Cal.3d 584, 487 P.2d 1241, 96 Cal. Rptr. 601 (1971).

13. Cal. Const. art. 1, § 21 (current version at § 7).

14. 411 U.S. 1 (1973).

15. *Serrano v. Priest* (Serrano II), 18 Cal.3d 728, 557 P.2d 929, 135 Cal. Rptr. 345 (1976), *cert. denied,* 432 U.S. 907 (1977).

16. *Bakke v. Regents of Univ. of Cal.,* 18 Cal.3d 34, 553 P.2d 1152, 132 Cal. Rptr. 680 (1977), *aff'd.* in part, *rev'd.* in part, 438 U.S. 265 (1978).

17. Cal. Const. art 1, § 24.

18. 18 Cal.3d 34, 553 P.2d 1152, 132 Cal. Rptr. 680 (1977), *aff'd.* in part, *rev'd.* in part, 438 U.S. 265 (1978).

19. Since this speech was delivered, the California Supreme Court has applied the state constitution rather than the federal equal protection clause as well as statutory law to hold that a public utility company unlawfully discriminated against employment of homosexuals. *Gay Law Students Ass'n. v. Pacific Telephone & Telegraph,* 24 Cal.3d 458, 595 P.2d 592, 156 Cal. Rptr. 14 (1979).

Other recent California decisions relying on state constitutional provisions include: *Van Atta v. Scott,* 27 Cal.3d 424, 613 P.2d 210, 166 Cal. Rptr. 149 (1980) (bail practices invalidated under state due process clause); *City of Santa Barbara v. Adamson,* 27 Cal.3d 123, 610 P.2d 436, 164 Cal. Rptr. 539 (1980) (ordinance prohibiting five or more unrelated persons from residing in single-family home violated state constitutional right of privacy); *San Francisco Labor Council v. Regents of Univ. of Cal.*, 26 Cal.3d 785, 608 P.2d 277, 163 Cal. Rptr. 460 (1980) (statute requiring university to pay prevailing wages in community violated state constitutional provision establishing independence of university); *People v. Rucker*, 26 Cal.3d 368, 605 P.2d 843, 162 Cal. Rptr. 13 (1980) (evidence of interviews between defendant and police violated state constitutional privilege against self-incrimination).

20. 308 F.Supp 128 (D. Or. 1970), *rev'd.*, 407 U.S. 551 (1972).

21. Ibid.

22. *Tanner v. Lloyd Corp., Ltd.*, 446 F.2d 545 (9th Cir. 1971), *rev'd.*, 407 U.S. 551 (1972).

23. *Lloyd Corp., Ltd. v. Tanner*, 407 U.S. 551 (1972), *rev'd.*, 446 F.2d 545 (9th Cir. 1971).

24. See *Lenrich Assocs. v. Heyda*, 264 Or. 122, 504 P.2d 112 (1972); 52 *Oregon Law Review* 338 (1973).

25. See *Robins v. Pruneyard Shopping Center*, 22 Cal.3d 899, 592 P.2d 341, (153 Cal. Rptr. 854 (1979), *aff'd.*, 48 U.S.L.W. 4650 (U.S. 1980).

26. The Supreme Court has reversed state supreme courts under these circumstances more than 20 times since the October 1972 term. The most recent decisions reaching this result include *Michigan v. DeFillippo*, 443 U.S. 31 (1979); *Fare v. Michael C.*, 442 U.S. 707 (1979); and *North Carolina v. Butler*, 441 U.S. 369 (1979).

27. *Gadsden Times Publishing Corp. v. Dean*, 49 Ala. App. 45, 268 So.2d 829, *cert. denied*, 289 Ala. 743, 268 So.2d 834 (1972), *rev'd.*, 412 U.S. 543 (1973).

28. *Alco Parking Corp. v. City of Pittsburgh*, 453 Pa. 245, 307 A.2d 851 (1973), *rev'd.*, 417 U.S. 369 (1974).

29. *Smith v. Idaho Dept. of Employment*, 98 Idaho 43, 557 P.2d 637 (1976), *rev'd.*, 434 U.S. 100 (1977).

30. 270 Md. 103, 311 A.2d 242 (1973).

31. See Linde, "Due Process of Lawmaking," 55 *Nebraska Law Review* 195 (1976).

32. See *North Dakota State Bd. of Pharmacy v. Snyder's Drug Stores, Inc.*, 414 U.S. 156 (1973).

33. 440 U.S. 648 (1979). Justice White's opinion states: "The [Delaware] court analyzed the various decisions interpreting the Federal Constitution, concluded that the Fourth Amendment foreclosed spot checks of automobiles, and summarily held that the state constitution was therefore also infringed. . . . Had state law not been mentioned at all, there would be no question about our jurisdiction, even though the state constitution might have provided an independent and adequate state ground. . . . The same result should follow here where the state constitutional holding depended upon the state court's view of the reach of the Fourth and Fourteenth amendments." Ibid., at 652-653. Justice White expanded this proposition: "Moreover, every case holding a search or seizure to be contrary to the state constitutional provision relies on cases interpreting the Fourth Amendment and simultaneously concludes that the search or seizure is contrary to that provision. . . ." Ibid., at 652-653 n.5. See also *New Jersey v. Portash*, 440 U.S. 450, 460-461 (1979) (Brennan, J., concurring).

23

Trends in the Relationship Between the Federal and State Courts

SANDRA D. O'CONNOR

*Justice, Supreme Court of the United States,
and former Judge, Arizona Court of Appeals*

We live in an imperfect world. Most people would agree our court system suffers from some of that imperfection. We appear to be the only major country with two parallel court systems. Among other things, such an arrangement affords most convicted criminal defendants opportunities for multiple post-conviction appellate court reviews. The labyrinth of judicial reviews of the various stages of a state criminal felony case would appear strange, indeed, to a rational person charged with devising an ideal criminal justice system. Changes and improvements come very slowly, if at all, and, more often than not, incrementally, in small case by case adjustments.

State courts, which annually process the great majority of all civil and criminal cases filed in this country, handle their workload for the most part without a great deal of concern about the federal court system which exists alongside them. Trial judges in both systems are busy hearing cases. Most state court trial judges do not have time to think about what jurisdiction the federal courts should have; they simply take each case assigned and do the best they can with it, whether or not it involves a federal legal question. On the other hand, state appellate court judges occasionally become so frustrated with the extent of federal court intervention that they simply abdicate in favor of the federal jurisdiction. For example, concern in the Supreme Court of Arizona with the extent of the exercise of federal jurisdiction of prisoner complaints led it to refuse to hear any prisoner complaints because of "preemption of the field" by the federal courts.[1]

It is my purpose to comment on some of the trends in the relationship between the state and federal courts as viewed from the practical perspective of a state court judge.

Criminal Proceedings

Application of federal constitutional law by state courts is made most often in state criminal prosecutions. A state criminal defendant gains access to the federal courts by alleging that a violation of the Federal Constitution occurred during the state proceedings. There is seldom a state criminal felony trial in which the defendant is convicted that does not result in an appeal at the state level alleging some federal constitutional error in order to exhaust the state remedies before seeking federal review. As noted by Justice Powell in his concurring opinion in *Rose v. Mitchell*: "Federal constitutional challenges are raised in almost every state criminal case, in part because every lawyer knows that such claims will provide nearly automatic federal habeas corpus review."[2]

Every state court trial judge realizes, of course, that federal constitutional challenges will be raised in almost every state criminal case and that, after the state appellate review is exhausted, further review will be attempted in the federal courts. As a result, state courts in urban areas have tended to assign certain judges to hear only criminal cases in order that they may become more familiar with applicable state and federal, substantive and procedural, criminal and constitutional law. In addition, the National Center for State Courts, the Institute of Judicial Administration, and the National Judicial College continually offer assistance to courts and to state judges on various aspects of how they can appropriately function within the state and federal constitutional parameters. There is a keen awareness among state court judges in state criminal cases of the federal constitutional protections of the defendant.

With the election of President Reagan, there is no reason to think the recent trend in the United States Supreme Court shifting to the state courts some additional responsibility for determination of federal constitutional questions in state criminal cases will not continue. As stated by Charles Whitebread:

> [T]he Warren Court, which was extremely energetic in expanding the scope of federal constitutional claims open to state prisoners, seemed to act on the premise that the state courts could not be depended upon to vindicate these newly created rights. Thus, it forged new law on the procedural as well as substantive front by providing greater access to federal court for state defendants. Federal habeas corpus became the principal remedy through which the newly created rights could be asserted and protected. By contrast, as the Burger Court has limited the substantive federal constitutional rights of the state criminal defendant, it has simultaneously reduced dramatically the avenues available for state prisoner access to the lower federal courts.[3]

A recent example of the increased reluctance of the United States Supreme Court to overturn by federal habeas corpus proceedings state court determinations in criminal cases is found in *Sumner v. Mata*.[4] The Court in *Sumner* held that a federal court that grants federal habeas corpus relief to a state criminal defendant is required by 28 U.S.C. § 2254(d) to presume the state appellate or trial court's factual findings are correct and to explain the reasons for determining that the state court's findings were not fairly supported by the record. The majority opinion states: "Federal habeas has been a source of friction between state and federal courts and Congress obviously meant to alleviate some of that friction when it enacted subsection (d) in 1966 as an amendment to the original Federal Habeas Act of 1867."[5]

In the next decade, there will probably be significant additional state court variations in cases involving the issue of illegal search and seizure under the Fourth Amendment. Since *Stone v. Powell*,[6] state criminal defendants who have had a "full and fair opportunity" to raise their claims of illegal search and seizure in the state courts may not, thereafter, obtain federal habeas corpus relief. We do not yet know the tests to be employed in determining what is a "full and fair opportunity." However, assuming that the state courts are providing a full and fair opportunity for the claims to be raised, and that federal habeas corpus review is unavailable, the state courts are more likely than their federal counterparts to reach widely varying results on search and seizure issues. Even the federal cases on search and seizure are not models of clarity and simplicity. The standards tend to be confusing and obtuse in some instances.[7]

One area where federal court review of state courts' determinations of federal constitutional questions may be expected to increase, however, is the area of state criminal defendants' waiver of their constitutional objections. State criminal defendants seeking habeas corpus relief in the federal court must raise their constitutional objections in a timely fashion in the state proceedings, or they will be held to have waived their claim for relief, absent a showing of cause why the objection was not raised and also a showing of actual prejudice.[8] We can expect a number of petitions to be filed for habeas corpus relief to test the extent to which failure of defense counsel to raise the issue in the state proceedings will establish good cause for avoiding the waiver. Competence of counsel may be relevant to the determination of good cause and of prejudice.[9]

Closely related to the question of waiver of the constitutional issue at the state level is the question of competence of counsel as a ground for collateral attack on state convictions on the basis of the Sixth Amendment. This issue is one which will undoubtedly be raised very frequently during the next few years. At present, it is the single issue raised most frequently in Arizona appellate courts in petitions for post-conviction relief in criminal cases.[10]

The United States Supreme Court has held that counsel must render legal services "within the range of competence demanded of attorneys in criminal cases."[11] This standard is far from definitive. No doubt the range of competence varies somewhat from community to community and from state to state. The older test of whether the proceedings were a "farce and mockery of justice" has been rejected in all but three of the federal circuits.[12] The other circuits have developed differing standards for determining the competence of counsel.[13]

The majority follow a "reasonable competency" or analogous standard.[14] The District of Columbia Circuit has adopted a standard which requires the defendant to show that his counsel performed measurably below accepted standards and that the inadequacy of his counsel had a "likely" effect on the outcome of the trial.[15] State standards for determining competency likewise vary.[16]

It is reasonable to expect that we will continue to see many state and federal cases dealing with the appropriate standard for effective assistance of counsel under the Sixth Amendment. In view of the conflicting holdings in the federal appellate courts, the Supreme Court may accept jurisdiction and attempt to establish a more definite standard. It is also likely that some strain may be felt by some state courts as their determinations of attorney competence are reviewed in the federal courts.

Civil Cases

Although the present trend in federal review of state criminal matters appears to be to restrict some of the federal jurisdiction, quite the reverse trend seems to be occurring in civil cases, both by federal judicial decisions and by congressional action. Although not arising as frequently as in the criminal area, federal constitutional law, as it applies to state legislative and executive action, is perhaps of more concern to state courts in terms of forcing significant decisions to be made in cases of great public interest. We have seen recently examples of acute confrontations between federal district courts and state courts in school busing and school desegregation cases. Application of the federal guaranty of equal protection of the laws has resulted in court review of state voting requirements,[17] state durational residence requirements for welfare benefits,[18] and other state welfare eligibility requirements,[19] in addition to public educational opportunities.[20] Application of the due process clause of the Fourteenth Amendment has resulted in court review of state prison regulations,[21] state procedures for garnishment,[22] and prejudgment attachment of property by creditors.[23]

The next decade is also likely to see continued expansion of litigation in the federal courts under 42 U.S.C. § 1983,[24] the civil rights statute, unless Congress decides to limit the availability of relief under that statute. Many, if not most, of the cases alleging due process or equal protection violations by the states, their officers, and employees are filed under Section 1983. Allegations that the plaintiff has been deprived of either personal liberty or property of any amount in violation of his civil rights will give the federal court jurisdiction to hear the claim. Even state court judges are not immune from a Section 1983 suit if the allegation is that the judge acted in the clear absence of jurisdiction in the matter.[25] Judge Aldisert has observed that each expansion of the use of Section 1983 to challenge state action has been prompted by a distrust of the state courts as proper forums to consider the issues raised.[26]

In the past, the United States Supreme Court has held that plaintiffs alleging state civil rights violations need not exhaust state remedies before filing suit in the federal court under Section 1983.[27] More recently, however, the Court has stated, "whether this is invariably the case . . . is a question we need not now decide."[28] In *Barry v. Barchi*,[29] the Court reaffirmed the *Gibson v. Berryhill*[30] holding that exhaustion of administrative remedies is not required when the question of the adequacy of the administrative remedies is for all practical purposes identical with the merits of the Section 1983 action. The United States courts of appeals are divided on the issue of whether exhaustion of state administrative remedies is a necessary prerequisite to the federal suit.[31]

Another area of federal civil case jurisdiction which Congress may examine in the next few years is the diversity jurisdiction. The debate over whether Congress should eliminate diversity jurisdiction from the federal courts has continued for some years.[32]

Any discussion of whether diversity jurisdiction should be eliminated, and any discussion of where the line should be drawn for the exercise of federal jurisdiction in state criminal and civil cases generally, requires examination of the assertion often heard that the federal courts are the preferred forum. Let us examine the arguments made to justify the conclusion that federal judges are preferred. First, it is argued that federal judges are better paid and have more prestige.[33] It is certainly true that most federal judges are better paid.[34] However, the higher pay does not necessarily attract only the most competent lawyers to the federal bench. Often political considerations are more important than pure competence in the appointing process. In addition, many appointments to the federal bench are made from state court benches.[35] When the state court judge puts on his or her new federal court robe he or she does *not* become immediately better equipped intellectually to do the job.

Second, it is said that life tenure insulates the judge from majoritarian pressure, and, therefore, the federal judges are more receptive to controversial principles.[36] In 20 states, however, we now have merit selection of state judges rather than popular elections.[37] These judges are relatively safe and secure in their positions. Even those state judges who are elected often have reasonably long terms of office.[38]

Third, it is argued that federal judges will be more receptive to federal constitutional claims. Yet, there is no reason to assume that state court judges cannot and will not provide a "hospitable forum" in litigating federal constitutional questions. As stated by Justice William H. Rehnquist in a recent opinion:

> State judges as well as federal judges swear allegiance to the Constitution of the United States, and there is no reason to think that because of their frequent differences of opinions as to how that document should be interpreted that all are not doing their mortal best to discharge their oath of office.[39]

Conclusion

If our nation's bifurcated judicial system is to be retained, as I am sure it will be, it is clear that we should strive to make both the federal and the state systems strong, independent, and viable. State courts will undoubtedly continue in the future to litigate federal constitutional questions. State judges in assuming office take an oath to support the federal as well as the state constitution. State judges do in fact rise to the occasion when given the responsibility and opportunity to do so. It is a step in the right direction to defer to the state courts and give finality to their judgments on federal constitutional questions where a *full* and *fair* adjudication has been given in the state court.

NOTES

1. *Patricella v. Arizona,* No. H 650 (24 April 1973).

2. 443 U.S. 545, 581 (1979) (Powell, J., concurring).

3. C. Whitebread, *Criminal Procedure* § 28.01, at 574 (Mineola, N.Y.: Foundation Press, 1980).

4. 101 S. Ct. 764 (1981).

5. Ibid., at 770.

6. 428 U.S. 465 (1976).

7. For some articles addressing the confusion in the case law in the Fourth Amendment area, see S. Burkoff " The Court that Devoured the Fourteenth Amendment: The Triumph of an Inconsistent Exclusionary Doctrine," 58 *Oregon Law Review* 151 (1979); and V. Countryman, "Search and Seizure in a Shambles? Recasting Fourth Amendment Law in the Mold of Justice Douglas," 64 *Iowa Law Review* 435 (1979).

8. *Francis v. Henderson,* 425 U.S. 536, 542 (1976).

9. See *Wainwright v. Sykes,* 433 U.S. 72, 94-96 (1977) (Stevens, J., concurring).

10. Seventy-five petitions for appellate post-conviction relief in criminal cases were filed in Arizona in 1980. Of these, 27, or 36 percent, raised the issue of competence of counsel. Letter from John Sticht, Staff Attorney, Arizona Court of Appeals to Judge Sandra D. O'Connor, Arizona Court of Appeals (25 February 1981).

Direct appeals from state criminal convictions frequently involve an allegation that there was a failure at trial to raise a defense, to make an evidentiary objection, or to request a jury instruction. Unless the failure resulted in "fundamental error," the state appellate court will ordinarily affirm the conviction. See, e.g., *State v. Workman,* 123 Ariz. 501, 500 P.2d 1133 (Ariz. Ct. App. 1979); *Bell v. State,* 598 S.W.2d 738 (Ark. 1980); *People v. Means,* 97 Mich. App. 641, 296 N.W.2d 14 (1980); *State v. Moon,* 602 S.W.2d 828 (Mo. Ct. App. 1980); *People v. Vasquez,* 430 N.Y.S.2d 501 (Sup. Ct. 1980); *State v. Foddrell,* 269 S.E.2d 854 (W.Va. 1980). The same is true in appeals to federal appellate courts from convictions in federal criminal cases. Fed. R. Crim. P.52; see, e.g., *McKissick v. United States,* 379 F.2d 754 (5th Cir. 1967).

11. *McMann v. Richardson,* 397 U.S. 759, 771 (1970).

12. W. Schwarzer, "Dealing with Incompetent Counsel—The Trial Judge's Role," 93 *Harvard Law Review* 633, 641 n.40 (1980); "Fifth Annual Ninth Circuit Survey— Criminal Law and Procedure—New Effective Assistance of Counsel Standard—Prejudice Required," 10 *Golden Gate University Law Review* 75, 79 n.29 (1980). See, generally, J. Strazzella, "Ineffective Assistance of Counsel Claims: New Uses, New Problems," 19 *Arizona Law Review* 443 (1977).

13. See authorities cited note 12 supra.

14. See *Cooper v. Fitzharris,* 586 F.2d 1325, 1328 n.3 (9th Cir. 1978), *cert. denied,* 440 U.S. 974 (1979).

15. *United States v. Decoster,* 624 F.2d 196 (D.C. Cir. 1976) (plurality opinion) (quoting *Commonwealth v. Saterian,* 366 Mass. 89, 96, 315 N.E.2d 878, 883 (1974).

16. See, e.g., *Bays v. State,* 240 Ind. 37, 159 N.E.2d 393 (1959) (requiring reasonable skill and diligence), *cert. denied,* 361 U.S. 972 (1960); *State v. Osgood,* 266 Minn. 315, 123 N.W.2d 593 (1963) (requiring consultations that adequately inform the accused of all his legal rights).

17. *Harper v. Virginia Bd. of Elections,* 383 U.S. 663 (1966).

18. *Shapiro v. Thompson,* 394 U.S. 618 (1969).

19. *Graham v. Richardson,* 403 U.S. 365 (1971).

20. *Keyes v. School Dist. No. 1,* 413 U.S. 189 (1973).

21. *Wolff v. McDonnell,* 418 U.S. 539 (1974).

22. *North Ga. Finishing, Inc. v. Di-Chem, Inc.,* 419 U.S. 601 (1975); *Sniadach v. Family Fin. Corp.,* 395 U.S. 337 (1969).

23. *Fuentes v. Shevin,* 407 U.S. 67 (1972).

24. 42 U.S.C. § 1983 (1976).

25. *Rankin v. Howard,* 633 F.2d 844, 849 (9th Cir. 1980).

26. R. Aldisert, "Judicial Expansion of Federal Jurisdiction: A Federal Judge's Thoughts on Section 1983, Comity and the Federal Caseload," 1973 *Law & Social Order* 557, 572.

27. *Wilwording v. Swenson,* 404 U.S. 249 (1971) (per curiam); *Damico v. California,* 389 U.S. 416 (1967) (per curiam); *McNeese v. Board of Educ.,* 373 U.S. 668 (1963).

28. *Gibson v. Berryhill,* 411 U.S. 564, 574-575 (1973).

29. 443 U.S. 55, 63 n.10 (1979).

30. 411 U.S. 564 (1973).

31. For cases holding exhaustion of state administrative remedies is required, see *Patsy v. Florida Int'l. Univ.,* 634 F.2d 900 (5th Cir. 1981); *Secret v. Brierton,* 584 F.2d 823 (7th Cir. 1978); *Gonzales v. Shanker,* 533 F.2d 832 (2d Cir. 1976); *Wishart v. McDonald,* 367 F.Supp. 530 (D. Mass. 1973), *aff'd.,* 500 F.2d 1110 (1st Cir. 1974).

For a case holding exhaustion of state administrative remedies is required only when prospective relief is sought, see *Canton v. Spokane School Dist. No. 81,* 498 F.2d 840 (9th Cir. 1974).

For cases holding exhaustion of state administrative remedies is not required, see *Simpson v. Weeks,* 570 F.2d 240 (8th Cir. 1978); *United States ex rel. Ricketts v. Lightcap,* 567 F.2d 1226 (3d Cir. 1977); *Gillette v. McNichols,* 517 F.2d 888 (10th Cir. 1975); *Hardwick v. Ault,* 517 F.2d 295 (5th Cir. 1975); *McCray v. Burrell,* 516 F.2d 357 (4th Cir. 1975), *cert. dismissed,* 426 U.S. 471 (1976); *Jones v. Metzger,* 456 F.2d 854 (6th Cir. 1972).

32. For an argument favoring abolition of federal diversity jurisdiction, see R. Kastenmeier and M. Remington, "Court Reform and Access to Justice; a Legislative Perspective," 16 *Harvard Journal on Legislation* 301, 311-318 (1979), and authorities cited therein. For an argument in support of maintaining federal diversity jurisdiction, see J. Frank, "The Case for Diversity Jurisdiction," 16 *Harvard Journal on Legislation* 403 (1979).

33. See, e.g., C. Neuborne, "The Myth of Parity," 90 *Harvard Law Review* 1105, 1121, 1124-1127 (1977).

34. From March 1977 to 31 December 1980, yearly salaries for federal district judges were $54,500 and for federal circuit judges, $57,500. *United States v. Will,* 101 S. Ct. 471, 476 (1980). Beginning 1 January 1981, yearly salaries for federal district judges are $67,100 and for circuit judges, $70,900. 67 *American Bar Association Journal* 162, 165 (1981).

As of 31 January 1979, the national average salary for association justices (excluding chief justices) of the highest state courts was $45,248; for state intermediate appellate court judges, $45,278; and for general trial court judges, $38,971. U.S. Department of Justice, Law Enforcement Assistance Administration, and National Criminal Justice Information and Statistics Service, *Sourcebook of Criminal Justice Statistics —* 1979 110, table 1.57 (1980). Hereinafter cited as 1979 *Sourcebook.*

However, the average salaries of state trial court judges increased by more than 90 percent between 1969 and 1980, while the salaries of federal courts of appeals and district court judges increased by less than 40 percent during the same period. 67 *American Bar Association Journal* 162, 164 (1981). And certain state judges receive salaries far higher than the averages given above. For instance, the chief justice of the state of California now receives $77,409 a year, and the chief judge of the highest New York court, the court of appeals, receives $75,000 a year. Ibid.

35. A study of characteristics of presidential nominees and appointees to United States court judgeships from 1963 to 27 August 1978, broken down by presidential administration, reveals that percentages of nominees who at the time of their nomination or appointment were employed by the judiciary ranged from 28.5 percent under President Nixon to 42.2 percent under President Carter. In addition, percentages of nominees with prior judicial experience ranged from 34.3 percent under President Johnson to 46.7 percent under President Carter. 1979 *Sourcebook,* supra note 34, at 115, table 1.60.

36. See, e.g., Neuborne, supra note 33, at 1105, 1127-1128.

37. S. Carbon, "Judicial Retention Elections: Are They Serving Their Intended Purpose?" 64 *Judicature* 210, 213-215 (1980).

38. D. Adamany and P. Dubois, "Electing State Judges," 1976 *Wisconsin Law Review* 731, 769.

39. *Sumner v. Mata,* 101 S. Ct. 764, 770 (1981).

PART VI

The Judicial Role in
a Litigious Society

IN HISTORICAL perspective, the role and power of the judiciary have always proven controversial, from the debates between Federalists and Antifederalists during the founding of the Republic to contemporary discussions of an "imperial judiciary" and "government by the judiciary."[1] Since *Marbury v. Madison,* the judiciary has assumed an important role in constitutional politics and shaped or given direction to public policy. Even as a forum for resolving private disputes, courts historically made policy. The "private law" of torts and contracts, for example, is actually "public law in disguise,"[2] inasmuch as it orders socio-economic relations and redistributes wealth.

The role of courts in our ever-litigious society has changed and become more important to the resolution of a growing range of public and private controversies. Increasingly in the twentieth century, Judge Irving Kaufman comments, "the judiciary has been an accelerator of government rather than a brake."[3] Judge Ruggero Aldisert, in chapter 24, points out that the changing role of courts is only partially due to judicial activism and intervention in the political process. The expanding role of courts, as Justice Lewis Powell among others also repeatedly emphasizes, has been encouraged by Congress's "enactment of remedial legislation deemed desirable to meet the social needs and technological developments of our time. This legislation, much of it creating new rights and inventing redress in courts, generates an ever-widening stream of litigation."[4] The growing prominence of the judiciary, moreover, may be due to more systemic political changes. Federal district Judge Jose Cabranes suggests that "as our politics have collapsed or proved unwieldy—the parties, the Congress, the post-Roosevelt presidency are widely believed to be in disarray— our least democratic branch of government has become the chief mechanism for serving democratic ends."[5] The contemporary judiciary has indeed come to be perceived as a forum for special-interest groups and so-called public-interest law firms to litigate issues of public policy, if not thereby to substitute the judicial process for the political process. Ultimately, Judge Aldisert concludes the prominence of courts in contemporary society is due to the people's high expectations of them and results from a "spreading judicialization" of political and social relationships.

Contemporary courts, Judge Aldisert underscores, make law and thus inexorably must address matters of public policy. In chapter 25, Judge Henry J. Friendly further discusses the issue of whether and when courts should decide questions of public policy and, if so, how and on what basis they should justify their decisions. Principles of law *and* considerations of public policy, he points out, long guided courts both in the private law of contracts, for example, and in areas of public law, such as the developing constitutional law of privacy. Judge Friendly departs from other judges who maintain that constitutional interpretation requires strict adherence to the text, to the language of the Constitution and Bill of Rights. Judge Robert Bork, for one, stresses that "the hard fact is . . . that there are no guidelines outside the Constitution that can control a judge [whether a judge turns to natural law, "conventional morality," "the idea of progress," or evolving social science and public policies]. . . . The truth is that the judge who looks outside the Constitution always looks inside himself and nowhere else."[6] By contrast, Judge Friendly argues that some clauses of the Constitution and Bill of Rights—for example, the First Amendment provision for freedom of speech and press or the Eighth Amendment ban on "cruel and unusual punishment"—are not only ambiguous but invite judges to develop and apply public policies. He illustrates the relationship between constitutional principles and public policy considerations by examining two of the Supreme Court's landmark rulings: the 1954 watershed school desegregation decision in *Brown v. Board of Education* and the 1973 abortion decision in *Roe v. Wade*. His discussion is particularly noteworthy in criticizing the former ruling for relying too much on social science data instead of articulating a persuasive constitutional principle, and in criticizing the latter for not paying enough attention to the social policy implications of the ruling while inventing an unconvincing constitutional "right of privacy" to justify its decision. Judge Friendly thus poses fundamental issues about the use of social and natural scientific evidence as a basis for judicial decision making and enforcement of civil rights and liberties.[7]

Along with Judges Aldisert and Friendly, Judge Frank Johnson, in chapter 26, argues the judicial role has always been an activist one, inexorably so given the judiciary's guardianship of civil rights and liberties. Judge Johnson concentrates on the role of the courts not in interpreting provisions of the Constitution but when enforcing their decisions and initiating and implementing policy with remedial decrees. Traditionally, courts have had a supervisory role in ensuring compliance with their decisions and have prescribed remedial changes in the operation of railroads in the late nineteenth century, for example, and more recently in the administration of public schools, mental health institutions, and prisons. Courts have accordingly been criticized for becoming, in Justice Benjamin Cardozo's words, "knight-errants," social-reform agencies and robed legislators. Judge Johnson nonetheless explains and defends such judicial intervention in terms of the judiciary's duty to enforce constitutional rights and liberties and the failure of other political branches to provide relief. He illustrates his view by detailing his decision and remedial decree in *Wyatt v. Stickney,* which mandated institutional reform of Alabama's largest state mental health facility and resulted in raising state annual expenditures "from $14 million before the suit was filed in 1971 to $58 million after the decree was rendered."[8]

Like Judge Johnson and Judge Ralph Winter (in chapter 28), Chief Judge Howard Markey in chapter 27 reiterates that judicial activism crosscuts both liberal and conservative political philosophies and Republican and Democratic party lines. Often, charges of judicial activism are a matter of "whose ox is getting gored." Both sides of the political spectrum would agree, Chief Judge Markey claims, that at least one form of judicial activism is always objectionable: that of "personal judicial activism," or "PJA" as he calls it, whereupon judges engage in social engineering based solely on their own idiosyncratic policy preferences and vision of "the good life." Given the tradition of judicial independence, the cure for such judicial activism, he concludes, must ultimately come from judges themselves—in Judge Peter Beer's words, from "the most difficult type of leadership example: leadership by restraint."[9]

Whereas Chief Judge Markey focuses on aspects of judicial activism on an individual level, Judge Winter in chapter 28 draws attention to more systemic changes in the American political system when examining "the activist judicial mind." The rise of special-interest groups, and therewith the rejection of the Madisonian model of governance and a two-party system, he suggests, has led to the dominance of interest-group pluralism and the ascendance of the judiciary as a forum for resolving disputes between groups that have either little or no access to political power or are unsatisfied with the outcome of the political process. Contemporary judicial activism, Judge Winter moreover argues, reflects not merely hostility toward a pluralistic political process but a demand for "rational" solutions to all governmental problems and a distrust of free markets.

Litigation, Justice William O. Douglas cautioned, "is not the cure-all, the solution for every conflict."[10] So too, courts neither create nor can solve all political and social problems. "We pay a price for our system of checks and balances," Justice Douglas also noted, "for the distribution of power among the three branches of government."[11] The Constitution was not designed, in Justice Louis Brandeis's words, "to promote efficiency but to preclude the exercise of arbitrary power. The purpose was, not to avoid friction, but, by means of the inevitable friction incident to the distribution of the governmental power among three departments, to save the people from autocracy."[12] In our constitutional system and in a "society in which rapid changes tend to upset all equilibrium," Justice Robert Jackson wisely observed, the judiciary, "without exceeding its own limited powers, must strive to maintain the great system of checks and balances upon which our free government is based."[13]

NOTES

1. See, e.g., H. Storing, *The Anti-Federalists,* 7 vols. (Chicago: University of Chicago Press, 1982); and R. Berger, *Government by Judiciary* (Cambridge: Harvard University Press, 1978).

2. L. Green, "Tort Law: Public Law in Disguise," 38 *Texas Law Review* 257 (1960).

3. I. Kaufman, "Chilling Judicial Independence," 88 *Yale Law Review* 681, 685 (1979).

4. L.F. Powell, Orison S. Marden Lecture, Association of the Bar of the City of New York, at 3 (18 October 1978).

5. J.A. Cabranes, "For the Record," *Washington Post* A31 (6 June 1982).

6. R. Bork, "The Struggle Over the Role of the Court," *National Review* 1137, 1138 (17 September 1982).

7. For a further discussion, see D.M. O'Brien, "The Seduction of the Judiciary: Social Science and the Courts," 64 *Judicature* 8-21 (1980).

8. D. Horowitz, *The Courts and Social Policy* 6 (Washington, D.C.: Brookings Institution, 1977).

9. P. Beer, "On Behalf of Judicial Restraint," 15 *Trial* 37 (1979).

10. W.O. Douglas, *We the Judges* 56 (New York: Doubleday, 1956).

11. *Youngstown Sheet & Tube Co. v. Sawyer,* 343 U.S. 579, 633 (1951).

12. *Meyers v. United States,* 272 U.S. 52, 293 (1926).

13. R. Jackson, *The Supreme Court in the American System of Government* 61 (Cambridge: Harvard University Press, 1955).

24

The Role of the Courts in Contemporary Society

RUGGERO J. ALDISERT

Judge, Court of Appeals, Third Circuit

To describe the role of the courts in contemporary American society is a Janus-faced assignment. It can be a description of what we are or an expression of what we should be. To propose what we should be requires that we know what we are; to know what we are, we must first know what we were; and to appreciate what we were requires an overview of two centuries of American judicial experience.

To be sure, our judicial systems were English in origin and in practice. Colonial courts had functioned from the beginning as integral parts of the British judicial system. When the colonies changed to statehood and separate courts were established within the state and federal sovereignties, an English model was adopted in each of the several jurisdictions. Aside from cutting the umbilical cord from the Privy Council, substantive laws and procedural rules of the original states did not undergo major revolutionary changes. By nationality we were Americans; by legal tradition we were still English. American judges in the early nineteenth century took a traditional view of their function. The English common law judge sat as a settler of disputes between private parties, deciding questions of "lawyer's law" and pronouncing what Roscoe Pound would later call "rules in the narrower sense," precepts attaching a definite legal consequence to a definite, detailed state of the facts.[1] But the American environment was different from the English, and soon began to make special demands on the courts. In America, unlike Great Britain,[2] a system of dual sovereignties existed. And, in America, a written constitution had been adopted—a primal document tracing its origins in part to the Magna Carta and the Petition of Right, and in part to the peculiar exigencies of the new "united states" where sovereign power was to be divided between the state governments and the national government.

Within 14 years of the Constitution's adoption, however, a new dimension was added to the judiciary's traditional role of dispute settler. Resolving a conflict between a private citizen, one William Marbury, and a public official, one James Madison, the Secretary of State, the Supreme Court set a precedential stage for a new judicial function—that of interpreter of a written constitution.[3] Thus the Court allocated to itself a role that would still serve as a source of criticism[4] of the American judicial function. It declared an act of a correlative branch of government unconstitutional, that is, null and void. Moreover, the Court designed to command the executive what it could and could not do under the Constitution. And so, early in our tradition, the judicial branch declared itself the overseer of the executive and legislative branches. Appropriately, perhaps, for present purposes, the Supreme Court did not "settle" the dispute between Marbury and Madison in the sense of resolving the conflict between two litigants. It dismissed Mr. Marbury's petition for lack of jurisdiction. Rather, *Marbury v. Madison* marked a departure from the traditional dispute-settling role of the courts, and an arrival of a new function, that of interpreting a written constitution. Said Chief Justice Marshall: "It is emphatically the province and duty of the judicial department, to say what the law is. Those who apply the rule to particular cases, must of necessity expound and interpret that rule."[5] Whether or not it was so intended, the judicial branch early established itself as protector of the Constitution and, thereby, as overseer of the constitutionality of actions of the executive and legislative branches of the federal government.

Having brought the coordinate branches of the federal government, and the state governments, within its "limited" jurisdiction, the Supreme Court began in the early decades of this century to interpret the substantive content of some of the more ambiguous phrases in the Constitution. But this was not ordinary interpretation, this was interpretation with a vengeance—what Dean Griswold has referred to as "decisional leapfrogging."[6] "[T]he first decision is distilled from the language of the Constitution, but the next expansion begins from the reasoning of the last decision, and so on down the line until we reach a point where the words of the Constitution are so far in the background that they are virtually ignored."[7] Operating in the common law tradition, reasoning from example and inbreeding newly distilled constitutional principles, the Supreme Court's interpretations authorized incursions by judges—both state and federal—into realms of policy traditionally entrusted to other public decision makers.

The march of federal judges into new decision-making fields continued through the era of substantive due process. Although Lochnerism[8] suffered a setback, replete with breast-beating apologies in which the Court publicly disavowed substantive due process as a method of substituting the Court's views of proper legislation for those of state legislatures,[9] it has returned recently under a new rubric and raiment: today American courts announce new vigors of the equal protection clause,[10] or delight in the surrealistic "penumbras" to the Bill of Rights,[11] or discover new rights of privacy extending from "the Fourteenth Amendment's concept of personal liberty" and "the Ninth Amendment's reservation of rights to the people."[12]

American courts reached the zenith of jurisdictional and jurisprudential expansion in 1963 when the Supreme Court cast another stout mooring line connecting the states' highest courts to the federal judicial system. Unlike that which tied the state judiciary to the apex of the federal court pyramid in 1816, this one wrapped around the very base of the federal judicial pyramid—the district courts. Under the guise of inquiry into "detention simpliciter" of state prisoners in actual custody, the Supreme Court vested federal district courts—*trial* courts—with authority to review fact-finding decisions and constitutional law interpretations of state court systems in criminal cases, including decisions of the states' *highest* courts.[13]

It has not been my purpose or intention to summarize American legal history, nor have I done so. Rather, I have attempted to point out a few distinctive landmarks on the journey from 1776; perhaps these can help in arriving at an appreciation of the contemporary legal landscape. . . .

The expansion of the American judicial function beyond the parameters of orthodox, private dispute settling, and the concomitant emergence of new emphases on sociological methodologies in decision making, highlight another respect in which contemporary American courts differ from those in which some of the Founding Fathers practiced: Today judges make, as well as interpret, law.

This truism may seem self-evident, but public acknowledgment of this proposition required a long gestation period. Judicial ears had long been cocked to venerable principles and aphorisms that disclaimed lawmaking as a proper judicial function. Francis Bacon admonished: "Judges ought to remember that the office is 'jus dicere,' and not 'jus dare'; to interpret law, and not to make law, or give law."[14] The Blackstonian view was that judges do not create law, they simply discover it, and even when they overrule precedent, they do not "make" law:

> For if it be found that the former decision is manifestly absurd or unjust, it is declared, not that such a sentence was *bad law,* but that it was *not law;* that is, that it is not the established custom of the realm, as has been erroneously determined.[15]

Modern jurisprudence, however, recognizes that the judge can, and indeed must, make law as well as apply it. Were it otherwise, there would be little room for the employment of public policy as a tool in judicial decision making. Yet there are limits. In 1917 Holmes counseled: "I recognize without hesitation that judges do and must legislate, but they can do so only interstitially; they are confined from molar to molecular motions."[16]

Although the precise limits of judicial lawmaking have not been staked out, the power undoubtedly is a broad one. Holmes and his followers propounded the "interstices" doctrine, but judicial lawmaking has often exceeded interstices. In practice it might appear that the only limitations are those which are "functional"—such as the inadequacy of facilities for extensive fact gathering, confinement to the facts of record, and the like. Ultimately the test of judge-made law, as with any law, is its effect on social welfare and its acceptance by society. The judge who makes law, therefore, must focus openly on policy considerations as he seeks to keep the law in tune with changing societal values.

It may be argued that this approach pays lip service only to the doctrine of separation of powers. The clear and obvious answer must be that the federal and state constitutions must be read against the backdrop of the common law tradition—which tradition has given to the courts the authority to interpret rules enacted by the legislature, and to fashion the aggregate of legal precepts that govern society.[17] Further, if legislative authority disagrees with judicial action, it can overrule that action by statute.[18] As the highly pragmatic legal philosopher John Chipman Gray would tell us, "The State requires that the acts of its legislative organ shall bind the courts, and so far as they go, shall be paramount to all other sources."[19]

Still another development in the American judicial function must be examined if we are to appreciate fully the role of the courts in contemporary American society. Phenomenally and somewhat paradoxically, as the courts have enlarged their lawmaking roles, so too have the legislatures enacted laws vesting the courts with greater responsibilities. At times the growth in statutory law—individual legislative acts as well as comprehensive codes—has seemed exponential. Simultaneously courts have been called upon to interpret volumes of exasperatingly detailed regulations promulgated by the executive branch. And where the legislature or the executive has not acted, prestigious private organizations—notably the American Bar Association[20] and the American Law Institute[21]—have suggested voluminous codes of substantive and procedural law which, while not possessing the sanctions of positive law, have exerted a potent, often persuasive, effect on the state and federal judiciaries.

A full generation ago Justice Frankfurter said that "even as late as 1875 more than 40 percent of the controversies before the [Supreme] Court were common-law litigation, 50 years later only 5 percent, while today cases not resting on statutes are reduced almost to zero."[22] If the court has not changed since Frankfurter's day, it is only because zero is so low. Judge Charles E. Wyzanski, Jr., has suggested that "[i]n two generations the law has moved in ways unforseeable by any nineteenth-century lawyer. The center has shifted from common law adjudged in the courts, to enacted law administered by executive agencies subject to limited judicial reviews."[23]

The annual grist for our separate, sovereign legislative mills must be measured in the hundreds of tons. "More than 26,000 bills were introduced during the last Congress. In the California Legislature alone, 7000 bills were proposed last year."[24] An average of 13,000 bills a year were introduced in the New York state legislature from 1973 to 1975.[25] How many bills may a legislator be expected to read? U.S. Senate Bill No. 1, a complete revision of the federal law[26] of crimes, has been described by Senator John McClellan as the lengthiest bill ever introduced in the Senate, surpassing even the Internal Revenue Code of 1954. How many members of Congress can be said to have read it? To have understood it?

Such legislative proliferation raises profound questions as to how our public policy is actually formulated. The reality that special legislative staffs—not elected legislators—draft many statutes draws into doubt the long-held notion that legislative enactments are the true expression of public policy, derived from the representatives elected by the people. Assuming, of course, that a statute does express some public policy—and I am convinced that many do not—the question arises whether that policy was derived from elected representatives of the people or from appointed specialists of the legislative staff.

Whatever reservations we may have about the process, the proliferation of legislation has made statutory construction the essence in the day to day work of American judges. Whatever the reason, the reality is that our society relies more heavily on the courts today than it has at any time in the past. This reliance is working a fundamental change in the nature of the judicial process. . . . Admittedly, American courts have never accepted the limited common law role of dispute settling. They have, almost from the beginning, been lawmakers, albeit, in Holmes's expression, "interstitial" lawmakers. But the courts' role today is expanding well beyond dispute settling and interstitial lawmaking into broader, more nebulous areas of societal problem solving. Judge Simon H. Rifkind describes the courts as "the problem solvers of our society: Shall we prosecute a war, or make peace? What is life; when does death begin? How should we operate prisons and hospitals? No problem seems to be beyond the desire of the American people to entrust to the courts."[27]

Problem-solving litigation might be described as litigation the purpose of which is not to compensate the plaintiff but to confront the defendant, and society, with the social costs of the activity in question.[28] The procedural vehicle is frequently, but not necessarily, the class action. The goals of problem-solving litigation are limited only by the human imagination—as one may readily discern by leafing through a few recent volumes of the legal reports. Most frequently, the object of dissatisfaction is government. It is now *de rigueur* to go to court whenever dissatisfied with governmental or private action that affects one.

As the emphasis in the subject matter of litigation has changed, so too have the litigators. Not too long ago, a caption in the Supreme Court reports often contained the names of only two individuals. Today's caption fare is more likely to involve governmental entities, private institutions or associations, or public interest groups. Part of this development reflects the change in subject matter. Not an insubstantial part, however, reflects the increasing cost of litigation; most private individuals no longer can afford to litigate "all the way to the Supreme Court if necessary." Judge Carl McGowan has commented on one aspect of this phenomenon as follows:

Meanwhile, there are to be seen in the burgeoning ranks of our litigants some new faces—those of the Congressmen themselves. With the decline of standing requirements, and the expansion of judicial remedies and review, a growing number of legislators have awakened to the political advantages of going to court to challenge executive, agency, and even legislative, action. This attracts publicity, and is likely to be popular with the constituents. It has few, if any, drawbacks, especially if there are *pro bono* groups or private law firms available, as they appear to be, to provide the legal representation.

I do not say that this is an undesirable development, but there may be implications of it not yet thought through with sufficient care. It might, for example, be unhealthy if the federal courts come to be regarded as a higher chamber where a legislator, who has failed to persuade his colleagues of the demerits of a particular bill, can always renew the battle.[29]

Another aspect of this new litigiousness is that courts are being asked to draft more and more complicated bottom lines. The judicial task is no longer to decide whether A injured B and, if so, how much should he pay. These days, "[t]he real concern is to confront the defendant (and the rest of society) with the right set of costs for different behavioral choices. . . ."[30] To quote Judge Shirley Hufstedler:

> We expect courts to encompass every reach of the law, and we expect law to encircle us in our earthly sphere and to travel with us to the alien vastness of our outer space. We want courts to sustain personal liberty, to end our racial tensions, to outlaw war, and to sweep the contaminants from the globe. We ask courts to shield us from public wrong and private temptation, to penalize us for our transgressions and to restrain those who would transgress against us, to adjust our private differences, to resuscitate our moribund businesses, to protect us prenatally, to marry us, to divorce us, and, if not to bury us, at least to see to it that our funeral expenses are paid. These services, and many more, are supposed to be quickly performed in temples of justice by a small priestly caste with the help of a few devoted retainers and an occasional vestal virgin. We are surprised and dismayed because the system is faltering.[31]

Judge Hufstedler is quite accurate, I think.

Why do we expect so much from courts? Perhaps it is the courts' own fault—for reaching out to take an activist role in so many matters, for moving beyond the limited common law role. From the beginning, American courts attracted the imagination and received the support of the public. The very openness of the judicial process may be the reason for this attraction. The trial judge on his bench is visible, so is the appellate judge. Moreover the Anglo-American tradition requires the court to write an opinion stating the result reached and the reasons for it. The opinions not only disclose the identity of the decision makers but also reveal internal conflict and expose dissenting views.

There may be other reasons for the phenomenon Judge Hufstedler describes. In the recent past, we have witnessed a decline in the power and prestige of private institutions. The decline of church, school, and family are well documented in the sociological literature. The courts cannot take the place of those institutions, but their decline has resulted in increased societal reliance on the courts to perform their functions. Juvenile crime is one, but not the only example, of the interrelationship. During the same time that we have witnessed the decline of private institutions, we have seen the expansion of government authority to regulate private activity. Correspondingly, private resistance to the authority has developed, often seeking to use the courts as a means of creating and enforcing limitations on government.

The product of all the foregoing forces is a "spreading judicialization of relationships."[32] I am not confident that a majority of the electorate in this nation of, by and for the people appreciates, much less condones, this development. Indeed, I am not even sure a majority of Congress recognizes and sanctions it. Nonetheless, after 200 years, the reality of judicialization can be neither gainsaid nor ignored.

NOTES

1. R. Pound, "Hierarchy of Sources and Forms in Different Systems of Law," 7 *Tulane Law Review* 475, 482 (1933).

2. See, generally, W. Holdsworth, *A History of English Law,* Vol. 1 (London: Methuen, 1903) (hereinafter cited as Holdsworth). An essentially centralized judicial apparatus evolved over a period of several centuries. Thus, such holdovers from Anglo-Saxon times as the courts of the County and the courts of the Hundred gradually were displaced by the King's Court, largely because the latter "offered better justice—[the King's] courts were selling a better and more reliable commodity." R. Jackson, *The Machinery of Justice in England* 2 (6th ed., Cambridge, England: Cambridge University Press, 1972).

   Appellate jurisdiction over foreign dominion within the British Empire—including, at least theoretically, the American colonies—was vested in the Judicial Committee of the Privy Council. See Holdsworth at 295. As a practical matter, however, law in the American colonies deviated from the course of law in England, depending on the perceived requirements of the moment. And the colonies varied in receptiveness to English law among themselves; thus, the Southern colonies accepted more of English law than did the New England colonies. L. Friedman, *A History of American Law* 16 (New York: Simon & Schuster, 1973).

3. *Marbury v. Madison,* 5 U.S. (1 Cranch) 137 (1803).

4. Compare R. Richardson, "Freedom of Expression and the Function of Courts," 65 *Harvard Law Review* 1 (1951), with E. Rostow, "The Democratic Character of Judicial Review," 66 *Harvard Law Review* 193 (1952).

5. 5 U.S. 1, at 177.

6. E. Griswold, "The Judicial Process," 28 *Record of New York City Bar Association* 14, 24 (1973), reprinted in 31 *Federal Bar Journal* 309, 317 (1972).

7. Ibid.

8. The term derives from the decision in *Lochner v. New York,* 198 U.S. 45 (1905). Other cases which have been criticized similarly include *Jay Burns Baking Co. v. Bryan,* 264 U.S. 504 (1924); *Adkins v. Children's Hosp.,* 261 U.S. 525 (1923); *Coppage v. Kansas,* 236 U.S. 1 (1915). See, generally, J. Ely, "The Wages of Crying Wolf: A Comment on *Roe v. Wade*," 82 *Yale Law Journal* 920 (1973).

9. *Ferguson v. Skrupa,* 372 U.S. 726, 730 (1963): "The doctrine . . . that due proc-

ess authorizes courts to hold laws unconstitutional when they believe the legislature has acted unwisely—has long since been discarded. We have returned to the original constitutional proposition that courts do not substitute their social and economic beliefs for the judgment of legislative bodies, who are elected to pass laws." But see *Roe v. Wade,* 410 U.S. 113, 167-168 (1973) (Stewart, J., concurring).

10. The Burger court has not used the equal protection clause expansively. See e.g., *San Antonio School Dist. v. Rodriguez,* 411 U.S. 1, 33-34 (1973). Compare G. Gunther, "The Supreme Court, 1971 Term—Foreword: In Search of Evolving Doctrine on a Changing Court: A Model for a Newer Equal Protection," 86 *Harvard Law Review* 1 (1972). See also R. Aldisert, *The Judicial Process* 594-598 (St. Paul: West, 1976).

11. E.g., *Griswold v. Connecticut,* 381 U.S. 479 (1965). But see Dean Griswold's comment: "I do not know where these penumbras come from, nor do I know their extent or limitations. . . . And I suspect that the true meaning of penumbra . . . is that the Constitution does not cover the subject but ought to because it does so much else that is desirable." Griswold, supra note 6, at 24.

12. E.g., *Roe v. Wade,* 410 U.S. 113, 153 (1973).

13. *Fay v. Noia,* 372 U.S. 319 (1963). There are indications that some members of the current Supreme Court have considered casting off the *Fay* line. See *Estelle v. Williams,* 425 U.S. 501 (1975); *Francis v. Henderson,* 425 U.S. 536 (1976); and especially the dissenting opinions of Mr. Justice Brennan.

14. F. Bacon, *Essays* 282 (1900; reprint, New York: Collier, 1909).

15. W. Blackstone, *Commentaries on the Laws of England,* Vol. 1 (Chicago: University of Chicago Press, 1980).

16. *Southern Pacific Co. v. Jensen,* 244 U.S. 205, 221 (1917) (Holmes, J., dissenting).

17. See, generally, R. Pound, "Hierarchy of Sources and Forms in Different Systems of Law," 7 *Tulane Law Review* 475 (1933).

18. See, e.g., *Molitor v. Kaneland Community Unit Dist. No. 302,* 18 Ill.2d 11, 42, 163 N.E.2d 89, 104 (1959) (Davis, J., dissenting), *cert. denied,* 362 U.S. 968 (1960); cf. W. Friedmann, *Legal Theory* 501-503 (5th ed., New York: Columbia University Press, 1967). See also B. Breitel, "The Lawmakers," 65 *Columbia Law Review* 749, 767-772 (1965).

19. J.C. Gray, *The Nature and Sources of Law* 124 (2d ed., New York: Macmillan, 1921).

20. See, e.g., *Standards of the ABA* on the following topics: The Prosecution Function and The Defense Function; The Urban Police Function; Post-Conviction Remedies; Providing Defense Services; Sentencing Alternatives and Procedures; The Function of the Trial Judge; Electronic Surveillance, Discovery and Procedure Before Trial; Trial by Jury; Joinder and Severance; Fair Trial and Free Press; Criminal Appeals; Probation; Pleas of Guilty; Pretrial Release; and Appellate Review of Sentences.

21. See, e.g., *Restatements of:* Agency; Conflicts of Laws; Contracts; Foreign Relations; Judgments; Property; Restitution; Security; Torts; and Trusts. See also Model Code of Pre-Arraignment Procedure; Model Penal Code; Model Land Development Code; Federal Securities Code—Tentative Drafts.

22. F. Frankfurter, "Some Reflections on the Reading of Statutes," 47 *Columbia Law Review* 527, 527 (1947).

23. C. Wyzanski, *Whereas—A Judge's Premises* xi (Boston: Little, Brown, 1964).

24. T. Ehrlich, "Legal Pollution," *New York Times,* 8 February 1976, § 6 (magazine), reprinted in *National Conference on the Causes of Popular Dissatisfaction with*

the Administration of Justice — Resource Materials 47, ed. R. Wheeler and L. Levin (St. Paul: West, 1976). Under the joint auspices of the American Bar Association, the Judicial Conference of the United States, and the Conference of Chief Justices, the April 1976 Conference convened in St. Paul, Minn., to commemorate Dean Pound's classic address to the ABA.

25. Letter from the Associated Press, 29 April 1976, on file in chambers of the writer.

26. S. 1, 93d Cong., 1st Sess. (1973); see H.R. 10047, 93d Cong., 1st Sess. (1973); S. 1400, 93 Cong., 1st Sess. (1973) (Administration's bill). See also H.R. 12504, 94th Cong., 2d Sess. (1976); H.R. 10850, 94th Cong., 1st Sess. (1975).

27. Address by Simon H. Rifkind to the National Conference on the Causes of Popular Dissatisfaction with the Administration of Justice in St. Paul, Minn., 8 April 1976, at 5.

28. See, generally, K. Scott, "Two Models of the Civil Process," 27 *Stanford Law Review* 937 (1975).

29. C. McGowan, "Congress and the Courts," University of Chicago Law School, Monograph Address, 17 April 1975. See, e.g., *Buckley v. Valeo*, 424 U.S. 1 (1976); *Kennedy v. Sampson*, 511 F.3d 430 (D.C. Cir. 1974); cf. *Hynes v. Mayor of Oradell*, 425 U.S. 610 (1976).

30. Scott, supra note 28, at 939.

31. S. Hufstedler, "New Blocks for Old Pyramids: Reshaping the Judicial System," 44 *Southern California Law Review* 901, 901 (1971).

32. E. Levi, Address to the National Conference on the Causes of Popular Dissatisfaction with the Administration of Justice (7 April 1976), at 7.

25

The Courts and Social Policy: Substance and Procedure

Henry J. Friendly

Senior Judge, Court of Appeals, Second Circuit

Should courts decide issues of social policy? If they do so, are some modifications of the adversary system desirable?

The courts must address themselves in some instances to issues of social policy, not because this is particularly desirable, but because often there is no feasible alternative. One is reminded of Sir Winston Churchill's remark that democracy is the worst form of government, except that no one has been able to think of a better one.[1] On the other hand, if an ascertainable jural principle will decide a case in a way the court finds acceptable,[2] it will do better not to support its decision on the basis of its conception of what is desirable social policy and particularly not on disputable social or economic data. When courts need to rely on such data, they should be careful to observe procedural fairness, both as a goal in its own right and as a tool toward getting information that is correct and complete. When the economic or social information is indeterminate, a court should refuse to use such data as a basis for its decision, although such a refusal should not foreclose a later attempt to convince the court when better information may be available.

Unlike legislatures, which may properly frame pragmatic rules having no relation to strict logic,[3] courts should render a principled decision that will apply to a great sweep of cases. Moreover, unlike legislatures, courts are generally confined to prohibiting or enforcing conduct, whether by the award of damages or, in the type of cases we are discussing, more frequently by injunction or declaratory judgment.[4] Legislatures, however, have many further options available to them, including taxation and subsidies. Also, the legislature can offer "sweeteners" in the form of increased benefits of a different sort that will justify the abolition of a rule which, however well conceived in its origin, has become unworkable.[5]

The adversary system, even at its best, is poorly calculated to arrive at the truth; the lawyer's duty is to win his case by any fair means. Moreover, the "best" advocacy is rarely seen. Fate may will it that even in the greatest cases one or both sides will be represented by counsel with far less than the highest degree of competence. Moreover, there often are marked inequalities in the resources of the two sides and the skill of their counsel.[6]

In the great debate about courts deciding policy issues, it is strange that so little attention has been paid to a long established instance where judges have been not simply permitted but required to enforce what they believe to be sound policy. None of us, I suppose, was particularly shocked to learn in the first year of law school that courts must refuse to enforce contracts that are "contrary to public policy." Perhaps we were told that an otherwise little known English judge had produced the aphorism: "[Public policy] is a very unruly horse and when once you get astride it you never know where it will carry you,"[7] and that a better known judge had later said: "[J]udges are more to be trusted as interpreters of the law than as expounders of what is called public policy,"[8] and that a Lord Chancellor had even attempted to freeze the categories of contracts contrary to public policy to what they were at the beginning of the twentieth century.[9] We were also taught, however, that in this country courts did not so limit themselves and have felt few inhibitions about expanding the categories of such contracts.[10] Here we encounter a "rule" requiring judges to consider policy, although our law school teachers did not tell us and scholars have not adequately discussed how judges should ascertain policy for this purpose when the legislature has not furnished them with guidance.

We have also witnessed, without much furor having been aroused, what I think to have been the creation of new common law rights due to a judicial perception of policy. The most striking example is the law concerning strict products liability. Fifty years ago, Judge Cardozo's then recent decision in *MacPherson v. Buick Motor Co.,*[11] that the duty of care of the manufacturer of an automobile extended beyond the immediate purchaser, was still a novel although quickly accepted doctrine.[12] However, it was well within the negligence model that had become received learning. Subsequently, a decision in Michigan[13] and a more widely known one in New Jersey[14] led to what Dean Prosser called "the most rapid and altogether spectacular overturn of an established rule in the entire history of the law of torts."[15] At first an attempt was made to cloak the revolution within the rubric of implied warranty, but this was a strange sort of warranty since no degree of contrary language could disclaim it.[16] The revolution culminated in section 402A of the American Law Institute's Second Restatement of Torts,[17] which is now regularly cited by courts as if it were a statute. Although "warranty" may initially have furnished a crutch that was soon discarded, the motive power behind the victory of strict products liability was a notion of social policy, just as the replacement of strict liability by negligence had been a century before.[18] What is this other than the courts deciding a question of social policy through the adversary process?[19] Yet, although there were some outcries from outraged manufacturers, few people today are concerned about this venture in applying judicial views of social policy.

I have dwelt on these two instances of the courts applying their notions of social policy not only because they are interesting in themselves but also because of the calm with which they have been received, in contrast to the storm over judicial policy making in other instances now to be considered, sheds some light on the problem under discussion. Refusal to enforce contracts that are contrary to public policy and the creation of products liability are entirely in the private sector.[20] The storm has arisen in the public sector and is particularly intense when courts resort to notions of social policy to set aside actions of other branches of government strongly supported by many citizens — notably invalidation of legislative or executive action on constitutional grounds and of administrative action pursuant to judicial review. The criticism is natural. If policy-making authority has been vested in another body, by what warrant does a court substitute its own contrary views? As was said by Professor Bickel: "All too many federal judges have been induced to view themselves as holding roving commissions as problem solvers, and as charged with a duty to act when majoritarian institutions do not."[21]

In the constitutional area, however, there are important distinctions. Some provisions of the Bill of Rights invite the courts to develop and then to apply notions of social policy. Perhaps the plainest example is the cruel and unusual punishment clause of the Eighth Amendment. Nearly everyone agrees with Chief Justice Warren's statement that the concept of cruelty is not static but must continually be reexamined in light of "the evolving standards of decency that mark the progress of a maturing society,"[22] although agreement as to exactly what those "evolving standards" are does not always exist.[23] Likewise, the First Amendment necessarily takes the courts into areas of policy. With all respect to Justice Black, "shall make no law" does not mean, and could never have been thought to mean, "shall make no law." Congress must make laws that impinge on absolute freedom of speech and of the press in order to protect the nation against foreign danger and internal subversion. Congress and the state legislatures may also make such laws to prevent disorders, to protect individual reputations and to deal with false advertising and pornography. The question is not whether but to what extent freedom of speech will be curtailed, with the First Amendment creating the need for an extremely strong justification. Here again, only a few criticize courts for making the policy decision, although many disagree with the results.

I move now from these relatively tranquil waters to the two cases where the Court's reliance on arguments of social policy has stirred the highest waves of criticism. I apologize for a renewed discussion of decisions that have been written and talked about extensively, but they are familiar and important and, therefore, perhaps can teach us the most.

The first is *Brown v. Board of Education,* and more particularly the psychological footnote.[24] There seems to be general agreement that while *Brown* was a good — indeed, as it now seems, an inevitable — decision, the decision was not, for whatever reasons,[25] embodied in a good opinion. Judge Learned Hand was quick to point out that although *Brown* was generally thought to have overruled the "separate but equal" doctrine of *Plessy v. Ferguson,*[26] and in fact, ultimately led to that result, the opinion did not do so at all. Rather, *Plessy* "was distinguished because of the increased importance of education in the 56 years that had elapsed since it was decided."[27] The reasoning was that: (1) education had become so important as to be "a right which must be made available to all on equal terms"; (2) the Kansas district court had "found" that " '[s]egregation with the sanction of law . . . has a tendency to [retard] the educational and mental development of negro children and to deprive them of some of the benefits they would receive in a racial[ly] integrated school system . . . ' "; and (3) the Court believed that "this finding is amply supported by modern authority."[28] All of this led to the crucial statement that "[s]eparate educational facilities are inherently unequal," and to the conclusion that the equal protection clause had thus been violated. Social policy entered the decision at two points—the Court's emphasis on the special importance of education and its determination that separate education was "inherently unequal."

If one looked only at the *Brown* opinion, it would be clear beyond peradventure that the decision was limited to public education. The opinion expressly stated the question to be "whether *Plessy v. Ferguson* should be held inapplicable to public education."[29] The entire discussion related to this specific area and the holding was that, because of the unique importance of public education, "the doctrine of 'separate but equal' has no place" in that field. The clear implication was that *Plessy* remained alive, although perhaps not entirely well, in other fields of lesser social importance and that an overruling of it in such fields would be done only by a fully explicated opinion, an opinion that would have been rather hard to write in light of the emphasis *Brown* placed on the unique importance of public education.

We know now, as the Court seemingly must have known then, that such conclusions would have been wholly wrong. One needed to read only a few pages beyond the *Brown* opinion itself to find the Court, in *Bolling v. Sharpe*,[30] invalidating school segregation in the District of Columbia, not on the basis of the unique importance of education or the adverse psychological effect of segregated schools on black children, but because "[c]lassifications based solely upon race must be scrutinized with particular care, since they are contrary to our traditions and hence constitutionally suspect."[31] At the beginning of the very next term, the Court proceeded to render "a series of subsequent per curiam decisions invalidating state-imposed racial segregation in virtually all areas of life."[32] Hence, "[i]t is not surprising . . . that constitutional scholars . . . have been reluctant to believe that the Court relied to any great extent on the 'modern authorities' cited in its opinion"[33] or on the "facts" found by the Kansas district court, and that these scholars have been busily engaged in rewriting the *Brown* opinion.[34]

Would not the Court have done better to decide *Brown* on the basis of a jural principle as it did in *Bolling*, rather than on the basis of supposed psychological facts? Several such bases could have been derived from the text and the history of the equal protection clause. The Court might have gone to the full extent of saying that any governmental classification based on race was a denial of equal protection. It might have said, less broadly, that any racial classification imposed by a majority upon a minority constituted such a denial. It might have said, still less broadly and with a view to the particular evil that gave rise to the writing of the Fourteenth Amendment, that any racial classification imposed upon blacks violated the equal protection clause.[35] It might have said, as Professor Goodman has suggested,[36] that since a racial classification is constitutionally suspect, the state had the burden of showing that such classification did no harm, and the finding of the Kansas district court and the opinions of the psychologists were relevant, although not really necessary, to show how far the state had fallen short of discharging that burden. Finally, in light of the doctrine that has since developed, the Court could have said that any racial classification must be shown to be required by a compelling interest and that the state had not done so.

If the Court had taken any of these courses, it would not have been subject to the criticism that it was using psychological evidence of dubious validity,[37] at least on an across-the-board basis,[38] as the justification for substituting its factual judgment that "[s]eparate educational facilities are inherently unequal" for the legislature's factual judgments that they were not. Admittedly, the jural bases suggested above are not interchangeable; each would have had consequences different from the *Brown* opinion and from each other for such issues as the appropriate remedy for de jure segregation, what was to be done about de facto segregation and the constitutionality of reverse discrimination.[39] But the Court and the country would have been better off if the Court had placed the *Brown* decision on jural considerations which were clearly within its province as the interpreter of the Constitution and which would have yielded readier and more acceptable answers in future controversies rather than on unestablished facts concerning segregation's psychological effects in public education.

If *Brown* could have been decided without the Court's plunging into the realm of social policy, it is not clear that this can be said of the abortion cases, *Roe v. Wade*[40] and *Doe v. Bolton*.[41] These decisions have alarmed not only those who dislike their result, but others who, as citizens, applaud their basic accomplishment, yet as scholars cannot conscientiously defend the Court's having proceeded as it did.[42] The Court recognized a woman's desire to have an abortion not only as a "liberty" protected by the due process clause, a proposition with which almost everyone would agree, but also as a right so "fundamental" that the state may do nothing in the first trimester of pregnancy except require consultation with and performance of the abortion by a licensed physician, and even in the later periods of pregnancy is subject to strict limitations in controlling abortions.

The considerations of social policy militating against both the strict Texas statute considered in *Roe* and the more modern Georgia statute considered in *Doe* were strong indeed. Justice Blackmun described these only partially when he wrote, in a passage that tends to be obscured by the mass of historical data, that:

> The detriment that the State would impose upon the pregnant woman by denying this choice altogether is apparent. Specific and direct harm medically diagnosable even in early pregnancy may be involved. Maternity, or additional offspring, may force upon the woman a distressful life and future. Psychological harm may be imminent. Mental and physical health may be taxed by child care. There is also the distress, for all concerned, associated with the unwanted child, and there is the problem of bringing a child into a family already unable, psychologically and otherwise, to care for it. In other cases, as in this one, the additional difficulties and continuing stigma of unwed motherhood may be involved.[43]

This I learned in preparing to hear an attack on the New York abortion statute, which happily was repealed, was only part of the sad story. Prohibition of abortions had no more prevented them than prohibition of alcohol had prevented drinking. Whereas the latter produced bootleggers and speakeasies operating in defiance of the law, the former created illegal abortion mills. While well-to-do women could afford a high-class, high-priced abortionist who rarely was subjected to prosecution, a hospital surgical procedure ostensibly for some other cause, or a trip to a foreign country where abortions were permitted, these options were not open to the poor. The woman of scant means was relegated to the choice between undergoing, or undertaking, procedures threatening her health of even her life, or carrying an unwanted child to term and rearing it thereafter, often alone. The problem had been aggravated by increased sexual permissiveness especially among teenagers; even the more liberal statutes afforded no help in most cases of voluntary intercourse, unless the girl was so young as to have been a victim of "statutory rape." As Justice Marshall was later to say in his eloquent dissent in *Beal v. Doe,* the abortion statutes "brutally coerce poor women to bear children whom society will scorn for every day of their lives."[44] Justice Blackmun must have been fully aware of all this, as witness the final paragraph of his subsequent dissent in *Beal* where he condemns the majority for refusing to recognize the realities of poverty. A detailed presentation of these considerations of social policy would, to my mind, have furnished a much more persuasive basis for judicial innovation than the opinion's lengthy discussion of the Hippocratic Oath[45] and the abortion practices of the ancient world or debate concerning the precise moment when a fetus becomes a person.[46]

Ultimately, however, one must face the question of how a case of such overwhelming social import could be translated into a principle of constitutional law, particularly in the face of what we now know to be deeply felt contrary views.[47] While the opinion rather convincingly demonstrated that during the first trimester the state's interest in the mother's health was an insufficient reason for prohibiting abortions, it provided no real answer to the argument that the state's interest in preserving the fetus was alone a sufficient justification for drastic limitation of abortions. The invocation of a "right of privacy" was not convincing. Not only is there nothing very private about an abortion, but the cases cited did not sustain the proposition for which they were relied upon.[48] Justice Brandeis's much-quoted reference to the "right to be let alone" in his *Olmstead* dissent[49] was in context of a protest against wiretapping. As his law clerk of that term, I can provide direct evidence that the Justice was not thinking about abortions and had no idea that he was framing a general principle that would include them. The Court's earlier decisions protecting sexual liberty, although superficially more to the point, likewise afforded no real support. Surely there is a recognizable distinction between invading the body to compel sterilization and forbidding such an invasion for the purpose of abortion; moreover, even the decision striking down the sterilization provision in Oklahoma's Habitual Criminal Sterilization Act had been placed on grounds of equal protection rather than on the basis of due process.[50] The equal protection clause furnished ample basis for the decision invalidating Virginia's statute prohibiting marriages between blacks and whites,[51] although the Court also relied on due process as well. Moreover, that case presented no questions of state interest relating to the health of the mother and the life of the fetus. The Connecticut contraception statute had conveniently provided a real basis for invoking the right of privacy since it prohibited the use rather than the sale of contraceptives,[52] and thereby enabled the opinion writer to paint a lurid picture of policemen secreted in marital bedrooms. In addition, the Court's only statement with respect to the distribution of contraceptives had rested on grounds of equal protection, not due process.[53] Thus, there was no real precedential support for the abortion decisions, and it was a bit disingenuous to rest them on a recognized "right of privacy." Still, that does not necessarily mean that they were wrong; indeed, I would like to believe that in their core—forbidding prohibition of abortions in the early months of pregnancy—they were right.

My problems with the decisions, in addition to the Court's failure to articulate a defensible principle, are two. One concern is the severity of the restrictions imposed on state abortion laws. Why should it be impermissible for a state to insist that an abortion, even in the first trimester, should be performed by a gynecologist or obstetrician if one were available, rather than by any licensed physician? Why does the due process clause forbid a state from insisting that such an abortion be performed in a hospital, at least in the absence of evidence that the cost would result in unfair discrimination? Granted that most abortions in the early stages of pregnancy are relatively safe, why is it unconstitutional for a state to want to make them as safe as practicable? Why in the third trimester must the state allow an abortion if only the "health" rather than the life of the mother may be imperiled? Should not the Court, after announcing some basic principles, have allowed the states leeway, as is normally accorded, in applying these principles? Was this not pressing social policy beyond anything demonstrated by the social data?

My other concern relates to the boundaries of the newly created constitutional right of personal autonomy—for it would be best to shed the "privacy" label and recognize that that is what it is. We now know, as we did not before the abortion cases, that a state may not require a pregnant woman to leave work too soon or return too late[54] and that a prohibition on the sale of contraceptives, as distinguished from a prohibition of their use, would violate due process.[55] We have just learned that the equal protection clause requires that any restrictions on the right to marry must be subjected to "rigorous scrutiny,"[56] the Supreme Court's euphemism for judicial invalidation of such restrictions. Two lower courts have recently held that the principle of the abortion cases invalidates regulations and legislation outlawing the use of laetrile.[57] The Supreme Court of New Jersey has recently decided that the right to privacy also includes the right of fornication.[58] Statutes making homosexual conduct and adultery crimes will surely be up for examination in the near future. And it will not end here. Indeed, is there any end short of holding that the due process clause enacted John Stuart Mill's *On Liberty?*[59] As a citizen, I might agree that we could do without statutes such as those just mentioned, but where do the courts get the power to decide this?

In summary, I think that the Court's abortion opinions should have dealt more with the evils of today and less with history. I also think the decisions would have been more justifiable and would have been somewhat better accepted if they had been less severe and less detailed. Finally, however unprincipled this may sound, I would have welcomed some language indicating that the decisions were limited to a social problem of the greatest moment and were not to be taken as announcing a set of rights to a liberty that had not been previously known.

However, the main lesson I wish to draw from the abortion cases relates to procedure—the use of social data offered by appellants and amici curiae for the first time in the Supreme Court itself. In the action attacking the former New York abortion statute, over which I presided, it was assumed from the outset that any social or medical facts or opinions on which the parties wished to rely, unless stipulated, should be offered in the three-judge district court and would be subject to cross-examination or, where the author was not readily available, to rebuttal. In *Roe,* no evidence was offered at the hearing before the three-judge court except affidavits of two physicians that legal abortions were extremely safe and illegal abortions were exceedingly dangerous. In contrast, appellants' brief in the Supreme Court had a supplementary appendix characterized as being "offset reproductions of particularly relevant legal, medical and social science publications, all of which are in the public domain,"[60] and amici briefs favoring the appellants also contained extensive factual statements of which the Court was asked to take judicial notice. So far as I have been able to determine, the "mass of data purporting to demonstrate that some facilities other than hospitals are entirely adequate to perform abortions," referred to in *Doe,*[61] was not before the trial court at all. The Court's conclusion in *Roe* that "[m]ortality rates for women undergoing early abortions, where the procedure is legal, appear to be as low as or lower than the rates for nor-

273

mal childbirth"[62] rested entirely on materials not of record in the trial court, and that conclusion constituted the underpinning for the holding that the asserted interest of the state "in protecting the woman from an inherently hazardous procedure" during the first trimester did not exist.

If an administrative agency, even in a rule-making proceeding, had used similar materials without having given the parties a fair opportunity to criticize or controvert them at the hearing stage, reversal would have come swiftly and inexorably. It will not do to answer that the Court was merely following the illustrious example of the "Brandeis brief."[63] The Brandeis brief was used to show that legislation was rational since a respectable body of opinion upheld it. It thereby supported the presumption of constitutionality. The only factual issues concerning the materials brought before the Supreme Court in such a brief were whether they in fact existed, a circumstance almost never in dispute, and how far their authors possessed at least some competence, a fact that was rarely controverted. It is altogether different when such materials are used to show that legislation is irrational; in such a case, the materials not only must exist but must be right. Experience has shown that economic, social, psychological, and other technical studies can be seriously flawed by lack of a sufficiently large or representative sample, by other improper methodology, by drawing conclusions outrunning the empirical data and otherwise. I am not suggesting that the articles relied on by the Court in Roe were in fact wrong, although one must wonder how well conclusions as to the safety of legal abortions during the first trimester correlate with the holding that the state may impose no safeguards during that period except that the woman must secure the blessing of and have the abortion performed by a licensed physician.[64] The Court should set an example of proper procedure and not follow a course which it would condemn if pursued by any other tribunal.

NOTES

1. J.F. Kennedy, *Profiles in Courage* 264 (New York: Harper & Row, 1956).

2. While I am acutely conscious of the question-begging character of this phrase, an effort to define it would require a lecture in itself. Generally, what I mean is a principle drawn primarily from the text of a constitution or a statute as illuminated by history and precedential development, or from the trend of common law decisions, rather than one derived directly from a consideration of social or economic views or data. The reader will find elucidation in A. Bickel, *The Supreme Court and the Idea of Progress* 86-87 (New York: Harper & Row, 1970); B. Cardozo, *The Nature of the Judicial Process* (third lecture) (New Haven: Yale University, 1921); H. Wechsler, "Toward Neutral Principles of Constitutional Law," 73 *Harvard Law Review* 1 (1959).

3. See W. Friedmann, *Law in a Changing Society* 155 (Berkeley: University of California Press, 1959) in reference to the Law Reform [Personal Injuries] Act, 1948, 11 & 12 Geo. 6, c. 41, § 2[1], concerning deduction of one half of industrial injury benefits

from recovery for loss of earnings in personal injury damage actions. See also Justice Douglas's statement: "The legislature may select one phase of one field and apply a remedy there, neglecting the others. . . . The prohibition of the Equal Protection Clause goes no further than the invidious discrimination." *Williamson v. Lee Optical Co.,* 348 U.S. 483, 489 (1955).

4. See A. Chayes, "The Role of the Judge in Public Law Litigation," 89 *Harvard Law Review* 1281, 1292-1296 (1976).

5. See, e.g., Longshoremen & Harbor Workers Compensation Act Amendments of 1972, Pub. L. 92-576, 86 Stat. 1251, where an increase in a scale of workman's compensation benefits that had become outmoded made it not only politically possible but morally defensible to abolish the triangular action for unseaworthiness of longshoremen versus ship versus stevedoring employer that was plaguing the federal courts. See *Pittston Stevedoring Corp. v. Dellaventura,* 544 F.2d 35, 40 (2d Cir. 1976), *aff'd. sub nom. Northeast Marine Terminal Co. v. Caputo,* 429 U.S. 998 (1977); S. Rpt. No. 92-1125, 92d Cong., 2d Sess. 4-5 (1976).

6. In cases involving states, the inequality of skill does not always weigh on the side of the state; public interest lawyers and private attorneys working "pro bono" often outclass hard pressed and underpaid offices of city counsel or even state attorneys general. Perhaps this is a neglected field for pro bono activity.

7. *Richardson v. Mellish,* 2 Bing. 229, 252 (1824).

8. *In re Mirams,* [1891] 1 Q.B. 594, 595.

9. *Janson v. Driefontein Consol. Mines, Ltd.,* [1902] A.C. 484, 491.

10. See A. Corbin, *Contracts,* Vol. 6 (St. Paul: West, 1962); L. Simpson, *The Law of Contracts* 430-434, 441-445 (2d ed., St. Paul: West, 1965); S. Williston, *Contracts,* Vol. 14, §§ 1628, 1629, 1629A (3d ed., Mount Kisco, N.Y.: Jaeger, 1972); *Restatement (Second) of Contracts,* ch. 14, Introduction, Note and Reporter's Note, § 320(2), Comments b and c (Tent. Draft No. 12, 1 March 1977). An outstanding example is *Henningsen v. Bloomfield Motors, Inc.,* 32 N.J. 358, 161 A.2d 69 (1960), which struck down, as contrary to public policy, an automobile manufacturer's disclaimer of an implied warranty of merchantability that had been widely used.

11. 217 N.Y. 382, 11 N.E. 1050 (1916).

12. See W. Prosser, *Torts* § 96, at 642-643 (4th ed., St. Paul: West, 1971). As the text points out, the initial limitation to "a thing of danger" was rapidly eroded.

13. *Spence v. Three Rivers Builders & Masonry Supply, Inc.,* 353 Mich. 120, 90 N.W.2d 873 (1958).

14. *Henningsen v. Bloomfield Motors, Inc.,* 32 N.J. 358, 161 A.2d 69 (1960).

15. W. Prosser, supra note 12, § 97, at 654. Dean Prosser himself played no small part in the revolution. See W. Prosser, "The Fall of the Citadel," 50 *Minnesota Law Review* 791 (1966); Prosser, "The Assault Upon the Citadel," 69 *Yale Law Journal* 1099 (1960).

16. The death knell of the "warranty" explanation was sounded by Justice Traynor in *Greenman v. Yuba Power Prods., Inc.,* 59 Cal.2d 57, 377 P.2d 897, 27 Cal. Rptr. 697 (1963).

17. As Dean Prosser, who was the reporter, noted, "[t]he change in the law was so rapid that the Section was actually drawn three times." W. Prosser, supra note 12, § 98, at 657 n.51.

18. See M. Horowitz, *The Transformation of American Law* 97-99 (Cambridge: Harvard University Press, 1977).

19. Recognizing the problem created for him in *Henningsen* and its progeny, Pro-

fessor Dworkin seeks to explain the new doctrine as the result of preexisting "principles." Dworkin, *Taking Rights Seriously* 24, 27 (Cambridge: Harvard University Press, 1977). But this merely moves the inquiry back to the question of where some of these principles come from and why they should be applied not only to manufacturers of automobiles but to all products manufacturers, although not to other persons. Dworkin answers that the "origin of these as legal principles lies not in a particular decision of some legislature or court, but in a sense of appropriateness developed in the profession of some public over time." Ibid., at 40. But that sense of "appropriateness," in my view, is nothing more or less than an opinion about policy, and whether mediately through the modulation of "principles" or immediately through direct influence, it was "policy" and not "principle" that caused the courts to shift the automobile manufacturer into the strict liability regime while leaving the automobile operator under the rule of negligence.

20. Sometimes the taking of a new direction in the private sector affects the wealth of only the first round of litigants. This was notably true of strict products liability. Once the doctrine was established, manufacturers simply marked up their prices to reflect the cost of insurance or self-insurance.

21. A. Bickel, supra note 2, at 134.

22. *Trop v. Dulles,* 356 U.S. 86, 101 (1958). See also *Robinson v. California,* 370 U.S. 660, 666 (1962). This had been anticipated by *Weems v. United States,* 217 U.S. 349, 373 (1910).

23. See *Furman v. Georgia,* 408 U.S. 238, 385-386 (1972) (Burger, C.J., dissenting); ibid., at 436-439 (Powell, J., dissenting) (discussing contemporary attitudes toward capital punishment).

24. 347 U.S. 483, 494-495 and n.11 (1954).

25. It has often been suggested that the *Brown* opinion had to be written as it was in order to obtain the desired unanimity and avoid concurring opinions. While the account in R. Kluger, *Simple Justice* 578-599 (New York: Random House, 1976), demonstrates that the Chief Justice had his problems in achieving this goal, it does not cast much light on why the opinion was written as it was (except for the inclusion of the final paragraph relating to the remedy, 347 U.S. at 495-496) or on the curious contrast between the opinion in *Brown* and that in the District of Columbia case, *Bolling v. Sharpe,* 347 U.S. 497 (1954).

26. 163 U.S. 537 (1896).

27. Learned Hand, *The Bill of Rights* 54 (Cambridge: Harvard University Press, 1958).

28. 347 U.S. at 492-495.

29. Ibid., at 492.

30. 347 U.S. 497 (1954).

31. Ibid., at 499.

32. F. Goodman, "De Facto School Segregation: A Constitutional and Empirical Analysis," 60 *California Law Review* 275, 278 and n.17 (1972).

33. Ibid., at 279-280 and n. 24.

34. For a summary of these efforts, see ibid., at 279-283 and nn. 24, 30 and 31.

35. This ground might have been too narrow to include the District of Columbia case, which had to rest on the due process clause of the Fifth Amendment.

36. Goodman, supra note 32, at 282-283.

37. Ibid., at 279; E. Epps, "The Impact of School Desegregation on Aspirations,

Self-Concepts and Other Aspects of Personality," 39 *Law & Contemporary Problems* 300, 303-313 (1975).

38. Professor Wechsler questioned early whether "the finding in Topeka [was] applicable without more to Clarendon County, South Carolina, with 2799 colored students and only 295 whites." Wechsler, supra note 2, at 33. Certainly it is not self-evident that black children are benefited psychologically by being bused to a distant predominantly white school where they may meet a blank or even hostile reception.

39. All this is carefully developed in Professor Goodman's article; see supra note 32. The foregoing, of course, was written several months before the decision in *Regents of the Univ. of Cal. v. Bakke,* 57 L. Ed. 750 (1978), upon which I have not attempted to reflect.

40. 410 U.S. 113 (1973).

41. 410 U.S. 179 (1973).

42. See, e.g., A. Cox, *The Role of the Supreme Court in American Government* 113-114 (New York: Oxford University Press, 1976); L. Lusky, *By What Right* 15-17, 100 (Charlottesville: Michie, 1976); J. Ely, "The Wages of Crying Wolf: A Comment on *Roe v. Wade,*" 82 *Yale Law Journal* 920 (1973).

43. *Roe v. Wade,* 410 U.S. 113, 154-155, 164-165 (1973).

44. Ibid., at 153.

45. *Roe v. Wade,* 410 U.S. 113, 130-132 (1973).

46. Ibid., at 159-162.

47. Some have doubted whether it is possible to find any acceptable articulable principle for the decision. See Cox, supra note 42, at 113-114. Still, the search for a principled rationale in *Roe* continues. A student commentator thought he found a possible approach in passages suggesting that the state lacks power to adopt "one theory" of life in light of the "wide divergence of thinking" on the subject. Note, "The Supreme Court, 1976 Term," 91 *Harvard Law Review* 70, 145 n.41 (1977) (citing *Roe v. Wade,* 410 U.S. 113, 160-162). But one must ask why does a state lack power to decide this question when it can decide so many others where thinking is equally divergent. See G. Gunther, *Constitutional Law: Cases and Materials* 651 (9th ed., Mineola, N.Y.: Foundation Press, 1975).

48. See the cases cited in *Roe v. Wade,* 410 U.S. 113, 152 (1973), which deal for the most part with issues of search and seizure and self-incrimination under the Fourth and Fifth amendments and issues discussed in the text accompanying notes 49-53 infra.

49. *Olmstead v. United States,* 277 U.S. 438, 478 (1928).

50. *Skinner v. Oklahoma,* 316 U.S. 535, 541 (1942).

51. *Loving v. Virginia,* 388 U.S. 1 (1967).

52. *Griswold v. Connecticut,* 381 U.S. 479 (1965).

53. *Eisenstadt v. Baird,* 405 U.S. 438, 443 (1972).

54. *Cleveland Bd. of Educ. v. LaFleur,* 414 U.S. 632 (1974).

55. See *Carey v. Population Serv. Int'l.,* 431 U.S. 678 (1977).

56. *Zablocki v. Redhail,* 98 S. Ct. 673, 679 (1978).

57. *Rutherford v. United States,* 438 F.Supp. 1287 (W.D. Okla. 1977); *California v. Privitera,* 74 Cal. App. 3d 936, 141 Cal. Rptr. 764 (Ct. App., 4th Dist. 1977).

58. *State v. Saunders,* 75 N.J. 200, 381 A.2d 333 (1977).

59. See P. Brest, *Processes of Constitutional Decisionmaking* 798 (Boston: Little, Brown, 1975). The reference, of course, is to Mill's statement: "The sole end for which mankind are warranted, individually or collectively, in interfering with the liberty of

any of their number, is self protection. . . . The only purpose for which power can be rightfully exercised over any member of a civilized community, against his will, is to prevent harm to others." Mill, "On Liberty," in *Essential Works of John Stuart Mill* 263, ed. M. Lerner (New York: Bantam, 1961).

60. See A.S. Miller and J.A. Barron, "The Supreme Court, the Adversary System, and the Flow of Information to the Justices: A Preliminary Inquiry," 61 *Virginia Law Review* 1187, 1189-1201 (1975).

61. *Doe v. Bolton,* 410 U.S. 179, 195 (1973).

62. *Roe v. Wade,* 410 U.S. 113, 149 (1973).

63. The name from the innovative brief submitted by Louis D. Brandeis in *Muller v. Oregon,* 208 U.S. 412 (1908).

64. 410 U.S. at 163-165. Although the former counsel to the Mayo Clinic surely does not regard physicians as fungible, these passages in the opinion, particularly the last, go to great pains to leave no room for doubt that any licensed physician will do. Earlier the opinion had recognized that the state's legitimate interest extended "to the performing physician and his staff, to the facilities involved, to the availability of after-care, and to adequate provision for any complication or emergency that might arise." Ibid., at 150. The opinion does not explain why the state may not insist on these interests in the first trimester. I have been told by physicians that although abortion during the early weeks of pregnancy is usually a safe and simple procedure, complications occasionally arise that are beyond the competence of those without special training in gynecology or obstetrics.

26

Judicial Activism Is a Duty—
Not an Intrusion

FRANK M. JOHNSON, JR.
Judge, Court of Appeals, Eleventh Circuit

The role of the federal courts in deciding constitutional questions is and always has been an activist one. It is not a role which has been usurped by the judiciary, however, but is one which is inextricably intertwined with its duty to interpret the Constitution. The federal courts have never acted directly on the states or assumed jurisdiction of mere political issues; but in cases involving individual rights and liberties, these courts are compelled to construe the law in order to determine such rights and liabilities.

As Chief Justice Marshall so eloquently expressed, in responding to Congressional attempts to take away the Supreme Court's power to review state supreme court decisions involving constitutional issues: "As this Court has never grasped at ungranted jurisdiction, so will it never, we trust, shrink from the exercise of that which is conferred upon it."[1]

In describing the role of the federal judiciary in deciding constitutional issues, I ascribe no particular political or social philosophy to the word "activist." Justice Sutherland, a staunch conservative on the court, was no more or no less "activist" in striking down social legislation and upholding governmental regulation of First Amendment rights than Justice Black was in upholding social legislation and invalidating state regulation of First Amendment rights. The activism I refer to is measured not by the end result but by how and under what circumstances the result is achieved.

Where the Decree Is Ongoing

Once having decided the issues, the court must then concern itself with the second and final phase of the adjudicatory process—the formulation and entry of an appropriate decree. If the evidence fails to disclose a constitutional violation, or if the evidence discloses a constitutional violation which can effectively be remedied by an award of damages or the issuance of a prohibitory injunction, the court's role is a limited one terminating upon entry of the decree. If the constitutional or statutory violation is one, however, which can be adequately remedied only by the issuance of a decree providing for affirmative, ongoing relief, the court's involvement is necessarily enlarged and prolonged.

The federal judiciary finds itself today being increasingly called upon to fashion and to render this latter type of decree, that is, one of an ongoing, remedial relief. This trend, I assure you, results not from the judiciary's masochistic yearning for hard work, but from several relatively recent developments in the law.

The most significant procedural change has been the adoption and promulgation by Congress and the courts of liberalized standing and joinder requirements. Under code pleading, for example, litigation used to involve but two individuals or at least two competing interests, diametrically opposed, with the winner taking all. Today, however, there are often competing, if not conflicting, interests among members of the same class, among different classes, and among parties and intervenors. This has made the task of formulating appropriate relief an increasingly complex and difficult one.

A significant development in the substantive area has been the shift in subject matter from business and economic issues to social issues. During the latter part of the nineteenth century and the first half of this century, the major focus in the area of constitutional law was the power of Congress and the states to enact statutes regulating and restricting private businesses and property. The constitutional theory most frequently advanced was substantive due process. Since only property rights were at stake, an award of damages to compensate the litigant for any economic loss and the issuance of a prohibitory injunction to restrain the operation of the statute provided the litigant with all the relief to which he was entitled.

During the past several decades, however, there have been in our society a growing awareness of and concern for the rights and freedoms of the individual. This awareness and this concern are reflected in the steady shift in emphasis in constitutional litigation from property rights to individual rights. Congress has enacted social welfare statutes in such areas as education, voting, consumer protection and environmental protection. Speaking through these enactments, Congress has made clear its desire that freedom, justice, and equality become a reality to and for all Americans. In many instances the responsibility for seeing that this salutary goal is accomplished lies with the federal judiciary.

Failure of Traditional Relief

The traditional forms of relief—an award of damages and the issuance of a prohibitory injunction—while adequate to remedy most constitutional violations of a business or economic nature, are but ingredients in remedying constitutional and statutory violations of a personal and social nature. The prisoner who lives in constant fear for his life and safety because of inadequate staffing and overcrowded conditions will not have his rights protected merely by an award of damages for the past injury sustained by him. If we, as judges, have learned anything from *Brown v. Board of Education* and its progeny, it is that prohibitory relief alone affords but a hollow protection to the basic and fundamental rights of citizens under equal protection of the law.

Once a constitutional deprivation has been shown, it becomes the duty of the court to render a decree which will as far as possible eliminate the effects of the past deprivations as well as bar like deprivations in the future. Because of the complexity and nature of the constitutional rights and issues involved, the traditional forms of relief have proven totally inadequate.

The courts have been left with two alternatives. They could throw up their hands in frustration and claim that, although the litigants have established a violation of constitutional or statutory rights, the courts have no satisfactory relief to grant them. This would, in addition to constituting judicial abdication, make a mockery of the Bill of Rights. Or, they could utilize their equitable powers to pursue the only reasonable and constitutionally accepted alternative: fashioning relief to fit the necessities of the particular case.

With acknowledgment that they are professionally trained in the law— not in penology, medicine or education—federal judges have approached these areas cautiously and hesitantly. Further, recognizing that many of the issues they are being asked to decide call for sensitive social and political policy judgments, the judges have shown great deference to those charged with making these judgments. The courts have intervened only when a constitutional or statutory violation has clearly and convincingly been established.

Nor have the courts attempted to enter these often murky and uncharted waters without navigational aids. In addition to seeking expert evidence, the court invites other parties, intervenors and *amici* to submit their recommendations and suggestions, usually in the form of proposed plans. This process, in addition to minimizing the need for judicial resolution of many of the remedial issues, increases the likelihood of voluntary compliance by the parties with the decree eventually adopted and entered by the court.

The courts have also turned to outside sources for advice and assistance. Biracial committees are, for example, now routinely provided for in school desegregation decisions in the Fifth Circuit.[2] In addition to putting forward their own remedial suggestions, these outside groups can and do play an invaluable role in implementing and, if necessary, monitoring the decree.

Implementing *Wyatt v. Stickney*

So that I might hopefully illustrate why these comprehensive remedial decrees are often necessary and how they are shaped and fashioned, I would like to briefly consider the case of *Wyatt v. Stickney*,[3] which I decided several years ago. I cite this not in any sense as a model of judicial perfection, but simply as one case that has been reviewed and approved by the United States Circuit Court of Appeals for the Fifth Circuit.

Wyatt v. Stickney was a class action lawsuit filed on behalf of all patients involuntarily confined at Bryce Hospital, Alabama's largest mental hospital, to determine whether and to what extent they were constitutionally entitled to minimum standards of care and treatment. Patients at Alabama's Searcy Hospital and residents at the Partlow State School and Hospital for the retarded were subsequently added as plaintiffs.

Resolution of these important constitutional issues necessitated a detailed and thorough examination of the state's entire mental health and retardation treatment and rehabilitation program. Because of the nature and scope of this inquiry, and with my conceded paucity of expertise in mental health and mental retardation areas, I solicited and was given assistance and advice from a number of outside sources. The Department of Justice, the American Civil Liberties Union, and the National Mental Health Law project acting on behalf of the United States of America were each allowed to intervene with full rights of a party. The leading experts in the country were called by the parties to testify and make recommendations.

The evidence presented at trial showed that Bryce Hospital, built in the 1850s, was grossly overcrowded, housing over 5000 patients. Of these 5000 persons ostensibly committed to Bryce Hospital for treatment of mental illness, about 1600 — or approximately one-third — were geriatrics neither in need of nor receiving any treatment for mental illness. Another 1000 or more of those confined at Bryce Hospital were mentally retarded rather than mentally ill. To serve these 5000 patients, there was a totally inadequate staff, only a small percentage of whom were professionally trained. There were only three medical doctors with psychiatric training, one Ph.D. psychologist and two social workers having master's degrees in social work.

The evidence indicated that the general living conditions and lack of individualized treatment programs were as intolerable and deplorable as the state's ranking of 50th among the states in per patient expenditures would suggest. By the way of example, less than 50 cents was spent per patient each day for food.

The evidence concerning Partlow State School and Hospital (for the retarded) was, if anything, even more dramatic than the evidence relating to mental hospitals. According to the testimony of the Associate Commissioner for Mental Retardation for the Alabama Department of Mental Health, Partlow was 60 percent overcrowded; he also testified that at least 300 residents could be discharged immediately, although the school had not undertaken to do so, *and that 70 percent of the residents should never have been committed at all.* The conclusion that there was no opportunity for rehabilitation for its residents was inescapable.

Mandating Patient Treatment

In evaluating the wealth of evidence adduced at trial, I began with the well settled principle that courts should not intervene in the affairs and activities of the coordinate branches of government without a clear showing of constitutional violation. However, upon a review of the complete record, I became convinced that in *Wyatt* such a showing was made. In the course of my opinion, I wrote:

> There can be no legal (or moral) justification for the state of Alabama's failing to afford treatment—and adequate treatment from a medical standpoint—to the several thousand patients who have been civilly committed to Bryce's for treatment purposes. To deprive any citizen of his or her liberty upon the altruistic theory that the confinement is for humane therapeutic reasons and then to provide inadequate treatment violates the very fundamentals of due process.[4]

Having found a constitutional violation, it then became necessary for me to formulate and render an appropriate decree. Clearly, monetary relief was not an appropriate remedy, nor would the mere issuance of an injunctive order restraining future constitutional violations suffice. The only constitutionally acceptable way to remedy the conditions existing in the state's mental health and mental retardation facilities was to issue a comprehensive remedial order.

The first stage was submission by the parties and *amici* of proposed plans for bringing the system up to Constitutional standards. It was only after two deadlines had passed during which acceptable progress had not been forthcoming that the court, itself, relying upon the proposals submitted, set forth the minimal constitutional standards of care, treatment, and rehabilitation for which the case of *Wyatt v. Stickney* is generally known.

Since the decree was one of an ongoing nature, human rights panels, comprised of individuals from all walks of life, were created to assist in implementing and monitoring the decree at each of the institutions. These panels, acting solely in an advisory capacity, have been of immeasurable assistance to both the various institutions and the court.

I should like to state that the conditions, while still not perfect, have improved dramatically in each of the institutions. The population at each facility has been reduced by approximately 50 percent, while staff has at least doubled at most institutions. A not altogether or unexpected benefit resulting from the public exposure given the problem has been a substantial increase in legislative appropriations for the state's mental health system.

I would again observe that, in an ideal society, all of these judgments and decisions should be made, in the first instance, by those whom we have entrusted with these responsibilities. It must be emphasized, that, when governmental institutions fail to make these judgments and decisions in a manner which comports with the Constitution, federal courts have a duty to remedy the violation. In summary, it is my firm belief that the judicial activism which has generated so much criticism is, in most instances, not activism at all. Courts do not relish making such hard decisions and certainly do not encourage litigation on social or political problems.

But the federal judiciary in this country has the paramount and the continuing duty to uphold the law. When a "case or controversy" is properly presented, the court may not shirk its sworn responsibility to uphold the Constitution and laws of the United States. The courts are bound to take jurisdiction and decide the issues, even though those decisions result in criticism. The basic strength of the federal judiciary has been, and continues to be, its independence from political or social pressures.

Finally, I submit that history has shown, with a few exceptions, that decisions of the federal judiciary over a period of time have become accepted and revered as monuments memorializing the strength and stability of this nation.

NOTES

1. *Fisher v. Cockerell,* 30 U.S. (5 Peters) 159, 167 (1831).

2. See *Calhoun v. Cook,* 362 F.Supp. 1249 (N.D. Ga., 1973), *aff'd.,* 522 F.2d 717 (5th Cir. 1975).

3. *Wyatt v. Stickney,* 325 F.Supp. 781; 344 F.Supp. 373 (1972); 344 F.Supp. 387 (M.D. Ala. 1972), modified on appeal, 503 F.2d 1305 (5th Cir. 1974).

4. Ibid., 325 F.Supp., at 785.

27

On the Cause and Treatment
of Judicial Activism

HOWARD T. MARKEY

Chief Judge, Court of Appeals, Federal Circuit

"Judicial activism" may mean different things to different people. One reason is because, like beauty, it can often be found "in the eye of the beholder." Judicial activism may be viewed, by those who look only at the result reached in a case, as routed toward different goals — toward management, labor, Republican, Democrat, capitalist, socialist, conservative, liberal goals — making the same conduct appear as "judicial activism" to some and as "judicial statesmanship" to others. Another reason is that judicial activism can be of different forms. It is on one of those forms that I primarily focus these remarks.

For want of a better term, I have called the form of judicial activism I have in mind "personal judicial activism," or "PJA."

It is the form of judicial activism to be feared most, because it would be anathema to that system of government we call "representative democracy." It would include ideological activism, in which result-oriented Federal judges would create new law in accord with their personal predilections, and would engage in social engineering and policy making to achieve personally perceived societal benefits. It would include operational activism, in which judges would take over and personally administer for years the day-to-day detail operation of any institution falling in any manner short of a judge's personal expectations.

All people have values of some sort, and judges are people. A person totally devoid of values would be a robot, an automaton. But at one end of the judicial spectrum, there are judges who hew to the Constitution and the law as they find it, honoring reason, precedent, logic, and the expressed intent of the drafters of the law at hand, making every conscientious effort to disregard their personal view of what the law "ought" to be, undertaking a balancing of values only when absolutely necessary, candidly admitting they are doing so and explaining why it was necessary. The term "personal" helps to pinpoint a type of judicial activism that would reside at the opposite end of the spectrum.

Not all judicial lawmaking can rightfully be labeled judicial activism, and only that judicial lawmaking designed to achieve a judge's personal societal goals can be labeled PJA. . . .

The litany of horrors likely to result from a rampant and widespread PJA is long indeed. We have time to list only the more obvious.

It could violate Article IV, section 4 of the Constitution. Justice Black, dissenting in *Griswold v. Connecticut,* pointed to the Framers' rejection of the suggestion that judges render advisory opinions and propose new laws to legislators. Most of the cases I found in a quick search dealt with protection of the right to vote. Many questions under the clause may be non-justiciable. In all events, it seems clear that Article IV, section 4 would prohibit imposition upon a state of a "Judicial Form of Government."

If we are approaching a point of peril for the American dream that the people can, through their representatives, govern themselves, the long-range solution is not for unelected, life-tenured judges to govern them. Nor can we, in these few moments, dig out a solution. The important thing is public awareness that the dream cannot long co-exist with government by the judiciary. A public dialogue on the threat would at least insure that the dream will not die unnoticed, unannounced, and unmourned.

The next horror is that PJA would give us Federal judges too much power. Unlike the beings that inhabited the cloud-draped heights of Olympus, we judges are not Gods. Be wary of the power you give us. Power is such a heady wine that even good men can become drunk on it.

Another horror is more insidious. Reliance on PJA has a currently hidden but fatal flaw. It builds expectations forlorn and foredoomed. With every human problem brought to court with all the people's eggs in the judicial basket, there is no way that the people's expectations can be met. The tragic awakening will come when the people learn a fundamental fact—judges can't solve all the people's problems. Certainly they cannot do so without lots of time, lots of investigators, lots of political input from numerous segments of society. There have been recent suggestions that judges be provided with staffs of investigators, social science advisors, accountants, and economists. Some of those suggestions read well, but they fail to recognize that a bureaucratization of the judiciary does two things: it locks in the notion that judges should govern, and it destroys the judiciary.

For the business of the judiciary is the administration of justice, not governance. Engagement of judges in ideological-legislative and operational-executive activities of the type I have lumped under "PJA" not only violates the separation of powers doctrine, it impedes performance of the judiciary's proper role. There is plenty for Federal judges, qua judges, to do now. Interpretation and application of the Constitution and Federal statutes, and keeping in balance the branches of government, including the judicial branch, are monumental tasks enough.

With 187,000 cases filed in one year before 450 trial judges, and 22,000 appeals filed before 40 appellate panels, the Federal judiciary has made yeoman, unprecedented efforts, under the dynamic and innovative leadership of the Chief Justice, to do what has been asked of it. With almost no timely help, Federal judges have so improved their efficiency and energy devotion that they are now annually rendering almost three times the number of decisions they did just a decade ago. But, unless there is a change in present trends, collapse is certain.

Last but not least among the horrors that would accompany a widespread PJA is the loss of the last hope for stability. As our pluralistic, multi-religious, multi-racial, multi-ideological society attempts to dispense equal justice under law and provide equal opportunity to all, as our society is beset with competing demands of single-issue pressure groups and unassimilated cultural differences, everybody is an activist. In a free society, controversy is endemic and taking sides is a national pastime. Somewhere is needed at least one stable and settled institution capable of applying rules of justice that rest on permanent principles, capable of resisting the seemingly sudden bursts of frenzied passion from which, as we have recently learned, even free societies are not immune.

That institution is a Federal judiciary protected by the law and protecting society by the law—a Federal judiciary of judges who refrain from the activist trends and temporary fads surrounding them—who diligently preserve the values of the centuries while their fellow citizens work out their destiny in freedom.

So, the problem is great and serious. As a beginning toward a solution-seeking dialogue, it would appear useful to outline some causes of the problem.

Perhaps a main cause has been the growth of government and the metamorphosis of our society into an administrative law state. In a few years we will be celebrating the 200th anniversary of the birth of the Constitution. Now would seem a good time to begin a review of where we are and how we got this way. Some things we find may be good. Some not so good. Consider the organization of the government under Articles I, II, and III, for example. We now have twice the number of "judges," called "Administrative Law Judges," in the Executive Branch as we have in the Judicial Branch. We have more "legislators," called "regulators," in the Executive Branch than we have in the Congress. With a Federal Register grown to 85,000 pages containing regulations "having the force of law," I am surprised that someone has not suggested changing the name of regulators to "Administrative Law Congressmen." No one would suggest a complete return to simpler times, but a review of where we are can help us retain, and where necessary, recapture the values inherent in the balance of powers when their exercise is separated.

With a growing number of regulatory agencies to the current level of 56, and the rapid increase in regulatory actions reflected in their budget growth since 1970 from less than $1 billion to more than $3 billion in constant dollars, it is not surprising that the courts have increasingly become major decision makers in resolving conflicts between regulators and segments of the public. Conflicts between the regulating agencies themselves have been increasingly brought to court. Appeals involving administrative agency action have become a growth industry. Between 1971 and 1979, the number of such appeals filed increased by 58 percent, and the number pending increased by 94 percent.

Congress, in the last decade, created 40 or 50 statutes, the last sentences of which read: "For details take this to the nearest courthouse." I emphasize with satire, and intend no attack on the wisdom or merits of any statute. But no one can list the causes for vastly increased activity of Federal judges without noting the statutory creation of new opportunities to go to Federal court. No one, least of all the judges, wants to deny access to the courts to any deserving party. But, as Griffin Bell pointed out, it is no good telling folks they can go to court if nothing happens when they get there. In sum, no one wants to slam the courthouse door—the problem is to avoid jamming that door by crowds who might not need to be there and are keeping out those who do.

Another cause, not to put too fine a point on it, is the refusal or inability of their branches to come to grips with and resolve some of the serious problems in our society, some of constitutional dimensions. When the pressure builds, and those responsible under the Constitution refuse to act, the people have felt compelled to turn to the only institution available, the courts. When courts enforce certain rights, the enforcement of which is constitutionally assigned to other branches of government, the danger is that those other branches will rest content to "leave it to the courts," and their interest in enforcing rights will atrophy. It is excruciatingly painful for the courts to abstain and watch the rights involved go unenforced. The charge of "judicial activism," though doubtless valid in many such instances, and if it is considered at all, seems at the time the lesser evil. Often an attractive "out" suggests itself—try to make it appear or sound like the court is just applying existing law.

Another cause may lie in an occasional judicial psyche. It would be foolish to pretend that no single Federal judge has ever, even subconsciously, viewed his or her role as one authorizing a personal policy-making function. The elements of office can lead to confusion of the terms "appointed" and "anointed." The temptation to "do good" can be strong. Judges harassed, harried, and hurried as they all are, may fall unknowing victim to various forms of judicial activism.

Some commentators have said, "After all, what is the judge to do? The case is there and must be decided." Until Congress or others act to create other decisional mechanisms to which some matters may be diverted for decision, those matters will continue to come "there." Absent a clearly defined and enforced set of legal parameters controlling the delegation of legislative powers to regulators, administrative agency cases will continue to come "there" to be decided. Judicial abstention, however desirable in a particular case, may be difficult to distinguish from judicial abdication. The line between restraint and retreat is not always clear.

There are doubtless other causes for what may seem to some a trend toward PJA. Whatever may be the fate of that trend, the level of judicial activity is likely to parallel that of government. If the role of government can be diminished, that of courts can also be. In any case, the trick is not only to limit the level of activity of judges, but to set its proper nature. PJA at any level of judicial activity is bad. The trick is to keep the judicial role judicial—to keep it from becoming either personal or political.

For two things are important to remember in discussing the role of the Federal courts in our society. Federal judges may be accountable in many ways, but they do not stand for election and thus are politically unaccountable. Judicial independence under our Constitution serves the people, not the judges, and is critical to the hope for continued freedom in this blessed land. But it must be factored into any evaluation of the role of the Federal courts. The other thing to remember is that courts have no armies. Their continued viability, the continuance of the very role of law in our society, depends upon respect for the courts and a consequent willingness to accept their judgments.

The treatment of judicial activism, in all its forms, must be rendered in the first instance by judges themselves. The news media, commentators in academe, law review writers, and others render yeoman service in pointing to instances of activism, but valuable as that service is, it is necessarily after the fact. Judges must be, or be made, constantly alert to temptations toward PJA, its dangers to society and the judiciary, and its "thief in the night" nature. Warned of the shoals, judges may sail safely by, deaf to the song of result-oriented sirens.

At the same time, judges alert to the activism syndrome, and forced to decide a case in a manner likely to appear activist, will treat the matter clearly in their opinions. To the extent that some form of limited lawmaking is absolutely required, the judge will "fess up," and will not pretend that the law announced has always existed. In this sense, a major treatment of judicial activism, as it is for so many things, is sunlight. Open and candid recognition that law is being made, accompanied by a clear explanation of why it must be made, if adopted as universal practice, could have two salutory effects. It could forestall unnecessary judicial lawmaking, when the effort to explain its necessity foundered. It could lead to reforms removing its necessity in future cases, when the reasons for an inescapable lawmaking are made public.

28

The Activist Judicial Mind

RALPH K. WINTER
Judge, Court of Appeals, Second Circuit

Although judicial activism has become a rather permanent fixture in the American political process during the last 20 years, we seem to know very little about its intellectual or attitudinal wellsprings. Those who praise it are usually political liberals and emphasize the desirability of the results of judicial activism as policy, typically by arguing that it has enlarged individual rights. Its critics, on the other hand, are usually politically conservative, and condemn it on policy grounds and attack the process itself as contrary to democracy.

The simplistic nature of the debate is, or so it seems to me, curious. First, judicial activism has entered an unprecedented era. While there have been previous occasions in which the Supreme Court has sought to impose its own political values upon the nation, these occasions have generally been limited to particular issues about which the Court felt strongly. Never has it sought to do so along as broad a political, social, and economic front as today. Legislative apportionment, voter eligibility rules, pupil assignment in public schools, abortion, welfare eligibility, public employment, birth control, landlord-tenant relations are areas where courts have changed existing laws and practices with only minimal support from conventional legal criteria other than the personal values of judges. Much of this has come from a Court, moreover, denounced by many as overly conservative.

Second, the activism appears not to have brought about policy results which are random in political direction. Rather, they seem consistently liberal or at least consistent with that branch of reformist, middle-class liberalism descended from the Progressive Era at the turn of the century. Critics generally attribute this to a variety of causes among which are the isolation of the Supreme Court in liberal Washington, the influence of, and dependence on, liberal law clerks, and an understandable desire for good reviews from a left-leaning media. Admirers attribute it to an enlightenment which has shaped judicial views of the good society in a fashion so similar to their own best judgment.

There is no doubt some truth in these observations however disparate their sources, but they hardly constitute a full explanation. So far as one can tell, many judges who have participated in the recent activism seem unlikely liberals.

Many were in fact appointed by a President who vowed to put an end to judicial activism. As for political liberals on the bench, there has been no ready explanation for the distrust of democratic procedures which judicial activism reflects. Surely something more than a desire for instant gratification explains their readiness to diminish the importance of the vote.

I emphasize what seems to me the shallowness of the discussion of the causes of judicial activism, for if these causes run deep in our modern polity and transcend to any degree common notions of "liberal" and "conservative," reversing the trend to judicial imperialism may be less easy than it seems to many.

Nor is there a single explanation, even of a complex sort. The growth of government itself, the coming to power of the New Class pressing for more regulation and social engineering, the leftist, activist tilt of legal education and legal educators, the growth of systematic "public interest" litigation and the reporting of the media on public affairs have all contributed in one measure or another to the growth of judicial power. . . .

The attitudes described, moreover, are by no means unique to lawyers or persons with legal training. To the contrary, judicial attitudes reflect, and probably always have, strains of thought found in a variety of pockets of the upper middle-class intellectual community. In particular, judicial activism today finds many of its sources in the Progressive movement of the turn of the century and contemporary reformist groups.

Contemporary judicial activism reflects, I believe, attitudes closely related to those of the reformist, in particular:

1. Hostility to a pluralist, party dominated, political process;
2. A demand for "rationality" in public policy;
3. Skepticism about the morality of capitalism.

Judicial Activism and Political Pluralism

Proponents of contemporary judicial activism emphasize the need to enlarge individual rights and protect "minorities" or "underrepresented" groups.* Critics emphasize the need to protect democratic processes from a non-elected branch of government.

This debate is as old, indeed, older than the Republic itself. In *Federalist No. 51,* Madison argued that there were two methods of protecting minorities from overreaching majorities. The first entailed "creating a will in the community independent of the majority that is, of the society itself," a method typified at the time by goverments with "an hereditary or self-appointed authority."

---

*Quotation marks are used, not because I deny the problem of minority protection, but because these terms have come to be used to include so many groups that they no longer necessarily have their traditional meaning. For example, one often hears discussions today which include as "minorities" all women, all blacks, all hispanics, and all orientals, perhaps 70 percent of the population.

Madison rejected this as rendering "but a precarious security . . . because a power independent of the society may as well espouse the unjust views of the major as the rightful interests of the minor party, and may possibly be turned against both parties."

Madison's second, and preferred, method, was a pluralistic political process. "Whilst all authority . . . will be derived from and dependent on the society, the society itself will be broken into so many parts, interests and classes of citizens, that the rights of individuals, or of the minority, will be in little danger from interested combinations of the majority."

In the evolved Madisonian system, minorities are protected in two ways. First, power is diffused in a government of checks and balances, with states exercising significant authority and the federal government organized in separate executive, legislative, and judicial branches. Second, each political branch represents differing constituencies and differing terms of office with the result that, in a socially, economically, and politically diverse nation, each branch generally has a distinct political outlook. The President, with a four-year term, must win a majority of electoral votes cast by state delegations under a unit rule, winner-take-all system. This tends to exaggerate, beyond their numerical proportion of the voting population, the power of majorities in the large states. Members of the House run every two years in winner-take-all districts within states. Senators hold six-year terms and are elected at large within states, each state having equal representation. Congressmen thus represent differing local majorities and each house has its distinct political complexion, while the Presidency reflects a national constituency generally tilted toward majorities in large states.

The franchise, of course, plays an important role in the evolved Madisonian system. All competing groups must be accorded the same voting rights accorded other competing groups. This convoluted formulation is necessary because the Madisonian system in no way depends on universal suffrage or even direct majority selection of representatives in each political branch. The creation of competing centers of powers representing differing constituencies requires only that no identifiable groups be disfranchised. For example, if every fifth person were randomly disfranchised but government was unable to distinguish between those who could and could not vote, the Madisonian system would continue to function exactly as expected. The vote is thus a right derived from the process and is more valuable for what it contributes to decentralization than for what it produces in the way of majoritarianism.

The formal structure of government does not by itself insure moderate political majorities, at least when viewed apart from other institutions, traditions, and laws. The Madisonian obsession with the representation of local majorities runs the real risk of political anarchy. The formation of an effective governing coalition is extremely difficult where so many competing centers of power exist. Once formed, moreover, such coalitions are inherently unstable as each group perceives its position in the coalition as indispensable and pushes its most extreme demand. The protection of political minorities would hardly seem a likely result.

Madison's vision was, therefore, never logical. What made the system work was the evolution of certain traditions and institutions, in combination with certain electoral laws, which operated both to produce coalitions with a measure of continuity and to moderate the demands of member groups. The result was in accord with Madison's vision, but for reasons which he did not foresee, a testament to what my late colleague, Alex Bickel, called the "mysteries" of democratic rule.

The most important institution is, of course, the political party, while the most important tradition is a competitive two-party system.

The parties themselves, in the evolved Madisonian system, were private groups managed and operated largely by persons active within the organization — or party leaders and workers as they have come to be called. Nominations were largely within their control through local caucuses or conventions, at which representation was largely restricted to the party establishment. These leaders and workers thus had a personal stake in the party organization and its electoral success—incentives which insured a working political organization at the grass roots level. In a two-party system, these incentives also tended to insure that party leaders would, in order to compete with their adversary, seek the broadest feasible coalition. Competition tended to force them to appeal to any group which might be attracted and which would not alienate other significant groups. They also had an incentive to select as the party nominee the candidate perceived to have the best chance of victory in the general election.

The party's success in turn depended upon formal political acts of platform adoption, campaign promises, voter registration, and get-out-the-vote drives. It also depended upon the party's relation to a multitude of groups in the society which affect our politics. American politics and American political parties involve a massive network of interconnected, overlapping groups, large and small, local, regional, and national, organized for economic, spiritual, recreational, professional, social, or educational purposes. The relationships are complex, subtle, and perhaps indescribable. Members of such groups were invited to become party workers while party workers became members of such groups. All served as channels of communication between the groups and the party organization. The overlapping membership of groups and political parties also gave party workers contact with both independents and with the opposition. What is clear, I think, is that parties in such circumstances must bid for the favor of groups which do not have clear and intensely desired political goals. The parties need these groups more than they need the parties. Other groups do have intensely felt political goals, however, and they need the parties as much as the parties need them. This, I believe, was a mighty force for moderation because party support for groups with defined political goals might be conditioned upon the groups' tailoring their claims so as not to alienate less politically concerned persons.

The consequence of this complex process was that competitive parties in a two-party system moved toward each other as party leaders sought a coalition which would produce majorities. Candidates were persons with whom party leaders felt comfortable and whom they believed had the best chance of victory. Sharp ideological stances were avoided, as were candidates who might attract the animosity of a particular group. A party seeking victory cannot afford to alienate any significant group, unless of course that alienation is prized by an even larger group.

The coalitions thus formed, moreover, were rarely temporary or *ad hoc,* for a measure of continuity is valuable to a competitive political party, just as a brand name provides good will for a manufacturer.

The two-party system thus accomplished in large part what Madison foresaw as the consequence of pluralism, namely a measure of protection for political minorities. As Richard Hofstadter has noted, what Madison hoped to achieve through pluralism among many factions was achieved through pluralism within two parties. The protection afforded minority interests came, of course, from the moderation produced by coalitions formed by the major parties. Because the aim of those putting the coalition together was electoral victory, groups hoping to share in that victory had to moderate their more extreme demands so that this contribution was not offset by losses among other groups.

This description of the evolved Madisonian system is, of course, an idealized version. In practice, the American political system has contained many of the elements of the evolved Madisonian system. In some regions, the two have come very close in practice. In others, any resemblance has been difficult to discern.

In the South, the two-party system was deliberately destroyed through a combination of devices including the use of a primary which prevented losing candidates from running in the general election. Moreover, blacks were disfranchised so no political group would be tempted to look to them for coalition building purposes. The result was an unstructured politics, heavily concentrated on individual candidates, prone to extremism and demagoguery. The failure was not a failure of the evolved Madisonian system but rather a failure to use it.

Lately, moreover, the Madisonian system has been assaulted on a national scale by modern day reformists who have roots in American history and in American political rhetoric. They are the descendants of the Progressive movement and their language is the language of high school civics classes.

To them the citizen is a person of good will who decides political questions on the merits alone, and only after study and deliberation. Whereas Madison extolled pluralism and the conflict between competing groups, a leading reform organization calls itself Common Cause. To the reformers, the Madisonian system is little more than an intricate set of rules and institutions designed to put impediments in the way of the citizen's quest of good government. Because the parties are more interested in winning than debating issues, the public is not adequately informed, and issue-oriented candidates are cast aside for those who survive by avoiding stands on important public questions while making covert commitments to special interest groups. Thus, it is believed that campaigns rely too heavily upon media promotion and not enough on "real" discussion of the issues. Because parties are "boss run," the rank and file of a party has little to say about the nominees of that party, a case of minority rule. Moreover, the minorities which rule the parties are usually selfish economic interests living off a public which is powerless to drive them from our politics.

This negative view of pluralism, I believe, is shared by judicial activists. In a pluralistic system, for example, legislative apportionment can be utilized to insure representation for distinct groups and to create legislative houses of differing political complexions. The "malapportionments" of the United States Senate and the Electoral College are thus essential elements of pluralistic politics at the federal level.

The reapportionment decisions of the Supreme Court, in opinions authored by Chief Justice Warren himself, were very much the work of judicial activism and were said to be his proudest achievement. Characterizing the issues as involving the "individual and personal" right to have all votes count equally, the Court held that apportionment schemes which contain legislative districts with unequal populations are constitutionally invalid.

The reasoning of the Court was decidedly negative so far as the value of a pluralistic political process was concerned. The argument that a constitution which provided for both the Senate and Electoral College would hardly compel the states to apportion more than one legislative house on a population basis was rejected. The Chief Justice's opinion found the "federal analogy" to be "inappropriate" where state legislative bodies are concerned. The federal system, he wrote, was a consequence of the fact that the original states were independent and concessions to small states were necessary to form the union. The Senate and the Electoral College were, in short, an undesirable but necessary result of a kind of extortion by the small states at the time of origin, which has served no useful function since.

That history indicated a persistent deviation from a population principle at both the federal and state levels and that enhancing group representation might be a legitimate goal were both flatly rejected in the name of individual rights. "But neither history alone, nor economic or other sorts of group interests, are permissible factors in attempting to justify disparities from population based representation. Citizens, not history or economic interest, cast "votes." What is important is "an individual citizen's ability to exercise an effective voice. . . ."

The judicial tendency to view politics as an aggregate of individual rights necessarily entails a view of the right to vote as inhering in the citizen rather than being derived from a particular political process.

As Alex Bickel described it, the Court was part of a more general populist movement.

There was a powerful strain of populism in the rhetoric by which the Court supported its one-man, one-vote doctrine, and after promulgating it the Court strove mightily to strike down all barriers—not only the poll tax, but duration of residence, all manner of special qualifications, and even in some measure, age—to the enlargement and true universalization of the franchise. In this the Court led successfully. It became irresistible dogma that no qualification for voting made any sense. It did not matter that you were a transient—and wherever the election catches you, you vote with no questions asked. No connection to place is relevant, there is no room for balancing interests and places, no need to structure institutions so that they be better able to generate consent. Every impediment, every distortion, including the electoral college, must go. All that matters is the people, told by the head!

In another line of decisions, the Court has frontally assaulted the patronage system by holding that governmental employees may not be discharged on grounds of party affiliation unless the nature of the employment is such that affiliation is related to effective performance of the job. Again, "individual rights" are elevated above the interests of groups, in this case those of political parties. That patronage is a method of creating and maintaining party organization was not denied but was held to be of insufficient weight to offset the intrusion on individual political beliefs and associations. Not only was party organization given little weight in the calculus, but by finding harm in the fact that a desire to gain or retain employment led to political activity, the Court struck at the very element which gave cohesion to many political organizations. Like the reformers, however, the majority obviously has a distaste for political activity which is not "issue" related and which increases the power of party organizations and party "bosses."

In the campaign finance area, judges normally associated with activism have strongly favored laws which, by limiting campaign contributions and expenditures, have sought to reduce very sharply traditional campaign activities. Not only is private campaign financing regarded as a source of undue or improper influence by "special interests" but political campaigns are viewed as media events which do not adequately inform the "citizen" as to the "issues." Thus, a majority of the Court of Appeals for the District of Columbia upheld the Federal Election Campaign Act as a way to "cleanse . . . democratic processes" of the "corrosive influence of money" while denigrating presidential campaigns as "quadrennial Romanesque political extravaganzas." That campaign activities would be sharply restricted was regarded as an "incidental" effect.

Given the facts that these judges also pride themselves on their vigor in protecting First Amendment rights, this attitude toward campaign financing is enormously significant. Campaign activities are political speech that cost money. If you limit the money, you limit the speech. And while you may limit the influence of organized economic interests, you also prevent the ideological groups from supporting candidates they favor, e.g., antiwar contributions to Eugene McCarthy in 1968. Nevertheless, the belief in the irrelevance of political campaigns to the "issues" and the outright hostility to "special interests" led these judges to the conclusion that mainstream political activity is entitled to less constitutional protection than they would routinely accord common pornographers.

The rejection of a pluralistic political process and an activist judiciary are closely related. Alex Bickel also noted the "paradox" that while contemporary populism exalts "the people," they may not vote for the results which populist ideology dictates. "But then," he wrote, "one can . . . identify the general will with the people despite their voices, and let the Supreme Court bespeak the people's general will when the vote comes out wrong."

At a conceptual level, the paradox results from viewing the right to vote as inherent in the citizen *qua* citizen, rather than derived from a particular kind of political process. When process is denigrated and individual rights are exalted, the power of courts necessarily increases because we culturally look to courts for the development and protection of rights. The judiciary, on the other hand, need have less respect for a process which lacks legitimacy and infringes on those protected rights. The right to vote and the right to use contraceptives—or any other right, for that matter—are relatively co-equal and must be balanced, much as a court balances a newspaper's right to a free press against a criminal defendant's right to a fair trial.

So long as we conceive of the right to vote as being absolute except where its exercise might infringe other rights, the conflict between judicial supremacy and democracy can be made to appear as an ordinary conflict between competing rights, the kind of problem routinely addressed by courts. That activism is in fact undermining the basic framework of government is thus concealed by a claim that judicial protection of rights is just business as usual.

Judicial attitudes toward a pluralistic political process lead to activism in yet another way. Academic defenders of judicial power repeatedly appeal to the protection of minorities, somehow defined, as a justification for expansion of judicial authority. Their position is not without logic, for the failure of the evolved Madisonian system, or its deliberate destruction in recent years, necessarily reopens the question of protection from "interested combinations of the majority," as argued by Madison in *Federalist No. 51*. Madison was prescient in noting that the alternative to pluralism so far as protection of minorities was concerned was a supreme "hereditary or self-appointed authority." American judges neither inherit their positions nor appoint themselves, but they more and more constitute "a will . . . independent of the majority."

In recent years, our political process has been revolutionized by a combination of reform and technology which has drastically affected Madisonian pluralism and, I believe, diminished its moderating effects on our politics. If this is the case, judicial activism protecting minorities from "interested combinations of the majority" may seem justified.

The competitive two-party system has been seriously, perhaps fatally, impaired by "party reform." The influence of party leaders upon the nomination process has been weakened, and the activities of party workers as intermediaries between the public and the party have declined. Nominees are increasingly chosen by a process which bypasses party organizations and which decidedly does not entail a professional judgment as to which candidate is more likely to attract a broad coalition of voters.

Campaign finance laws limit the amounts parties can raise and spend on behalf of candidates and force candidates to centralize their campaign activities under a separate candidate-operated committee. Candidates necessarily view themselves as independent from the party. The weakening process feeds on itself. Party workers let up or even disappear as they feel a diminishing of their influence. Candidates see the party withering away and rely even less upon it.

As the role of parties declines, the role of individual candidates increases. Indeed, the nation has turned more to the model of the one-party South than the other way around. Technology has made this possible by enabling candidates to appeal directly to the public through television and computerized mailing lists, while sophisticated polling techniques allow candidates to gather information about the public mood while bypassing the party. The campaign finance laws give enormous advantages to candidates with independent fundraising capabilities and institutionalized ideological groups such as NCPAC, and other interests such as unions or corporations, which can bypass the party and give help directly to candidates.

Our politics are exhibiting an increasing lack of moderation. One hears constant concern over the rise of single-issue groups pressing their claims upon candidates. What else would one expect, however, from a system which subjects strategic points in the political process to direct control by small numbers of issue activists? The campaign finance laws, the open nominating process, and the lack of party organizations encourage, not to say force, candidates to attend to the wants of small cohesive groups. A working two-party system would either ignore such groups or force them to moderate their more extreme claims. An "open" system allows them to go direct to candidates and press for all they can get.

The point is that a plausible case can be made for the proposition that the moderating effect of evolved Madisonian pluralism has been drastically reduced by a combination of technological innovation and conscious change in the name of reform. Calls for judicial activism in the face of this are not wholly implausible, as Madison's own discussion of minority protection indicated, even when it comes from those who have done so much to impair the moderating forces of pluralism.

The Supreme Court, it can be argued, is less subject to influence by single-issue or special interest groups, and it can thus serve as a moderating force. Justices are, after all, freed from transitory political pressures and thereby able to respond to more stable values. Judicial proceedings tend, as a consequence of the adversary process, to expose judges to all relevant arguments and not just the vocal demands of committed zealots.

I am not arguing, it should be stressed, the merit of this position. Rather I am describing what seems to me to be an attitude which helps to explain the apparent imperviousness of many judges to equally plausible claims that courts are usurping the powers of the democratically elected branches of government.

Judicial Activism and the Quest for Rational Solutions

A second attitude, closely related to hostility to a pluralistic political process, which underlies judicial activism is a belief in the need for rational solutions to public issues. A pluralistic political process tends to arrive at solutions which are essentially compromises accommodating conflicting goals in an untidy fashion. Policies tend to be unintelligible mixes of political power, legislative judgment, historical accident, and conventional wisdom, funded according to standards only remotely related to merit or need.

Once courts embark on an activist course, it is probably inevitable that they will seek to reshape governmental institutions which seem to embody significant irrational components. The judicial process, after all, stresses "right" solutions rather than compromises or half measures tempered by political considerations. I am, persuaded, for example, that the reapportionment decisions were heavily influenced by a quest for rationality.

Malapportionment was always partly the product of historical accident and unforeseen demographic changes as well as conscious design. The real evil it entailed—preventing democratic majorities from registering an opinion on apportionment as a consequence of the abiding self-interest of incumbent legislators—could easily be remedied by requiring the establishment of processes which allowed the people a choice as to apportionment schemes. This solution, however, would not have eliminated accidental or irrational apportionment schemes, whereas "one-person, one-vote" seems a relevant, quantifiable criterion. What other value it has is difficult to discern, since so long as single-member, winner-take-all districts are permitted, a majority of elected legislators may represent a minority of voters.

Much of this is true in other areas. It is still part of the standard activist program to attack local funding of education on the grounds that the tax bases available to each community vary widely. That is of course true, but it is also the case that each community has varying educational needs and desires and that an amount of self-selection in choosing where to live occurs. The activists occasionally mask their goal by arguing that some form of equalization of tax bases would help poor children, but in many places the tax base of inner cities is greater than that of the suburbs. Nevertheless, the attack on local financing continues unabated. At bottom, the factor which stirs the activists to action is neither poverty nor discrimination but the seeming irrationality of local financing which results from the lack of central planning.

The same is true in the area of school busing in which courts attempt to find the "right" racial mix based upon population data and findings as to "tipping points." The fact that racial integration—defined in terms of people being in the same building—has a quantifiable dimension has itself, I believe, made it more attractive as a goal for judicial activism.

Activist judges also are quite confident about the superiority of judicial processes. The urge to take over a school system, welfare program, prison, or mental hospital is based not only on righteous indignation over governmental inertia and inefficiency but on an abiding belief that courts, unlike other agencies of government, can exclude from consideration "irrational" factors such as public reaction or problems in raising revenue while taking into account the latest teaching of the social sciences. Only courts can concentrate fully on reaching the right solution by taking into account all of the "relevant" considerations. Only they can engage in really successful social engineering.

A yen for social engineering is not all that is at work, however, for legal training itself emphasizes the search for rationality and coherence in legal rules. Unless tempered by an understanding of what kinds of problems can never be solved by rules, most lawyers will utilize a technocratic approach.

Judicial Activism and Hostility to Free Markets

The negative attitude toward a pluralistic political process and the desire to find rational solutions to governmental problems are closely related to a third attitude, hostility to free markets.

Activist doubt about the value of free markets is reflected in a variety of areas. In antitrust, the most activist judges generally adopt a posture of protectionism toward small business. There are many decisions, for example, which in effect make it illegal to be a superior competitor and expose companies to treble damage liability for harm suffered by less efficient rivals. While activist judges universally take the position that "economic" regulation may not be subjected to constitutional challenge, they generally scrutinize the regulation of welfare carefully. Finally, activists have sought to analogize poverty to race and to work out legal theories under the Equal Protection Clause which would reduce economic inequality. In each case, their attitude reflects profound doubt about the value of free markets.

This doubt, however, is not Marxist in any strict sense. Rather, it stems from two characteristics of free market systems to which judicial activists are particularly sensitive. First, a free market system is the antithesis of central planning. As a consequence, the results it produces seem irrational or accidental and certainly a deviation from "right" solutions. There is a contemporary mindset which associates the lack of central planning with irrationality, anarchy, and a lack of social purpose. An elitist group such as judges will have tastes different from those of the mass of consumers. It is not unnatural for them to view many of the products produced by free markets as having no intrinsic value and being little more than a response to irrational demands induced by advertising.

A second source of doubt about free markets is more serious. Activist judges deal in moral values, in "justice." Chief Justice Warren was fond of asking questions which ignored traditional rules or technicalities and focused on "Is it right? Is it fair?" Such an attitude about the judicial role is almost inevitably associated with hostility to free markets. Those markets do not reward those who adhere most closely to conventional moral values. Rather, they reward the efficient, and efficiency is often found in company with a singleminded greed, if not even more distasteful personal qualities.

Judicial activists . . . have no intention of destroying capitalism; they only want to make it more rational and more moral, a goal that they view as fully consistent with diminishing the power of "special interests" in the political system. Here their attention is focused on protecting the "small," "local" (and implicitly the more worthy) businessman from the rigors of competition, ameliorating the lot of the very poor and reducing economic inequality to some degree.

Conclusion

If this speculation about the attitudes of judicial activists is correct, two conclusions follow: (1) political conservatism in a judge is no absolute guarantee against judicial activism; (2) judicial activism rests on an intellectual base which is dangerous to the nation.

First, the attitudes described above are found to some degree in political conservatives as well as political liberals. Political pluralism is neutral to the liberal/conservative distinction. . . . A political conservative may be a different kind of judge than a political liberal, therefore, but not necessarily less activist. A reduction in activism can be achieved only when courts understand and value the political process and have a sense of the limitations of social engineering and the judicial process.

Second, the intellectual and attitudinal wellsprings of activism do not bode well for the nation. When Madison posed a supreme authority "independent of the majority" as the alternative to pluralism as protection for the minority, he also rejected it as being a threat to majority and minority alike. The belief that an activist court will do only good things and be a successful moderating influence is more a matter of faith than of logic, of political religion than of experience. In fact we are in a time when extreme groups are exerting great pressure on judicial appointments. The Carter administration's "merit selection" panels appear to have been, in true Orwellian fashion, a vehicle for politicizing the lower courts, while the Republican platform appears to limit appointments to persons with fixed positions on certain issues. If anything, therefore, it appears that the special interest or single-issue groups are insisting on representation in the judicial branch.

The quest for rational solutions, moreover, carries the seeds of future disasters. Government must respond to intangibles with policies which are never fully logical, much less quantifiable. There are mysteries in democratic government which are never fully understood or articulated. What works in one community will be an utter failure in another, as the search for the right racial balance in schools indicates. Local financing of education may be irrational but it may also be a rough compromise and in the end superior to the alternatives. In truth, our information is always inadequate and the quest for the right solution is a game of blind man's bluff rather than a comprehensive inquiry. Moreover, since the search for the right solution ignores the most important factor in a democratic society, generation of consent among the people, it is always disaster prone.

The hostility to capitalism is less dangerous, although quite as mistaken. Judicial activists have no system to replace free markets and no principled theory of reform. What they generally offer are solutions arrived at in innocence of their economic effects, which often may be a reduction in economic activity injurious to the very persons they were trying to protect.

The cumulative impact of these attitudes ought to be a source of apprehension. They reflect a lack of understanding of the full political process and of the mysteries of government along with a generalized hostility to important institutions in our society which they seek to weaken but not replace.

NOTE

1. Alexander Bickel, *The Morality of Consent* 121 (New Haven: Yale University Press, 1980).

Appendix A

Selected Bibliography
of Off-the-Bench
Commentaries

The items selected provide illuminating commentaries on the nature of judicial review, the judicial process and the administration of justice, the dynamics of constitutional and statutory interpretation, as well as on the role of the judiciary in a litigious society. They are arranged according to the subject matter of each section in order to facilitate further research. The list is inevitably selective and incomplete due to the long, rich history of extrajudicial writing, the large number of individuals who have sat on federal and state benches, and the wide range of issues addressed.

The collection was guided by two objectives: (1) inclusion of representative expressions of different judicial philosophies and views from the bench; and (2) that selection of commentaries provide some historical perspective and insights on the operation of the judiciary principally by members of the Supreme Court of the United States and leading members of the contemporary federal and state judiciaries.

Those interested in further exploring particular justices' views should consult Adrienne deVergie and Mary Kate Kell, *Location Guide to the Manuscripts of Supreme Court Justices* (1981), and A.K. Wigdor, *A Survey of the Collections of Personal Papers of Supreme Court Justices: Their Locations, Size, Provenance, and Character* (1977).

The list here does not include items in either of these volumes, nor justices' memorial remarks (which may be found in *United States Reports*) and speeches delivered to the American Law Institute (since they may be located in the *Proceedings* of the Institute).

Albert P. Blaustein and Roy M. Mersky's *The First One Hundred Justices* (1978) contains some vital statistics on the Supreme Court of the United States and a useful bibliography of secondary literature on the judiciary and constitutional politics; as does Henry J. Abraham's *The Judicial Process: An Introductory Analysis of the Courts of the United States, England, and France* (5th ed., 1985). The *Index to Legal Periodicals* provides the most reliable and up-to-date reference to the extrajudicial writings of contemporary justices and judges.

Judicial Review and American Politics: Historical and Political Perspectives

BALDWIN, HENRY. *A General View of the Origin and Nature of the Constitution and Government of the United States.* Philadelphia: Clark, 1837.

BRADLEY, JOSEPH P. "Office and Nature of Law as the Basis and Bond of Society." 41 *Legal Intelligencer* 396 (1884).

BREWER, DAVID. "The Supreme Court of the United States." 33 *Scribner's* 273 (1903).

BURGER, WARREN E. "The Doctrine of Judicial Review: Mr. Marshall, Mr. Jefferson, and Mr. Marbury." Presidential Address, Bentham Club, University College, London, England, 1 February 1972.

BURTON, HAROLD. "The Cornerstone of American Constitutional Law: The Extraordinary Case of *Marbury v. Madison.*" 36 *American Bar Association Journal* 805 (1950).

_____. "Justice the Guardian of Liberty: John Marshall at the Trial of Aaron Burr." 37 *American Bar Association Journal* 735 (1951).

_____. "The Dartmouth College Case: A Dramatization." 38 *American Bar Association Journal* 991 (1952).

_____. "An Independent Judiciary: The Keystone of Our Freedom." 39 *American Bar Association Journal* 1067 (1953).

_____. "John Marshall—The Man." 104 *University of Pennsylvania Law Review* 3 (1955).

CLARKE, JOHN H. "History and the 1937 Court Proposal." 3 *Vital Speeches* 369 (1937).

COOLEY, THOMAS M. *A Treatise on Constitutional Limitations.* Boston: Little, Brown, 1868.

CURTIS, BENJAMIN R. *Jurisdiction, Practice, and Peculiar Jurisprudence of the Courts of the United States.* Boston: Little, Brown, 1880.

FIELD, STEPHEN J. Address, "The Supreme Court of the United States." Centennial Celebration of the Organization of the Federal Judiciary, New York, N.Y., 134 U.S. 729 (1890).

FULLER, MELVILLE W. "Centennial of the Constitution of the United States." 21 *Chicago Legal News* 303 (1889).

HARLAN, JOHN M. "The Courts in the American System of Government." 37 *Chicago Legal News* 271 (1905).

_____. "Government Under the Constitution." *Law Notes* 206 (1908).

HUGHES, CHARLES EVANS. *The Supreme Court of the United States.* New York: Columbia University Press, 1928.

_____. "An Imperishable Ideal of Liberty Under Law." 25 *Journal of the American Judicature Society* 99 (1941).

JACKSON, ROBERT H. *The Supreme Court in the American System of Government.* Cambridge: Harvard University Press, 1955.

_____. "The Task of Maintaining Our Liberties: The Role of the Judiciary." 39 *American Bar Association Journal* 961 (1953).

_____. *The Struggle for Judicial Supremacy.* New York: Knopf, 1941.

JAY, JOHN. *The Correspondence and Public Papers of John Jay.* New York: Putnam's, 1890-1893.

KAUFMAN, IRVING R. "The Essence of Judicial Independence." 80 *Columbia Law Review* 671 (1980).

_____. "Chilling Judicial Independence." 88 *Yale Law Journal* 681 (1979).

MARSHALL, JOHN. Letter to the editor (under pseudonym "A Friend to the Union"). *Philadelphia Union* (18 April, 1 May, 1819).

MILLER, SAMUEL. *Lectures on the Constitution.* Washington, D.C.: Morrison, 1880.

REED, STANLEY. "Our Constitutional Philosophy: Concerning the Significance of Judicial Review in the Evolution of American Democracy." 21 *Kentucky State Bar Journal* 136 (1957).

_____. "The Living Law." Address, Columbia University Law School, 8 November 1958.

ROBERTS, OWEN J. *The Court and the Constitution.* Cambridge: Harvard University Press, 1951.

_____. "American Constitutional Government: The Blueprint and Structure." 29 *Boston University Law Review* 1 (1953).

RUTLEDGE, WILEY. *A Declaration of Legal Faith.* Lawrence: University of Kansas Press, 1947.

STORY, JOSEPH. *Commentaries on the Constitution of the United States.* Boston: Little, Brown, 1833.

_____. "Life, Character, and Service of Chief Justice Marshall." In *Miscellaneous Writings of Joseph Story.* Boston: Little, Brown, 1852.

VINSON, FRED. "Our Enduring Constitution." *Washington and Lee Law Review* 1 (1949).

WILSON, JAMES. "Of the Judicial Department." In *The Works of James Wilson,* Vol. 2. Chicago: Callaghan, 1896.

The Dynamics of the Judicial Process

ALARCON, ARTHUR. "Political Appointments and Judicial Independence—An Unreasonable Expectation." 16 *Loyola of Los Angeles Law Review* 9 (1983).

BAZELON, DAVID. Address. School of Law, University of Washington, 11 June 1983.

BLACK, HUGO. "The Lawyer and Individual Freedom." 21 *Tennessee Law Review* 461 (1950).

_____. "Mr. Justice Rutledge." 25 *Indiana Law Review* 541 (1950).

_____. "Mr. Justice Murphy." 48 *Michigan Law Review* 739 (1950).

BLACKMUN, HARRY A. "A Candid Talk with Justice Blackmun." *New York Times Magazine,* Sec. 6 (20 February 1983).

_____. "A Justice Speaks Out." Cable News Network, Inc., 4 December 1982.

BRANDEIS, LOUIS D. *Miscellaneous Papers.* Edited by O.K. Fraenkel. New York: Viking Press, 1934.

_____. *The Words of Justice Brandeis.* Edited by S. Goldman. New York: Schuman, 1953.

_____. *Letters of Louis D. Brandeis.* Edited by M.I. Urofsky and D. Levy. Albany: State University of New York Press, 1971.

BRENNAN, WILLIAM J., JR. "The National Court of Appeals: Another Dissent." 40 *University of Chicago Law Review* 473 (1973).

_____. "The Proposed New National Court of Appeals." 28 *Record of the Association of the Bar of New York City* 627 (1973).

_____. "Remarks." Third Circuit Judicial Conference, Philadelphia, Pa., 8 September 1982.

BREWER, DAVID. "The Work of the Supreme Court." *Law Notes* 167 (1898).

_____. "The Federal Judiciary." 12 *Kansas State Bar Association Proceedings* 81 (1895).

_____. "The Nation's Anchor." 57 *Alabama Law Review* 166 (1898).

_____. "The Supreme Court of the United States." 33 *Scribner's* 273 (1903).

_____. "Organized Wealth and the Judiciary." *Chicago Legal News* (27 August 1904).

_____. "Two Periods in the History of the Supreme Court." 19 *Virginia State Bar Association Report* 113 (1906).

BROWN, HENRY. "The Judiciary." *Addresses on the Celebration of the One Hundredth Anniversary of the Laying of the Cornerstone of the Capitol of the United States* 74 (1896).

BURGER, WARREN E. "Deferred Maintenance of Judiciary Machinery." Remarks, National Conference on the Judiciary, Williamsburg, Va., 12 March 1971.

_____. "The Special Skills of Advocacy." 42 *Fordham Law Review* 227 (1973).

_____. "Rx for Justice: Modernize the Courts." *Nation's Business* 60 (September 1974).

_____. "Agenda for 2000 A.D.—A Need for Systematic Anticipation." Address, National Conference on the Causes of Popular Dissatisfaction with the Administration of Justice, St. Paul, Minn., 7 April 1976.

_____. "Some Further Reflections on the Problem of Adequacy of Trial Counsel." 49 *Fordham Law Review* 1 (1980).

_____. "Annual Report on the State of the Judiciary." Mid-Year Meeting of the American Bar Association, New Orleans, La., 6 February 1983.

_____, and WARREN, EARL. "Retired Chief Justice Warren Attacks, Chief Justice Burger Defends Freund Study Group's Composition and Proposal." 59 *American Bar Association Journal* 721 (1973).

BURTON, HAROLD H. "Judging Is Also Administration." Address, Section on Judicial Administration, ABA Convention, Cleveland, Ohio, 1947.

_____. "Unsung Services of the Supreme Court of the United States." 24 *Fordham Law Review* 169 (1955).

BUTLER, PIERCE. "Some Opportunities and Duties of Lawyers." 9 *American Bar Association Journal* 583 (1923).

BYRNES, JAMES F. *All in One Lifetime.* New York: Harper & Bros., 1958.

CAMERON, JAMES DUKE. "Federal Review, Finality of State Court Decision, and a Proposal for a National Court of Appeals—A State Judge's Solution to a Continuing Problem." 3 *Brigham Young University Law Review* 545 (1981).

CAMPBELL, JOHN. "Address." 6 *Alabama State Bar Association Proceedings* 75 (1884).

CARDOZO, BENJAMIN. *The Nature of the Judicial Process.* New Haven: Yale University Press, 1921.

_____. *The Growth of Law.* New Haven: Yale University Press, 1924.

CLARK, TOM C. "The Court and Its Functions." 34 *Albany Law Review* 497 (1970).

_____. Address, "Some Thoughts on Supreme Court Practice." 13 April 1959.

_____. "The Supreme Court Conference." 19 *Federal Decision Rules* 303 (1956).

_____. "The Internal Operation of the United States Supreme Court." 43 *Journal of the American Judicature Society* 45 (1959).

_____. "Introduction, Judicial Reform: A Symposium." 23 *University of Florida Law Review* 217 (1971).

CLARKE, JOHN H. "Practice Before the Supreme Court." 8 *Virginia Law Review* 241 (1922).

_____. "Methods of Work of the United States Supreme Court Judges." 9 *American Bar Association Journal* 80 (1923).

COFFIN, FRANK. *The Ways of a Judge: Reflections from the Federal Appellate Bench.* Boston: Houghton Mifflin, 1980.

DAVIS, JOHN W. "The Argument of an Appeal." 26 *American Bar Association Review* 895 (1940).

DOUGLAS, WILLIAM O. "Mr. Justice Douglas." CBS Reports, 6 September 1972.

_____. "Stare Decisis." 49 *Columbia Law Review* 735 (1949).

_____. "On Misconception of the Judicial Function and the Responsibility of the Bar." 59 *Columbia Law Review* 227 (1959).

_____. "The Supreme Court and Its Case Load." 45 *Cornell Law Quarterly* 401 (1960).

_____. *We the Judges.* Garden City, N.Y.: Doubleday, 1956.

_____. "Mr. Justice Black." 65 *Yale Law Journal* 449 (1956).

_____. "Chief Justice Stone." 46 *Columbia Law Review* 693 (1946).

_____. "The Lasting Influence of Mr. Justice Brandeis." 19 *Temple Law Quarterly* 361 (1946).

_____. "In Forma Pauperis Practice in the United States." 2 *New Hampshire Bar Journal* 5 (1959).

_____. "The Role of the Lawyer." 12 *Oklahoma Law Review* 1 (1959).

_____. "Mr. Justice Cardozo." 58 *Michigan Law Review* 549 (1960).

EDWARDS, HARRY T. "A Judge's View on Justice, Bureaucracy, and Legal Method." 80 *Michigan Law Review* 248 (1981).

FIELD, STEPHEN J. "The Late Chief Justice Chase." 11 *Overland Monthly* 305 (1873).

_____. Address, "The Supreme Court of the United States." Centennial Celebration of the Organization of the Federal Judiciary, New York, N.Y., 4 February 1890, 134 U.S. 729 (1890).

_____. "Farewell to the Supreme Court." 5 *American Law Review* 537 (1897).

FORTAS, ABE. "Chief Justice Warren: The Enigma of Leadership." 84 *Yale Law Journal* 405 (1970).

FRANK, JEROME. *Courts on Trial: Myth and Reality in American Justice.* Princeton: Princeton University Press, 1959.

_____. *Law and the Modern Mind.* New York: Brentano's, 1930.

FRANKEL, MARVIN E. *Partisan Justice.* New York: Hill and Wang, 1980.

_____. "The Adversary Judge." 54 *Texas Law Review* 465 (1976).

_____. "The Search for Truth: An Umperial View." 123 *University of Pennsylvania Law Review* 1031 (1975).

_____. "From Private Fights Toward Public Justice." 51 *New York University Law Review* 516 (1976).

FRANKFURTER, FELIX. "Personal Ambitions of Judges: Should a Judge 'Think Beyond the Judicial'?" 34 *American Bar Association Journal* 656 (1948).

_____. "The 'Administrative Side' of Chief Justice Hughes." 63 *Harvard Law Review* 1 (1949).

_____. "Chief Justices I Have Known." 39 *Virginia Law Review* 883 (1953).

_____. "The Job of a Supreme Court Justice." *New York Times Magazine* 14 (28 November 1954).

_____. "Mr. Justice Brandeis." 55 *Harvard Law Review* 181 (1941).

_____. "Harlan Fiske Stone." *American Philosophical Society Year Book* 334 (1946).

_____. "Benjamin Nathan Cardozo." 22 *Dictionary of American Biography* 93 (1949).

_____. " 'Moral Grandeur' of Justice Brandeis." *New York Times Magazine* Sec. 6, at 26 (11 November 1956).

_____. "Some Observations on the Nature of the Judicial Process of Supreme Court Litigation." 98 *American Philosophical Society Proceedings* 233 (1954).

_____. "John Marshall and the Judicial Function." 69 *Harvard Law Review* 217 (1955).

_____. "Mr. Justice Jackson." 68 *Harvard Law Review* 937 (1955).

_____. "Mr. Justice Roberts." 104 *University of Pennsylvania Law Review* 311 (1955).

_____. *Of Law and Men: Papers and Addresses, 1939-1956.* New York: Harcourt, Brace, 1956.

_____. "The Supreme Court in the Mirror of the Justices." 105 *University of Pennsylvania Law Review* 781 (1957).

FRIENDLY, HENRY J. "Averting the Flood by Lessening the Flow." 59 *Cornell Law Review* 634 (1974).

_____. "Indiscretion About Discretion." 31 *Emory Law Journal* 747 (1982).

GODBOLD, JOHN C. "Twenty Pages and Twenty Minutes—Effective Advocacy on Appeal." 30 *Southwestern Law Journal* 801 (1976).

GOLDBERG, ARTHUR. *The Supreme Court of the United States.* Evanston, Ill.: Northwestern University Press, 1971.

GRAY, HORACE. "An Address on the Life, Character, and Influence of Chief Justice Marshall." 14 *Virginia State Bar Association Report* 365 (1901).

GUNDERSON, ELMER. "Jurisprudential Character: The Typology of James David Barber in a Judicial Context." 13 *Southwestern University Law Review* 396 (1983).

HAND, LEARNED. "Chief Justice Stone's Conception of the Judicial Function." 46 *Columbia Law Review* 696 (1946).

HARLAN, JOHN M. "The Supreme Court of the United States and Its Work." 30 *American Law Review* 900 (1896).

_____. "James Wilson and the Formation of the Constitution." 34 *American Law Review* 481 (1900).

HARLAN, JOHN M., JR. "What Part Does the Oral Argument Play in the Conduct of an Appeal?" Address, Judicial Conference, Asheville, N.C., 1955.

_____. "Some Aspects of Handling a Case in the United States Supreme Court." Address, New York State Bar Association, N.Y., 1957.

_____. "Manning the Dikes." 13 *Record of the New York City Bar Association* 541 (1958).

_____. "A Glimpse of the Supreme Court at Work." 11 *University of Chicago Law School Record* 1 (1963).

_____. "Some Aspects of the Judicial Process in the Supreme Court of the United States." 33 *Australian Law Journal* 108 (1959).

HAYNSWORTH, CLEMENT F. "A New Court to Improve the Administration of Justice." 59 *American Bar Association Journal* 841 (1973).

HIGGINBOTHAM, PATRICK E. "Bureaucracy—The Carcinoma of the Federal Judiciary." 31 *Alabama Law Review* 261 (1980).

HOFFMAN, WALTER. "Plea Bargaining and the Role of the Judge." 53 *Federal Rules Decisions* 499 (1971).

HOLMES, OLIVER WENDELL. *The Mind and Faith of Justice Holmes.* Edited by R. Lenner. Boston: Little, Brown, 1943.

_____. *The Common Law.* Boston: Little, Brown, 1881.

_____. *The Holmes-Laski Letters, 1916-1935.* Edited by M. De Wolfe Howe. Cambridge: Harvard University Press, 1953.

_____. *The Holmes-Pollock Letters, 1874-1932.* Edited by M. De Wolfe Howe. Cambridge: Harvard University Press, 1941.

HUFSTEDLER, SHIRLEY. "New Blocks for Old Pyramids: Reshaping the Judicial System." 44 *Southern California Law Review* 901 (1971).

HUGHES, CHARLES E. *Addresses.* New York: Harper, 2d ed., 1916.

_____. "Mr. Justice Holmes." 44 *Harvard Law Review* 677 (1932).

_____. "Roger Brooke Taney." 17 *American Bar Association Journal* 785 (1931).

_____. "The Social Thought of Mr. Justice Brandeis." In *Mr. Justice Brandeis,* ed. by F. Frankfurter. New Haven: Yale University Press, 1932.

JACKSON, ROBERT H. "Advocacy Before the Supreme Court: Suggestions for Effective Case Presentations." 37 *American Bar Association Journal* 801 (1951).

_____. "Decisional Law and Stare Decisis." 30 *American Bar Association Journal* 334 (1944).

_____. "Decline of Stare Decisis Is Due to Volume of Opinions." 28 *Journal of American Judicature Society* 6 (1944).

_____. "Progress in Federal Judicial Administration." 23 *Journal of the American Judicature Society* 60 (1939).

KAUFMAN, IRVING. "Judicial Reform in the Next Century." 29 *Stanford Law Review* 1 (1976).

LEVENTHAL, HAROLD. "A Modest Proposal for a Multi-Circuit Court of Appeals." 24 *American University Law Review* 881 (1975).

LUMBARD, J. EDWARD. "The Place of the Federal Judicial Councils in the Administration of the Courts." 47 *American Bar Association Journal* 169 (1961).

LURTON, HORACE. "A Government of Law or a Government of Men." 193 *North American Review* 9 (1911).

McCREE, WADE H., JR. "Bureaucratic Justice: An Early Warning." 129 *University of Pennsylvania Law Review* 777 (1981).

McGOWAN, CARL. "The View from an Inferior Court." 19 *San Diego Law Review* 659 (1983).

McMILLAN, JAMES B. "Social Science and the District Court: The Observations of a Journeyman Trial Judge." 39 *Law and Contemporary Problems* 157 (1975).

MARKEY, HOWARD. "Judicial Administration—The Human Factors." 3 *Brigham Young University Law Review* 535 (1981).

MATTHEWS, STANLEY. "The Judicial Power of the United States." Yale Law School, 26 June 1898.

_____. "The Federal Judiciary." 2 *History of the Celebration of the One Hundredth Anniversary of the Promulgation of the Constitution of the United States* 370 (Carson ed., 1889).

MILLER, JUSTIN. "Oral Argument." 9 *District of Columbia Bar Association Journal* 196 (1942).

MILLER, SAMUEL F. "The Study and Practice of Law in the United States." 48 *Law Times* 171 (1870).

_____. "Judicial Reform." 6 *Western Jurist* 49 (1872).

_____. "Legislation in This Country as It Affects the Administration of Justice." 2 *New York State Bar Association Proceedings* 31 (1879).

_____. "The System of Trial by Jury." 21 *American Law Review* 859 (1887).

O'CONNOR, SANDRA DAY. "Comments on the Supreme Court's Caseload." National Conference of the American Bar Association, 6 February 1983.

POSNER, RICHARD. "Will the Federal Courts of Appeals Survive Until 1984? An Essay on Delegation and Specialization of the Judicial Function." 56 *Southern California Law Review* 761 (1983).

POWELL, LEWIS F. "Are the Federal Courts Becoming Bureaucracies?" 68 *American Bar Association Journal* 1370 (1982).

_____. "What the Justices Are Saying. . . ." 62 *American Bar Association Journal* 1454 (1976).

_____. Remarks. Southwestern Legal Foundation, 1 May 1980.

_____. "Myths and Misconceptions about the Supreme Court." 48 *New York University Law Review* 6 (1976).

_____. "Of Politics and the Court." *Yearbook of the Supreme Court Historical Society* (1982).

PRETTYMAN, E. BARRETT. "Some Observations Concerning Appellate Advocacy." 39 *Virginia Law Review* 285 (1953).

REHNQUIST, WILLIAM H. "Sunshine in the Third Branch." 16 *Washburn Law Journal* 559 (1977).

_____. "The Open and Closed Nature of the Supreme Court." *IPS Byliner* release (United States Information Service, October 1977).

_____. "The Supreme Court: Past and Present." 59 *American Bar Association Journal* 361 (1973).

_____. Remarks. Mac Swinford Lecture, University of Kentucky, 23 September 1982.

ROSSMAN, GEORGE. "Appellate Court Advocacy." 45 *American Bar Association Journal* 675 (1959).

RUBIN, ALVIN. "Managing Problems in the Federal Courts: Curbing Bureaucratization and Reducing Other Tensions Between Justice and Efficiency." 55 *Notre Dame Lawyer* 648 (1980).

_____. "Views from the Lower Court." 23 *U.C.L.A. Law Review* 448 (1976).

RUTLEDGE, WILEY. "The Appellate Brief." 28 *American Bar Association Journal* 251 (1942).

SCHAEFER. WALTER V. "Precedent and Policy." The Ernst Freund Lecture, University of Chicago Law School, 1956.

_____. "The Appellate Court." 3 *University of Chicago Law School Record* 10 (1954).

STEVENS, JOHN PAUL. "The Life Span of a Judge-made Rule." New York University School of Law, 27 October 1982.

_____. "Some Thoughts on Judicial Restraint." 66 *Judicature* 177 (1982).

STEWART, POTTER. "Reflections on the Supreme Court." 8 *Litigation* 8 (1982).

_____. "The Indigent Defendant and the Supreme Court of the United States." 58 *Legal Aid Review* 3 (1960).

STONE, HARLAN F. "Fifty Years Work of the United States Supreme Court." 14 *American Bar Association Journal* 428 (1928).

_____. "The Chief Justice." 27 *American Bar Association Journal* 407 (1941).

_____. "Dissenting Opinions Are Not Without Value." 26 *Journal of American Judicature Society* 78 (1942).

_____. "Functions of the Circuit Conferences." 28 *American Bar Association Journal* 579 (1942).

STRONG, WILLIAM. "The Needs of the Supreme Court." 132 *North American Review* 437 (1881).

_____. "Relief for the Supreme Court." 151 *North American Review* 567 (1890).

TAFT, WILLIAM H. " The Jurisdiction of the Supreme Court Under the Act of February 13, 1925." 35 *Yale Law Journal* 1 (1925).

_____. "Delays and Defects in the Enforcement of Laws in this Country." 183 *North American Review* 851 (June 1908).

_____. "Possible and Needed Reforms in Administration of Justice in Federal Courts."

8 *American Bar Association Journal* 601 (1922).

_____. *Present Day Problems.* New York: Dodd, Mead, 1908.

_____. "Adequate Machinery for Judicial Business." 7 *American Bar Association Journal* 453 (1921).

_____. "Salmon P. Chase Memorial." 9 *American Bar Association Journal* 348 (1923).

TAMM, EDWARD A., and REARDON, PAUL C. "Warren E. Burger and the Administration of Justice." 3 *Brigham Young University Law Review* 447 (1981).

VANDERBILT, ARTHUR T. *The Challenge of Law Reform.* Princeton: Princeton University Press, 1955.

VAN DEVANTER, WILLIS. Statement. *Hearing Before the Committee on the Judiciary,* 98th Cong., 2d Sess., 18 December 1924.

VINSON, FRED M. "The Work of the United States Supreme Court." 12 *Texas Bar Journal* 551 (1948).

_____. "The Supreme Court's Work: Opinion and Dissents." 20 *Oklahoma Bar Journal* 1296 (1949).

_____. "The Business of Judicial Administration: Suggestions to the Conference of Chief Justices." 35 *American Bar Association Journal* 893 (1949).

WAITE, MORRISON, JR. "The Supreme Court of the United States." 36 *Alabama Law Journal* 318 (1887).

WALLACE, J. CLIFFORD. "Working Paper—Future of the Judiciary." 94 *Federal Rules Decisions* 225 (1981).

_____. "The Nature and Extent of Intercircuit Conflict: A Solution Needed for a Mountain or a Molehill?" Address, University of California School of Law (Berkeley), 1982.

WARREN, EARL. "Chief Justice Marshall." 41 *American Bar Association Journal* 1008 (1955).

_____. "Chief Justice Taney." 41 *American Bar Association Journal* 504 (1955).

_____. "Chief Justice William Howard Taft." 67 *Yale Law Journal* 353 (1958).

_____. *The Public Papers of Chief Justice Earl Warren.* Edited by Henry Christman. New York: Simon & Schuster, 1959.

_____. *Hughes and the Court.* Hamilton, N.Y.: Colgate University Press, 1962.

_____. "Delay and Congestion in the Federal Courts." 42 *Journal of the American Judicature Society* 6 (1958).

WHITE, BYRON. "Challenges for the U.S. Supreme Court and the Bar: Contemporary Reflections." 51 *Antitrust Law Journal* 275 (1982).

_____. "The Work of the Supreme Court: A Nuts and Bolts Description." 54 *New York State Bar Journal* 346 (1982).

WHITE, EDWARD D. "The Supreme Court of the United States." 7 *American Bar Association Journal* 341 (1921).

WHITTAKER, CHARLES E. "Judicial Discretion." Address, Illinois Division of the Federal Bar Association, Chicago, Ill., 1960.

WISDOM, JOHN MINOR. "Random Remarks on the Role of Social Sciences in the Judicial Decision-Making Process in School Disegregation Cases." 39 *Law and Contemporary Problems* 134 (1975).

WYZANSKI, CHARLES E., JR. "Judicial Review in America: Opening Statement." In *Constitutional Government in America,* ed. by R.K.L. Collins. Durham, N.C.: Carolina Academic Press, 1980.

The Judiciary and the Constitution

BRENNAN, WILLIAM J. "Constitutional Adjudication." *Notre Dame Lawyer* 559 (1965).

BREWER, DAVID. "Protection of Private Property from Public Attack." 10 *Railway and Corporation Law Review* 281 (1891).

BROWN, HENRY B. "The Distribution of Property." 16 *American Bar Association Report* 213 (1893).

BURGER, WARREN E. "Remarks to the Ohio Judicial Conference." Columbus, Ohio, 4 September 1968.

_____. "Causes of Dissatisfaction with Criminal Justice." Seminar of Investigative and Enforcement Officials, Washington, D.C., 15 November 1967.

BURTON, HAROLD. "*Ex parte Milligan* and *Ex parte McCardle*." 41 *American Bar Association Journal* 176 (1955).

_____. "The Legal Tender Cases." 42 *American Bar Association Journal* 231 (1956).

CARDOZO, BENJAMIN. *Law and Literature and Other Essays.* New York: Harcourt, Brace, 1931.

CLARK, TOM C. "Constitutional Adjudication and the Supreme Court." 9 *Drake Law Review* 59 (1960).

CURTIS, BENJAMIN. *Executive Power.* Boston: Little, Brown, 1862.

DOUGLAS, WILLIAM O. "Recent Trends in Constitutional Law." 30 *Oregon Law Review* 279 (1951).

FRANKFURTER, FELIX. *The Commerce Clause Under Marshall, Taney, and Waite.* Chapel Hill: University of North Carolina Press, 1937.

_____. *Extrajudicial Essays on the Court and the Constitution,* ed. by P. Kurland. Cambridge: Harvard University Press, 1970.

_____. "Address." 98 *Proceedings of the American Philosophical Society* 233 (1954).

HUGHES, CHARLES E. "War Powers Under the Constitution." Address, American Bar Association Meeting, 1917.

JACKSON, ROBERT. "Decisional Law and Stare Decisis." 30 *American Bar Association Journal* 334 (1945).

JUSTICE, WILLIAM WAYNE. "A Relativistic Constitution." 52 *University of Colorado Law Review* 19 (1980).

MILLER, SAMUEL F. "Introduction to Constitutional Law." 4 *Scotland Law Review* 79 (1878).

_____. *The Constitution of the United States.* 1880.

_____. "The Weight of Authorities." 10 *Virginia Law Journal* 582 (1886).

_____. "The Use and Value of Authorities." 23 *American Law Review* 165 (1889).

_____. *Lectures on the Constitution.* New York: Banks & Brothers, 1891.

OAKS, DALLIN H. "When Judges Legislate." Speech, Utah State University, 29 April 1982.

_____. "Judicial Activism." Address, Federalist Society, University of Chicago School of Law, 1983.

POWELL, LEWIS F. "Constitutional Interpretation." An Interview. *Kenyon College Alumni Bulletin* 14 (Summer 1979).

_____. "*Carolene Products* Revisited." 82 *Columbia Law Review* 1087 (1982).

REED, STANLEY. "Stare Decisis and Constitutional Law." 35 *Pennsylvania Bar Association Quarterly* 131 (1938).

REHNQUIST, WILLIAM H. "The Cult of the Robe." 15 *Judges' Journal* 74 (1976).

_____. "The Notion of a Living Constitution." 54 *Texas Law Review* 693 (1976).

RUTLEDGE, WILEY B. Foreword to "Symposium on Constitutional Rights During War-time." 29 *Iowa Law Review* 379 (1944).

SNEED, JOSEPH T. "When Should the Lions Be on the Throne? Reflections on Judicial Supremacy." 21 *Arizonia Law Review* 925 (1979).

STEVENS, JOHN PAUL. "Some Thoughts About a General Rule." 21 *Arizonia Law Review* 599 (1979).

STONE, HARLAN F. "The Constitution of the United States." Address, League of Republican Women of the District of Columbia, 1924.

SUTHERLAND, GEORGE. "The Courts and the Constitution." Address, American Bar Association, 1912.

_____. *Constitutional Power and World Affairs.* New York: Columbia University Press, 1919.

TAFT, WILLIAM H. *Liberty Under Law, an Interpretation of the Principles of Our Constitutional Government.* New Haven: Yale University Press, 1922.

TRAYNOR, ROGER. "Quo Vadis, Prospective Overruling: A Question of Judiciary Responsibility." 28 *Hastings Law Journal* 533 (1977).

VANDERBILT, ARTHUR T. *The Doctrine of the Separation of Powers and Its Present Day Significance.* Lincoln: University of Nebraska Press, 1963.

WALLACE, J. CLIFFORD. "The Jurisprudence of Judicial Restraint: A Return to the Moorings." 50 *George Washington Law Review* 1 (1981).

WHITE, BYRON R. "The Role of Judicial Review." *Horizons* 52 (1970).

WHITTAKER, CHARLES E. "Judicial Discretion." Address, Federal Bar Association, 1960.

Judiciary and Federal Regulation:
Line Drawing and Statutory Construction

BAZELON, DAVID L. "Science and Uncertainty: A Jurist's View." 5 *Harvard Environmental Law Review* 209 (1981).

_____. "The Court and the Public: Policy Decisions About High Technology and Risk." Remarks. "Saturday at the University," University of Pennsylvania, 4 April 1981.

FRANKFURTER, FELIX. "Some Reflections on the Reading of Statutes." 2 *Record of the Association of the Bar of the City of New York* 213 (1947).

FRIENDLY, HENRY J. "Judicial Control of Discretionary Administrative Action." 23 *Journal of Legal Education* 63 (1970).

_____. "Mr. Justice Frankfurter and the Reading of Statutes." In *Benchmarks,* ed. by H.J. Friendly. Chicago: University of Chicago Press, 1967.

_____. "The Gap in Lawmaking: Judges Who Can't and Legislators Who Won't." 63 *Columbia Law Review* 787 (1963).

JACKSON, ROBERT H. "The Meaning of Statutes: What Congress Says or What the Court Says." 34 *American Bar Association Journal* 535 (1948).

LEVENTHAL, HAROLD. "Environmental Decisionmaking and the Role of the Courts." 122 *University of Pennsylvania Law Review* 509 (1974).

_____. "Principled Fairness and Regulatory Urgency." 25 *Case Western Reserve Law Review* 66 (1974).

McGOWAN, CARL. "Congress, Court, and Control of Delegated Power." 77 *Columbia Law Review* 1119 (1977).

MARKEY, HOWARD T. "A Forum for Technology?" 60 *Judicature* 365 (1977).

POSNER, RICHARD A. "Economics, Politics, and the Reading of Statutes and the Constitution." 49 *University of Chicago Law Review* 263 (1982).

RE, EDWARD. "Stare Decisis." Presentation, Federal Judicial Center, 1975.

REHNQUIST, WILLIAM H. "A Government of Laws and of Men: A Bicentennial View of the Judicial Branch." Remarks, Indiana University, 1975.

TAFT, WILLIAM H. *The Anti-Trust Act and the Supreme Court.* New York: Harper & Bros., 1914.

TRAYNOR, ROGER. "Statutes Revolving in Common Law Orbits." 17 *Catholic University Law Review* 401 (1968).

WALD, PATRICIA M. "Some Observations on the Use of Legislative History in the 1981 Supreme Court Term." 68 *Iowa Law Review* 195 (1983).

WRIGHT, J. SKELLY. "Beyond Discretionary Justice." 81 *Yale Law Journal* 575 (1972).

_____. "Courts and the Rulemaking Process: The Limits of Judicial Review." 59 *Cornell Law Review* 375 (1974).

_____. "Court of Appeals Review of Federal Regulatory Agency Rulemaking." 26 *Administrative Law Review* 199 (1974).

_____. "New Judicial Requisites for Informal Rulemaking: Implications for the Environmental Impact Statement Process." 29 *Administrative Law Review* 59 (1977).

_____. "Rulemaking and Judicial Review." 30 *Administrative Law Review* 461 (1978).

Our Dual Constitutional System: The Bill of Rights and the States

BLACK, HUGO. "The Bill of Rights." 35 *New York University Law Review* 865 (1960).

_____. *A Constitutional Faith.* New York: Knopf, 1969.

_____. "Justice Black and the Bill of Rights." CBS News Special, 3 December 1968.

BRENNAN, WILLIAM J. "The Criminal Prosecution: Sporting Event or Quest for Truth?" 1963 *Washington University Law Quarterly* 279 (1963).

_____. "State Supreme Court Judge Versus United States Supreme Court Justice: A Change in Function and Perspective." 19 *University of Florida Law Review* 225 (1966).

_____. "Landmarks of Legal Liberty." In *The Fourteenth Amendment,* ed. by Bernard Schwartz. New York: New York University Press, 1970.

_____. "The Bill of Rights and the States." 36 *New York University Law Review* 761 (1961).

_____. "State Constitutions and the Protection of Individual Rights." *Harvard Law Review* (1977).

_____. "Address." 32 *Rutgers Law Review* 1 (1979).

BROWN, HENRY B. "Liberty of the Press." 23 *New York State Bar Association Proceedings* 133 (1900).

BYRNES, JAMES F. Address, "Preserve People's Rights." 16 *Vital Speeches* 450 (1952).

_____. "Segregation." 50 *Vermont Bar Association Proceedings* 86 (1956).

_____. Address, "The South Respects the Written Constitution: Supreme Court Has No Power to Amend the Constitution." 23 *Vital Speeches* 331 (1957).

_____. "The Supreme Court and States Rights." 20 *Alabama Lawyer* 396 (1959).

CLARK, TOM C. "Random Thoughts on the Court's Interpretation of Individual Rights." 1 *Houston Law Review* 75 (1963).

DOUGLAS, WILLIAM O. "Procedural Safeguards in the Bill of Rights." 31 *Journal of the American Judicature Society* 166 (1948).

_____. *The Right of the People.* Garden City, N.Y.: Doubleday, 1958.

_____. "Bill of Rights Is Not Enough." 38 *New York University Law Review* 207 (1963).

FRIENDLY, HENRY J. *Benchmarks.* Chicago: University of Chicago Press, 1967.

GOLDBERG, ARTHUR. *Equal Justice: The Supreme Court in the Warren Era*. Evanston, Ill.: Northwestern University Press, 1971.

HAND, LEARNED. *The Bill of Rights*. Cambridge: Harvard University Press, 1958.

LINDE, HANS. "First Things First: Rediscovering the States' Bill of Rights." 9 *University of Baltimore Law Review* 379 (1980).

MARSHALL, THURGOOD. "Group Action in the Pursuit of Justice." 44 *New York University Law Review* 661 (1969).

———. "Law and the Quest for Equality." 1 *Washington University Law Quarterly* 1 (1967).

MOSK, STANLEY. "Rediscovering the 10th Amendment." 20 *Judges' Journal* 16 (1981).

OAKES, JAMES L. "The Proper Role of the Federal Courts in Enforcing the Bill of Rights." 54 *New York University Law Review* 911 (1979).

O'CONNOR, SANDRA DAY. "Trends in the Relationship Between the Federal and State Courts from the Perspective of a State Court Judge." 22 *William and Mary Law Review* 801 (1981).

REHNQUIST, WILLIAM H. "The First Amendment: Freedom, Philosophy, and the Law." 12 *Gonzaga Law Review* 1 (1976).

SCHAEFER, WALTER V. "Federalism and State Criminal Procedure." 70 *Harvard Law Review* 1 (1956).

STEWART, POTTER. "Or of the Press." 26 *Hastings Constitutional Law Journal* 631 (1975).

TAFT, WILLIAM H. "Administration of Criminal Law." 15 *Yale Law Journal* 1 (1905-1906).

WARREN, EARL. "A Conversation with Earl Warren." WGBH-TV, Boston, 1972.

———. "Fourteenth Amendment: Retrospective and Prospective." In *The Fourteenth Amendment,* ed. by B. Schwartz. New York: New York University Press, 1970.

———. "The Bill of Rights and the Military." 37 *New York University Law Review* 181 (1962).

WRIGHT, J. SKELLY. "Judicial Review and the Equal Protection Clause." 15 *Harvard Civil Liberty—Civil Rights Law Review* 1 (1980).

The Judicial Role in a Litigious Society

ALDISERT, RUGGERO J. "The Role of the Courts in Contemporary Society." 38 *University of Pittsburgh Law Review* 437 (1977).

———. "Judicial Expansion of Federal Jurisdiction: A Federal Judge's Thoughts on Section 1983, Comity and the Federal Caseload." 1973 *Arizona State University Law Review* 557.

BAZELON, DAVID L. "Coping with Technology Through the Legal Process." 62 *Cornell Law Review* 817 (1977).

———. "New Gods for Old: 'Efficient' Courts in a Democratic Society." 46 *New York University Law Review* 653 (1971).

———. "The Impact of the Courts on Public Administration." 52 *Indiana Law Review* 101 (1976).

BEER, PETER. "On Behalf of Judicial Restraint." 15 *Trial* 37 (1979).

BURGER, WARREN E. "Who Will Watch the Watchman?" 14 *American University Law Review* 1 (1964).

———. "Arbitration, Not Litigation." *Nation's Business* 52 (August 1982).

DAY, WILLIAM R. "The Judicial Power of the Nation." 17 *Michigan Alumnus* 357 (1911).

FRANKFURTER, FELIX. *The Public and Its Government*. New York: Oxford University Press, 1930.

———. *Law and Politics.* New York: Harcourt, Brace, 1939.

FRIENDLY, HENRY J. "The Courts and Social Policy." 33 *University of Miami Law Review* 21 (1978).

———. "Some Kind of Hearing." 123 *University of Pennsylvania Law Review* 1267 (1975).

———. *Federal Jurisdiction: A General View.* New York: Columbia University Press, 1973.

JOHNSON, FRANK. "Judge: The Law and Frank Johnson." *Bill Moyer's Journal,* WNET, 24 July 1980.

———. "Judicial Activism Is a Duty—Not an Intrusion." 16 *Judges' Journal* 4 (1977).

MARKEY, HOWARD T. "On the Cause and Treatment of Judicial Activism." *Federal Bar News* 296 (December 1982).

NEELY, RICHARD. *How Courts Govern America.* New Haven: Yale University Press, 1981.

OAKES, JAMES L. "The Role of Courts in Government Today." 22 *Akron Law Review* 1775 (1980).

REHNQUIST, WILLIAM H. "The Adversary Society." Keynote Address of the Third Annual Baron de Hirsch Meyer Lecture Series. 33 *University of Miami Law Review* 1 (1978).

RUTLEDGE, WILEY B. *A Declaration of Legal Faith.* Lawrence: University of Kansas Press, 1947.

STONE, HARLAN F. *Law and Its Administration.* New York: Columbia University Press, 1915.

———. *Public Control of Business.* N.p.: Howell, Soskin, 1940.

TAFT, WILLIAM H. *Popular Government.* New Haven: Yale University Press, 1913.

TRAYNOR, ROGER. "The Limits of Judicial Creativity." 63 *Iowa Law Review* 1 (1977).

WALLACE, J. CLIFFORD. "How Judicial Restraint Encourages the Democratic Process in a Free Society." Speech, Washington, D.C., 13 October 1982.

WINTER, RALPH. "The Activist Judicial Mind." Remarks, American Enterprise Institute, 1978.

WYZANSKI, CHARLES. *Whereas—A Judge's Premises.* Boston: Little, Brown, 1964.

Time Chart of Members of the Supreme Court of the United States

Name	Appointed by President	Term of Office
CHIEF JUSTICES:		
Jay, John	Washington	1789-1795
Rutledge, John	Washington	1795
Ellsworth, Oliver	Washington	1796-1800
Marshall, John	Adams, J.	1801-1835
Taney, Roger B.	Jackson	1836-1864
Chase, Salmon P.	Lincoln	1864-1873
Waite, Morrison R.	Grant	1874-1888
Fuller, Melville W.	Cleveland	1888-1910
White, Edward D.	Taft	1910-1921
Taft, William Howard	Harding	1921-1930
Hughes, Charles Evans	Hoover	1930-1941
Stone, Harlan Fiske	Roosevelt, F.	1941-1946
Vinson, Frederick M.	Truman	1946-1953
Warren, Earl	Eisenhower	1953-1969
Burger, Warren E.	Nixon	1969-
ASSOCIATE JUDGES:		
Rutledge, John	Washington	1790-1791
Cushing, William	Washington	1790-1810
Wilson, James	Washington	1789-1798
Blair, John	Washington	1790-1796
Iredell, James	Washington	1790-1799
Johnson, Thomas	Washington	1792-1793
Paterson, William	Washington	1793-1806
Chase, Samuel	Washington	1796-1811
Washington, Bushrod	Adams, J.	1799-1829
Moore, Alfred	Adams, J.	1800-1804
Johnson, William	Jefferson	1804-1834
Livingston, Henry B.	Jefferson	1807-1823
Todd, Thomas	Jefferson	1807-1826
Duvall, Gabriel	Madison	1811-1835
Story, Joseph	Madison	1812-1845
Thompson, Smith	Monroe	1823-1843

Name	Appointed by President	Term of Office
Trimble, Robert	Adams, J.Q.	1826-1828
McLean, John	Jackson	1830-1861
Baldwin, Henry	Jackson	1830-1844
Wayne, James M.	Jackson	1835-1867
Barbour, Philip P.	Jackson	1836-1841
Catron, John	Van Buren	1837-1865
McKinley, John	Van Buren	1838-1852
Daniel, Peter V.	Van Buren	1842-1860
Nelson, Samuel	Tyler	1845-1872
Woodbury, Levi	Polk	1845-1851
Grier, Robert C.	Polk	1846-1870
Curtis, Benjamin R.	Fillmore	1851-1857
Cambell, John A.	Pierce	1853-1861
Clifford, Nathan	Buchanan	1858-1881
Swayne, Noah H.	Lincoln	1862-1881
Miller, Samuel F.	Lincoln	1862-1890
Davis, David	Lincoln	1862-1877
Field, Stephen J.	Lincoln	1863-1897
Strong, William	Grant	1870-1880
Bradley, Joseph P.	Grant	1870-1892
Hunt, Ward	Grant	1873-1882
Harlan, John M.	Hayes	1877-1911
Woods, William B.	Hayes	1881-1887
Matthews, Stanley	Garfield	1881-1889
Gray, Horace	Arthur	1882-1902
Blatchford, Samuel	Arthur	1882-1893
Lamar, Lucius Q.	Cleveland	1888-1893
Brewer, David J.	Harrison, B.	1890-1910
Brown, Henry B.	Harrison, B.	1891-1906
Shiras, George, Jr.	Harrison, B.	1892-1903
Jackson, Howell E.	Harrison, B.	1893-1895
White, Edward D.	Cleveland	1894-1910
Peckham, Rufus W.	Cleveland	1896-1909
McKenna, Joseph	McKinley	1898-1925
Holmes, Oliver Wendell	Roosevelt, T.	1902-1932
Day, William R.	Roosevelt, T.	1903-1922
Moody,William H.	Roosevelt, T.	1906-1910
Lurton, Horace H.	Taft	1910-1914
Hughes, Charles Evans	Taft	1910-1916
Van Devanter, Willis	Taft	1911-1937
Lamar, Joseph R.	Taft	1911-1916
Pitney, Mahlon	Taft	1912-1922
McReynolds, James C.	Wilson	1914-1941
Brandeis, Louis D.	Wilson	1916-1939
Clarke, John H.	Wilson	1916-1922
Sutherland, George	Harding	1911-1938

Time Chart of Members of the Supreme Court

Name	Appointed by President	Term of Office
Butler, Pierce	Harding	1923-1939
Sanford, Edward T.	Harding	1923-1930
Stone, Harlan Fiske	Coolidge	1925-1941
Roberts, Owen J.	Hoover	1930-1945
Cardozo, Benjamin N.	Hoover	1932-1938
Black, Hugo L.	Roosevelt, F.	1937-1971
Reed, Stanley F.	Roosevelt, F.	1938-1957
Frankfurter, Felix	Roosevelt, F.	1939-1962
Douglas, William O.	Roosevelt, F.	1939-1975
Murphy, Frank	Roosevelt, F.	1940-1949
Byrnes, James F.	Roosevelt, F.	1941-1942
Jackson, Robert H.	Roosevelt, F.	1941-1954
Rutledge, Wiley B.	Roosevelt, F.	1943-1949
Burton, Harold H.	Truman	1945-1958
Clark, Thomas C.	Truman	1949-1967
Minton, Sherman	Truman	1949-1956
Harlan, John Marshall	Eisenhower	1955-1971
Brennan, William J., Jr.	Eisenhower	1956-
Whittaker, Charles E.	Eisenhower	1957-1962
Stewart, Potter	Eisenhower	1958-1981
White, Bryon R.	Kennedy	1962-
Goldberg, Arthur J.	Kennedy	1962-1965
Fortas, Abe	Johnson, L.	1965-1969
Marshall, Thurgood	Johnson, L.	1967-
Blackmun, Harry A.	Nixon	1970-
Powell, Lewis F., Jr.	Nixon	1972-
Rehnquist, William H.	Nixon	1972-
Stevens, John Paul	Ford	1975-
O'Connor, Sandra Day	Reagan	1981-

NOTE: The acceptance of the appointment and commission by the appointee, as evidenced by the taking of the prescribed oaths, is here implied; otherwise the individual is not carried on this list of the Members of the Court. Examples: Robert H. Harrison is not carried, as a letter from President Washington of 9 February 1790 states Harrison declined to serve. Neither is Edwin M. Stanton, who died before he could take the necessary steps toward becoming a Member of the Court. Chief Justice Rutledge is included because he took his oaths, presided over the August Term of 1795, and his name appears on two opinions of the Court for that term. This material was adapted from a chart prepared by the Marshal of the Supreme Court of the United States.

Appendix C

NOTE: The Court of Appeals for the Federal Circuit is located in the District of Columbia.

Jurisdictional Map of
the U.S. Court of Appeals and U.S. District Courts

Puerto Rico **1**

Maine **1**

Minnesota

Michigan Western

Vermont

New Hampshire

Wisconsin Western

Wisconsin Eastern

Michigan Eastern

New York Northern

2

Massachusetts

Conn. R I

Michigan Western

New York Western

Pennsylvania Middle

N.Y. Southern

New York Eastern

8

Iowa Northern

Illinois Northern

Indiana Northern

Ohio Northern

Pennsylvania Western

3

Penn Eastern

New Jersey

Iowa Southern

Ohio Southern

West Virginia Northern

Maryland

Delaware

District of Columbia

Illinois Central

7

Indiana Southern

6

West Virginia Southern

4

Virginia Eastern

Missouri Western

Illinois Southern

Kentucky Eastern

Virginia Western

North Carolina Eastern

Missouri Eastern

Kentucky Western

Virginia Western

Virgin Islands

Oklahoma Northern

Tennessee Middle

Tennessee Eastern

North Carolina Western

Middle

Virgin Islands

3

Arkansas Eastern

Tennessee Western

Georgia Northern

South Carolina

Oklahoma Eastern

Mississippi Northern

Alabama Northern

Arkansas Western

11

Georgia Southern

Texas Eastern

Louisiana Western

Mississippi Southern

Alabama Middle

Georgia Middle

LEGEND:

5

Alabama Southern

Florida Northern

———— Circuit boundaries

Louisiana Middle

———— State boundaries

Louisiana Eastern

·········· District boundaries

Florida Middle

Florida Southern

General Subject Index

Court Case Index

About the Editors

MARK W. CANNON is the first person to fill the position of Administrative Assistant to the Chief Justice of the Supreme Court of the United States, a position created by Congress in 1972. Mr. Cannon received his B.A. from the University of Utah, and his M.A., M.P.A., and Ph.D. from Harvard University. Prior to serving as Administrative Assistant to the Chief Justice, Mr. Cannon was Director of the Institute of Public Administration in New York, and previously Chairman of the Department of Political Science at Brigham Young University. He also has had extensive legislative experience in the U.S. House of Representatives and the Senate. Mr. Cannon has lectured at over 50 universities and institutions throughout the world and has written numerous articles on the administration of justice and public policy, as well as five books, including co-authorship of *The Makers of Public Policy: American Power Groups and Their Ideologies.*

DAVID M. O'BRIEN is an Associate Professor in the Woodrow Wilson Department of Government and Foreign Affairs at the University of Virginia. He received his B.A., M.A., and Ph.D. from the University of California (Santa Barbara). Prior to teaching at the University of Virginia, he taught at the University of California and the University of Puget Sound, where he was Chairman of the Department of Politics. He also has served as Research Associate in the Office of the Administrative Assistant to the Chief Justice. During 1982-1983 he was a Judicial Fellow at the Supreme Court, and in 1981-1982 a Visiting Postdoctoral Fellow at the Russell Sage Foundation in New York. Mr. O'Brien has written numerous articles and is the author of *Privacy, Law, and Public Policy* (1979) and *The Public's Right to Know: The Supreme Court and the First Amendment* (1981), as well as co-author of *The Politics of Technology Assessment: Institutions, Processes, and Policy Disputes* (1982).